SUPREME INJUSTICE

Guilty until proven not Catholic?

John I Fleming

Supreme Injustice: Guilty until proven not Catholic?

ISBN: 978-0-646-88935-1 (paperback)

Published in Australia by John I Fleming.

This book was substantially written a few years ago. It did not proceed to publication because, to protect both my family and the Catholic Church, I did not want to see these matters publicly canvassed all over again believing that The Advertiser/Sunday Mail would not hesitate to use its bully pulpit against me if I did publish.

All that changed when Sean Fewster decided to use 11 hours of radio time from August 2023 to make further inaccurate claims about me and the defamation case in which I was involved. Fewster, the journalist in the employ of The Advertiser who reported on the defamation matter for that paper, decided to use his Sunday evening programme on Radio FIVEaa to publicly canvas all over again these defamatory matters made against me in 2008 and in what I and many others consider to be a highly inaccurate, one-sided, and high-handed manner.

In these circumstances I have, after all, decided to publish this book. The book demonstrates how some judges in the Supreme Court of South Australia and the High Court of Australia have, in my opinion, unjustly treated me. Unable to have a trial by jury I have been tried first by The Advertiser, then the individual judges of the Supreme Court, and now by Sean Fewster and radio station FIVEaa.

> **No free man shall be** seized or imprisoned, or stripped of his rights or possessions, or outlawed or exiled, or **deprived of his standing in any way**, nor will we proceed with force against him, or send others to do so, **except by the lawful judgment of his equals or by the law of the land**. [Magna Carta Liberatum, 15 June 1215]

Contents

Note on style 1

Acknowledgements 3

Foreword
David Flint AM. 5

Foreword
Gabriël A. Moens AM 11

Foreword
Augusto Zimmermann 19

Introduction
Dr Paul Collits 23

Chapter One
Legal Processes Begin 37

Chapter Two
Contextual Truth. 55

Chapter Three
Appeals to Prejudice. 69

Chapter Four
Justice Gray Questions Credibility of Two Major Witnesses 81

Chapter Five
Analysis of Jane's First Major Allegation 153

Chapter Six
Ten Reasons to Mistrust Gray's Findings Concerning Meningie 171

Chapter Seven
The Meningie Finding Became the Prism Through Which Justice Gray Considered Other Allegations 205

Chapter Eight
Dr Michelle Arnold: Expert Witness 239

Chapter Nine
Justice Gray's Misapplication of
the *Briginshaw* Rule 297

Chapter Ten
Appeal to the Full Court of the Supreme Court
in South Australia 303

Chapter Eleven
High Court Refuses Application for Leave to Appeal .361

Chapter Twelve
The Case Against the Judges in Brief –
What is to be Done? .391

Chapter Thirteen
Allegations of Bias or Improper Motive 433

Chapter Fourteen
Afterword. 441

Chapter Fifteen
The Behaviour of Journalists for *The Advertiser* and *The Sunday Mail* 443

Chapter Sixteen
Churches Respond to Allegations Against Father
Fleming 2008-2022 455

Appendix A
Timeline. 483

Appendix B
Application to the High Court of Australia Special for
Leave to Appeal 485

Index of Proper Names i

Note on style

Throughout the book, words in **bold** signify emphasis that has been added in the quotations where it occurs. Otherwise, it is the author wanting to emphasise a particular point.

Acknowledgements

It has taken many years to complete this book. It might never have seen the light of day were it not for the encouragement and solicitude of so many people outside of my family. My barrister, Paul Heywood KC, provided me with kind and generous legal and personal support. I received professional guidance also from David Flint, Paul Collits, Gabriël Moens, and Augusto Zimmermann. The book has greatly benefited from the extraordinary editing skills of Melissa Collits, a specialist in legal editing. Of course, I take full responsibility for the contents of this book. Any errors, inadvertent as they may be, are mine. And to my benefactors who have made publication of this book possible, I am grateful beyond measure.

Foreword

David Flint AM

I have known Father John Fleming for what is now approaching one quarter of a century. During all of those years I have been impressed not only by his intellect and his abilities, but especially by his courage and his decency. If there is a wrong in the case the subject of this book, apart from the original defamation, it is that our legal system has proven itself unable, or its custodians unwilling, to render justice when decency and fairness demand precisely that.

My first meeting with Dr Fleming was in Old Parliament House, Canberra in February 1998. He had just been elected by South Australians as an unpaid delegate to the 1998 Constitutional Convention to consider the question of Australia becoming a republic. He contested the election under the banner of Australians for Constitutional Monarchy. From my experience and those of colleagues, this was a time when coming out in support of the constitutional monarchy was not popular in media and other elite circles. The result was that many supporters deemed it prudent to keep their views to themselves. Not Father Fleming who was already well known for his achievements in the media and the academy.

I soon realised that I should never be surprised by either Fr Fleming's courage or his integrity. He has constantly shown these in relation to issues which are distinctly out of fashion. I suspect that some of his misfortune could well have been as a consequence of his stand on some of these issues, issues such as religion itself and his conversion to Catholicism, as well as on the moral issues of abortion and euthanasia.

Nevertheless, his intellect and learning have attracted recognition internationally in the academy, in the church, and in education where he had been appointed foundation president of a unique venture, Campion College, in Sydney.

As my colleagues Professor Moens and Professor Zimmerman detail in their forewords, Dr Fleming's world has been visited by a calumny which has seriously damaged his life and that of his family, but for which he has been unable to find that quality of justice which any advanced civilised society must provide to all citizens.

Since 2008, he has been the subject of defamatory accusations of a sexual nature involving the commission of crime which proved so unsubstantiated and so implausible that the South Australia police declined to take any action whatsoever. But he was unsuccessful in a defamation case which was upheld on appeal with the High Court declining twice to hear an appeal. The result is that an innocent man and his family have suffered a serious miscarriage of justice.

As the distinguished academic Dr Paul Collits writes in the Introduction to this book, the errors in the original judgement are many and significant, as are those in the South Australian Court of Appeal.

Where a solution should lie is in the High Court, but the Court has declined to act.

In the absence of the High Court, the only answer now would lie in a Royal Commission undertaken by a former judge of as sound criminal law experience as the dissenting judge in the Victorian Court of Appeal in *George Pell v The Queen*, Justice Mark Weinberg. Alone on that bench, he instantly understood why the conviction of Cardinal Pell could not for a moment stand, a conclusion endorsed by a unanimous High Court.

Justice Weinberg understood something which is at the very basis of our legal system, the presumption of innocence. This applies to everyone, including a prince of the church. The Victorian police did not accept this, otherwise they would not have opened an investigation without a complaint. The other judges on the Victorian Court of Appeal were distracted from the principle by a need to believe the victim. Only Justice Weinberg and then the full High Court returned to the fundamental principle that, in a criminal case, the Crown must prove guilt beyond reasonable doubt.

But Father Fleming's case was not a criminal case. Remember, the South Australian police had thought there was nothing in the newspaper story and had declined to act. Father Fleming, unwilling to allow his name to be dragged in the mud, was forced to react. If he did not, people could have believed what was being reported. So, he took out a defamation writ where the civil and not the criminal standard of proof applies. This is proof not beyond reasonable doubt but at a lower standard. This is proof on the balance of probabilities.

But what is the correct standard when *The Advertiser* and *The Sunday Mail* were alleging criminal conduct?

The common law is pragmatic. As long ago as 1938 the High Court developed a solution for this, the

Briginshaw principle. While the standard remains on the balance of probabilities, a court in a civil action should not lightly find that a party has engaged in criminal conduct. Because the consequences are so grave, the evidence should be of high probative value.

Arguing the *Briginshaw* principle, but losing in the lower court, Father Fleming appealed and lost again in the South Australian Supreme Court in 2016. The Court surprisingly played down *Briginshaw,* claiming later High Court judgments did not import that presumption into the civil arena and that it was incorrect to raise it to an 'onus', 'standard' or 'principle'.

Yet in a subsequent case concerning allegations of fraud and not sex abuse, *Poniatowska vs Channel Seven* (2019), the same court applied *Briginshaw,* restoring it to the status of a 'principle'.

The principle has found its way into some legislation. Thus section 140(2) of the NSW and similarly in the Commonwealth Evidence Act requires a court to consider the following matters when determining whether a case is proved on the balance of probabilities: the nature of the cause of action or defence; and the nature of the subject matter of the proceeding; and the gravity of the matters alleged. No such provision has been enacted in South Australia. If one were now, it would be unusual to legislate with retrospective effect.

As we saw in the *Geoffrey Rush v Nationwide News* (2020), this principle is crucial for those accused of sexual abuse. There the Federal Court had recourse to the statutory incorporation of the *Briginshaw* principle. But the High Court has twice inexplicably refused to review Fleming and clean up the confusion in South Australia, and possibly other courts, where there has been no statutory incorporation of *Briginshaw*.

There is no automatic right of appeal to the High Court; there is an approximately one-in-ten chance of a hearing.

Clarifying an area of the law where there is such inconsistency, and when the result can be so devastating, is surely one matter which needs the Court's attention.

As argued above, the only answer to this grave injustice would seem to lie in a Royal Commission undertaken by a former judge of as sound criminal law understanding as the dissenting judge in the Victorian Court of Appeal Justice Mark Weinberg in *George Pell v The Queen*.

Father Fleming and his family deserve to be saved from this supreme injustice.

David Flint AM is an Emeritus Professor of Law, having read law and economics at the Universities of Sydney, London, and Paris. He has served as Chairman of the Australian Press Council and of the Australian Broadcasting Authority and was made a Member of the Order of Australia in 1995. He writes regularly in the press and comments on radio and television and has published books and articles on topics such as foreign investment law, European Union law, the media, international economic law, and Australia's Constitution.

Foreword

Gabriël A. Moens AM

Supreme Injustice: Guilty until proven not Catholic? details Fr John Fleming's abominable treatment by Australia's judicial system.

Fr Fleming is a Catholic priest who, since 2008, has been the subject of an intense campaign by *The Advertiser/Sunday Mail,* a newspaper in Adelaide, to discredit his character and smear his reputation by accusing him of historical sex crimes. However, these allegations are unsubstantiated and implausible. He sued *The Advertiser/Sunday Mail* for publicising defamatory material about him, even though the police did not pursue the matter. However, Fr Fleming lost his defamation case in the first instance, a decision which was upheld by the Full Supreme Court of South Australia, and the High Court twice decided not to intervene.

The book is an eye-opening harrowing narrative that illustrates how a person's reputation could be thoroughly and irretrievably trashed by uncorroborated allegations made by some persons who hide behind the cloak of anonymity. Indeed, one complainant, "Jane", was underage at the time when the alleged abuse is said to have taken place and, therefore, her name could not be revealed. Although the names of two complaining adults are disclosed in the book, *The Advertiser/Sunday*

Mail still has not published their names. However, Fr Fleming's identity has been splashed all over the papers and in the media. Such treatment is more reminiscent of an authoritarian, dictatorial regime bent on maintaining its power by encouraging people to betray those who oppose the regime. One would not expect this tactic in a liberal democracy governed by the rule of law.

The obvious injustice suffered by Fr Fleming was compounded when, in the defamation action against the newspaper that published the unsubstantiated allegations, he was expected to prove that he did not commit the alleged acts.

Moreover, Fr Fleming's judicial trajectory reveals that policymakers and trendsetters seem to assume uncritically that, if you are a Catholic priest, you are certainly guilty because of your association with the Catholic Church. The author of *Supreme Injustice* confirms the existence of that assumption when he indicates that "once a Catholic priest is accused of a serious sexual offence, he is assumed to be guilty".

Of course, there have been cases where clerics have abused their position of trust by grooming young girls and boys to serve their perverse sexual interests, but paedophilia is clearly not limited to clerics. To assume that clerics must necessarily be guilty because of their association with a Church is an apt example of present-day persecution of religion in Australia, and throughout the world.

Religious persecution takes many forms. It ranges from complete disdain for what religions have to offer, to violent repression of religious activity. The former is exemplified by the Australian Curriculum, Assessment and Reporting Authority's revision of the high school curriculum which ostensibly disregards the Christian heritage of Australia. The latter may be illustrated by the vicious persecution of the Falun Gong faith and the Moslem Uyghurs in China, or religious minorities in Iran and Yemen where members of the Baha'i faith are treated horribly and imprisoned. The Western world's devaluation of the importance of the role of religion must necessarily impact on its ability, or even willingness, to condemn persecution of religion and people of faith.

Powerful or well-connected people, like Cardinal George Pell and former Attorney-General, the Hon Christian Porter MP have been accused of historical sex abuse offences. The former has since been completely exonerated by the High Court, while the latter initiated, and then settled, an action for defamation. Cardinal Pell and the Hon Porter are merely examples of what could happen to a person's reputation when allegations of sexual impropriety are made against them.

In Fr Fleming's case, both the trial judge and the appeal judges were not motivated to render a judgement based on a logical, impartial, and thorough analysis of the evidence presented to them. The book compellingly highlights the many logical inconsistencies in the statements made, and arguments developed, by the judges.

The judges proceeded on the basis that the complainant must always be believed, even if her allegations are riddled with uncertainties, discrepancies, inconsistencies, and contradictory statements. The "I hear, I listen, I believe" mantra, so boldly promoted by progressive politicians, policymakers, and judges, permeated the judicial proceedings, and inexcusably and irreparably influenced the judges' decision.

The judgments rendered by the courts in Fr Fleming's case are examples of crude utilitarianism. Proponents of utilitarianism would look at the judges' decision in the case and, considering the consequences of the judgment, they might conclude that it yields measurable benefits for society. These benefits include, but would not be limited to, the expectation that society would be a safer place for impressionable young people, even if occasionally a few innocent people get sacrificed in the process. However, such an approach distorts the rule of law, which requires that innocent people should go free. Nevertheless, this utilitarian approach has recently become very trendy, especially in our @meToo times. Fr Fleming is undoubtedly one of the victims of this illiberal trend.

The @meToo movement has facilitated the uncritical acceptance of the 'I hear, I listen, I believe' mantra according to which persons who say they are victims of sexual abuse must necessarily be believed regardless of the implausibility of their allegations. Although such allegations may prove to be true in some cases, there is always a distinct possibility that they are fictitious narratives because of the complainant's faulty memory, or because they are made in a malicious, revengeful manner.

One of the contentious points in the book's narrative relates to the onus of proof in defamation cases. As the complainant is always to be believed, the onus of proving that a person did not and could not possibly have done the acts accused of, is shifted to the plaintiff. This is a violation of the *Briginshaw* rule – a rule developed by the Australian High Court in 1938 – which appears to be consistently applied in Australia's jurisdictions, except in South Australia. The *Briginshaw* rule, which requires a complainant to prove the veracity of their allegations, is uniformly used in defamation cases. The only case in which judges have ruled that *Briginshaw* did not apply was Fr Fleming's case. The Full Supreme Court of South Australia commented on this issue:

> **We would add that, although in *Briginshaw* Dixon J referred to a person against whom are alleged serious matters enjoying the "presumption of innocence" and the consequent requirement of "exactness of proof", the later High Court judgments do not import that presumption into the civil arena. Furthermore, from the above it would appear that any references to *Briginshaw* as establishing an "onus" or a "standard" are incorrect. Additionally, in the several High Court cases referred to, there is no reference to *Briginshaw* establishing a "principle".**[1]

However, the same Supreme Court which ruled that *Briginshaw* was not to be applied in Fr Fleming's case, applied *Briginshaw* to a subsequent case in which the plaintiff was represented by the same lawyer who advised Fr Fleming. Hence, it is reasonable to speculate that *Briginshaw* has not been applied in Fr Fleming's case because he is Catholic priest. Be that as it may, the reality

1 *Fleming v Advertiser-News Weekend Publishing Company Pty Ltd & ANOR* [2016] SASCFC 109, Supreme Court (Full Court) (SA, Australia) at [108].

is that Fr Fleming was deprived of the presumption of innocence and, therefore, he had to prove his innocence.

In such circumstances, it is surprising that the High Court did not intervene in the one case in which the existing *Briginshaw* rule was not applied. The High Court should have accepted the appeal to clarify the application of the rule in defamation cases. The judgment in Fr Fleming's case means that, while the presumption of innocence prevails in criminal cases, the presumption does not appear to be applicable in defamation cases, which are civil cases.

The court's bizarre treatment of the concept of "contextual truth" and its rejuvenation of an ancient, and discredited view of a wife's role in giving evidence are perplexing. The courts' implication that Fleming's wife is untrustworthy because she is married to him, is disturbing. The courts' treatment of a reputable witness and expert, Dr Michelle Arnold, is also disgraceful.

I hope that the book facilitates a review of the judicial trajectory of Fr Fleming's case. This book may incentivise Australia's political and legislative authorities to explore the injustices suffered by Fr Fleming and other victims of historical sex abuse cases. An appeal to Australia's political rulers is indeed a road well-travelled by other litigants, but experience indicates that the chances of success are limited. This is because politicians are typically uninterested and, more importantly, are likely to hide behind the excuse that they cannot interfere with the work of judges in order not to violate the separation of powers doctrine. It is also unlikely that the *Briginshaw* rule will be embedded in the law of defamation because the relevant law is a creature of the common law – judge-made law.

Fr Fleming has written a powerful book that illustrates nicely that the uncritical embrace of the "I hear, I listen, I believe" mantra may eventually have fatal consequences for the application of the rule of law in Australia. Indeed, if the application of the mantra were to result in the crucifixion of many innocent people, a marked deterioration in the application of the rule of law would be observed over time. The ineluctable conclusion is that the "I hear, I listen, I believe" mantra has no place in a liberal democracy which is based on the rule of law. An important value of the book thus lies in revealing an egregious violation of the rule of law, which requires that all people be treated equally, regardless of their rank in society, sex, race, religion, or political affiliation.

I recommend this book to all people who are interested in the nefarious consequences of the illiberalism that is dividing, and possibly destroying, Australia at present. Although a reading of the book would benefit those who are interested in the nurturing of the rule of law, it will especially appeal to lawyers working in the field of defamation and politicians whose responsibility it is to see that the intentions of legislators are properly understood and applied.

This book will be valued by people of goodwill who still believe in the power of goodness, decency, and Australian fair play. As such, *Supreme Injustice* will become a classic in the literature that describes the perceptible deterioration of these values of a liberal Australia.

Gabriël A. Moens AM is Emeritus Professor of Law at the University of Queensland. He served as pro vice-chancellor and dean at Murdoch University, Western Australia. In 2003, Professor Moens was awarded the Australian Centenary Medal by the Prime Minister for services to education. He has taught extensively across Australia, Asia, Europe, and the United States.

Foreword

Augusto Zimmermann

I am honoured and delighted to write this foreword to *Supreme Injustice.* This book by John Fleming concerns his appalling treatment by the Australian justice system.

John Fleming is a Catholic priest living in retirement in South Australia. He was initially a married Anglican priest. An eminent, widely published scholar with an international reputation in the field of bioethics, Fr Fleming was the inaugural President of Campion College, Australia's highly regarded liberal arts institution located in Western Sydney.

Fleming's career, reputation, financial security, and family life were seriously compromised when, in 2008, the local Adelaide paper (*The Sunday Mail*) ran a series of unsubstantiated allegations made by the journalist Nigel Hunt against Fleming related to the historic sexual abuse of a minor. These allegations had been previously examined and dismissed by the South Australian police, casting extreme doubt on their veracity. There were other allegations made, but the claim by witness "Jane" was the most serious, as it alleged the criminal sexual abuse of a minor.

Fleming subsequently sued *The Sunday Mail* for defamation, and the case was heard in 2014. *The Sunday Mail* fought the action on the claim that the allegations it had published were true.

When Justice Gray's decision finally appeared in early 2016 after an inordinate and unexplained delay, Fleming's defamation case was dismissed, the judge having accepted as truthful the stories published by *The Sunday Mail* against Fleming. Fleming then appealed the decision, unsuccessfully, before the South Australian Supreme Court and finally, to the High Court of Australia where special leave was denied.

This was an appalling outcome. In a few words, the judge in the Fleming trial and subsequently the judicial members of the South Australian Supreme Court have completely overturned the presumption of innocence and held that some people are simply not to be believed.

While questions of natural justice and procedural fairness are extremely important, at the end of the day the harm done to Fleming's reputation is considerably irreversible and immeasurable. Being labelled with vile accusations due to a bungled court case can result in being permanently labelled this way. Following the court's decision, the Archdiocese of Adelaide denied Fleming the opportunity to re-engage in Catholic ministry. As Dr Paul Collits pointed out,

> **Sacked from his most important of jobs, Fleming and his family have been put through hell. Fleming's PhD thesis (Griffith University, 1992), was, ironically, about human rights and natural law. The law, in this case, has let down very badly an innocent man, convicted not by the police but in the court of public opinion, on the back of fanciful allegations of criminal conduct by one (witness Jane) who is clearly**

> **a deeply troubled soul. The legal battle to clear his name may not be over yet ... but John Fleming will never get back either his job or the lost peace of mind that has ruined his life since 2008.**[2]

As can be seen, this book is about the treatment envisaged by the Australian justice system on an innocent person. The Fleming judgement reported in the pages of this book reveals that something terribly wrong is happening with the Australian justice system. Accordingly, *Supreme Injustice* provides a sober reminder of what might happen to an innocent person when the system fails to uphold elementary principles of judicial fairness and natural justice.

To conclude, the scandalous outcome of this notorious case has compromised not only the life and reputation of an entirely innocent person but also the very image and reputation of the nation's court system in the eyes of the world. It is my hope that this book becomes a classic on the subject of miscarriage of justice in Australia.

Augusto Zimmermann is Professor and Head of Law at Sheridan Institute of Higher Education in Perth, WA. He is also Adjunct Professor of Law at the University of Notre Dame Australia, Sydney campus and President of the Western Australian Legal Theory Association (WALTA). From 2012 to 2017, he served as a Law Reform Commissioner in Western

2 Paul Collits, 'The Crucifixion of John Fleming', The Freedoms Project, 18 May 2020, at https://thefreedomsproject.com/item/522-the-crucifixion-of-john-fleming

Australia. While serving as Associate Dean (Research) at Murdoch School of Law, he was awarded the Vice Chancellor's Award for Excellence in Research, in 2012.

Introduction

Dr Paul Collits

The April 2020 High Court decision exonerating George Pell has lifted the spirits of his many supporters and has set the Get Pell brigade back on its heels.

The rabid anti-Catholicism of the secular press has been exposed. The manifest deformities of Victoria's "justice" system have been exposed. The utterly contemptible behaviour of our national broadcaster is patently obvious. Calls for the resignation of Victoria's Supreme Court justices who ludicrously upheld the conviction of Pell have multiplied since the High Court decision.

Yet there is a danger that all the media attention to the Pell case might have kept other cases of the maladministration of justice off the front pages. Perversely.

Other Catholic priests have suffered from the same toxic anti-Catholicism, the "guilt by accusation" referred to by Professor David Flint among others, that felled Pell. Only their stories, not having the star appeal of Pell, have remained under the radar.

Their stories deserve to be told. Not just to accord justice to the wrongly accused, but to bring to the surface in Australia's public consciousness a vicious campaign to bury the Catholic Church. To consign it to irrelevance in Australia.

The manifest injustices flowing from the perfect storm of Royal Commission led piles on, MeTooism "we believe you" ideology, victim activism weaponised by powerful interest groups and their favoured priest chasing lawyers, and residual sectarian impulses are, sadly, not confined to the good and innocent Cardinal.

The case of Dr Fleming is another, very regrettably not so fortunate, encounter with a faulty legal system that finally – finally – got around to delivering justice in these other cases, as, for example, that of Archbishop Phillip Wilson. Dr Fleming is an ageing Catholic priest, now living in uneasy and anxious retirement and poor health in South Australia, following his own trip to hell-on-earth.

Prior to becoming a member of the Catholic Church, he was an ordained minister of the Anglican Church of Australia. He enjoyed a long career as a broadcaster in commercial radio, had been a columnist for the local newspaper for 13 years, and enjoyed both a national and international reputation as an academic specialising in bioethics and public policy. Having completed degrees in theology and the arts, he was awarded his PhD at Griffith University (Queensland) in 1992 in philosophy and medical ethics.

Fleming has been an eminent Catholic scholar; a "star" convert to Catholicism from the Anglicanism of his upbringing; internationally recognised for his scholarly contributions to life issues and bio-ethics; a well-known and feted radio personality in South Australia; a weekly columnist for – of all things – the Adelaide Advertiser; a Doctor of Philosophy; a delegate to the Constitutional Convention in 1998; a faithful, orthodox priest; a highly respected inaugural President of Campion College in Western Sydney, much loved by his students and colleagues; a considerable presence in Adelaide over several decades; and indeed a public figure in that city. Oh, and highly unusual for the Catholic Church, Dr Fleming is married with three children, his ordination made possible by the outcome of a Papal dispensation (from St John Paul II) in 1995.

He indeed has a Wikipedia entry – potentially a mixed blessing in these times. Sadly, what Dr Fleming seems destined to be most remembered for is entirely another matter. For in 2008, his world fell apart under allegations of historical sexual impropriety and in one case alleged criminal abuse.

A Catholic public figure, a defender of traditional morality and so one with enemies as well as friends in a highly secularised city. At a time of virile anti-Catholicism, the subsequent Fleming court case occurring right at the height of the McClelland Royal Commission into child sex abuse and the Pell pile on occurring through the SANO Taskforce and Operation Tethering across the border in Victoria, it was a perfect storm for Father Fleming.

The Publication of Slanderous Allegations Against Dr Fleming

A happy life and a successful career as both priest and academic came crashing to earth in August 2008.

It was then that the publishers of *The Advertiser/ Sunday Mail* (*The Advertiser*), two newspapers owned by the same company (News Limited), decided to publish stories written by journalist Nigel Hunt concerning John Irving Fleming. Dr Fleming had been unsuccessfully targeted by *The Advertiser* before. This time the paper proceeded with allegations.

On the back of utterly spurious allegations of sexual impropriety, including accusations of criminal abuse many decades ago, the *Adelaide Advertiser's* Sunday tabloid (*The Sunday Mail*) went after Fleming, starting in August 2008 and continuing into 2009.

The allegations gave rise to no fewer than five defamatory articles in the Adelaide Murdoch press in 2008 and 2009. They related to three complainants, given the pseudonyms "Jane", "Jenny" and "Richard". The latter two complainants subsequently had their real names revealed – Diane Lynch and Peter Kay.

Absent police charges before or since the journalistic outing of Dr Fleming and on the basis of the thinnest plausibility, the newspaper conducted a campaign of public vilification and career destroying "journalism". They published allegations of a criminal nature that traduced a family and blighted an entire career, and in a way that revealed a ruthless determination to destroy Fleming and reflected secularist small town hubris disguised as investigative journalism. As is the way of it these days, the complainant in the alleged criminal matter has been allowed to keep her anonymity, her career, her reputation, and her life.

Here is what happened in August 2008.

Nigel Hunt sent emails to Dr Fleming in the days after World Youth Day 2008. In those emails Hunt said that he was coming to Sydney the next day and wanted to talk to him about his "activities" when he was an

Anglican priest in Adelaide. Dr Fleming told him that he could not see him that week because his schedule was already full. Subsequently, he received a tip-off from a friend that Hunt wanted to talk to him because he was going to soon run a story accusing him of misconduct.

Dr Fleming cancelled his appointments and stayed at home. The following day, Hunt arrived at Campion College with a photographer. He was told that Dr Fleming was not in. He then drove to his home and parked his car a couple of doors away from his house.

Hunt and his photographer came to the door and asked to speak to Dr Fleming. Through his wife he declined because Hunt would not provide him with the substance of the matters he wished to talk about. In any case, his solicitor strongly advised him not to speak to Hunt. Hunt was advised of Dr Fleming's response by his wife. His wife asked Hunt what he really wanted, and whether he would be considering anything that Dr Fleming might have to say before he wrote his story. Hunt replied that the story was already written, and he just wanted a response to it from Father Fleming.

In short, Hunt wanted Dr Fleming to respond to a story that he had not read and to do so without advanced notice of what he wanted to discuss with him. In the end Hunt provided a scrappy piece of paper on which he had written a short dot point list of things he wanted to discuss in the hope that Dr Fleming might change his mind. That short list was not full disclosure with crucial elements (such as names of complainants and all relevant details) withheld.

It should be clear, even to journalists at *The Advertiser*, that public accusations of the kind they were making would have a devastating effect on the person being accused. This is the case whether the accusations are true or not true. *The Advertiser* could provide no corroboration for the accusations being made, nor did they investigate the motives of the people concerned. Blindly following the slogan "always believe the accuser", Nigel Hunt did his worst. Where the principal accuser is concerned, there was available to Nigel Hunt an abundance of persons who could, and later did, corroborate Dr Fleming's account, and were in a good position to be able to explain the mental instability of the accuser and what her motivations would almost certainly be.

Nigel Hunt seems to have done nothing more than believe the accusers, and especially the person with the pseudonym "Jane".

Fleming subsequently sued the *Adelaide Advertiser* for defamation and lost when his case finally came to trial six years later, in 2014. It then took around a year following the trial for a judgement to be handed down.

Hence the allegations stood. He then appealed to the South Australian Supreme Court and lost. He then applied for the matter to be heard on appeal at the High Court, but the High Court refused to hear the appeal. These decisions do not mean that Fleming is guilty. Far from it. Important matters of law and of evidence were overlooked by the South Australian legal system in similar ways to the appalling treatment meted out to George Pell in Victoria. And in Dr Fleming's case, there weren't even police charges.

All the claims related to alleged events from as far back as the 1970s. It was not until August 2008 that Dr Fleming even knew of the allegations, although each of them had previously been raised with Church authorities, and in the case of Jane, with the South Australian Police.

In 2000, "Jane" complained to the Anglican Church Hotline, and gave a statement to police in 2007.

These were heinous allegations, and those making them, at least initially, had their anonymity preserved. One of the complainants, Jane, alleged criminal offences had been committed. The two other allegations, even if true, were not criminal offences.

Two of the three complainants received substantial cash and in-kind payments from the Anglican Church even before there had been any process to establish the truth or otherwise of the allegations.

None of these allegations is true. The events portrayed never happened. Dr Fleming released the following statement in response to the publication of the first article.

> *Public Statement of Dr Fleming*
>
> *The Sunday Mail said today that I am the subject of a police investigation.*
>
> *I know nothing of any such investigation. No police officer or other person has ever to this day approached me in relation to any criminal investigation: I have seen no statements: I have been given no particulars of any kind by anyone of any alleged criminal behaviour. I know nothing about any such investigation having ever occurred.*
>
> *I am shocked and sickened by what has been written about me in this article.*
>
> *I will deal with the three allegations contained in it separately.*

Firstly, as to the allegation relating to "Jane" I utterly refute that I have ever engaged in sexual or other inappropriate behaviour with a minor. It is an outrageous lie for anyone to suggest otherwise. As I have been told nothing of this person's identity or her circumstances or of what I'm alleged to have done to her, I cannot respond with more particularity. I can only say that the allegations are totally false, and I can say that because I have never behaved this way to any person. It is a wicked attack upon my character and upon my reputation. I urge "Jane" to go to the police immediately if she has not already done so.

Secondly, as to the allegation relating to "Jenny", while the particulars given are very scant, enough is revealed in relation to this allegation for me to identify the alleged "victim" as a woman known to me from previous unsubstantiated allegations made by her to my church.

She does not even allege on her own account anything that could constitute criminal behaviour. But further than that, I utterly refute any allegation of any inappropriate behaviour of any kind, sexual or otherwise, in relation to her.

She was a troubled young woman who I met as a member of my Anglican congregation at St Paul's Church in the 1970s. She was well known to my wife and to many other members of the congregation for the profoundly mistaken and inappropriate assumptions she made as to the nature of the assistance I was offering her.

Her complaint, such that it was, was dealt with appropriately by the Vicar General of the Church over twelve years ago. She took it no further until 2004 when she wrote to Cardinal Pell. She refused to take up the opportunity subsequently offered her at the Cardinal's request by my local bishop to have the matter reinvestigated.

If there is any substance in the suggestion that she has approached the police I welcome the opportunity to deal with her false allegations finally and comprehensively.

Finally, as to the allegations relating to "Richard", I utterly refute the suggestion in the article that at any time there was any impropriety in the discharge of my responsibilities as a counsellor or priest. It is utterly false to suggest we were in any kind of a "relationship" for six years. He, too, was a member of my St Paul's congregation. He and his wife later became close friends of my wife and me. Our relationships became personally complicated, but I had thought we had remained friends. He attended my ordination as a priest in 1995. His marriage was subsequently annulled following the processes of the Marriage Tribunal of the Church and he is now openly homosexual.

I cannot understand what has caused him to participate in this false attack upon me. I am shocked and dismayed at what he is alleged to have said.

As to the contentions in the article that there has been any irregularity or impropriety of any kind associated with my ordination as a priest or with my appointment to my present academic role, they are totally false and I utterly refute them. I welcome the investigation by Mr. Abbott KC as to these matters which Archbishop Wilson in Adelaide has apparently commissioned, though I knew nothing of it until I read about it in the article. I will co-operate fully with it and with any other investigation.

I have retained the best legal advice to assist me in responding to this outrageous attack upon me.

Over the years I know that some have been discomforted with my personal exposition of my understanding of my faith. We live in an age of increasing hostility, particular in sections of the media, to the Church and its teaching. It remains possible that this may explain in part this terrible attack upon me. There may be more mercenary explanations. I am determined to find out.

In accordance with long – established protocol in the church, it is appropriate that I stand down from my duties as a priest while these investigations are undertaken and completed. Similarly, and because I do not wish to cause any distraction or inconvenience to the wonderful College of which I am President or to its student body, I will not resume my duties at the college until these investigations have been brought to an end.

Thank you to all my friends and colleagues for their support at this time.

> *I will not be offering further comment until the investigations are complete.*

On 24 February 2016 the Supreme Court of South Australia found in favour of *The Sunday Mail,* ruling that the articles truthfully conveyed imputations that Dr Fleming was engaged in "sexual misconduct, predatory sexual behaviour, morally reprehensible and deceitful conduct, an immoral, adulterous, homosexual affair, hypocrisy, abuse of trust, moral cowardice and false denial of sexual involvement", with costs awarded against him.

The judgement was especially vicious, as well as being beyond incompetent. Fleming had to wait over a year even to get this judgement!

The judge in Fleming's initial defamation case was Justice Malcolm Gray. Those who have argued for judge only trials involving historical abuse allegations because of the poisoning of the public mind and therefore the difficulties in finding an unbiased jury, might want to think again post the Fleming saga. Judges get it palpably wrong too.

Gray's performance in the Fleming case makes Victorian Justices Ferguson and Maxwell look like some combination of William Rehnquist and Lord Denning. It seems that, when it comes to judges in Australia, you just can't get good help anymore. Gray took over a year to deliver his verdict and judgement, an inexcusable delay, and a matter where the High Court had earlier confirmed that Gray "had form".

Whether more motivated by incompetence – and there is plenty, as this book will reveal – or latter-day anti-Catholicism is a question without a definite answer. Either way, the judge involved here can only be described as failing to deliver justice, both in relation to the law and to his treatment of the evidence.

Following the High Court's decision not to hear Dr Fleming's final appeals in 2017, the Archdiocese of Adelaide proceeded to deny Dr Fleming the opportunity to engage in any Catholic ministry. So, Dr Fleming was sacked from his most important of jobs, as well as he and his family having been put through hell.

Dr Fleming's PhD thesis (Griffith University, 1992), was, ironically, about human rights and natural law. The law in this case has let down very badly an innocent man, convicted not by the police but in the court of public opinion, on the back of fanciful allegations of criminal conduct by one (witness Jane) who is clearly a deeply troubled soul. The legal battle to clear his name may not be over yet, with discussions ongoing in relation to one last (re-)appeal to the High Court, but Dr Fleming will never get back either his job or the lost peace of mind that has ruined his life since 2008.

The campaign by *The Advertiser* (*Sunday Mail*) to destroy Dr Fleming tapped into three contemporary powerful beliefs in society – #MeTooism, aka always believe the accuser; get the Catholic priests; and punish them for the many past sins of the Church in relation to sex abuse.

Sadly, the travesty of justice masquerading as a legal system in South Australia allowed the defamations of August 2008 to stand. The whole saga started with a single journalist. The journalist Nigel Hunt came to hear of the allegations against Dr Fleming and he went a trawling. He tracked down the complainants – they didn't come to him – and hence initiated a Fleming pile on. It was all about Nigel Hunt, like Louise Milligan feted with awards for her journalism.

Hunt was even able to get in a swipe at Pell, following the judgement in the Fleming defamation case. "Pell knew!"

The Court's decision meant that Hunt and colleagues could engage in further gloating and that words like "disgraced", "predator", "moral coward", "victim" and "liar" could continue to be bandied about without fear of reprisal from the one real victim in this case.

Because Dr Fleming is not a famous prelate like Cardinal Pell, despite his public persona, and because the Fleming case was very much an Adelaide only affair not subject to East Coast, let alone international media interest, it all occurred under the radar and hence Fleming's supporters have been fewer and less vocal. Ultimately it was all down to Dr Fleming to seek justice for himself, at the cost of all his savings. (Even Pell, of course, was virtually disowned by the Australian bishops who, almost to a man, took to fence sitting on the very odd occasions on which they ventured an opinion on Pell's guilt or innocence).

This book sets out to tell the story of Dr Fleming's search for justice and details the ways in which the justice system has so badly let him down. In doing so, it uncovers serious, unresolved legal issues that apply to every case of uncorroborated, historical sex abuse allegations. It also highlights the context in which men, especially men of religion, are considered fair game in the light of legal #MeTooism, the moral panic associated with Church sex abuse, and the pile-on culture in the secular media. We now inhabit a culture of "guilt by accusation" in which the odds are clearly stacked against the accused.

Dr Fleming's is a story that must be told.

Dr Paul Collits
Senior Political Commentator, Politicom
Freelance Writer

Chapter One

Legal Processes Begin

This is a case where the defendants were aware of a police investigation into the plaintiff's relations with three young persons. The defendants decided that they were not interested in the results of that investigation – *The Sunday Mail* has, apparently, the right to be judge and jury. *The Sunday Mail* convicted the plaintiff of criminal conduct in the court of public opinion before he had even been given the opportunity to be interviewed by police.

A few short months after the publications by *The Sunday Mail* of a serious allegation of a criminal offense, Dr John Fleming was interviewed by the police. In November 2008, and following that police interview, SAPOL wrote to Dr Fleming's solicitor:

> **I would like to advise that matter of sexual allegations made by [JANE] against FLEMING has been finalised by police. There will be no formal charges laid against FLEMING. This matter will now be filed by police; however, can be re-opened and investigated at any stage due to further evidence or alleged victim/s.**
>
> **Kind regards**
>
> **Senior Constable Mel Worden**

Father Fleming's involvement with the Police ended there. He was not to be charged with anything. The Police believed his side of the story, or at least found there was no compelling evidence in favour of Jane which meant that they would take the matter no further. The matter was "filed" by the Police.

That should have been the end of the matter. But it was not to be.

Decision to sue

Faced with what is right, to leave it undone shows a lack of courage.[3]

Courage is going from failure to failure without losing enthusiasm.[4]

Dr Fleming sued the media publishers for defamation because (a) he believed that *The Advertiser* was never going to let the matter go, and (b) he knew that the Catholic Archbishop of Adelaide, Philip Wilson, had decided to end his career even though these matters had been dismissed by the Church and by the police. Archbishop Wilson forbade him to return to work, a rule which he did not apply to himself even though he, himself, had been charged [unfairly I believe] with a serious criminal offence.

In summary, as a priest and academic, Father Fleming had been severely damaged as a direct result of those publications.

---

3 Robert Eno, translator and editor, *The Analects of Confucius, An Online Teaching Translation*, 2015 (Version 2.2), at 2.24.

4 Attributed to Winston Churchill and equally to Abraham Lincoln.

1. He lost his position as President of Campion College, a liberal arts tertiary institution in Sydney. The financial cost of that loss was enormous, especially for a man of 65 years as he was at the time.
2. He effectively became unemployable in the positions in life in which he had excelled including employment in radio and as head of any other academic institute.
3. He was given no appointment when he moved back to Adelaide by Archbishop Wilson, and ever since has had no position of responsibility anywhere either in Church or State.
4. His personal health has been substantially damaged.
5. His wife and children have suffered greatly.
6. The stories about these allegations are on the webpage of *Adelaide Now,* the website of *The Advertiser/Sunday Mail,* and so continue to be broadcast every day, not only within Australia but to the whole world.

In the present political and social climate in Adelaide, South Australia, like that which obtains throughout Australia, it is the case that once a Catholic priest is accused of a serious sexual offence, he is assumed to be guilty. Even if he can establish the high improbability that he committed the offence, he will not be listened to by large sections of the community, much if not most of the judiciary, the hierarchy of the Catholic Church, and large sections of the mainstream media.

A classic example of the present mentality, although not involving a Catholic priest, is the American case of

Professor Alan Dershowitz, former professor of law at Harvard and now retired. Dershowitz is quite rightly "proud of the way I've conducted my private and professional life during my long career as a professor, lawyer and public intellectual".[5]

Although Dershowitz had never been convicted in a court of law of any offence, still he lost his position as a political and legal commentator on television, his reputation, and his sense of who he really is as a human being.

> **In the minds of some, including some in the media, the presumption, indeed the certainty, of guilt that flows from an accusation by a woman cannot be overcome by evidence or the lack thereof.** Though there is not a scintilla of evidence to support the accusation against me—no photographs, no witnesses, no documents, no contemporaneous accusation—and though the accuser has a long history of falsely accusing prominent men, and though she communicated to her friends she did not have sex with me, and though her lawyer admitted she was "wrong," the media persists in portraying me as possibly guilty. **The result of this media portrayal is that I am now presumed guilty—or at least suspect—and at age 81 my life and career are no longer being honoured but dishonoured.** An obituary writer for the Washington Post called to tell

5 Alan Dershowitz, *Guilt by Accusation: The Challenge of Proving Innocence in the Age of #MeToo*, Hot Books, New York 2019, Kindle Edition, Location 1780-1789.

> me that he was drafting my obituary, which would include references to the accusation. All this because of a demonstrably false accusation by a woman with a long history of lying.[6]

Dershowitz points out the difficulty of the accused person publicly denying the allegation, let alone to cast aspersions on the trustworthiness of the accuser.

> For a man to call a false accuser a liar became a political sin, even if the accused had hard evidence of the accuser's lies, as I did. Much of the media, especially but not exclusively the social media, bought into the narrative of guilt by accusation instead of by proof. They refused to report on evidence of innocence that contradicted the narrative of guilt.[7]

As things turned out, his accuser recently withdrew her allegations where Dershowitz is concerned. She[8] reportedly stated 'she may have been mistaken'.

Dr Fleming found himself in a similar situation to Dershowitz. *The Advertiser/Sunday Mail* is the only newspaper published in Adelaide. No other media, including the whole of the Adelaide electronic media, was really interested in this story. The Catholic Church ran an inquiry which did not incriminate Dr Fleming.

---

6 Alan Dershowitz, *Guilt by Accusation: The Challenge of Proving Innocence in the Age of #MeToo*, Hot Books, New York 2019, Kindle Edition, Location 220 – 226.

7 Alan Dershowitz, *Guilt by Accusation: The Challenge of Proving Innocence in the Age of #MeToo*, Hot Books, New York 2019, Kindle Edition, Location 201 – 208.

8 Maria Puente, "Woman who accused Prince Andrew drops 'mistaken' allegations against Alan Dershowitz", USA Today, 8 November 2022, www.usatoday.com

The Anglican Church also conducted an inquiry even though, as it later recognised, it had no standing to do so, Dr Fleming having abandoned Anglicanism in 1987 and was neither a member of their Church nor their clergy. There was no public way to fight back. Even during the defamation trial, it was *The Advertiser* alone (the defendant) which published news of the trial, and that in a biased way, and without even the slightest shame at their conflict of interest. All that was left was the hope of justice in the SA Supreme Court. He chose to sue.

Dr Fleming was suing only on the Jane accusations because they were allegations involving serious criminality on his part if proved to be true. Dealing with all three of them would mean a long and costly trial which he could not sustain economically.

The media publishers responded by choosing to run also with Peter Kay and Dianne Lynch as contextual truth. If they failed to show that the Jane allegations were true, then they could use the other two matters to demonstrate that Dr Fleming's reputation had not been further damaged by the publishing of the Jane allegations.

In August 2010 Dr Fleming applied to have the contextual truth defence of *The Advertiser* struck out and the names of the three complainants revealed.

Section 24 of the South Australian *Defamation Act 2005* reads thus:

> 24—Defence of contextual truth
>
> It is a defence to the publication of defamatory matter if the defendant proves that—
>
> the matter carried, in addition to the defamatory imputations of which the plaintiff

> complains, one or more other imputations ("contextual imputations") that are substantially true; and
>
> the defamatory imputations do not further harm the reputation of the plaintiff because of the substantial truth of the contextual imputations.

Dr Fleming's legal team argued that it is simply incorrect, indeed risible, to say that the suggestion that a young Anglican minister having had unlawful sexual intercourse with a minor does not further injure that minister's reputation from allegations of adult consensual sex. So, lawyers for Dr Fleming applied to have the other two items struck from *The Advertiser*'s defence arguing that it would seem to be obvious that as far as the State is concerned, consensual adult sex provides no context for an allegation of criminal sexual misconduct with a minor. The Court refused that application.

Judge Burley (a Master of the Supreme Court of South Australia) handed down his decision rejecting both key elements of the application. This, he said, is a matter for the Judge at trial to determine whether the defence had made out the pleading of contextual truth.[9]

The matters of contextual truth and revealing the names of the complainants were the subject of another application to the Supreme Court in June 2013. Judge Dart refused the application.[10]

---

9 Judgment of Judge Burley a Master of the Supreme Court, *Fleming v Advertiser-News Weekend Publishing Company Pty Limited and ANOR* [2010] SASC 255, 18 August 2010.

10 Judge Dart, *Fleming v Advertiser-News Weekend Publishing Co Pty Ltd & ANOR* [2013] SASC 92 (19 June 2013).

There was a third and final hearing on these matters in April 2013. Justice Peek also refused the application.[11] In the event, Diane Lynch's allegations were not accepted by the judge acting in the defamation trial.

The crucial legal issues at stake in defamation – the importance of Briginshaw v Briginshaw

To understand the context within which a civil action is heard in Australian courts one must have regard to the longstanding Australian High Court case of *Briginshaw v Briginshaw* which defined the way in which courts are expected to make their judgements. The following elements to be satisfied in defamation cases involving the publication of an accusation of criminal behaviour are these:

1. The standard of proof required is that the accusation is substantially true on the balance of probabilities as guided by the *Briginshaw* rule.
2. According to the Melbourne Law Review:

   > The *Briginshaw* approach is based on the principle that a court in a civil action should not lightly find that a party has engaged in criminal conduct. As accusations of wrongdoing usually involve serious consequences for the defendant, justice demands that the

11 Judgement of Judge Peek, Fleming v Advertiser-News Weekend Publishing Company Pty Ltd and Advertiser Newspapers Pty Ltd [2012] SASC 58 (13 April 2012)

accuser, whether in civil or criminal matters, carries the burden of proof to the requisite standard. It is not surprising that this issue was at the forefront of Dixon J's mind in *Briginshaw*, as he had but recently commented on it extra-curially in relation to Australian criminal law.

Briginshaw therefore directs a court to proceed cautiously in a civil case where a serious allegation has been made or the facts are improbable. If the finding is likely to produce grave consequences, the evidence should be of high probative value. The *Briginshaw* test focuses attention on the standard of the evidence required to prove the case to the ordinary civil standard—it is not a change in the standard of proof. There is no third standard of proof in the common law. More proof means nothing more than better evidence.

3. Emphasis is placed on the need for 'clear' or 'cogent' evidence to bring about the reasonable degree of satisfaction required in the particular case. The following passage from Dixon J's judgment in *Briginshaw* continues to be cited by subsequent courts:

    Except upon criminal issues to be proved by the prosecution, it is enough that the affirmative of an allegation is made out to the reasonable satisfaction of the tribunal. But reasonable satisfaction is

> **not a state of mind that is attained or established independently of the nature and consequence of the fact or facts to be proved. The seriousness of an allegation made, the inherent unlikelihood of an occurrence of a given description, or the gravity of the consequences flowing from a particular finding are considerations which must affect the answer to the question whether the issue has been proved to the reasonable satisfaction of the tribunal. In such matters "reasonable satisfaction" should not be produced by inexact proofs, indefinite testimony, or indirect inferences. Everyone must feel that, when, for instance, the issue is on which of two dates an admitted occurrence took place, a satisfactory conclusion may be reached on materials of a kind that would not satisfy any sound and prudent judgment if the question was whether some act had been done involving grave moral delinquency.**[12]

4. As *Briginshaw* expressed it: "In such matters 'reasonable satisfaction' should not be produced by inexact proofs, indefinite testimony or indirect inferences."
5. In *Rejfek v McElroy* (1965) 112 CLR 517 at [10] the Court spoke of **"(T)he degree of satisfaction**

12 *Briginshaw v Briginshaw*, [1938] HCA 34, 60 CLR 336 at p 362, Dixon J.

for which the civil standard of proof calls may vary according to the gravity of the fact to be proved."

6. *Briginshaw* was seen to import a certain degree of flexibility into the civil standard of proof. In 1992, the High Court in *Neat Holdings Pty Ltd v Karajan Holdings Pty Ltd* stated: "**The ordinary standard of proof required of a party who bears the onus in civil litigation in this country is proof on the balance of probabilities. That remains so even where the matter to be proved involves criminal conduct or fraud. On the other hand, the strength of the evidence necessary to establish a fact or facts on the balance of probabilities may vary according to the nature of what it is sought to prove.**[13]
7. In 2018 Justice Rachel Pepper summarised the position thus: "put simply... *Briginshaw* should be seen not as a standard of proof, but as a standard of satisfaction. That is to say, that the more serious the allegation, the more serious or anxious should be the consideration given by the decision maker that he or she has attained the necessary state of reasonable satisfaction or persuasion that the facts in dispute are more likely than not to exist."[14]
8. In defamation proceedings, publications are presumed to be false until proven otherwise.

13 *Neat Holdings Pty Ltd v Karajan Holdings Pty Ltd* [1992] HCA 66, 110 CLR 445 at p 449-50, High Court.

14 Pepper, Rachel, "*Briginshaw* in Land and Environment Court Proceedings - Introductory Observations from the Judicial Perspective", (2013) Judicial Commission of NSW.

> In contrast to criminal law, and even civil law in general, the burden of proof falls to the defendant to prove that they did not defame the plaintiff.[15] In other words, the onus of proof is on the defendant, the one who published the allegations.

In the case of Dr Fleming Justice Gray did not apply *Briginshaw* correctly, but he seemed to recognise that it ought to be applied.

But the Full Court of the Supreme Court of South Australia [108] not only did not properly apply *Briginshaw*, it addressed the reference by Dixon J to a "presumption of innocence" in a dismissive way asserting that "later High Court judgments do not import that presumption into the civil arena". Whilst that might be the case since it was already there, more importantly neither do they remove it. Justices Vanstone, Nicholson, and Bampton then went on to say that "... it would appear that any references to *Briginshaw* as establishing an 'onus' or a 'standard' are incorrect."[16]

This book will demonstrate that the appellant (Dr John Fleming) was denied the presumption of innocence, that the *Briginshaw* rule was either not properly applied or not applied at all in his case, and that the appellant was being forced to prove his innocence in undocumented and uncorroborated events said to have occurred 40 years previously and for which he had witnesses who

---

15 Jackie Olling, "Defamation Law in Australia: 5 Things You Need to Know", *Lawpath*, 3 October 2018, https://lawpath.com.au/blog/defamation-law-australia-5-things-need-know

16 *Fleming v Advertiser-News Weekend Publishing Company Pty Ltd & ANOR* [2016] SASCFC 109 (29 September 2016), at paragraph 108.

would corroborate much of what he said in his own defence.

Summary of allegations against Dr Fleming

The central issue at stake in the defamation case against *The Advertiser/Sunday Mail* was the allegation of criminal sexual misbehaviour. In its various publications, *The Advertiser* outlined certain criminal sexual acts said to have been committed by Dr Fleming against a 14-year-old girl at a country town in South Australia, Meningie, in his car at Brighton, and at his flat in North Adelaide.

Dr Fleming was suing *The Advertiser* for defamation, and this was the matter on which he wished to sue. *The Advertiser* promoted the allegations of Peter Kay and Diane Lynch as contextual truth.

Social worker Diane Lynch's allegation was not proved according to Justice Gray, nor indeed was her evidence accepted by the Anglican Church who nevertheless paid her a large sum of money in compensation despite having conducted no process involving Dr Fleming to determine what were the facts of the matter. Peter Kay's allegations were believed by Justice Gray. His allegations, if they were true, involved consensual adult sex. Jane's allegations were far more serious because they entailed criminal behaviour with a minor. But Justice Gray not only accepted the Kay allegations as substantially true with the implications for damages had Dr Fleming succeeded where Jane was concerned, he also used the Kay matter as a means of proving the Jane matter which he was not entitled to do.

Moreover. Justice Gray should then have rejected the entire contextual truth submission because he had dismissed one half of it (Diane Lynch) as being not proved.

In summary, Jane's allegations in the Court were these:

1. **The "Meningie incident"**: That she had gone with the McNicol family for a holiday in Meningie at the Anglican Rectory where Dr Fleming was the *locum tenens*. She claimed that the sleeping arrangements in the house involved her and her 14-year-old friend, Alison McNicol, sleeping in the same room as then 27-year-old Anglican priest, Dr Fleming. On the first night Jane claims that she had engaged in a sexual act (touching) with Dr Fleming while *Alison* was, at the same time, passionately kissing him. Jane had two other entirely different and mutually contradictory versions of her story which will be dealt with later.
2. **The "Brighton Beach" incidents**: Jane further claimed that she had performed sexual acts on Dr Fleming in his "bubble car" near Brighton Beach. Justice Gray found that these were not proved.
3. **The "St Mark's College" incidents**: Jane also claimed that she had visited Dr Fleming's flat in North Adelaide and performed oral sex on him.

The trial *Fleming v The Advertiser*

The matter was heard before a single judge of the Supreme Court of South Australia. Dr Fleming appealed against that decision to the Full Court (3 judges) of the Supreme Court, an appeal which failed. Finally, Dr Fleming twice sought leave to appeal to the High Court of Australia and each time it was refused.

The defendant carried the onus of proving justification. In this case the defendant sought to justify 'criminal sexual conduct'. The standard of proof was meant to be in accordance with *Briginshaw* principles. The *Briginshaw* principles enable the Court to say to a defendant in the circumstances of a case such as this: you will be held to at least a burden approaching the criminal burden. For it to be otherwise would undermine the rule of law and constitutional protections upon which every member of society relies. There is good reason for this. It is the police who are charged with the responsibility of investigating crime: Police Act 1988 (SA), s.5. When the police investigate and prosecute a case they are bound by certain strict rules of conduct and procedure. Further, had police charged the plaintiff with an offence concerning Jane the publications would almost certainly have been a contempt: *Hinch v AG (1987) 164 CLR* 15. Matters pertaining to Ms Lynch and Peter Kay could not conceivably have been given in evidence in prosecuting the plaintiff in respect of an alleged offence involving Jane. Note in particular Mason CJ at pp.19, and 25-26, and Deane J at pp. 58-59. In summary, therefore, on the issue of the burden of proof, the decision does not boil down to "who does the Court believe?" The real question is not one that requires the Court having to make a "choice" between the witnesses. The evidence of the complainant witnesses is to be considered in conjunction with the content of the plaintiff's evidence and all the other evidence. Where there is a conflict between the defendants' witnesses and the plaintiff (and witnesses he called), **the question is not whose evidence is to be preferred, but whether the defendants have proved their case in accordance with *Briginshaw* principles.**

The aim of this book

It is the aim of this book to show that the judges of the Supreme Court involved in this matter were wrong in finding that the allegations of Jane and Peter Kay involved events which were substantially true because

a) they failed to interpret and apply the law correctly, fairly, and impartially;
b) they reversed the onus of proof;
c) they broke the ordinary rules of logic;
d) in some instances, they misunderstood and misstated the evidence before them; and
e) they indulged their penchant for two main prejudices: the errant belief that an adult woman complaining of sexual abuse is presumed to be telling the objective truth and her evidence is always to be preferred to that of the one accused of the abuse, and that Catholic priests and clergy generally are not to be believed.

In schematic form what seems to have been the strategy employed by Justice Gray makes clear how some of the mistakes made in his judgement occurred, mistakes which, as will be shown, seem also to have strongly influenced the judges in the Full Court of Appeal.

Justice Gray's Strategy

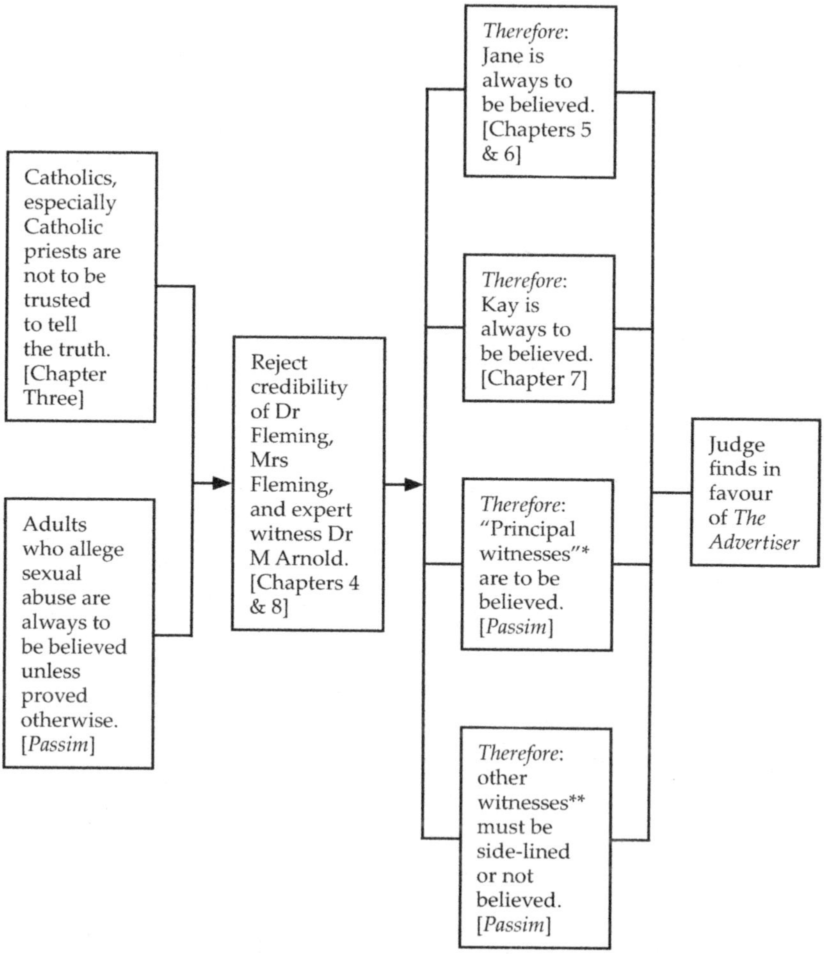

*The "principal witnesses" in this trial are only those witnesses who appeared for The Advertiser. Witnesses who appeared in support of Dr Fleming were not to be considered "principal" and so were not part of that favoured list.

The other witnesses** who gave evidence in support of Dr Fleming, included a former judge, a lawyer, two Anglican clerics, a teacher, a retired senior public servant, a retired businessman, a social worker specialising in sex abuse and family therapy, and an academic expert in cognitive memory.

Chapter Two

Contextual Truth

A critical element of the defendants' case was the defence of contextual truth. To clarify:

> *Truth (or justification) is a complete defence to an action for defamation.*
>
> *The defendant (the alleged defamer) must prove that the defamatory imputation carried by the material published is substantially true.*
>
> ...
>
> *Where the defendant (the alleged defamer) proves that the matter carried 1 or more imputations that are substantially true (contextual imputations) and that any defamatory imputations of which the plaintiff complains that are not contextual imputations (ie because they are not proved to be true) do not further harm the reputation of the plaintiff because of the substantial truth of the contextual imputations, then the defence of contextual truth succeeds.*
>
> *The contextual imputations on which the defendant may rely to establish the defence of contextual truth can include imputations of which the plaintiff has complained. In other words, in order to establish the defence, a defendant may*

> *plead back (as contextual imputations) any substantially true imputations originally pleaded by the plaintiff. For example, if a publication carries imputations that a professional person has intentionally deceived a client and has also stolen another client's money and only one of the imputations is proved to be true, that may be sufficient to defend the whole publication through the defence of contextual truth.*[17]

In pre-trial proceedings to the defamation action relating to publication of allegations made by Jane, *The Advertiser* and *The Sunday Mail* (the defendants) sought to use their publication of the allegations made by Peter Kay and Diane Lynch as contextual truth to assist in their defence. Section 24 of the *Defamation Act 2005* (SA) states:

> **24—Defence of contextual truth**
>
> **It is a defence to the publication of defamatory matter if the defendant proves that—**
>
> **(a) the matter carried, in addition to the defamatory imputations of which the plaintiff complains, one or more other imputations (contextual imputations) that are substantially true; and**
>
> **(b) the defamatory imputations do not further harm the reputation of the plaintiff because of the substantial truth of the contextual imputations.**

17 *Law Handbook*, Legal Services Commission of South Australia, https://lawhandbook.sa.gov.au/

The defendants argued that if they proved the truth of the Kay and Lynch allegations, irrespective of whether the truth of Jane's allegations of underage sexual relations with the plaintiff was proved, the defence case would be won because the imputations of Jane's allegations would not have further damaged the reputation of the plaintiff (Dr Fleming). They argued there would be no additional damage to the plaintiff's reputation by the publication of Jane's allegations involving unlawful sex with a minor if what Kay claimed concerning homosexual acts with the plaintiff, and Lynch's claims of having an unspecified sexual act with him, were true, even though those allegations concerned acts between consenting adults.

The plaintiff unsuccessfully applied to have the contextual truth defence struck out prior to the main trial and then during the trial itself. As a comparatively recent piece of legislation, there was limited authority available on the application of section 24 of the *Defamation Act 2005* (SA). Section 16 of the *Defamation Act 1974* (NSW) is of assistance notwithstanding that the contextual truth defence created by that section requires public interest to be established.

An early authority on section 16 of the NSW Act is *Jackson v John Fairfax* [1981] 1 NSWLR 36 at 40:

> **... From this discussion, it is apparent that the following issues of law will arise in relation to a defence of contextual truth (it having already been found that the matter complained of is capable of conveying the imputation pleaded by the plaintiff to which the defence of contextual truth is pleaded by the defendant):**

> **(1) Does the contextual imputation relied upon by the defendant differ in substance from that pleaded by the plaintiff?**
>
> **(2) Is the contextual imputation capable of being conveyed by the matter complained of at the same time as and in addition to the imputation pleaded by the plaintiff?**
>
> **(3) Is the nature of the contextual imputation such that its substantial truth is capable of being rationally considered by the jury as so affecting the plaintiff's reputation that the imputation of which the plaintiff complains did not further injure that reputation?**

The defamatory imputations pleaded by the plaintiff were:

> **Paragraph 5A**
>
> **(1) That the Plaintiff as an Anglican priest had committed criminal offences of unlawful sexual intercourse with a vulnerable minor in her formative adolescent years who might be as young as 13 thereby resulting in irreversible effects; or alternatively**
>
> **(2) That there were reasonable grounds to suspect that the Plaintiff as an Anglican priest had committed criminal offences of unlawful sexual intercourse with a vulnerable minor in her formative adolescent years who might be as young as 13 thereby resulting in irreversible effects.**

Paragraph 7A

(1) That the Plaintiff as an Anglican priest had committed criminal offences of unlawful sexual intercourse with a minor who might be as young as 13; or alternatively

(2) There were reasonable grounds to suspect that the Plaintiff as an Anglican priest had committed criminal offences of unlawful sexual intercourse with a minor who might be as young as 13.

Paragraph 9A

(1) That the Plaintiff as an Anglican priest had committed criminal offences of unlawful sexual intercourse with a minor who might be younger than 13; or alternatively

(2) There were reasonable grounds to suspect that the Plaintiff as an Anglican priest had committed criminal offences of unlawful sexual intercourse with a minor who might be younger than 13.

Paragraph 11A

(1) That the Plaintiff as an Anglican priest had committed criminal offences of unlawful sexual intercourse with a minor who might be as young as 13; or alternatively

(2) There were reasonable grounds to suspect that the Plaintiff as an Anglican priest had committed criminal offences of

unlawful sexual intercourse with a minor who might be as young as 13.

Paragraph 12A

(1) That the Plaintiff as an Anglican priest had committed criminal offences of unlawful sexual intercourse with a minor who might be younger than 13 in respect of whom he stood in a professional relationship; or alternatively

(2) There were reasonable grounds to suspect that the Plaintiff as an Anglican priest had committed criminal offences of unlawful sexual intercourse with a minor who might be younger than 13 in respect of whom he stood in a professional relationship.

The defence's response included imputations of contextual truth in so far as they concerned the allegations by Kay and Lynch of consensual adult sexual activity.

In seeking to have this application of the law regarding contextual truth refused as a matter of law, the plaintiff argued that it would be simply incorrect to hold that the allegation that a young Anglican priest having unlawful sexual intercourse with a minor did not further injure that priest's reputation than the injury caused by the allegation that he engaged in consensual sexual activity with an adult member of his congregation. The plaintiff pointed out that the allegation concerning unlawful sexual intercourse with a minor is an offence with a maximum penalty of a term of imprisonment for life (*Criminal Law Consolidation Act 1935* (SA), section 49(1)). But where the contextual imputations pleaded by the defendant are concerned, the law imposes no offence.

This would also mean that the two matters pleaded as contextual truth by the defendants could not also be pleaded as partial justification in mitigation of damages. *The Law of Defamation in Australia and New Zealand,*[18] states:

> **Leaving aside the defence of contextual truth, evidence may not be led in order to justify imputations other than the ones complained of, even if they are conveyed by the very same matter: NRMA Insurance v Amalgamated Television Services [1989] A Def R 40,371 at 40,371-2.**[19]

Particulars of justification are liable to be struck out where they are incapable of supporting a defamatory meaning of "reasonable grounds to suspect". The principle to be applied on that question was set out in *Manock v Advertiser News-Weekend Publishing Co Ltd* where Besanko J stated:

> **If it is not reasonably arguable that a particular of a plea of justification is capable of supporting the plea then it should be struck out. It should be struck out because it discloses no reasonable defence (r 46.18(a)) or because it has a tendency to cause**

18 Michael Gillooly, The Law of Defamation in Australia and New Zealand, Federation Press, 1998, p 115.

19 See also *Herald & Weekly Times Ltd v Popovic* (2003) 9 VR 1 at [323, 324].

> **prejudice, embarrassment or delay in the proceedings (r 46.18(c)).**[20]

The plaintiff argued that this test (that if it is not reasonably arguable that a particular of a plea of justification is capable of supporting the plea then it should be struck out) is the sort of test which the Court should adopt when considering the strike out of a plea of contextual truth. It is suggested that it is reasonably arguable that the plea complies with the parameters of section 24.

The plaintiff also argued that the 'leeway' (in the sense of only needing to be 'capable' of supporting the plea) associated with the pleading of imputations by the plaintiff should not be adopted for this separate purpose for the following reasons:

> **(1) the Act does not require it;**
>
> **(2) South Australia does not have juries where defamation trials are concerned;**
>
> **(3) it is an appropriate decision at the interlocutory stage which in this instance will ensure that 'the proper conduct of the action' is not prejudiced; in other words there is no reason to read down Chapter 5, Part 2, Div. 2 of the Supreme Court Rules, particularly rr.98, 100, and 104;**
>
> **(4) the suggestion would appear to be foreign to NSW practice in respect of section 16 of the Defamation Act 1975 (NSW): Pavy**

20 Manock v Advertiser News-Weekend Publishing Co Ltd (2004) 88 SASR 495 at 510.

v John Fairfax Publications [2000] NSWSC 328; Sutherland v ACP Publishing Pty Ltd [2000] NSWSC 1139 at [28-36];

(5) the issue here is not whether the contextual imputations pleaded are 'capable' of arising; the issue is rather whether the imputations pleaded can comply with the strictures of section 24, particularly section 24(b).

It was also argued that further prejudice would follow to the plaintiff in this case for the following reasons:

1. The plaintiff is entitled to pursue the separate and distinct defamatory meaning that he has chosen. In justifying that imputation – of serious criminal conduct – the defendant would not be entitled to adduce evidence of consensual sexual acts with two adults.
2. For the defendant to be allowed to plead these alleged contextual imputations would be to allow evidence into the proceeding which will no doubt be reported – the plaintiff is a prominent theologian – to the plaintiff's detriment whatever the result of the proceedings.
3. Moreover, although there will not be a jury, it is inappropriate that the judge be exposed to such evidence.

In the event, these concerns appear justified. *The Advertiser* published further highly prejudicial articles discussing the case after the judgement was handed down to damage Dr Fleming as much as they could.

In addition, Dr Fleming was denied the opportunity to properly defend himself against the allegation of serious criminal sexual behaviour.

Why did the judges not allow the striking out of the contextual truth allegations?

Judge Burley, Master of the Supreme Court, who first heard the strike out applications, approached the comparison exercise by considering the cumulative of the various contextual imputations pleaded by the defendant: see for example [56].[21]

> **As with the first two articles, the contextual imputations are supported by particulars given between paragraphs 40 and 45 of the amended defence. The determination required of the Court in respect of this aspect of the application is whether or not the contextual imputations set out in paragraph 38 of the amended defence are capable of satisfying the requirements of s 24 of the Defamation Act. In my opinion, the cumulative effect of the contextual imputations is capable of satisfying a jury that the defamatory imputations set out in subparagraphs 14(1) and 14(2) of the Further Amended Statement of Claim do not further harm the reputation of the plaintiff.**

---

21 *Fleming v Advertiser-News Weekend Publishing Company Pty Limited* ANOR [2010] SASC 255 Judgment of Judge Burley a Master of the Supreme Court 18 August 2010

It is suggested that instead Justice Burley should have examined cumulatively the allegations of Kay and Lynch and compared that examination with Jane's allegations. Instead, he included all three sets of allegations (of Lynch, Kay, and Jane) in one column and compared that cumulation with the allegations made by Jane.

In each of the following published articles Justice Burley does not isolate the particular imputation which asserts sex with a minor, the focus of the plaintiff's complaint. Necessarily, if the plaintiff's complained of imputation is part of the cumulative conduct which forms part of the **comparison exercise required by section 24(b)** the defendant will always establish that what the plaintiff complains of does "not further harm the reputation of the plaintiff" because somehow Jane's allegations are included in the assessment of contextual truth. If you cumulate all three together, and then separately cumulate Kay and Lynch then clearly the cumulation of the 3 overwhelms the two. What the judge needed to do was to compare the cumulation of Kay and Lynch with that of Jane. It is strongly suggested that Justice Burley misunderstood what was required.

The matter was appealed on two further occasions, first to Justice Lunn and then to Justice Peek. There were many changes to the defendants' pleadings before the matter was heard by Justice Peek and a different approach was taken by the Court in each appeal.

In contrast to Judge Burley, it would appear that Judges Lunn and Peek did compare the imputations of Kay and Lynch cumulatively but without including the imputations concerning Jane. Discussing the issue of contextual truth Justice Peek stated:

> Judge Lunn correctly appreciated that the imputations relied upon by the defendant must be different to those pleaded by the plaintiff and also adopted the correct approach, as adumbrated in *Hepburn v TCN Channel Nine Pty Ltd*,[6] that:
>
> [28] the relevant comparison is not simply between individual imputations, but whether **the defendants' contextual imputations, taken in aggregate and including the facts and matters pleaded by the defendants**, are such that they are capable of so affecting the plaintiff's reputation that **the defendant's pleaded imputations, assuming they are established**, do not further injure his reputation.[22]

Thereafter, Justice Peek, in agreement with Justice Lunn, stated:

> [30] ... Against the seriousness of the criminal conduct alleged in the plaintiff's imputation must be weighed the extent and the frequency of the sexual improprieties as pleaded by the defendant as contextual truth.

In rejecting this ground of appeal, Justice Peek ruled:

> On reconsideration, taking the correct approach to be as I have formulated it above, but bearing in mind "the extent and the frequency of the sexual improprieties as pleaded by the defendants as contextual truth", I am not satisfied that the defendants

22 Hepburn v TCN Channel Nine Pty Ltd (1984) 1 NSWLR 386, 400.

> will not be able to satisfy the trial Judge, that the publication of the plaintiff's imputation did not cause additional injury to the plaintiff's reputation notwithstanding the substantial truth of the defendants' pleaded imputations.[23]

These judgements by Justices Peek and Lunn appear extraordinary. To suggest that allegations of personal private sexual activity between consenting adults in a secular society is in any way to be compared to an allegation of a serious criminal sexual event is, on its face, sheer nonsense. The Church may (and should) deal with the moral aspects of personal behaviour in terms of what she holds the essential role of her ordained priests to be. But that is not the business of the secular courts.

However, allegations of criminal behaviour are the business of the court. The plaintiff chose not to sue on the Lynch and Kay matters, arguing that there is no comparison in seriousness of character defect regarding those matters compared to that of a criminal sexual offence involving a minor. That Justices Peek and Lunn (and Burley) can make the kind of subjective judgement they have raises serious questions regarding the whole concept of contextual truth. The context of a criminal offence occasioning up to life imprisonment if proved cannot sensibly be equated with the context of behaviour which, as far as the law is concerned, is perfectly legal.

---

23 *Fleming v Advertiser-News Weekend Publishing Company Pty Ltd and Advertiser Newspapers Pty Ltd* [2012] SASC 58, Judgment of The Honourable Justice Peek, 13 April 2012. http://www.austlii.edu.au/cgi-bin/viewdoc/au/cases/sa/SASC/2012/58.html?context=1;query=John%20Fleming;mask_path=au/cases/sa/SASC

Chapter Three

Appeals to Prejudice

Public opinion is a compound of folly, weakness, prejudice, wrong feeling, right feeling, obstinacy, and newspaper paragraphs.[24]

When you have no basis for an argument, abuse the plaintiff.[25]

Andrew Harris, Counsel for the defendant, began his cross examination of Dr Fleming by questioning him about the oath that he took at the start of his evidence and his attitude, as a Catholic priest, to lying. A little history will provide the context within which this approach should be evaluated.

The protestant cleric and novelist, Charles Kingsley, in his review of an English history book, published in 1864, accused John Henry Newman (a well-known 19th century English convert from Protestantism to Catholicism, now Saint John Henry Newman) of supporting the position that Catholic clergymen could lie following the principle of mental reservation.

What Kingsley said was this:

> **Truth for its own sake had never been a virtue with the Roman clergy. Father**

24 Robert Peel (1788–1850)

25 Marcus Tullius Cicero, 106 BC – 43 BC

> **Newman informs us that it need not be, and on the whole ought not to be; — that cunning is the weapon which Heaven has given to the saints wherewith to withstand the brute male force of the wicked world which marries and is given in marriage. Whether his notion be doctrinally correct or not, it is, at least, historically so.**[26]

Kingsley offered no evidence of any kind to support this accusation. The then Father Newman responded in a series of letters, these letters subsequently inspiring Newman to write his majestic book, *Apologia Pro Vita Sua,* which was published in 1864. Kingsley was saying Catholic priests lie on system and so cannot be trusted where the truth is concerned. Newman exposed that lie for the foul calumny that it was.

The history[27] of the discussion on mental reservation according to the explanation given at *New Advent* describes there being two opinions on mental reservation. The first of these, the doctrine of "wide mental reservation", as formulated by St Raymund of Pennafort in his *Summa* (1235), dealt with the problem of when the demands of truth conflict with the demands of justice. He acknowledged St Augustine's strong teaching (following St Paul) that we must not do evil to achieve good and nor may we slay our own soul to preserve the life of another. Then he added this:

> **I believe, as at present advised, that when one is asked by murderers bent on taking the**

26 JM Cameron, *John Henry Newman,* Longmans, Green and Co, London, 1956, at page 31

27 http://www.newadvent.org/cathen/10195b.htm

> **life of someone hiding in the house whether he is in, no answer should be given; and if this betrays him, his death will be imputable to the murderers, not to the other's silence. Or he may use an equivocal expression, and say 'He is not at home,' or something like that. And this can be defended by a great number of instances found in the Old Testament. Or he may say simply that he is not there, and if his conscience tells him that he ought to say that, then he will not speak against his conscience, nor will he sin. Nor is St. Augustine really opposed to any of these methods.**

Thus, if, in 1938, the Gestapo had called at your home looking to see if you were harbouring any Jews, it would have been legitimate to equivocate because the Gestapo had no right to the knowledge that would allow them the opportunity to kill the innocent. You could answer, "he is not at home", by which you mean he is not at home **for you**. And so on.

Is this a licence to lie? No. The suggested response referred to in the previous paragraph, and others like them, are not lies. Those who hear them may understand them in a sense which is not true, but their self-deception may be permitted by the speaker for a good reason. If there is no good reason to the contrary, the demands of truthfulness require all to speak frankly and openly in such a way as to be understood by those who are addressed.

A sin is committed if mental reservations are used without just cause, or in cases when the questioner has a right to the naked truth.

Hundreds of years later, moral theologians were challenged with new problems when some moralists wanted to extend the accepted doctrine of wide mental reservation to a greater range of cases.

A typical instance of the type of case in which the proposed new doctrine of "strict mental reservation" could be used was the following:

> **Titius, who privately said to a woman 'I take thee for my wife' without the intention of marrying her, answered the judge, who asked him whether he had said those words, that he did not say them, understanding mentally that he did not say them with the intention of marrying the woman.**[28]

Martin Aspilcueta, an important sixteenth century Spanish canonist and theologian commonly known as "Doctor Navarrus", was one of the primary authors of what became known as the doctrine of strict mental reservation, to distinguish it from wide mental reservation. He produced an elaborate argument to show why strict mental reservation would not be a lie, maintaining that Titius neither lied, nor committed perjury, nor any sin whatever, on the supposition that he had a good reason for answering as he did.

In strict mental reservation, the speaker mentally adds some qualification to the words which he utters, and the words together with the mental qualification make a true statement in accordance with fact, whereas in wide mental reservation, the qualification comes from the ambiguity of the words themselves, or from the

28 *Ibid.*

circumstances of time, place, or person in which they are uttered.

The theory of strict mental reservation was strongly rejected by Paul Laymann SJ (1574 – c 1635) and others. He argued that such mental reservations were lies. The matter was freely debated in the Church and was ultimately resolved by the Supreme Pontiff. Pope Innocent XI condemned the doctrine of strict mental reservation on the 2nd of March 1679.[29] and since then no Catholic theologian has defended the lawfulness of this doctrine. In other words, for several hundred years the notion of strict mental reservation has been explicitly condemned. Despite this, Kingsley used this line in the 19th century against Newman,[30] as did Andrew Harris KC in his cross-examination of Dr Fleming in the 21st century.

In his examination of Dr Fleming, Harris approached this subject by referring to the doctrine of wide mental reservation and discussed with Dr Fleming answers that might genuinely be given in the hypothetical case of a German during the Nazi period harbouring a Jewish fugitive. Then, subtly, he switched to the doctrine of strict mental reservation, a doctrine, as discussed above, condemned by the Church as endorsing lying. He did

29 Pope Innocent XI, *Sanctissimus Dominus,* 1679. "Condemned Proposition 28: Whoever is promoted to a magistracy or public office by a recommendation or a gift can with a mental reservation take the oath customarily required of such persons by order of the King, having no regard for the intention of the one exacting it, because he is not bound to admit an occult crime." (Denzinger 2128)

30 Newman's discussion on "Lying and Equivocation" may be found in "Note G" of his *Apologia pro vita sua,* London, Longmans, Green, Reader, and Dyer, 1875, at pages 348-363

it in such a manner that Dr Fleming initially seemed unaware of what was happening.

> **Harris: But there is also a situation, is this strict mental reservation where the person knows that they are telling an untruth but they do it for a proper - what is regarded in their own mind as a proper purpose and having created that reservation in their mind they commit no sin.**[31]

Dr Fleming's response was in line with the doctrine of wide mental reservation not having picked up this sudden change of subject. It should be noted that it was acknowledged in Court earlier that Dr Fleming suffered from a significant hearing deficit.[32] He struggled to catch up with Harris's sleight of hand.

Harris continued with this new line:

> **Harris: When you gave your oath to tell the truth in this matter yesterday, in any sense did you reserve to yourself the ability to create such a strict mental reservation from time to time and not tell the truth.**
>
> **Fleming: I can't answer that question.**
>
> **Harris: Do you allow for the possibility that when I am asking you questions and you are giving answers that you might say something that you know is untrue but because you have made a strict mental**

31 *Transcript of evidence given in Court* at page 220 line 35-page 221 line 2.

32 *Transcript of evidence given in Court* at page 34 lines 11-14.

> **reservation in your mind, that's not a sin and you are prepared to do it?**
>
> **Fleming: No.**
>
> **Harris: So we can be confident in the evidence that you give based on the oath that you gave yesterday that it will in every respect be the truth?**
>
> **Fleming: Yes.**[33]

This line of questioning was disgraceful and demeaned Dr Fleming in open Court. Harris was implying that Dr Fleming, as a faithful Catholic, was a natural liar and could tell lies in accordance with a discredited doctrine condemned in the Catholic Church for over 300 years. It was never a doctrine of the Church. At best, it was once an opinion held by some theologians in the Church but opposed by many others. Dr Fleming did his best to answer Harris within the strict limits of the questions put to him, but he was given no opportunity to expose what he considered the unpleasant bigotry which lay behind this line of questioning. The definition of 'lying' in Catholic teaching is this:

> **Lying is the most direct offence against the truth. To lie is to speak or act against the truth in order to lead into error someone who has the right to know the truth.**[34]

And where veracity conflicts with justice it is resolved on the side of justice.

---

33 *Transcript of evidence given in Court* at page 221 lines 8-22.

34 *Catechism of the Catholic Church,* n 2483.

> **According to the common Catholic teaching it is never allowable to tell a lie, not even to save human life. A lie is something intrinsically evil, and as evil may not be done that good may come of it, we are never allowed to tell a lie. However, we are also under an obligation to keep secrets faithfully, and sometimes the easiest way of fulfilling that duty is to say what is false, or to tell a lie. Writers of all creeds and of none, both ancient and modern, have frankly accepted this position. They admit the doctrine of the lie of necessity, and maintain that when there is a conflict between justice and veracity it is justice that should prevail. The common Catholic teaching has formulated the theory of mental reservation as a means by which the claims of both justice and veracity can be satisfied.**[35]

Perhaps Harris might, instead, have paid more attention to these words from the *Catechism of the Catholic Church* which are relevant in this case.

> **Detraction and calumny destroy the reputation and honour of one's neighbour. Honour is the social witness given to human dignity, and everyone enjoys a natural right to the honour of his name and reputation and to respect. Thus, detraction and calumny offend against the virtues of justice and charity.**[36]

---

35 http://www.newadvent.org/cathen/10195b.htm

36 *Catechism of the Catholic Church*, n 2479

Harris continued with his approach regarding the subject of confession about which Dr Fleming stated he would answer no questions, including neither affirming nor denying the identity of anyone who may have come to him, as a priest, for that purpose.

> **Harris: So it doesn't matter that something might be out in the public domain, the prohibition is absolute in respect of something inside the confessional or anything outside the confessional which might inform what happened in it, isn't that it?**
>
> **Fleming: Yes, but I'm the one who is in a position to know that. I am sorry but I am not going to divulge information about whether or not I heard a confession or any information that may have been given to me at that time. You should draw your own conclusions.**
>
> **Harris: The first conclusion is that that is terribly convenient for you, isn't it? Really convenient in this case. It gives you a bolt hole any time you want it, doesn't it?**
>
> **Fleming: I think that, your Honour, that is a regrettable statement to make. I am simply doing what is well-known is the role of a priest and I haven't invoked that and I haven't invoked it in any other situation.**
>
> **Harris: When you gave your answer earlier on that there had been no mental reservation in relation to any of the sworn evidence that**

> **you gave in this court, was that answer the subject of mental reservation?**
>
> **Fleming: Not as I understand it to be. I understand it is part of my duty.**[37]

This approach by Harris is insulting, prejudicial, and hypocritical. Taking the last of these adjectives first, it is hypocritical of Harris to assume that a priest would misuse the Sacrament of Holy Penance for his own self-interest while at the same time not questioning whether a lawyer would use 'legal privilege' dishonestly. No lawyer is in a position to question the confidentiality of the confessional while they see no problem with lawyers not having to disclose anything their client tells them. What they justify for their own profession they have no moral right to question in a priest. Lawyers protect the interests of their clients whose advocates they are and for which they are paid large sums of money. Priests protect secrets which belong to God and in which they have no financial interest. Lawyers questioning the confidentiality of the confessional is humbug, pure and simple.

Next, Harris states clearly that he thinks a Catholic priest would use the Holy Sacrament of Penance as a personal convenience to get himself out of trouble, and that Dr Fleming specifically would manipulate that convenience for his own benefit "in this case". He even goes so far as to allege that Dr Fleming would, in his own personal self-interest, use the Sacrament as "a bolt-hole any time you want it".

---

37 *Transcript of evidence given in Court* at page 255 line 32-page 256 line 16

This line of questioning reflected no credit on either Harris or his client.

Not being satisfied with this appalling line of questioning, Harris returned to the earlier mischievous question about the doctrine of mental reservation by asking a question that was too smart by half:

> **When you gave your answer earlier on that there had been no mental reservation in relation to any of the sworn evidence that you gave in this court, was that answer the subject of mental reservation?**[38]

At the very least, in his judgement, Auxiliary Justice Gray should have mentioned this and rejected it. One can only speculate on the effect that this attack on Dr Fleming might have had on the Judge and his subsequent judgement. This perceived prejudice against the Catholic Church as an institution and officials of the Catholic Church in general where sex abuse is concerned was even more clearly evident in the Appeal Judgement of the Full Court of South Australia and will be discussed later.

The historical context of the general animus to Catholics (and especially to convert Catholic priests) is this. Following the already discussed very public contretemps between Charles Kingsley and St John Henry Newman in 1864 the full onslaught of anti-Catholic sentiment was played out just ten years later when William Ewart Gladstone Prime Minister of Britain, reacting to the recently defined doctrine of Papal Infallibility, claimed that "**no one can now become her**

38 *Transcript of evidence given in Court* at page 256 lines 11-14

convert without renouncing his moral and mental freedom, and placing his civil loyalty and duty at the mercy of another."[39] Gladstone was also to claim that the Pope wanted to destroy the rule of law and replace it with arbitrary tyranny and then to hide these "crimes against liberty beneath a suffocating cloud of incense".[40]

The central platform of much anti-Catholicism is that the Catholic religion, and especially since the definition of Papal Infallibility proclaimed at the First Vatican Council in 1870, puts the Church and her adherents in fundamental conflict.

Dr Fleming is a convert to Catholicism. He would put his loyalty to Catholic teaching before his duty to the State. Therefore, he would lie to the Court in violation of his duty as a citizen. This prejudice, apparently, still lingers.

---

39 William Ewart Gladstone, *The Vatican Decrees in Their Bearing on Civil Allegiance: A Political Expostulation*, (Kindle Locations 142-143). Harper. Kindle Edition.

40 Philip Magnus, *Gladstone: A Biography*, London: John Murray, 1963), 235–6.

Chapter Four

Justice Gray Questions Credibility of Two Major Witnesses

Justice has been described as a lady who has been subject to so many miscarriages as to cast serious reflections upon her virtue.[41]

On the 24th of February 2016, Justice Malcolm Gray of the Supreme Court of South Australia handed down his judgement in the civil matter of *Fleming v Advertiser-News Weekend Publishing Co P/L & Anor (No 2)*. Dr Fleming had instituted defamation proceedings against *Advertiser-News Weekend Publishing*.

Justice Gray found in favour of *The Advertiser*. Specifically, Justice Gray found that "the defendants make out their defence that the imputation that the plaintiff engaged in criminal sexual behaviour while an Anglican priest is substantially true, and that the contextual imputations upon which the defendants relied are substantially true".[42]

It is important to examine the reasoning Justice Gray used in coming to this conclusion. It is suggested

41 William L. Prosser, *The Judicial Humorist* (1952), p. viii.

42 Justice Gray judgement, n. 427, at page 118

that Justice Gray, based his reasoning on the following propositions:

1. The credibility of the plaintiff, Dr Fleming, was questionable.
2. The credibility of the plaintiff's wife, Alison Fleming, was questionable.
3. The evidence of Jane, the principal witness for the defence who alleged that the plaintiff had engaged in criminal misconduct with her, was compelling and to be believed; and
4. The evidence of Peter Kay, who alleged he and the plaintiff had a sexual relationship, was to be believed, while that of Diane Lynch was not accepted.

Justice Gray's reasoning will be examined as to why he accepted those propositions which he claims led him to his conclusions. Dr Fleming, who brought the action for defamation will be referred to as the plaintiff, or as Dr Fleming,[43] and Advertiser-News Weekend Publishing will be referred to as the defendant or *The Advertiser*. "Richard" will be identified by his real name, which is Peter Kay,[44] "Jenny" by her real name, which is Diane Lynch,[45] while the third person will, for legal reasons, be identified only by her pseudonym "Jane".

This chapter will deal only with the issue of the credibility of witnesses as detailed above and the

43 The Rev'd Dr John Fleming, Catholic priest, scholar of international repute, and radio broadcaster.

44 Dr Peter Kay has a doctorate in "public health", and is a public servant.

45 Ms Lynch is a social worker.

evidence given by Jane will be examined as to whether it was sufficient to prove that the allegation that Dr Fleming engaged in criminal misconduct was "substantially true".

Reactions of Flemings show consciousness of guilt

It seems clear to the present writer that unfounded submissions made by Andrew Harris KC (Harris) on behalf of *The Advertiser* were, in large measure, accepted uncritically by Justice Gray. In the adversarial setting of our Court system one can understand that counsel for both sides must put their arguments to the judge with the assumption either that it is their client who is in the right or there is no sustainable case against their client. It is Justice Gray's judgement, and that of the Full Court, to which most of the attention is drawn in this book because these judgements are meant to be about finding the truth and should not be opportunities for judicial advocacy. Harris made several predictable submissions to which I shall refer later. For now, I limit myself to just one reference in his work. In this reference Harris acts as psychologist and mind-reader when he says this:

> **When the Plaintiff and Alison Fleming were informed there was a journalist wanting to speak to the Plaintiff about sexual misconduct and that one of the complainants was [Jane] they both knew the lies of a lifetime were about to become public. There is no other plausible explanation for the sudden and extreme deterioration in the**

> **Plaintiff's mental state, and for his wife felt the need to take the day off work.**[46]

First, the evidence in Dr Fleming's hospital records from that time, and the report from his psychologist (see below) to the Court make no such assertion and give the lie to Harris' bald assertions. The Advertiser had every opportunity to seek an alternative expert opinion but didn't, relying only on Harris' baseless assertions. Judges should be able to detect when a barrister makes assertions not based on evidence before the Court and give credit to the unchallenged expert evidence which had actually been provided and passed into evidence.

Second, Harris suggested that Dr Fleming had misled his wife about the nature of his interview with the Police and that it was the habit of Dr Fleming to shape "his story to fit the facts". The evidence given was this. After the Police interview, Dr Fleming told his wife about the allegation of a threesome in Meningie. At the trial, Mrs Fleming said that Dr Fleming had told her that this event had taken place in a car. First, if the "Meningie event" had occurred as Harris had alleged, why would Mrs Fleming get her remembrance of events at Meningie wrong at trial since she was said to have been an active player in the event? That makes no sense. When Dr Fleming was confronted by his wife's account at trial in cross examination by Harris, this is what happened:

> **Harris: ... Now, I just want to follow up with one further question on that topic. When you went over to the Hilton did you sanitise for one reason or another what had been**

46 Andrew Harris, *Second Closing Submissions of the Defendants*, 9th of February 2015

said to you by the police when you relayed it to your wife?

Fleming: Absolutely not. In the time at the Hilton and then of course following when we were alone I told my wife all that I could remember. Neither she nor I have discussed these matters over the last five and a half years because of advice from our solicitor that we should not - given that this matter was going to go to the courts - we shouldn't discuss it. My memory of it is accurate and I think my wife's is inaccurate, it's understandable given the passage of time. I told her completely everything that I could recall of the police interview.[47]

The evidence shows that Mrs Fleming's inexact recall of what she was told, some five or more years earlier, of an allegation given to her husband by the police, an event in which she was alleged to be a player, is consistent with the event never, in fact, having occurred. If it had occurred, she would have not had trouble in recalling it. Harris' statement that "they both knew the lies of a lifetime were about to become public" is contrary to his other insinuation that Dr Fleming "sanitised" what the police had told him when reporting to his wife what the police had said to him. On this point, Harris makes no sense and Justice Gray should have been alive to it, as should also Justices Vanstone, Nicholson, and Bampton meeting as the Full Court and if they were doing their job properly and thoroughly.

47 *Transcript of evidence given in Court* at page 2308 line 30 to page 2309 line 8.

And when it comes to his assertion that "there is no other plausible explanation for the sudden and extreme deterioration in the Plaintiff's mental state ...", not only was there no evidence led which would establish that as an expert opinion, but Harris takes on the authority of a professional psychologist which manifestly he is not. The evidence in Dr Fleming's hospital records from that time, and the report from his psychologist to the Court make no such assertion.

The unchallenged evidence of Dr Fleming's psychologist was this:

> **His symptoms meet the criteria for Post Traumatic Stress Disorder (DSM-5 309.87).**[48]
>
> **His life history is of him experiencing bouts of depression. The cycle he entered when he received the news was of being traumatised. He recounts feelings of shock and horror. These feelings were to do with his beliefs that anyone accused of sexual offences is likely to defend themselves, to say they are innocent, but in fact are guilty, that is, that victims, especially children, do not lie. Given this, his reaction was that he simply could not see how the allegations could have been made and, if they were, how they could have been published. If they were, did that mean that others would believe, as he had, that an allegation of sexual abuse especially by a child was true and so he**

48 See Exhibit P1. *Report of Clinical Psychologist Ms Fiona Stevens*, dated the 13th of June 2013, to be found at page 5 of the report and page 597 of Exhibit P1.

> **had no defence. Since that time he has re-evaluated the situation and is very clear that the complainants were not all children and that there were circumstances associated with his knowledge of them which explains his innocence. It was that in the immediate knowledge of these publications he knew that his first response, that is that all paedophiles and sex offenders say they are innocent when the literature tells us this is not true and so how could he defend himself. This sudden onset of powerlessness to defend himself and with the allegations the loss of his livelihood and his reputation led to him developing suicidal ideation which was so severe he needed to be hospitalised. His acceptance that this was the only solution was traumatising to him as he knew then and certainly knows now that this response is not healthy, it reflects the hopelessness he felt at that time.**[49]

It is concerning to note the style of advocacy employed by Harris. He is a hired gun giving evidence on a matter (psychology) on which he lacked professional competence. His submissions are not much more than unsupported allegations about Dr Fleming's character based upon a crude and malicious misstatement and abuse of Catholic moral theology, Dr Fleming's alleged duplicity, and his alleged predatorial instincts. What needed to be done, but was not done,

---

49 See Exhibit P1. *Report of Clinical Psychologist Ms Fiona Stevens*, 13th of June 2013, at page 6.

was an honest assessment of the facts in evidence, including **the evidence of the psychologist**, leading to a rational conclusion. What we got from Harris were assertions about Dr Fleming's character, assertions devoid of reasoned argument based upon fact, assertions conditioned by his crude appeal to anti-Catholic and anti-clerical prejudices, and assertions in which he makes magisterial statements even though they are based upon his conspicuous lack of competence where the psychological sciences are concerned. By contrast, it should be noted that Dr Fleming and his counsel were careful not to engage in gratuitous assertions amounting to character assassination to promote the case for the plaintiff.

It should also be pointed out that while Harris is not an expert where psychology is concerned but a "hired gun", he has no compunction in labelling as a "hired gun" an expert in psychology called to give evidence on Dr Fleming's behalf. And Justice Gray seemed to have bought it, reflecting very badly on himself as one not competent in the psychological sciences but seeming to want to reject evidence which would upset his apparent prejudice that alleged "victims" are always to be believed.

Principal witnesses and reversal of onus of proof

Five witnesses were named by Justice Gray in his judgement as "principal witnesses" and were given priority throughout the judgement. These five witnesses all appeared for the defence. It can be questioned why, for example, the wife of the plaintiff, or an expert witness on memory, were not included. Even though witnesses called by the plaintiff gave crucial corroborating evidence in support of Dr Fleming's evidence none were listed as a principal witness.[50]

Herein lies a problem for Dr Fleming. In practice, he has become the defendant who must defend himself against uncorroborated allegations made about him, which is suggestive of a reversal of the onus of proof. None of the witnesses which corroborate Dr Fleming's account are to be regarded as "principal". At best, they are to be side-lined as 'bit players' and their evidence hardly referred to at all let alone treated seriously. Dr Fleming is on his own. He called *The Advertiser* to account to prove that its published allegations were true, but Justice Gray has proceeded on the basis that it is Dr Fleming who must prove himself innocent and that with at least one hand tied behind his back. This reversal of onus is initially subtle in Justice Gray's judgement, but it is there, nevertheless, and became even clearer and more explicit as Justice Gray's written judgement developed.

The credibility of the plaintiff

Justice Gray prefaced his consideration of the evidence of the "principal witnesses" in his judgement by saying that the plaintiff was not to be believed.

> **Although the plaintiff said that he was only answering the questions put to him, I do not regard that to be a credible explanation in the case of plainly volunteered evidence.**

50 Justice Gray *judgement*, 24 February 2016, at paragraph 380.

> **The emphatic nature of the plaintiff's denials of the use of the term "ménage à trois" to Monsignor Cappo and the evidence volunteered about the rumour, strongly tell against any confidence that I might have in accepting or giving weight to his emphatic and positive denials in other aspects of his evidence.**[51]

This proposition, it is suggested, conditioned the way he evaluated the trial evidence. Having suggested that the plaintiff's evidence was unreliable and therefore he was guilty of the allegations made against him, he then looks at what others had to say. **The others are the favoured "principal witnesses" called by *The Advertiser*** and exclude the appellant, the appellant's expert witness on memory, and all other witnesses called by the appellant.

It is necessary to consider what formed the basis of Justice Gray's view of the plaintiff's credibility. The following matters were established during the trial.

In 1995, Monsignor David Cappo conducted an inquiry into allegations made by Dianne Lynch to the Catholic Church in Adelaide. The matter was subsequently resolved at a meeting between all parties. In the report prepared by Monsignor Cappo for the then Archbishop of Adelaide, the Most Reverend Leonard Faulkner, he recorded that he had questioned Dr Fleming about his awareness of any rumours about him. Dr Fleming responded that, as a public media person, of course he had heard that there were rumours about him and related what he had heard to Monsignor Cappo.

51 Justice Gray judgement, 24 February 2016, at paragraph 203.

Also included in the Cappo Report was the information that Dr Fleming had once been accused of engaging in a ménage à trois.[52]

When questioned in Court by counsel for the defendant, Andrew Harris, the plaintiff strongly denied that he had ever said any such thing to Monsignor Cappo:

> **Dr Fleming: This is clearly, in my view, something written after a non-note-taking event and I think some of it is creative.**[53]
>
> Harris: So that's not just 'It's possible I did, but more likely or not'. You are saying unequivocally on your oath 'I did not use those words to Monsignor Cappo'. Is that your evidence?
>
> Dr Fleming: What my evidence is is I'm saying on oath that **I certainly do not recall using those terms**, I do not believe I used those terms because it would seem to me to be not an accurate description of what I was reporting to him.[54]

Dr Fleming was very strong in his denial, saying that he could not "recall" using that term.

Harris began by asking the plaintiff questions about a ménage à trois said to have occurred in January 1971 at Meningie to which he testified that the first he had heard of such an accusation was from the police when they

---

52 Exhibit D8: *Confidential memorandum from Monsignor Cappo to Archbishop Faulkner*, 26 June 1995, at pages 1-2

53 *Transcript of evidence given in Court* at page 321, lines 16-18

54 *Transcript of evidence given in Court* at page 322, lines 17-27

interviewed him in November 2008. Harris's approach was to suggest that Dr Fleming had, in fact, engaged in a ménage à trois at Meningie in 1971, and had mentioned this to Monsignor Cappo in 1995 in a guarded way to prepare for any allegation that might come out in the future. Hence the reference to the ménage à trois in the Cappo report

> Harris: You said, 'The first allegation that I was involved in a kind of ménage à trois with my wife Alison and [JANE] when she was under-age, both of them were under-age' then jumping to the next answer, you say 'I was really shocked about the first one. I really - that really - I mean, it hit me for six'. That's the allegation about participating in the ménage à trois.
>
> Dr Fleming: Yes.
>
> Harris: The allegation specifically was with two 13-year-old-girls.[55]
>
> Dr Fleming: Absolutely.
>
> Harris: Forgive me for probing into your personal life to some extent but is a ménage à trois an activity that otherwise you might have engaged in with other people?[56]
>
> Dr Fleming: I read, I am literate, I've seen the expression used, that's the only reason I

55 This is factually incorrect. The age was 14 years. However, that small error in no way changes the seriousness of the allegation.

56 A gratuitously insulting question. Harris was not asking to be "forgiven" for his implied defamatory insult.

would've used it. No, of course not. Never in a fit.

Harris: The understanding of that term to mean a sexual encounter with two other people at the same time.

Dr Fleming: That's as I would understand it.

Harris: And so out of the blue when Constable Warden raised that with you in November 2008 was the suggestion that you'd engaged in a sexual activity of a ménage à trois.

Dr Fleming: Yes.

Harris: And that was untrue not only in relation to your now wife and *[JANE]* but in relation to anybody.

Dr Fleming: Absolutely.

Harris: And you had never been aware of anybody making such an allegation against you previously.

Dr Fleming: Never.

Harris: That's not true, is it?

Dr Fleming: Well I just said. I would - never had anybody ever suggested to me before or since that I would engage in a ménage à trois.

Harris: When you were interviewed by Monsignor Cappo in 1995, that interview taking place in June 1995, one of the things that Monsignor Cappo asked you, I suggest, apart from the allegations that have been raised by Diane Lynch, was whether or not there were any other rumours or issues relating to other people that you might like to tell Monsignor Cappo about; that's correct, isn't it.

Dr Fleming: I believe he wrote that. You asked me did he say that to me?

Harris: Did he say that?

Dr Fleming: He did.

Harris: Because you've seen that he wrote that in a memorandum to Archbishop Faulkner in 1995, haven't you?

Dr Fleming: I think that's where it was.

Harris: It would be unusual if Monsignor Cappo wouldn't be writing what actually happened to his archbishop in 1995. Isn't it the case that you told Monsignor Cappo that at one stage you had been accused of being a marijuana smoker?

Dr Fleming: Correct.

Harris: Did you also tell him that on another occasion many years ago, that is many years before 1995, you were accused of engaging in a ménage à trois?

Dr Fleming: Never.

Harris: I beg your pardon.

Dr Fleming: I did not say that to him.

Harris: So if Monsignor Cappo wrote to Archbishop Faulkner in 5 June 1995 that you told him that, he is wrong.

> Dr Fleming: Absolutely wrong. Absolutely. I'm just amazed.
>
> Harris: Because it's a pretty sort of focused piece of information, isn't it? The reference to ménage à trois does not exactly immediately spring to mind in terms of activity in one's day-to-day life and yet Monsignor Cappo got it from somewhere to write it to Archbishop Faulkner in 1995.[57]

Harris immediately went on to clarify what he was implying:

> Harris: Might it have been the case that you were actually giving him some advance notice of the possibility that it might come out that in about 1969[58] in Meningie you engaged in sexual activity with *[JANE]* and your now wife Alison in the way that *[JANE]* has described it?
>
> Dr Fleming: No, and the suggestion is of course repulsive to me.[59]

Dr Fleming may have been too quick and strong with his denial that he had said any such thing to Monsignor Cappo. Be that as it may, it was clear to Dr Fleming that Harris was suggesting that Dr Fleming knew he had sexually assaulted two young girls in a threesome and had mentioned it to Monsignor Cappo in a guarded

57 *Transcript of evidence given in Court* at page 306, line 21 to page 308, line 13.

58 The year stated was wrong. It could only have been January 1971..

59 *Transcript of evidence given in Court* at page 308 lines 17-22.

manner, describing it as a rumour to protect himself if it were to come out at some later time.

However, the assault was denied not only by the plaintiff but also by the alleged third party, Alison, who later became his wife. Dr Fleming knew that it had never happened and that the first time he had ever heard of the allegation was from the police in November 2008.

Giving evidence the following day, Dr Fleming drew the attention of the Court to another rumour maliciously spread about him. It could not in any way be construed as a ménage à trois but it was the only other thing that Dr Fleming could think of which he might have said to Monsignor Cappo. That there was such a rumour could be attested to by the Hon Mark Brindal, a former Minister of the Crown in South Australia.

Monsignor Cappo was subpoenaed by the defence and brought with him his personal contemporaneous notes from the meeting with Dr Fleming upon which he relied. This evidence was crucial in establishing whether Dr Fleming had used the term "ménage à trois", and if he had, in what context it was used and whether the information was accurately reflected by Monsignor Cappo in his report to Archbishop Faulkner.

It was clear that there were contemporaneous notes taken by Monsignor Cappo. Dr Fleming had no knowledge of this, and the notes were not provided at discovery.[60] These notes did contain the words "ménage à

60 Discovery is a "category of procedural devices employed by a party to a civil or criminal action, prior to trial, to require the adverse party to disclose information that is essential for the preparation of the requesting party's case and that the other party alone knows or possesses". Cf http://legal-dictionary.thefreedictionary.com/discovery

trois" but not in relation to a rumour, but to an allegation put to Dr Fleming in late January or February 1974.

The clue to the correct context was in the notes but not in the report. That is, where the words "ménage à trois" occurred in the notes there was an arrow to the margin with the name "Macdonald" circled, and reference was made to the "ménage à trois" having taken place "in his flat". No reference was made to Meningie, but only to "his flat" which had to be his flat at St Mark's College in North Adelaide.[61] This immediately triggered Dr Fleming's memory as to what the correct context was.

The context was this: in January 1974 Dr Fleming took his holidays in Perth, WA. He gave the keys to his flat to Arlene Macdonald so that she and Dr Fleming's now wife, Alison, could have use of its various facilities while he was absent. They returned the keys to Dr Fleming upon his return home. The woman who lived next door to the flat and was a parishioner at St Paul's where Dr Fleming was the Rector, complained to the People's Warden that Dr Fleming was conducting a live-in arrangement with two young women. The People's Warden put the allegation to Dr Fleming who clarified the situation and reminded the Warden that Dr Fleming had told him in advance of his trip to Perth.

This account of the context was subsequently confirmed by both women in evidence to the Court which Justice Gray acknowledged.[62]

Monsignor Cappo's account in his report did not give the context and so his report was, to that

---

61 Dr Fleming had not moved into his flat at St Mark's until later February 1971. The so-called Meningie incident was said to have occurred in January 1971.

62 Justice Gray judgement, 24 February 2016, para 202.

extent inaccurate. The report did not reflect what the contemporaneous notes recorded as having been told to him by Dr Fleming.

Further, Monsignor Cappo clearly stated in his evidence that at no time did he think that the ménage à trois in his notes referred to anything to do with teenage girls and that if he had thought that he would have had to follow that up.[63] When asked by counsel for the plaintiff, Heywood-Smith KC, "When he used the phrase 'in my flat' you understood him to be referring to his residence", Monsignor Cappo answered, "I did".[64]

In summary, then, Dr Fleming's memory was faulty when he denied that Monsignor Cappo took notes, and that he had ever used the words "ménage à trois" in that conversation which had taken place some 21 years previously. It must be remembered that Monsignor Cappo's notes were not made available during discovery. If they had been, then these misunderstandings would not have arisen. Dr Fleming was right to deny using the French term in the context in which it was put to him.

Justice Gray's erroneous conclusion as to the meaning of the evidence

Having summarised this evidence in a highly selective way, Justice Gray made the following astonishingly inaccurate and plainly false set of conclusions, conclusions which he used to justify his claim that he was

63 *Transcript of evidence given in Court* at page 876 line 29 – page 877 line 3.

64 *Transcript of evidence given in Court* at page 877 line 6.

right not to give "weight to his [Dr Fleming's] emphatic and positive denials in other aspects of his evidence".

> The plaintiff conceded that his evidence as to the term "ménage à trois" was mistaken, however, it was evidence given in emphatic terms without qualification. **Whilst I accept there is nothing adverse to be drawn from the plaintiff's mistake which would imply knowledge or involvement in the incident recounted by Jane, his categorical denial of the use of the expression is concerning.** The plaintiff also admitted that the evidence he gave of the rumour about having a child with a Member of Parliament was wrong. By way of explanation the plaintiff said that he gave that evidence because it was the only rumour of great significance to him. My concern about this evidence is that it was in the first instance volunteered and given as an absolute fact without any qualification at all. Although the plaintiff said that he was only answering the questions put to him, I do not regard that to be a credible explanation in the case of plainly volunteered evidence. **The emphatic nature of the plaintiff's denials of the use of the term "ménage à trois" to Monsignor Cappo and the evidence volunteered about the rumour, strongly tell against any confidence that I might have in accepting or giving weight to his emphatic and positive denials in other aspects of his evidence.**[65]

65 Justice Gray *judgement*, para 203.

Justice Gray provides a footnote to justify his first three sentences. But Dr Fleming's evidence about his usage of the term "ménage à trois" was not mistaken. He did not use the term in the context in which the expression was put to him. There never was such a rumour and so he could not have told Mons Cappo about a rumour of which he had never heard. That he had no memory of incidental issues such as Mons Cappo's notes is not surprising since, until that time, their existence had not been disclosed. And why should Dr Fleming's "categorical denial" of the use of the expression be concerning? He denied using the term because it in no way fitted any rumour of which he was aware. That he did use the term not in relation to a rumour but in relation to an incident he at first did not recall, is the truth of the matter. **In other words, he denied using the term in the context in which it was put to him.** Justice Gray also falsely asserted that the evidence given of a rumour about having a child with a Member of Parliament was wrong and against the evidence provided at trial.

Now Justice Gray's provision of a footnote by way of justification for his conclusions in these first three sentences is curious. It reads:

> Dr Fleming: I was wrong, my memory was triggered by the notes of Monsignor Cappo which acted as an aide-mémoire for me.[66]

But wrong about what? The immediately preceding text from the *Transcript of evidence given in Court,* **but not referenced by Justice Gray**, makes that clear.

> Harris: So is this the position, your now evidence is that you did not tell Monsignor

66 *Transcript of evidence given in Court* at page 2289 line 17.

> Cappo in the interview in June of 1995 about a rumour that Mark Brindal had passed on to you about you having a child with a member of parliament.[67]
>
> Dr Fleming: That is correct.

From the transcript, it can in no way be logically concluded, as Justice Gray does, "that the plaintiff also admitted that the evidence he gave of the rumour about having a child with a Member of Parliament was wrong". That the evidence he gave was true was corroborated by the Hon Mark Brindal. The only thing about which Dr Fleming was mistaken was that he surmised that he may have told Mons Cappo about it in 1995. But then Dr Fleming was racking his brain to try to think back to a conversation he had with Mons Cappo some 21 years previously, to remember exactly what he might have told Mons Cappo. The existence of Mons Cappo's notes were not available to him and consequently those notes were not known by him.

So, who can remember every detail of a conversation they had had with someone else 21 years previously? No one really. Yet Justice Gray holds Dr Fleming to account on this in a way that he does not hold to account any of the witnesses for *The Advertiser*.

When Brindal came to Court to give evidence of the truthfulness of Dr Fleming's evidence about the rumour involving an MP, he was stopped from doing so on the ground that it was not 'relevant'. This ruling was made by Justice Gray after Harris objected to that line of questioning. The gist of it was that Harris said he

67 *Transcript of evidence given in Court* at page 2289 lines 10-15.

was not challenging the truth about the existence of that rumour.[68] So, it was not relevant to question Brindal on it. Instead Brindal gave reputation evidence. All, then, that is left for Justice Gray to do is to refer to the reputation evidence provided by Brindal.

> As the defendants point out other witnesses have described the plaintiff as intimidating.[69] [footnote 371 of the judgement includes "Mr Mark Brindal"]
>
> In the present case, the plaintiff led impressive evidence of his general good reputation from a number of witnesses: Malcolm McKenzie, Reverend Joan Claring-Bould, Kirsty Henning, Arlene MacDonald, Mark Brindal, Stuart Lindsay, and Lorraine Dohnt.[70]

Here, the witness Brindal was marginalised and prevented from giving his evidence about the rumour according to the arcane procedures of the law when in fact what he had to say was very important to show that Dr Fleming was a truth-teller.

'Curiouser and curiouser', as Alice said in surprise, is the next part of Justice Gray's conclusions as to Dr Fleming's credibility.

> My concern about this evidence is that it was in the first instance volunteered and given as an absolute fact without any qualification at all. Although the plaintiff said that he was

68 Cf *Transcript of evidence given in Court* at page 2446 line 36 – page 2447 line 12.

69 Justice Gray *judgement*, paragraph 367.

70 Justice Gray *judgement*, paragraph, 469.

> only answering the questions put to him, I do not regard that to be a credible explanation in the case of plainly volunteered evidence.[71]

The fact of the matter is that Dr Fleming was, indeed, being questioned by Harris about the whole of the conversation that had taken place between Dr Fleming and Mons Cappo. The following day Dr Fleming asked Justice Gray a question:

> Dr Fleming: May I ask you a question?
>
> HIS HONOUR
>
> Q. I think so.
>
> Dr Fleming: At the end of yesterday's session there was a question put to me in relation to Monsignor Cappo's memorandum in relation to two rumours that have been spread about me and which I said one of them was incorrect. I would like to tell you about what I actually did say to Monsignor Cappo, if that's acceptable?
>
> Justice Gray: I'll leave it to Mr Harris. Mr Heywood-Smith is on notice of your concern with respect to that, he has an opportunity to re-examine you in relation to it and I think I would prefer to leave it to that at this stage.
>
> Dr Fleming: That's fine.
>
> Harris: I'll grasp the nettle and deal with it straight away.[72]

71 Justice Gray *judgement*, para 203.

72 *Transcript of evidence given in Court* at page 315 line 24-page 316 line 1.

So, the particulars of Dr Fleming's evidence were then given in answer to questions directly put to him by Harris. All Dr Fleming sought to do was to clarify, to the best of his ability, what he believed he might have said to Mons Cappo. Which is what he said to the judge. The detail was not provided until Harris asked a question about it, a question which he was under no obligation to ask. It was not "volunteered" in the sense in which Justice Gray intends to use the word, ie "say or suggest something without being asked".[73] But even if it had been "volunteered", what is wrong with that? Why is it wrong, or suspicious, that someone tries to be helpful when answering questions by giving as much information as he can. There is something sinister here about the attribution of bad motive to someone who, *in good faith*, volunteers information.

Moreover, if Dr Fleming had not so strongly denied what Harris was putting to him, Mons Cappo would not have been subpoenaed and his exculpatory notes never made available. The strength of Dr Fleming's denial forced the truth out into the open.

Justice Gray also objects that the information was given "as an absolute fact without any qualification at all". What sort of qualification did Dr Fleming need to give? It was demonstrated to be true that such a rumour had been in existence. Dr Fleming said that, of course, this rumour was not a "ménage à trois".[74] Dr Fleming believed he may have told Mons Cappo of this and that is what he averred. Justice Gray's unqualified assertion

73 *Concise Oxford English Dictionary*, 12th edition 2011, at page 1620.

74 *Transcript of evidence given in Court*, at page 321, lines 25-26.

that the information supplied was "without any qualification" is just not true because Dr Fleming had qualified it by saying that it did not fit the term "ménage à trois".

In other parts of his judgement, Justice Gray makes excuse after excuse for the multitude of memory lapses, self-contradictions, and inconsistencies of the complainants, Jane,[75] Diane Lynch, and Peter Kay.[76] But no allowance is to be made for Dr Fleming.

The bottom line as far as Justice Gray is concerned, is that the issues connected with the much-overblown significance of the "ménage à trois" reference, and about which the judge errs in nearly every particular,

> **strongly tell against any confidence that I [Justice Gray] might have in accepting or giving weight to his emphatic and positive denials in other aspects of his evidence.**

This means that Justice Gray, because he has no confidence in the appellant's denial believes that Dr Fleming is a dissembler, a liar, a concealer of the truth. Justice Gray admits that

> **The plaintiff conceded that his evidence as to the term "ménage à trois" was mistaken, however, it was evidence given in emphatic terms without qualification. Whilst I accept there is nothing adverse to be drawn from the plaintiff's mistake which would imply knowledge or involvement in the incident**

---

75 Justice Gray *judgement,* paragraphs 364-427 *passim.*

76 Justice Gray *judgement,* paragraph 256ff and *passim,* and see particularly the last sentence in para 245.

> **recounted by Jane, his categorical denial of the use of the expression is concerning.**[77]

So, while Justice Gray concedes that there was "nothing adverse to be drawn" over the ménage à trois controversy, nevertheless he does draw something adverse, namely that Dr Fleming cannot be trusted in his denials.

Justice Gray misrepresents evidence and displays an astonishingly poor grasp of the basic elements of logic such that his account of the matter, and the conclusions he draws from it, strongly tell against any confidence an independent observer might have in accepting or giving weight to the rest of his [Justice Gray's] judgement.

Logic

The conclusion to a deductive argument can be no stronger than the premisses upon which it is based. If the premisses fail, so must the conclusion. Putting Justice Gray's argument about Dr Fleming's credit in terms of a syllogism, this what Justice Gray argued in paragraph 203 of his judgement:

> Premiss 1: The plaintiff concedes his evidence re the term "ménage à trois" is "mistaken";
>
> Premiss 2: His "categorical denial of use of the expression is concerning";
>
> Premiss 3: The plaintiff "admitted that the evidence he gave of the rumour about having a child with a member of parliament was wrong";

77 Justice Gray *judgement,* at paragraph 203.

Premiss 4: His evidence concerning the Member of Parliament was "volunteered";

Conclusion: Therefore, the plaintiff's evidence of "emphatic and positive denials in other aspects of his evidence" must be given no weight.

The problem here is that, as we have seen, premisses 1 and 3 are factually wrong, premiss 2 is based upon a false reading of the evidence which locates that "expression" in another context, premiss 4 is a statement without any definition, and therefore Justice Gray's conclusion logically fails.

Where the accusation of Dr Fleming being an unreliable witness is concerned, the Justice Gray argument would go something like this:

Premiss 1: Dr Fleming denied using those words;

Premiss 2: Dr Fleming knew that he did use those words;

Premiss 3: Dr Fleming was trying to cover up or conceal esoteric knowledge of Meningie;

Premiss 4: It was clear that he did use those words;

Conclusion: Therefore, Dr Fleming is a person who is less than frank about the truth and any further denials he might make should not be given any weight.

However, while premiss 1 is true, premiss 2 was not established, and premiss 3 was not true. His use of the French term in a completely different context was shown to be factual. The conclusion does not follow, because proof of concealment was not established. In fact, the contrary was shown.

Justice Gray made it clear that in his view Dr Fleming deliberately misled the court.

> **My concern about this evidence is that it was in the first instance volunteered and given as an absolute fact without any qualification at all. Although the plaintiff said that he was only answering the questions put to him, I do not regard that to be a credible explanation in the case of plainly volunteered evidence.**

Where this allegation that Dr Fleming misled the Court is concerned, Justice Gray's argument could, in the alternative, be further subject to this analysis:

> **Premiss 1: Dr Fleming denied use of those words, "ménage à trois" in the context put to him;**
>
> **Premiss 2: The context within which he was said to have used those words was wrongly suggested as Meningie;**
>
> **Premiss 3: Dr Fleming did use those words but not in the context in which it was put to him;**
>
> **Premiss 4: There is no evidence that Dr Fleming sought to deliberately mislead, conceal, or knowingly tell an untruth;**
>
> **Conclusion: Dr Fleming used those words but in a different context from the way the**

> **question was put to him. His denial does not amount to unreliability. His denial was understandable in the circumstances and does not justify the sweeping adverse credit finding.**

Dr Fleming's denial can be further logically supported in these terms:

> Premiss 1: The 'Meningie incident' did not occur;
>
> Premiss 2: When he was interviewed by Monsignor Cappo, the plaintiff did not know of any rumour concerning a 'Meningie incident';
>
> **Conclusion: Therefore the plaintiff could categorically deny that he ever said that to Monsignor Cappo.**

How could Justice Gray get it so wrong? Lies and lapses in memory

Justice Gray got wrong his argument about Dr Fleming's trustworthiness in giving evidence because, it seems, he failed to make a very simple philosophical distinction between 'failure of memory' and being unreliable or even 'telling a lie'.

Where 'failure of memory' is concerned, regard should be had to the age of the witness, the health of the witness (especially psychological health), how long ago were the events which were said to have occurred, and the nature of the event itself. In Dr Fleming's case, the circumstances were these:

a) He is a man in his seventies;
b) He is trying to recall what he said in conversation some 21 years previously;
c) No notes of that conversation were available to him; and
d) He accurately recalled most (more than 90%) of what he said to Mons Cappo at that time.

What is a lie? A lie is "an **intentionally false** statement. **A situation involving deception** or founded on a mistaken impression; she had been living a lie."[78]

It is elementary philosophy to understand the distinction between a lie and a failure of memory. Nearly everything Dr Fleming said was corroborated by other witnesses. He neither told lies nor was his memory regarding the "ménage à trois" matter in error. On the contrary, he was very forthcoming, volunteering information where necessary.

Justice Gray made no distinction between being unreliable, lying (acting deceitfully, intending to mislead), on the one hand, and the frailty of human memory on the other hand. Indeed, he has appeared to collate the two concepts which is why he can conclude as he did. Even worse is Justice Gray's inconsistency in his methodology. Justice Gray does not follow the same process where other witnesses favourable to The Advertiser's case are concerned, even when those witnesses change their minds about their story, are proved wrong, and show persistent unreliability in their testimony. How much was Justice Gray influenced by the anti-Catholic line of questioning with which Harris

78 *Concise Oxford English Dictionary*, 12th edition 2011, at page 823.

began his cross-examination of Dr Fleming, that Catholic priests hide behind a spurious and long-discredited doctrinal opinion to escape telling the truth?

How could Justice Gray not take full account of Jane's unreliability as evidenced by:

1. Her telling three very different stories about the Meningie incident she alleged had occurred and the eyewitness who corroborated Dr Fleming's denial.
2. Her admission that her memory was unreliable, "I do not remember exactly what occurred" together with the scientific evidence given in Court (and uncontested) about how memory works.
3. Her giving many different accounts about what she said happened at St Mark's and the evidence given by witnesses which would make these assignations highly unlikely.

These matters and more will be canvassed in referenced detail in Chapter Five. The standard used to assess Dr Fleming's reliability was very different to the standard used for Jane's reliability.

It is risible to suggest, as Justice Gray does, that Dr Fleming's manner (robust denial) and his very, very occasional memory lapses, give any just cause to treat **every one of his denials** of uncorroborated allegations made against him as being unreliable. This is yet another instance of flawed logic on Justice Gray's part because it is logically impermissible to simply move from the particular to the general. This apple is green; therefore, all apples are green. This man got one fact wrong; therefore, everything he says must be mistrusted.

All this calls into question Justice Gray's capacity for rational thought and rational argument, more of which will be shown later in this book.

And there is a second main reason to explain why Justice Gray is so wrong about this and looking back into Justice Gray's judicial history gives us reason to understand part of what has happened here.

Justice Gray's "deplorable" delay in handing down his judgement

In the matter of *Fleming v The Advertiser*, Justice Gray took 12 months to hand down his judgement. On the 13th of January 2016, concerned at the extraordinary delay in judgement being handed down, Dr Fleming's solicitor, Michael Sykes, wrote to the Honourable Chris Kourakis, Chief Justice of the Supreme Court of South Australia, in these terms:

> Final addresses in the action were heard on 20 February 2015 and Judgment was reserved.[79]
>
> My purpose in writing to you is to draw to your attention this outstanding Judgment and to respectfully enquire when it might be delivered.[80]

The Honourable Chris Kourakis responded very quickly. In a letter dated the 18th of January 2016 he said:

---

79 The matter was reserved on the 24th of February 2015.

80 Michael Sykes, Sykes Bidstrup Barristers and Solicitors, *Letter to the Chief Justice of the Supreme Court of South Australia*, 13th January 2016

Dear Mr Sykes

SCCIV-10-488 Dr Fleming ats Advertiser-News Weekend Publishing Co Pty Ltd & Anor

I refer to the letter of 13 January 2016 enquiring about the delivery of judgment in this matter.

Acting Justice Gray informs me that he expects to deliver judgment on or before Friday 26 February 2016.

Justice Gray needed prompting from the Chief Justice to do his duty. Even then, it took a further 43 days (more than six weeks) for the judgement to be handed down. Why so long? Speculation might reasonably have it that not much work on it had been done over the preceding 9-10 months. Justice Gray, himself, offered no explanation for his delay in handing down his judgement in the case of *Fleming v The Advertiser*.

But what we do know is that Justice Gray has form when it comes to this kind of dilatoriness.

In *Aon Risk Services Australia Limited v Australian National University* 2009, Justice Gray was on the receiving end of caustic criticism from the judges of the High Court of Australia. He had taken some 10 months to hand down his judgement in an interlocutory matter.[81] Apart from the fact that the High Court upheld an appeal against this judgement, Justice Gray, as the primary judge, received this admonition:

---

81 *Aon Risk Services Australia Limited v Australian National University* [2009] HCA 27 (5 August 2009), at paragraph 151.

> **There may be some good explanation for the primary judge's delay in giving judgment. However, the materials before this Court do not indicate, and the parties did not suggest, any good explanation. Unless there is some good explanation for that delay which has not been revealed to this Court, it is deplorable.**[82]

Specifically commenting on the 10-month delay, the judges of the High Court went on to observe:

> **Authority both in England and in intermediate appellate courts in this country would correctly regard ten months as an excessive period of reservation, even for the most complex of trials or appeals.** In relation to a fairly routine procedural application, even assuming a short period of reservation were justifiable, the delay in giving judgment in this case is alien to every axiom of modern litigation.

To be sure there were other causes of delay in the *Aon Risk Services* matter, including the Court of Appeal. Justice Heydon, in considering all the persons responsible for delays in this matter said this:

> **Conclusion. The presentation and adjudication of the case in the courts below do cause it to merit a place in the precedent books. The reasons for placing it there turn on the numerous examples it affords of**

82 *Aon Risk Services Australia Limited v Australian National University* [2009] HCA 27 (5 August 2009), at paragraph 152.

> **how litigation should not be conducted or dealt with. The proceedings reveal a strange alliance. A party which has a duty to assist the court in achieving certain objectives fails to do so. A court which has a duty to achieve those objectives does not achieve them. The torpid languor of one hand washes the drowsy procrastination of the other. Are these phenomena indications of something chronic in the modern state of litigation? Or are they merely acute and atypical breakdowns in an otherwise functional system? Are they signs of a trend, or do they reveal only an anomaly? One hopes for one set of answers. One fears that, in reality, there must be another.**[83]

In the matter of *Fleming v Advertiser-News Weekend Publishing CO P/L & Anor (No 2)*, the delay was 12 months, even though Justice Gray had previously been categorically admonished by the High Court, that a much shorter delay of 10 months was "deplorable" "even for the most complex of trials or appeals".

Notwithstanding the very clear judgement of the High Court on the matter of judicial delay, the Full Court of the Supreme Court in South Australia (Justices Vanstone, Nicholson and Bampton) sought to justify Justice Gray's "deplorable" delay in delivering judgment because they did not **believe** it "had any impact on the ability of the Judge to do justice to the parties". How Justices Vanstone, Nicholson, and Bampton reached this

83 *Aon Risk Services Australia Limited v Australian National University [2009] HCA 27 (5 August 2009)*, at paragraph 156

"belief" is not stated, just asserted. Even worse, these judges absurdly sought to blame "Counsel for both sides" for the delay rather than Justice Gray.

> There is another topic relating to the matter of delay which, although not figuring in any ground of appeal, was mentioned in the appellant's written submissions. It is the delay in delivery of the Judge's decision and reasons. Exactly one year elapsed between the day upon which judgment was reserved and the day of delivery.
>
> A delay of this length is rarely acceptable. We do not wish to appear to condone such a delay, but there are some countervailing aspects which are relevant to the question whether the delivery of justice has been affected and which should be mentioned.
>
> This trial occupied 37 sitting days. The transcript runs to 2970 pages. **A long list of exhibits were (*sic*) tendered, many of them inadmissible. As has already been outlined, a good deal of inadmissible evidence was admitted, almost entirely without objection.**[84] Ultimately, the Judge's consideration of the matter was thereby made more difficult. Without wishing to detract from the complexity of the pleadings and the fact that the respondents' defence involved three principal witnesses, in our

84 No justification of this criticism of Justice Gray is provided by *Vanstone et al.*

> view the trial was simply not adequately contained. ***Counsel for both sides must bear some responsibility for that.*** The scope of the issues to be examined in the trial did not justify a trial of this length. While trial judges in this jurisdiction do not as a rule impose time limits upon counsel – particularly senior counsel – the time seems to be approaching when that will become necessary and appellate courts will be asked to respect the right of trial judges to do so where counsels' judgment appears to be lacking.
>
> As has already been observed, the reasons for decision in this case are lengthy. They are also detailed. They demonstrate a sure understanding of the issues and of the appellant's arguments and an ample grasp of the fine detail of the evidence. In our view, it cannot be said that the delay in delivering judgment has had any impact on the ability of the Judge to do justice to the parties.[85]

They say they do not wish "to appear to condone" Justice Gray's delay. **But they do condone it**, even making excuses for Justice Gray, excuses which he, himself, did not make and which they were in no position to know were true reasons for delay! This was judicial surmise, judicial advocacy to support a "mate", and masquerading as solemn judicial fact finding.

---

85 *Fleming v Advertiser*News *Weekend Publishing Company Pty Ltd & ANOR* [2016] SASCFC 109 (29 September 2016) Supreme Court of South Australia, paragraphs 185-188

The fact of the matter is that, *pace* the justices of the Supreme Court of South Australia, if the High Court has ruled that ten months is "an excessive period of reservation, even for the most complex of trials or appeals" then it follows *a fortiori* that a delay of 12 months is excessive and accordingly "deplorable". What part of the word "deplorable" do they not understand? The High Court used that descriptive for a reason.

It also behoves the judges in the Supreme Court to understand why that strong word was used and, when they do understand it, see why they should not *de facto* condone such delays and why they should have taken it into account when considering the appeal. Such a delay deprives the judge of his advantage of having just heard the evidence. He must now rely more and more on his memory. And as the expert Dr Michelle Arnold pointed out so well, memory is a very tricky thing. What we are left with, if we are not to be held in the thrall of what Justice Gray might remember eleven months later, is the transcript of evidence, and all the documents received into evidence at trial.

By his own dilatoriness, Justice Gray lost whatever advantage he may have had.

So why does the High Court regard such delays as deplorable? Because in and of themselves they may lead to injustice.

> Aon rightly submitted that the judgment was "infected by heavy delay ". Aon also rightly suggested that the delay led to some of its deficiencies – failure to refer to the affidavit evidence or the cross-examination of ANU's solicitor, failure to appreciate the gulf

> between what counsel for ANU said were the reasons for the amendment and what the evidence on the point was, and failure to identify what factors, if any, there were which explained ANU's failure to appreciate and raise the new claims earlier.[86]

With such delays, trial judges have weakened their advantage of having just heard the evidence,[87] and will require the judge to give reasons why one witness is preferred over another.[88] Justice Gray provided no satisfactory reasons why he preferred his privileged pantheon of "principal witnesses" (all from *The Advertiser*) over all other witnesses. He just did. Indeed, long delays (in this case 12 months) may have led to some of the many fatal deficiencies in the judgement.[89]

Justices Vanstone, Nicholson, and Bampton say they did not believe it "had any impact on the ability of the Judge to do justice to the parties". Why did they have this "belief"? This is what Justices Vanstone, Nicholson, and Bampton said in defence of Justice Gray and in support of their own "belief".

> As has already been observed, the reasons for decision in this case are lengthy. They are also detailed. **They demonstrate a sure understanding of the issues and of the**

86 Heydon J, Aon Risk Services Australia Limited v Australian National University [2009] HCA 27, 5 August 2009 C1/2009 at page 153.

87 Expectation Pty Ltd v PRD Realty Pty Ltd (2004) 140 FCR 127 at [70].

88 *Hadid v Redpath* (2001) 35 MVR at 152 at [34] and [53].

89 Aon Risk Services v ANU (2009) 239 CLR 175.

> **appellant's arguments and an ample grasp of the fine detail of the evidence.**[90]

This is pure speculation and assertion on the part of Justices Vanstone et al. It seems that they simply did not want to face the fact that there was a very good reason why Justice Gray's sense of the case should be mistrusted. The statements in the second sentence are merely obiter dicta, remarks in passing, and in this case amount to no more than self-serving assertions, for which the reader can find little evidence in the written judgement.

The contention of this book is that these judges discharged their duty in this matter in a very superficial manner, shared the prejudices of their fellow judge, Justice Gray, and seemed more intent on protecting a colleague than giving the appellant, Dr Fleming, a fair and just hearing such that the evidence was looked at afresh and rational responses made to the grounds of appeal. In their judgement, they provide no evidence that they engaged in the kind of scrutiny that such an appeal demands, a scrutiny which seems to be not much more than a quick reading of the transcript of proceedings and the Justice Gray judgement. Moreover, an independent assessment of the Justice Gray judgement demonstrates that, whatever Justice Gray had, it was not "a sure understanding of the issues and of the appellant's arguments", let alone "an ample grasp of the fine detail of the evidence", and that his memory was certainly faulty.

90 *Fleming v AdvertiserNews Weekend Publishing Company Pty Ltd & ANOR* [2016] SASCFC 109 (29 September 2016) Last Updated: 29 September 2016 Supreme Court of South Australia (Full Court: Civil), paragraph 188.

It seems reasonable to conclude that the lengthy delay in writing his judgement, and the last-minute rush to write it, led to Justice Gray's numerous interpretive and logical errors in this case. On this basis alone, one is entitled to question just why Justices Vanstone, Nicholas, and Bampton felt that they had to go to such lengths to justify the unjustifiable.

Justice Gray fails to give due weight to the delay in complaints being made

Delay and forensic disadvantage. The accusers' failure to raise any allegations for many years made it almost impossible for the plaintiff to refute the allegations properly and the defendants, in choosing to publish the allegations, must bear the prejudice that flows from the delay.[91]

The trial judge made a passing reference to deceased witnesses and long-lost diaries [J192] – [J193] but he did not subsequently bring to bear the significance that such delay in bringing the allegations has caused the plaintiff. To the contrary, the benefit of any prejudice is given to the media defendants. The plaintiff can only guess at the potential witnesses and evidence that may have been available to him but has been lost. Documentation such as his own diaries is a clear example, but potentially others may have discarded their own diaries and memorabilia.

Jane claimed a lack of memory over matters upon which the plaintiff would necessarily cross-examine. Examples are:

---

91 Cf the reasons of Peek J in *R v Maiolo* (No.2) [2013] SASCFC 36 at [171] to [199].

> **Jane has no idea how she came to be with the plaintiff on Brighton beach.**[92]
>
> **Jane has no idea how she knew where to go in St. Mark's College.**[93]
>
> **Jane's ability to give any credible account of the interior of the St Mark's flat.**[94]
>
> **Jane doesn't remember the morning after at Meningie.**[95]

This gives rise to a subtle application of the rule in *Browne v Dunn*.[96] The plaintiff is denied the opportunity of having a case put to him which he can reject. The respondents should have been made to wear such prejudice as attaches to this.

One example of prejudice is readily apparent. If the defendant had failed to call the Reverend John Stephenson the plaintiff would have invoked the rule in *Jones v Dunkel*.[97] Because Mr Stephenson was dead by the time of trial, the plaintiff was deprived of the opportunity of cross-examining him or, indeed, of calling him.

Another example is given by the evidence concerning the 'ménage à-trois' issue. The defence case became a

---

92 Transcript of evidence, 1553-7.

93 Transcript of evidence, 1568 –

94 Transcript of evidence, 1573-6

95 Transcript of evidence, 1591

96 The rule *Brown v Dunn* entails that a cross examiner cannot rely on evidence that is contradictory to the testimony of the witness without putting the evidence to the witness in order to allow them to attempt to justify the contradiction.

97 The *Jones v Dunkel* rule is a rule of evidence relating to situations where one party fails to lead evidence, and this failure is unexplained.

criticism of how a witness (in this case the plaintiff) was forced to struggle with his memory over many years of something that he said and why he said it. This in circumstances where the plaintiff's explanation is totally cogent and supported by other evidence, namely that of Alison Fleming, Arlene Macdonald, and "D34".

The danger of an innocent man's human rights being trammelled by a court 'getting it wrong' throws a strong *(Briginshaw)* burden on the media entity concerned when reporting historical allegations of criminal behaviour.

Justice Gray does not give due weight to reputation evidence

The plaintiff was entitled to adduce evidence as to both his reputation and his good character.[98] Such evidence is relevant to the "seriousness of the allegation made, the inherent unlikelihood of an occurrence of a given description, or the gravity of consequences" and hence impacts upon the application of the *Briginshaw* standard. It was not so considered by the trial judge.

Justice Gray's final attack on Dr Fleming's credibility - the circular argument rules!

Justice Gray's final attack on Dr Fleming's credit or credibility is found later in his judgement at paragraph 322. In this section of his judgement, Justice Gray is reviewing Peter Kay's evidence. He concludes that section thus:

98 Gatley, 12th Edit. [32.62], [32.63]

> I am, however, satisfied that the plaintiff did not have conversations with Dr Kay or Ms Kay in which he denied to them Dr Kay's allegations of a relationship involving masturbation to ejaculation and mutual masturbation, or that either Dr Kay or his wife accepted such a denial and were prepared to speak to others about it. I do not accept the plaintiffs' evidence to the contrary. That is a finding which seriously affects the plaintiff's credibility and the reliance that I can place on his evidence generally.[99]

Again, logic fails Justice Gray when he again has recourse to a circular argument. His argument goes like this:

1. First, in relation to the "ménage à trois" matter, Justice Gray concludes: "The emphatic nature of the plaintiff's denials of the use of the term "ménage à trois " to Monsignor Cappo and the evidence volunteered about the rumour, strongly tell against any confidence that I might have in accepting or giving weight to his emphatic and positive denials in other aspects of his evidence." So, at paragraph 203 of his judgement, Justice Gray has already indicated that he simply cannot rely on Dr Fleming's credibility or on his evidence generally.
2. Justice Gray then immediately proceeds to evaluate the evidence concerning the allegations made by "principal witness" Peter Kay in

---

99 Justice Gray *judgement*, paragraph 322.

dialectical relationship to Dr Fleming's evidence, and no doubt through the prism already established in paragraph 203 of his judgement. This evaluation is contained in paragraphs 204 to 325, an evaluation which gives very sparse attention to the evidence of Dr Fleming and the witnesses he called. More of that later. Given what he said of Dr Fleming before he began this part of his judgement, his harsh treatment of Dr Fleming must be understood in the context that, as far as Justice Gray is concerned, Dr Fleming is not to be believed.

3. And then, the circle is completed. *Mirabile dictu*! "I do not accept the plaintiff's evidence to the contrary", he says. "That is a finding which seriously affects the plaintiff's credibility and the reliance that I can place on his evidence generally."[100]

Put simply, this is what Justice Gray's circular argument amounts to.

Premiss 1 Dr Fleming is not to believed (para 203).

Premiss 2 Having decided that, I now evaluate evidence concerning Peter Kay (paras 204-325). Since Dr Fleming is not to be believed, Peter Kay is believed.

Conclusion Therefore, with respect to his evidence which disagrees with "principal witnesses" of which Peter Kay is one, Dr Fleming is not to be believed.

---

100 *Ibid.*

Such argumentation coming from a judge of the Supreme Court is risible. That it seems to have been upheld by three more judges on appeal is deeply concerning.

Credibility of Alison Fleming questioned

Justice Gray's conclusions about the credibility of Alison Fleming are, perhaps, the most puzzling aspect of Justice Gray's judgement. It was certainly the part that Dr Fleming found most offensive.

These conclusions seemingly turned upon the recollections of a conversation at a lunch in November 1994 involving the plaintiff, Alison Fleming, and Peter Kay's former wife Sue Kay.

In late 1994, the plaintiff advised Peter Kay that he was soon to be ordained as a Catholic priest. The dispensation, required as the plaintiff was a married former protestant minister, had been granted. Peter Kay expressed support and then told Dr Fleming he had decided to leave his wife and live with another man as a homosexual. Peter Kay said that he knew this was something of which Dr Fleming would not approve and asked for his understanding. Soon after, Peter Kay's wife inquired at the Catholic Marriage Tribunal about an annulment. She told the person she spoke to that her marriage had broken down because of a sexual relationship her husband had had with the plaintiff. Archbishop Faulkner reported the allegation to Dr Fleming and that he, as Archbishop, was resolved to investigate it. Dr Fleming informed his wife of the allegation. Subsequently, the Flemings invited Ms Kay to lunch at their home. In evidence before the Court, the three participants gave their accounts of what they remembered being discussed at that luncheon.

It is clear from Justice Gray's judgment that he accepted everything that Ms Kay, a privileged "principal witness", had to say, and that any matters upon which there were different recollections would be decided in Ms Kay's favour. Examples of this are these:

1. What was the purpose of the luncheon?
2. Was the matter of Ms Kay going to the media discussed or not and in what context?
3. Did the luncheon occur before or after Archbishop Faulkner had resolved to proceed with the ordination having decided that Dr Fleming was indeed a fit and proper person free of scandal?

As to the first question, the only evidence given on this was from Dr Fleming and from his wife. They had not colluded since they gave answers that, while not contradictory, were not verbally identical.

According to Justice Gray, Dr Fleming said, "that the only purpose of the lunch with Ms Kay was that his wife and Ms Kay were good friends and he and his wife wanted to make sure things were okay."[101] But Dr Fleming did not say that that was the "only" purpose. Justice Gray has intruded the word "only", and in a way that puts a quite different complexion on what he actually said.

Justice Gray then went on to describe Alison Fleming's description of the purpose of the meeting. Alison Fleming said that the purpose

---

101 Justice Gray *judgement* at paragraph 298.

> was not only to know where their friendship was with Ms Kay, but also whether Ms Kay was going to not see them ever again, **or whether Ms Kay was going to take it further**.[102]

Justice Gray's gloss on the evidence (which he misquotes) is this:

> That [Dr Fleming's version of the purpose] is quite different to what Alison Fleming said was the purpose of the lunch. She said that the purpose of the lunch was not only to know where their friendship was with Ms Kay, but also whether Ms Kay was going to not see them ever again, or whether Ms Kay was going to take it further. Alison Fleming also said that Ms Kay was asked if there was any chance she was planning to talk to the media and if this was going to impact on the plaintiff's ordination at all.[103]

How is it quite different? The only extra thing Alison Fleming says is "or whether she was going to take it further", an extra thing which is really just part of the generality of wanting to see where their friendship was. There is nothing that justifies Justice Gray trying to pit Alison Fleming against the plaintiff, one against the other in this matter, and certainly not by wrongly adding the extra word "only" to the plaintiff's words. That in no way justifies either why he should prefer the version of Sue Kay.

---

102 *Ibid.*

103 *Ibid.*

Dr Fleming's version is more general but in no way at odds with what his wife said. And given that all parties were trying to remember undocumented events of some 21 years earlier, it is remarkable that there is this degree of coincidence. Moreover, it demonstrated that the Flemings had not colluded with each other to give 'identical' answers.

As to the second question, not surprisingly recollections of the discussion differed between the three participants. Just who got it exactly right is not able to be objectively determined from the evidence. The best that can be said is that it was probable that the matter of the media was discussed in some form since both Alison Fleming and Ms Kay agree on that. But what this has to do with anything is not made clear by Justice Gray except that Justice Gray has it in his head that any disagreement between those whom he arbitrarily describes as his favoured and privileged "principal witnesses" tells against the overall credibility of those who disagree with his "principal witnesses".

As to the third question, whether the luncheon occurred before or after Archbishop Faulkner had resolved to proceed with the ordination, again there is a variation in recollection. What needs to be said, however, are these things:

1. The issue is minor even to the point of irrelevance.
2. Neither Dr Fleming nor his wife could possibly have known when any private meetings between the Kays and Archbishop Faulkner occurred. And nor could the Kays have known when were the meetings between Dr Fleming and Archbishop Faulkner.

3. *The Advertiser* was very keen to establish why they were not calling Archbishop Faulkner for evidence to support in what order things occurred. Harris was very keen to get Dr Fleming to agree with him that Archbishop Faulkner was not fit to give evidence because of dementia.[104] That being the case, there is no way that the sequence of events could be independently corroborated.

Dr Fleming's recollection was that the luncheon occurred after Archbishop Faulkner had finalised his investigations and informed him that the ordination would proceed. The evidence of the Kays suggested otherwise. Why, then, does the judge proceed to give credence only to the account of his "principal witnesses"? He just does, furthering his reversal of the onus of proof, accepting that uncorroborated evidence can be accepted as objective fact. He states all this clearly enough when he concludes:

> Given my acceptance of the sequence of events deposed to by Dr Kay and Ms Kay, I do not accept the plaintiff when he says that before Ms Kay came to lunch he had been informed by the Archbishop that the matter had been resolved and that the ordination would proceed.[105]

Alison Fleming is deemed to be not credible when she has different recollections from the Kays. There is

104 *Transcript of evidence given in Court* at page 682 lines 4-29.
105 Justice Gray *judgement*, paragraph 299.

no way that this can be logically deduced from the evidence, and unfair to so label someone when there was absolutely no evidence led to suggest that she was this kind of person.

The logical error here is the **false dichotomy error** (also called "the either/or fallacy", "the black and white fallacy", "the excluded middle"). Justice Gray thinks that he must decide either that Ms Kay is to be believed or Alison Fleming is to be believed. But that is not the case here. In the first place, what is at stake is an issue of no great moment. Second, there is at least one other alternative (middle ground) finding possible, namely that one cannot decide whose memory of every detail of a long-ago luncheon conversation is correct. In short, this issue provides no safe basis upon which one could conclude that either of these two women is lying, deceiving, or unreliable.

The strategy here being employed by the judge is that anyone who disagrees with one of his "principal witnesses" is *ipso facto* not credible. Consider what this judge says when confronted with the fact that both Dr Fleming and Alison Fleming deny Jane's allegation of a threesome in which Jane claims Alison Fleming was involved. Alison Fleming is not to be believed because she had recollections of the details of a luncheon conversation about an entirely different matter with Ms Kay, recollections that were different from Ms Kay's recollections in some, but by no means all, respects. Justice Gray, quite irrationally, moves that forward into his consideration of Alison Fleming's evidence that the alleged sexual threesome with Jane in Meningie did not occur.

> That leaves me to deal with the denial by Alison Fleming as "absolutely untrue" that any such incident occurred.
>
> The defendants say that I should reject that denial. They theorise that Alison Fleming is a "loyal protectionist" of her family unit and that she can rationalise the incident because of what has later become of her life. Her evidence involves an unequivocal denial that the plaintiff slept in the same room as the two young girls and that she engaged in passionate kissing of the plaintiff.
>
> **I have earlier indicated that I do not accept Mrs Fleming's denial of Ms Kay's evidence concerning the meeting that she had with her and the plaintiff where Ms Kay was asked to deny her husband's allegations concerning the plaintiff. I am similarly not prepared to accept Mrs Fleming's denial of the occurrence of this incident concerning Jane.**
>
> To my mind there is considerable force in the fact that Jane has steadfastly persisted in her account of this incident with an embellishment of a fact so readily liable to be rebutted. I am satisfied that the incident took place as Jane has described.[106]

At no time did *The Advertiser* lead evidence to show that Alison Fleming was a "loyal protectionist" of her

106 Justice Gray *judgement*, paragraphs 393-396.

family unit such that she would lie and dissemble under oath. Justice Gray uncritically quotes the defendants' theory about Alison Fleming (a theory which is no more than unjustified character assassination) even though this is a theory about motive not based on any established facts. But to buttress his own personal narrative, he needed more. So, he added to the fanciful Harris speculation an irrational preference for one person's remembrance of an undocumented lunch conversation twenty-one years previously, and, for good measure, contrary to the evidence, he wrongly states that Jane has "steadfastly persisted in her account of this incident". To that last matter, I will return later.

In his closing submissions Harris made this unwarranted personal attack on Mrs Fleming. In his judgement Justice Gray referred to what Harris said about Alison Fleming being a "loyal protectionist". If this caricature did not affect his thinking why mention it? And since he did it raises serious questions about bias. This is what Harris said in his closing remarks.

> **- whatever might be the truth of the matter Mrs Fleming's denial of that event is utterly unsurprising even if it happened. What she did, as we put in our submissions, is kissed the man she loved and who she ended up marrying and with whom she's made a life, and a proud life with her family. She's never going to admit to something like that, even though by her lights and what her involvement was, given what happened afterwards, that's actually relatively minor.**

> **The point is, as has been said in another context, if the suggestion was, well, Alison Fleming denies that, the answer will be, well, she would say that. The point is, why would someone in Jane's position who is going to create a fantasy or a fabrication introduce as one of the actors to it someone who was always going to deny it? That makes no sense at all.**[107]

This is a manifestly illogical way of mounting an argument. You assume the moral character of the witness concerned, that she is the kind of person who, through self-interest, **would lie** about these matters. You then say **she must have lied** and then conclude that **therefore she did lie**. Even worse, Harris says it really makes no sense to evaluate Alison Fleming in any other way, and Justice Gray seemed to go along with that as his judgement implies *passim*. If this is Justice Gray's baseline opinion about Alison Fleming, then again we have an example of the circular argument, this time based upon assumptions and expecting it to be believed as an objective conclusion even though it is based upon unsound premisses.

Moreover, Harris seems unconcerned about the objective truth here when he says, "whatever might be the truth of the matter Mrs Fleming's denial of that event is utterly unsurprising even if it happened". So, whether the "Meningie incident" (whichever version) actually happened you can discount anything Alison Fleming might have to say because she is married to Dr Fleming. A neat way of discrediting the evidence given

107 *Transcript of evidence given in Court* at page 2865 lines 15-32.

by the third party to the alleged event when that person's evidence clearly contradicts the one who alleged the event.

Again, the onus of proof is to be reversed. The working assumption is that Dr Fleming must prove his innocence, and with at least one hand tied behind his back, specifically that the only eyewitness (Alison Fleming) is to have her evidence rejected without proper cause.

Harris KC leads return to the nineteenth century view of spousal evidence

As I have just remarked, counsel for *The Advertiser*, Andrew Harris, theorised that Alison Fleming was a "loyal protectionist" of her family and Justice Gray seemed attracted to that proposition. Is this a throwback to the early nineteenth century legal position when wives and husbands were prohibited from giving evidence in which one or the other was on trial? As WS Holdsworth has noted,

> **It was the one case in which relationship is allowed to disqualify.**[108]

That prohibition was discussed in these terms by the *Law Reform Committee South Australia* in a report (1978) to the then Attorney-General, The Honourable Peter Duncan, M.P:

---

108 WS Holdsworth, KC, DCL, *A History of English Law, Volume 1X*, 1922, Methuen & Co Ltd, London, 197.

The common law position is well summed up in Bacon's Abridgement (Bac. Ab. Evidence A.1.). Husband and wife "are considered as one and the same person in law, and to have the same affections and interests; from whence it has been established as a general rule that the husband cannot be a witness for or against the wife, nor the wife be a witness for or against the husband, by reason of the implacable dissention which might be caused by it, and the great danger of perjury from taking the oaths of persons under so great a bias, and the extreme hardship of the case".

As far as the law of evidence is concerned, the prohibition was connected with the common law rule that the plaintiff and the defendant in civil proceedings in the common law courts with very minor exceptions could not give evidence on their own behalf. Accordingly as husband and wife were one flesh both in scripture (St. Matthew XIX: 5) and in law, if one of the spouses was interested in the result of an action so was the other.

In criminal cases an accused person could not give evidence in his own defence, though by a merciful bending of the rules the practice gradually grew up that the accused could make an unsworn statement from the dock as he still can. The general prohibition on a wife giving evidence for her husband or vice

> versa applied to criminal as well as to civil proceedings.[109]

That prohibition was lifted many years ago by way of amendments to the *Evidence Act 1929.*

As remarked by John Huxley Buzzard, Richard May and MN Howard, some exceptions to this general prohibition were allowed in common law.

> **By statute also this general incompetency has been gradually removed ... in civil cases[110] ... by a series of Acts culminating in the Criminal Evidence Act 1898 ... and the Theft Act 1968.[111]**

Today the South Australian *Evidence Act 1929* makes it clear that wives and husbands may participate in civil proceedings.

An Act to consolidate certain Acts relating to evidence.

> **16—Parties, their wives and husbands competent and compellable in civil proceedings**

---

109 *Forty-fifth Report of the Law Reform Committee South Australia to the Attorney-General Relating to the Competence of Spouses as Witnesses in Criminal Prosecutions for Injuries Causing Death or Serious Bodily Injury to Children (1978),* at pages 3-4. The members of the Law Reform Committee at that time were The Honourable Mrs Justice Zelling, C.B.E., Chairman, The Honourable Mr Justice King, Deputy Chairman, B. R. Cox, Q.C., S.-G., Deputy Chairman, The Honourable Mr Justice White, D. W. Bollen, Q.C, J. F. Keeler, and K. T. Griffin.

110 Footnotes provided by *Buzzard et al*: See Jac. 1, c.19, s. 6; the *County Courts Act 1846*, s. 83; the *Evidence Amendment Act 1853*, s. 1; the *Evidence Further Amendment Act 1869*, s. 3; and the *Law Reform* (miscellaneous Provisions) Act 1949, s. 7 (see now M.C.A. 1973, s. 48).

111 John Huxley Buzzard, Richard May, and MN Howard, *Philipson on Evidence: Thirteenth Edition*, London, Sweet & Maxwell, 1982, at pages 692-693.

> **In any proceeding not being a criminal proceeding the parties thereto and the persons on whose behalf such proceeding is brought or defended, and the husbands and wives of such parties or persons respectively, shall, subject to the provisions of this Act, be competent and compellable to give evidence on behalf of either or any of the parties to such proceeding.**[112]

Depicting Alison Fleming as a "loyal protectionist" as Harris does and as Justice Gray seems to accept, a label for which no evidence was led to justify it, is redolent of the ancient idea that a woman could not possibly be regarded as an independent and objective teller of truth where her husband is concerned. This is highly prejudicial, sexist, and based on an outdated mode of legal thinking.

Harris KC depicts Alison Fleming as a victim of her husband

The defence needed to get over the fact that Alison Fleming denied that any such event(s) alleged to have happened at Meningie had ever occurred.[113] Harris does this by assertion after assertion which, in today's Courts, is meant to pass for an argument. Each assertion is bereft of evidence. Harris even lays claim to be a mind-reader.

---

112 *Evidence Act, 1929*: An Act to consolidate certain Acts relating to evidence.

113 Andrew Harris, *Second Closing Submissions of the Defendants*, 9th February 2015, Paragraph 277.

First, he makes the following assertions:

1. "Alison is also a victim of the Plaintiff's predatory behaviour."[114] No evidence provided.
2. "She is able to rationalise the incident because of what has later become of her life." Theory without evidence to support it.
3. "She was an innocent and naïve young teenager who, on [Jane's] account, did no more than passionately kiss the man she went on to marry and with whom she raised a family." BUT ... denied by Alison Fleming and contradicted by Jane herself in evidence.
4. "In her eyes there was really no harm done by the incident at Meningie." Harris now claims to be a mind reader.[115]

He then concludes from these four assertions that "she is a loyal protectionist of her family unit". But none of the premisses 1, 2, and 4 preceding this conclusion are factual, while number 3 requires an uncritical acceptance of one version of the evidence that Jane has given. But in other places, Jane falsely depicts Alison Fleming as having been sexually abused by her father,[116] as having had a pre-marital sexual relationship with Dr Fleming,[117] and in yet another place as being mean and vindictive

114 *Ibid*, 278.

115 *Ibid*.

116 *Case Book, Volume One*, page 504 in document Exhibit P49: "I actually think that she knew the value of sex because she'd been abused by her father".

117 *Case Book, Volume One*, page 504 in document Exhibit P48: "I know that if he was passionately kissing her when we were 13 he probably had a sexual relationship with her."

and the more so because she became a Catholic.[118] Apparently, when you become a Catholic your propensity for meanness and vindictiveness escalates by virtue of being a Catholic.

Since one of Jane's assessments of the character of Alison Fleming was that she was neither naïve nor innocent, this would seem to contradict Harris's appraisal of Alison Fleming in 3 above.

To try and shore up his illogical conclusion, Harris then refers to Alison Fleming acting as a protectionist on two occasions:

a) When Alison Fleming "deliberately collected Peter Kay from the train station in Sydney, not wanting her husband to be alone in the car with him". He cites as evidence from the Transcript at page 2161 lines 18-26.
b) "She and the Plaintiff invited Sue Kay over for lunch to ensure knowledge of her husband's homosexual relationship would not go further." Evidence for this is cited from Transcript at page 2125 line 25 – page 2126 line 21.

In each case, Harris misrepresents the evidence.

118 *Case Book, Volume One,* page 463 in document Exhibit P48. "At the risk of sounding slightly paranoid you know one of the things with the police was finding out what would happen you know if he got in touch with me, could he get in touch with me, could Alison get in touch with me. I have been afraid for what Alison would do even more than Fleming actually. She would be vicious as well, now yeah." Cf also Transcript at page 1670 line 8, and Case Book, Volume One at page 595, Exhibit P54A: Transcript of witness interview of [Jane] by Nigel Hunt 7 August 2008: "opportunity, I mean she is very nasty when they went to, the Catholics."

Harris KC's claim about Alison Fleming and the luncheon with Sue Kay

Harris misstates the evidence when he says that the purpose in having "Sue Kay over for lunch [was to] to ensure knowledge of her husband's homosexual relationship would not go further." This is caricature pure and simple. Neither Alison Fleming nor Dr Fleming agreed that there had been a "homosexual relationship" between Dr Fleming and Peter Kay. What was discussed was what Sue Kay said to an officer of the Marriage Tribunal and which, according to Dr Fleming, she later retracted. This evidence is from Transcript at pages 2125-2126. The issue was Kay's unwanted sexual advance to Dr Fleming to which Harris would soon allude at Transcript page 2161 lines 10-14:

> **Harris: At the time that your husband told you about the marriage tribunal and about this one-off incident, did he say to you words to the effect that he would make certain that he wasn't in situations alone with young men anymore?**
>
> **Mrs Fleming: No.**
>
> **Harris: Or words to that effect?**
>
> **Alison Fleming: No, he said he would not be in a situation alone with Peter Kay anymore.**

It seems reasonable to suppose that Justice Gray uncritically accepted Harris's version of the evidence without checking that evidence for himself. This gave him a basis for accepting Harris's rather old-fashioned and clearly sexist views about women in the context of a modern marriage. That Justices Vanstone, Nicholson, and Bampton (the judges conducting the appeal) did not see the illogic of this and other arguments strongly suggests that they shared the prejudice against women embraced by Justice Gray and Harris, or they didn't do their homework or, if they did, they weren't up to the job.

The evidence shows that Dr Fleming and Alison Fleming were in a marriage where both parties worked equally together for the good of their marriage and their family. Yes of course Alison Fleming is a protector of her family just as her husband is protector of his wife and family. To suggest that accepting those roles in a marriage of equal partnership means that both parties will necessarily engage in lies and deception to protect each other and the family is to adopt the very attitudes deemed unreasonable at law from the nineteenth century.

Justice Gray's refusal to allow character evidence for Alison Fleming

> ***Heywood-Smith*: There has also been evidence given by one of the complainants that Alison Fleming is 'a really nasty person'. I take it that you've known Alison Fleming for as long as you've known John Fleming.**
>
> ***Stuart Lindsay*: Yes, just about.**
>
> **Heywood-Smith: Are you aware of people who know her?**
>
> **Lindsay: Yes.**

> **Heywood-Smith: And are you able to speak to her reputation?**
>
> **Lindsay: Yes.**
>
> **OBJECTION: MR HARRIS OBJECTS**
>
> **MR HARRIS: Mrs Fleming is not a plaintiff in these proceedings. Your Honour will make an assessment about her as a witness. There is no licence across the spectrum to have one witness give reputation or character evidence about another witness in the case who is not the plaintiff.**
>
> **MR HEYWOOD-SMITH: An issue in this case is the reliability of the evidence of Jane. If JANE is making totally unfounded allegations that have no basis, that may impact upon your Honour's assessment as to her reliability as a witness. This assertion was made by JANE and in my submission.**
>
> **HIS HONOUR: In the context in which it was made though, no, I don't think it's appropriate to obtain character evidence.**[119]

What was going on here? Jane was permitted to comment on Alison Fleming's character describing her as 'a really nasty person', but Mr Lindsay, a former judge in the Federal Magistrate's Court, was not permitted to testify to Alison Fleming's good character. And given that Justice Gray was going to traduce the character of Alison Fleming, her evidence having been already

119 *Transcript of evidence given in Court* at page 2498 lines 2-26.

given, why did he not seek "assistance" from someone well placed to assist him in assessing her character. All Justice Gray seemed to need was Alison Fleming's slight difference with Mrs Kay in remembering a conversation held more than 21 years previously, plus Harris' baseless suggestion that she would dissemble in order to protect her family, for him to dismiss anything she might have to say when it disagreed with one of the "principal witnesses". In the circumstances, it was wrong, indeed unjust, of Justice Gray not to allow character evidence by one witness with respect to another witness when he had already allowed a "principal witness" to cast serious aspersions on the character of that other witness, and especially as his disallowance had no solid legal basis to it. Again, Justice Gray seemingly discriminates against the appellant Dr Fleming and his wife to sustain the narrative he has chosen.

Why should a good, truthful, and reliable witness such as Alison Fleming be treated in such a disgraceful and unjust manner? The serious and ineluctable conclusion to which the present writer is drawn is that this judge was so determined to find against Dr Fleming that he would do all in his power to undermine the characters of Dr Fleming, Alison Fleming, and Dr Arnold.

Justice Gray accepts the 'grooming' theory as fact

How did Justice Gray arrive at his conclusion about Dr Fleming's relationship with Jane and Alison Fleming when they were 13 – 14 years of age? He did this by simply discounting the evidence of both Dr Fleming and

Alison Fleming about the contact that occurred when Dr Fleming lived in the flat at the bottom of the McNicols' garden.

> **As far as the plaintiff's evidence was concerned he said that he could not recall seeing Jane at the McNicol house during weekdays as he returned there around 6 to half past 6 at night and that there were very few occasions when Jane visited the McNicol house when he was there. He said that the two girls were infrequently in his flat with him and that he did not recall dancing in his flat with the girls. In summary, the plaintiff said, "on very few occasions" Jane came to visit him in the flat and "she just turned up, she didn't stay long and there was nothing untoward in it". In seeking to determine the extent of contact between the plaintiff and Jane, I do not consider that Jane can be taken as exaggerating the position to the extent that I should judge her evidence on this matter as unreliable. I also regard the contact that took place was to a greater extent than the plaintiff would allow in his evidence and, at least through the eyes of a thirteen year old girl, encouraged a familiarity which the plaintiff does not now acknowledge but must have been apparent to him at the time.**[120]

In fact, Justice Gray can mount no argument from the evidence to defend his conclusions, conclusions which

120 Justice Gray *judgement* at paragraph 370

are no more than what he "considers" and "regards". To begin with, Jane's evidence was remarkably different from that of the other two witnesses involved. But that was to change under cross examination. And Justice Gray positions himself as a mind-reader when he opines what "must have been apparent to him [Dr Fleming] at the time".

Looking at all the evidence on this point, what do we see?

Jane had stated in evidence that she was frequently in Dr Fleming's flat at Seacliff during his curacy at St Jude's Brighton from 1969-1970. That flat was in the garden of Alison Fleming's parents' home as a separate unit. She claimed Dr Fleming was always around in his flat after school and that the two girls (she and Alison Fleming) were always with him in the flat after school listening to music, dancing and so on. Here *The Advertiser* was claiming that the two girls were being "groomed" by Dr Fleming for sexual purposes. Dr Fleming's evidence was that he was rarely home before 5 pm and usually as late as 6 pm. He agreed that on some occasions the two girls and the two boys [Alison Fleming's brothers] came into his flat but those occasions were comparatively rare.

Alison Fleming corroborated Dr Fleming's account of his comings and goings when he was a curate at Brighton.

> Heywood-Smith: In the two years, which I think were your first two years of high school, what, if any, interaction did you have with John Fleming as a result of him living in the back of your house.

Alison Fleming: He would come to my parents' house and sit with them in the evening sometimes and discuss things. Occasionally Mum would invite him to join us for dinner and we would see him walking from his car down the side of the house to the granny flat, so we might see him if we were in the garden, and sometimes he would invite us into his flat to listen to records.

Heywood-Smith: What time would you get home from school in the ordinary course in those two years.

Alison Fleming: Depending on whether there were after school activities, if we went straight from school I would get home probably close to 4 o'clock or maybe just before that. If I had sports practice after school I wouldn't get home 'til maybe 5 o'clock.

Heywood-Smith: Was John Fleming usually at home at that time when you got home or what.

Alison Fleming: No, very rarely, if at all.

Heywood-Smith: What observation did you make, if any, as to when he would normally get home of an evening.

Alison Fleming: It would be around about dinnertime, around about tea time, sixish, that sort of time I believe.[121]

---

121 *Transcript of evidence given in Court* at page 1936 line 20 – page 1937 line 6.

However, Judge Justice Gray is having none of it. Jane must be right.

> In seeking to determine the extent of contact between the plaintiff and Jane, I do not **consider** that Jane can be taken as exaggerating the position to the extent that I should **judge** her evidence on this matter as unreliable. I also **regard** the contact that took place was to a greater extent than the plaintiff would allow in his evidence and, at least through the eyes of a thirteen year old girl, encouraged a familiarity which the plaintiff does not now acknowledge but must have been apparent to him at the time.[122]

All we have from Justice Gray here is what he "considers" and "regards". But Justice Gray makes no reference to Jane's admissions and qualifications to the evidence upon which Justice Gray has chosen to rely, admissions and qualifications made under examination and cross-examination. For example:

1. Jane originally claimed that in 1969, Dr Fleming's first year in the Brighton parish, she would see him "almost every day". She further said that over time she would go into his flat (with Alison) and that "It built up to that kind of contact so it was, **towards the end we would, we would be in the flat regularly watching** - playing, playing records and dancing".[123]

---

122 Justice Gray *judgement* at paragraph 370

123 *Transcript of evidence given in Court* at page 1362 lines 16-19

2. Under cross examination, however, Jane told a different story. Her evidence now is that it was only "**towards the end of his tenure" (ie end of 1970**) that she would spend time in Dr Fleming's flat, and that "it wasn't every day".

   Heywood-Smith: How many times a week do you say you would spend time in his flat up the back?

   Jane: **That was towards the end of his tenure**. It wasn't immediately that he arrived and **it wasn't every day**, it was frequently.[124]

   Jane: I was assuming **the end of his tenure** but what I mean is when we knew him better we did that. I can't be sure of the time.[125]

3. Jane accepted that it was "possible" that Father Fleming would very rarely arrive home before 6.00 pm during the week.[126]

It appears that Justice Gray was not cognisant of this evidence because he not only doesn't specifically refer to it, he doesn't take it into account when he unfairly suggests that, despite the evidence of Dr Fleming and Alison Fleming, and the evidence given by Jane herself, he regards "the contact that took place was to a greater extent than the plaintiff would allow in his evidence".[127]

---

124 *Transcript of evidence given in Court* at page 1473 lines 21-25.

125 *Transcript of evidence given in Court* at page 1474 line 6.

126 *Transcript of evidence given in Court* at page 1474 lines 27-30.

127 Justice Gray *judgement* at paragraph 370.

What Jane said under cross-examination was close to the evidence that Dr Fleming gave. On this point, Justice Gray's evaluation of the evidence is clearly inadequate and highly suggestive in a negative way about Dr Fleming's truthfulness.

Notwithstanding that, and in the face of the plaintiff's evidence corroborated by Alison Fleming, Justice Gray arbitrarily sides with Jane's first account of Dr Fleming's comings and goings when he lived at Seacliff, ignores Jane's major qualifications to that evidence, and fails to take into full account the evidence of Alison Fleming. The only reason Justice Gray proffers is what he "considers" and "regards" to be the case. Never mind the evidence. Dr Fleming was 'grooming'.

Justice Gray uses Alison Fleming's credibility when it suits him

Justice Gray picks and chooses in relation to Alison Fleming's credibility very selectively. Sometimes she is reliable, sometimes not. It all depends upon with whom she is agreeing. **When she disagrees with favoured witnesses, called "principal witnesses", she is not to be believed. At other times, she is used to back up the Justice Gray narrative.** Some examples:

1. The Judge accepts Alison Fleming's credibility in general, using her evidence to support other contentious issues. A stand-out is the issue of whether Debbie Munro found Alison McNicol and Jane at St Barnabas' Theological College in student David Richardson's room or in a room with the plaintiff. Alison Fleming supported

Jane's account that they had been in Mr Richardson's room. Justice Gray uses evidence from Alison Fleming to support Jane's account.[128]

2. Justice Gray accepts as true Alison Fleming's evidence when it confirms much of the background as described by [Jane] in those early days at St Jude's.
3. Conversely, when Alison Fleming supports Dr Fleming in describing the amount of interaction between the two girls and the plaintiff, Justice Gray accepts Jane's original version not her later version, and Alison Fleming is disbelieved.[129]
4. The Judge then uses the evidence of Alison Fleming against her husband. The question was whether Jane left Meningie, where the threesome was alleged to have occurred, earlier than everyone else. She is to be believed because her account is supported by Alison Fleming.

The plaintiff further criticised Jane's evidence concerning her leaving to go home the next morning. Firstly, on the basis that her assertion that she did so was not established by any other evidence. That is not entirely so. Alison Fleming believed that Jane left sooner than the family did.[130]

There are many other occasions when Justice Gray adopts his either/or approach to evidence and his selective use of "credibility". This allows the judge to

128 Justice Gray *judgement* at paragraphs 335-339.

129 *Ibid*, paragraph 370.

130 *Ibid.*, paragraph 389.

"use" Alison Fleming when he wants to, as reliable, and "reject" her as unreliable when it doesn't fit his narrative.

A final example of Justice Gray's arbitrary preference for only one side of the argument is his refusal to accept any evidence from Alison Fleming and Dr Fleming when their evidence agrees and does not support Jane. This was the case in relation to the "Meningie incident" and the evidence about how often Dr Fleming was around the two girls when he lived in his Seacliff flat.

In summary

It seemed that Justice Gray, once having adopted his Narrative of the course of events, used certain evidence to support that Narrative while finding reason to ether disbelieve evidence to the contrary or reasons to dismiss evidence that called that Narrative into question. His Narrative? That persons making accusations of sexual misconduct against a Catholic priest are always to be believed.

Chapter Five

Analysis of Jane's First Major Allegation

The "Meningie incident"

Reference has already been made to the nature of the incident that Jane alleged to have occurred at Meningie, a country town in South Australia. The plaintiff, Dr Fleming had accepted an invitation from the Anglican cleric at Meningie to be locum of his parish while he was away on holidays in the first week of January 1971. At the time, Dr Fleming had been living for nearly two years in a rented flat separately situated in the garden of a property owned by the McNicol family in Seacliff. Tom McNicol asked Dr Fleming if he could bring his family to the Rectory at Meningie/Tailem Bend parish for a holiday. Having sought permission from the Anglican cleric at Meningie, Dr Fleming agreed. The McNicols brought with them their daughter, Alison, two of their three sons, and Jane.[131] Jane was Alison's best friend at the time and would keep her company.

Jane claimed that the sleeping arrangements at the Rectory had Dr Fleming and the two girls sleeping in

131 Dr Fleming did not recall *Jane's* presence at Meningie but did not dispute the clear recollection of others.

the same room unsupervised. She described an incident where, she said, the two girls found their way to Dr Fleming's bed and were kissing him while Jane, herself, claimed to have touched Dr Fleming's penis.

Justice Gray found that:

- Jane's evidence was "inherently credible and compelling";
- "I am satisfied on the balance of probabilities that it is an event that in fact took place"; and
- "I am satisfied Jane's allegation is true".[132]

But there was nothing "inherently credible" about Jane's story at all. Indeed, her account is inherently implausible, glaringly improbable.

Timeline and general observations as to the reliability of Jane's evidence

The plaintiff's case for defamation centred on the truth of the claims made by the witness Jane that she had been the victim of illegal sexual acts by the plaintiff, Dr Fleming, when she was underage.

The first thing to note is that Jane's accounts of the alleged incidents of sexual impropriety involving the plaintiff varied markedly depending on to whom she was talking. The timeline setting out just when she alleged the various acts occurred reveals remarkable confusion and unreliability on her part. The documents tendered as evidence give three different sets of timelines:

1. Allegations made by Jane to various authorities before commencement of the trial;

132 Justice Gray *judgement* at page 108 paragraph 392.

2. Allegations alleged by *The Advertiser* as defence particulars; and
3. *Jane's* evidence at trial.

A timeline of Jane's evidence including evidence given before and during the trial, overlaid against uncontroversial evidence and the defence particulars, indicates the highly improbable nature of the allegations she made (see Appendix A).

This timeline was made available at trial and subsequently at the appeal and to the High Court to clarify how wide the variations in Jane's story were. Another way of expressing Jane's variations in her evidence is this:

First: Timeline according to Jane's statements to authorities pre-trial. Jane gave two different dates when she says sexual acts commenced and stopped.

1. Commencement of sexual acts: **Early 1969 or mid-1969**
2. Last sexual act: Between 9 November 1974 and 4 January 1975[133]
3. Last sexual act: **Winter of 1975.** Timeline provided as defence particulars

Second: Timeline according to Jane's evidence at trial which is very different:

1. Commencement of sexual acts: **Early 1971**
2. Last sexual act: **Mid 1972**

At trial, Jane reduced the dates of alleged sexual acts from between February 1969 and the winter of 1975,

133 After *Jane's* 18th birthday (the ninth of November 1974) and before the marriage of the Dr Flemings (the fourth of January 1975).

down to between early 1971 and mid-1972. Put another way, in statements before the trial Jane alleged acts of sexual misconduct occurred over a period of six and a half years, whereas in her evidence at trial this timeframe had shrunk to approximately one and a half years, showing a clear and very significant inconsistency in her claims.

The Advertiser's claims also shrank from five and a half years to one and a half years, ie by 73%

This timeline overlaid against objective evidence (evidence of independent witnesses), the respondent's pleadings, and prior statements of Jane, shows not only the confused nature of Jane's account, but the highly improbable nature of the allegations she makes. Such improbability cannot be explained away by a witness "getting the dates wrong".

In his judgement, Justice Gray accepted Jane's evidence that she travelled to Meningie with the McNicols and that, whilst there, she touched the appellant's penis whilst he was passionately kissing Alison McNicol.[134] Why did he accept that?

That the incident occurred was denied by both Dr Fleming and Alison Fleming (née McNicol). The trial judge turned to consider Alison Fleming's evidence only after stating that Jane's account had been accepted.[135] This approach was symptomatic of a tendency on the part of the trial judge, Justice Gray, to consider the evidence of Jane in isolation and subsequently endeavour to dispose of evidence to the contrary, rather than to consider the

134 *Ibid.*, at paragraphs 344-351 and 383-397.

135 *Ibid.*, at paragraphs 392-395.

evidence of Jane together with other competing evidence. **There were, on Jane's evidence, three people in the room at Meningie. The evidence of all three ought to have been considered before findings of fact were made.**

In parenthesis, it is unacceptable that a witness in Alison Fleming's position is dismissed in a sentence. She is a wife of forty-two years, a mother of three and grandmother, a registered teacher for approximately 40 years, a devout Christian, and a woman of unblemished character. Her oath should count for something. Had she not been called the respondents would have been quick to invoke *Jones v Dunkel*.[136]

The only other potentially corroborating witness called was Alison Fleming's brother, Douglas McNicol. All other people who were at the premises were, at the time of the trial, deceased. Douglas McNicol's evidence, which was not referred to by the trial judge, was that he could not recall the sleeping arrangements at Meningie but that his "mum was really conservative and dad was very protective".[137] Rhetorically, how likely is it that

136 The failure of a party to call a witness does not necessarily give rise to an adverse inference being drawn in accordance with *Jones v Dunkel* (1959) 101 CLR 298. An unfavourable inference is drawn only if evidence otherwise provides a basis on which that unfavourable inference can be drawn. An unfavourable inference cannot be drawn solely on the basis that the witness was not called, there must be a basis elsewhere in evidence to support that inference. The rule in *Jones v Dunkel* (1959) 101 CLR 298 relates to the unexplained failure of a party to give evidence which may, in appropriate circumstances, lead to an inference that the uncalled evidence would not have assisted that party's case. http://www.mondaq.com/australia/x/59640/Insurance/Exhibit Principle+in+Jones+v+Dunkel+an+adverse+inference+must+be+supported+by+other+unfavourable+evidence

137 *Transcript of evidence given in Court* at page 2474 lines 28-32.

a "really conservative" mother and a "very protective father" would allow two teenage girls to sleep in the same room with a young adult man unsupervised?

That evidence, as well as the inability of the appellant to call witnesses who were also present at Meningie because they were already deceased at the time of trial, demonstrates the prejudice occasioned upon the plaintiff in endeavouring to restore his reputation in the face of allegations published by the respondents nearly 40 years after the alleged events.

Aside from the fact that Jane's evidence was both uncorroborated and contradicted by a third-party witness, and that in the civil matter of defamation, *Briginshaw* requires the presumption of innocence where the appellant (Dr Fleming) has been accused of a serious criminal offence, there were several very significant inconsistencies between her evidence given in Court and the statements she had previously made to police and Church authorities:

1. Her position when the alleged touching of the penis was occurring. Jane's evidence was that she was sitting on the edge of the bed, whilst she had told police that she was kneeling. Her explanation for the discrepancy was that she was:

   > conflagrating [*sic*] – I love that word – the experience of being in servitude, to, to Father Fleming and, and that the church, being at church and, and praying and (indicates) having him at the front of the church, so I think in my mind it was, that was why I said 'kneeling' and I – when I

> examine the memory without the distress
> I see myself sitting ...[138]

Notwithstanding that the trial judge described this explanation as being a "rationalisation", he held that it did not demonstrate unreliability either of her memory or of her fantasising.[139]

2. Jane's evidence as to with which hand she touched the appellant's penis differed from what she had told police. The trial judge stated that Jane "readily admitted the difference", apparently using that fact in support of Jane's reliability about the incident rather than drawing the contrary conclusion.[140] Having established the inconsistency, counsel is apparently criticized for having "not further pressed (her) about it".[141] Jane had 40 years to resolve any confusion in her mind as to whether it was her left or right hand.
3. How Jane came to be touching the appellant's penis. Jane, in a manner consistent with the vagueness of her evidence as a whole, described her recollection of this aspect as "an assumption based on a memory".[142] This evidence was not referred to by the trial judge.
4. Whether the appellant touched his own penis during the incident.[143] Jane's evidence was that

138 *Transcript of evidence given in Court* at page 1590 line 27 – page 1591 line 1.

139 Justice Gray *judgement* at paragraph 386.

140 Justice Gray *judgement* at paragraph 387.

141 Justice Gray *judgement* at paragraph 387.

142 *Transcript of evidence given in Court* at page 1537 lines 29-33.

143 Referred to without further comment. See Justice Gray *judgement* at paragraph at 388.

she could not recall telling a Catholic Church inquiry conducted by Michael Abbott KC that she saw the appellant touching his own penis.[144]

5. Jane gave evidence of what she and Alison McNicol were wearing in circumstances where she had told police that she could not remember what they were wearing. The only explanation proffered for the apparent improvement in Jane's memory was given by the trial judge in his reasons, namely that Jane had been told in her police interview that if she could not remember, she could not remember.[145] This, it is respectfully submitted, does not militate in favour of Jane's reliability on this or any other topic.

Jane's evidence as to how she came home from Meningie was confused and inconsistent with several of her previous statements. In evidence in chief, she said that the morning after the alleged incident she spoke to Mrs. McNicol and said she wanted to go home because of 'women's business'.[146] That explanation had not been given in any previous statement.[147] She said she was driven back to Adelaide by Alan Hudson who was at the church service that morning.[148] In her SAPOL interview she said that her first recollection on the morning following the alleged incident was

---

144 The transcript of her interview suggests she did so: Exhibit P48 at page 3.

145 Justice Gray *judgement* at paragraph 384.

146 *Transcript of evidence given in Court* at page 1378 lines 17-19 and page 1399 lines 10-18.

147 *Transcript of evidence given in Court* at page 1548 line 25 – T1549 line 24.

148 *Transcript of evidence given in Court* at page 1378 lines 24-32.

> being in a car with an actor person…I… don't really remember demanding to go home, I don't remember anything of that.[149]

Her police statement asserted that she did not go to a church service the next morning.[150] In her interview with Mr Cannons of the Anglican Church in May 2010 she didn't recall going to church the following morning.[151] She identified the driver as 'Alan' or 'Darryl Hilton' alternately interspersed with saying she had hitchhiked.[152] Hilton was contacted by police but denied any involvement. Hilton suggests Alan Hudson as a possibility, but Jane denied he was the driver when shown a photo. Ultimately, when shown a photo of Hudson that is in evidence Jane adopted him as the driver.[153] Hudson was deceased by the time of the publications. She had described the driver to police as in his 'early 20s'.[154] In 1971 Hudson was in his 30s. Her evidence on this issue was labelled as a "reconstruction" by the trial judge.[155] Notwithstanding that, Justice Gray does not ask himself what else in her story might be

149 Exhibit P50: *Transcript of police Interview with [Jane],* 10th of October 2007, at page 14.

150 Exhibit P47: *Statement of [Jane] to South Australia Police,* made on the 10th of October 2007 but not signed by Jane until 30th July 2008, at page 15.

151 Exhibit P49, question 401. But her cross-examination at *Transcript of evidence given in Court* page 1625 lines 9-19 has her saying the ride back was arranged in church the driver being a member of the congregation.

152 Worden's Running Sheet, "Exhibit P82".

153 *Transcript of evidence given in Court* at page 1380 L30-34.

154 Exhibit P47, p.15.

155 Justice Gray *judgement* at paragraph 390.

reconstruction. To the contrary, Justice Gray is prepared to turn it to her advantage.

> On the other hand, Jane's belief and conviction that she left the next morning and returned by car to Adelaide as a result of the events the previous evening seems to be supported by the earnest effort that she made to attempt to identify and locate the person whom she said had driven her.[156]

In fact, the "earnest effort" to identify her driver was made by the police, not Jane.

One of the most unbelievable aspects of Jane's account of the Meningie allegation relates to the events that immediately followed. Jane had told an Anglican Church inquiry that it was her and Alison McNicol's goal to seduce the appellant.[157] In cross-examination, Jane confirmed that was a goal she had discussed with Alison.[158] However, it was Jane's evidence that she and Alison never discussed the events of Meningie on the night that it occurred or at any time thereafter.[159] In the circumstances, that they should never discuss their success defies credulity. That submission was made at trial[160] but was not referred to by the trial judge.

Given that Jane's evidence regarding the "Meningie incident" was uncorroborated, was contrary to other versions she gave of the alleged event, inconsistent in

156 *Ibid.*, at paragraph 391.

157 Exhibit P 49 at Question 302.

158 *Transcript of evidence given in Court* at page 1623 lines 13-17.

159 *Transcript of evidence given in Court* at page 1378 lines 10-16.

160 Appendix A of the Plaintiff's Outline of Submissions at [37]-[41].

material respects with statements she had previously made, and inherently improbable, the trial judge erred seriously in accepting it on any view, let alone in circumstances where the *Briginshaw* principle should have been brought to account. The trial judge erred by excusing and, in some cases, entirely overlooking, those aspects of Jane's evidence which told against her credibility and/or reliability. Whilst it might be said that any of the matters referred to above were, in isolation, not sufficient to definitively dispose of Jane's account, in combination they tell of precisely the type of "uncertain proof" that *Briginshaw* warns against accepting in a case such as this.

Corroboration

It was clear throughout the trial that Jane's allegations lacked corroboration, whereas the plaintiff had up to half a dozen witnesses who corroborated his statements. It is suggested the evidence these witnesses provided should have given any reasonable judge reason to question Jane's allegations and to find that the defendant had not proved them to the *Briginshaw* standard.

When one considers the evidence as a whole, and whose evidence was the most strongly supported by other witnesses, two things stand out:

1. Those witnesses who corroborated the plaintiff's evidence did not do so based on what the plaintiff had once told them, ie hearsay, but what they actually observed and knew for themselves because they were there at the relevant times; and
2. Those same witnesses agreed with each other, and with the plaintiff, in detail.

The Plaintiff's evidence and corroborating evidence in response to Jane's allegations

Subject	Corroborated by	Contradicted by	Could have corroborated but deceased
The plaintiff did not sleep in same room at Meningie as Jane and Alison.	Alison Fleming; Douglas McNicol impliedly	Jane	Tom, Jean, and Malcolm McNicol
There was no threesome.	Alison Fleming	Jane	Tom, Jean, and Malcolm McNicol
The plaintiff was not always at his flat in Seacliff after school as Jane alleged.	Alison Fleming	Jane, but later she greatly modified her assertions on this matter.	In first year, Jean McNicol always at home. Thereafter, Tom and Jean McNicol, now school teachers, were home early.
The plaintiff was not only not always in Brighton Parish after his term as Curate finished. He was never there.	Alison Fleming, Kirsty Henning, Rev Russell Simmonds, and Rev Joan-Claring-Bould	Jane	
The plaintiff did not attend choir practices at St Jude's.	Alison Fleming, Kirsty Henning, Rev Russell Simmonds, Rev Joan Claring-Bould. D Munro did not say he was ever at choir practice, and she was "in charge of the girls' choir".[161]	Jane	
The plaintiff at football every Saturday during the winter	Peter Fleming, Alison Fleming		
The plaintiff never owned or wore red "trackies" and dressed clerically nearly all the time	Arlene Macdonald, Rev Joan Claring-Bould, Kirsty Henning, Alison Fleming	Jane claims to have seen The plaintiff wearing such "trackies"	
The plaintiff's reference to a ménage à trois to Mons Cappo was not a reference to Meningie	Arlene Macdonald, Alison Fleming, Monsignor Cappo		
The plaintiff's evidence re a rumour involving an SA MP	Mark Brindal		

161 Transcript of evidence given in Court at page 1785 line 22.

On these key matters, it is the evidence of the plaintiff that is corroborated. Jane had no witness to corroborate her allegations. Justice Gray's assertion that the plaintiff lacked credibility, does not deal with the fact that his evidence was corroborated by independent witnesses.

Jane stated unequivocally that, based upon her memory, the plaintiff engaged in criminal sexual abuse with her at Meningie. Jane's memory, and that alone, was relied upon because there were no corroborating witnesses. Even though there was an eyewitness who corroborated the plaintiff's denial, Justice Gray believed Jane's uncorroborated and contradicted claim provided a sound basis for the historical allegation being established as fact.

Specific qualifications made by Jane to what she says she "remembers"

Throughout her examination in chief, Jane qualified what she had previously said occurred, testifying that she didn't really remember exactly, or at all, those events. Here are four examples from Jane's testimony:

> ***Harris:* Are you able to remember now how you came to be holding the plaintiff's penis?**
>
> ***Jane:* I don't remember exactly. I remember that his hand was along the wall - wall side and close to his erect penis but I don't - I don't remember the action of actually him holding my hand onto his penis. I do remember feeling that I had been directed to do so.**[162]

162 *Transcript of evidence given in Court* at page 1376 lines 4-10.

> ***Harris*: Do you have any recollection of what you did, if anything, while you had the plaintiff's erect penis in your hand?**
>
> ***Jane:* I can't remember.**[163]
>
> ***Harris*: Do you remember what you did the following morning?**
>
> ***Jane:* I think I sought out Alison's mum and said 'I want to go home'.**[164]

In his cross examination of Jane, counsel for the plaintiff exposed Jane's admission that her memory was quite unreliable.

> ***Heywood-Smith*: You say in the paragraph that I've directed your attention to in the second line, 'I believe I was directed to Fleming's erect penis'.**[165] **Do you say that?**
>
> ***Jane*: Yes.**
>
> ***Heywood-Smith*: That's a belief rather than a memory?**
>
> ***Jane*: Yes, well no, I mean, I'm not sure what you're asking. Do I believe that I, do I believe, do I, is my memory that I went to John's penis or that I was directed? It's my, I don't, the bit that, I'm not, I can't, I can't say with absolute certainty how I ended up holding his penis.**[166]

---

163 *Transcript of evidence given in Court* at page 1377 lines 5-8.

164 *Transcript of evidence given in Court* at page 1378 lines 17-19.

165 Exhibit P5O: *Transcript of police Interview with [Jane]*, 10 October 2007, at page 8.

166 *Transcript of evidence given in Court* at page 1536 lines 1-11.

> *Jane*: **No, I can't remember exactly how my hand ended up on his penis.**[167]
>
> *Heywood-Smith*: **To be quite clear about it you have no recollection of Father Fleming touching his own penis.**
>
> *Jane*: **No.**[168]

Jane gave evidence of returning to Adelaide the first morning after arriving at Meningie. But she said she thought she might have gone to Tailem Bend for a church service first. Counsel for the plaintiff sought to establish how uncertain her memory was and that she was possibly re-constructing.

> *Heywood-Smith*: **Do you recall whether after the church service you went and packed up your bag and got your things together?**
>
> *Jane:* **I don't remember.**[169]
>
> *Heywood-Smith*: **Do you recall having to drive back to Meningie to get your personal effects?**
>
> *Jane:* **I don't remember.**
>
> *Heywood-Smith*: **As I understand your evidence, you spoke to Mrs McNichol about reasons why you wanted to go home.**
>
> *Jane:* **I don't remember. I'm assuming that that's - I certainly didn't - I just remember**

---

167 *Transcript of evidence given in Court* at page 1536 lines 36-37.

168 *Transcript of evidence given in Court* at page 1540 lines 11-13.

169 *Transcript of evidence given in Court* at page 1548 lines 25-27.

> **saying 'I don't remember who'. I just remember saying I wanted to go home.**[170]

Mr Heywood-Smith KC directed Jane's attention to the transcript of an interview she had with Michael Abbott KC[171] who was investigating matters on behalf of the Catholic Church. Again, Jane's answers in cross-examination, qualify her earlier testimony and further emphasise the confused and confusing nature of Jane's evidence because, as she admits, she really doesn't remember anything.

> *Heywood-Smith*: **Can I take you firstly to p.3 of the transcript. Towards the top of the page, the third answer that you give on that page, at the end of the answer you give these words 'I remember seeing him touching his erect penis'. Do you see that?**
>
> *Jane:* **Yeah, well, again, I think - I don't remember saying that. It is a transcript. I don't remember saying that.**
>
> *Heywood-Smith*: **Do you have any recollection of seeing Father Fleming touching his penis?**
>
> *Jane:* **No, I don't.**
>
> *Heywood-Smith*: **You say halfway down that page an answer that you give commencing**

170 *Transcript of evidence given in Court* at page 1548/28-36.

171 Exhibit P48: *In the Matter of an Inquiry Conducted by Michael Abbott KC and in the Matter of the Catholic Archdiocese of Adelaide RE: Complaints Concerning Fr John Fleming,* "Transcript of interview conducted by Mr Abbott KC with [Jane], Tuesday, 24th of February 2009".

> **with the words 'I guessed'. Do you see that answer?**
>
> ***Jane:* Yes.**
>
> ***Heywood-Smith*: You say there that you've been 'quite good at forgetting'.**
>
> ***Jane:* Yes.**
>
> ***Heywood-Smith*: What did you mean by that? What were you referring to?**
>
> ***Jane:* As I've explained before, I mean that I don't have to think about those things. I've been very good at not thinking about those things.**[172]

These are just some of the many examples where the accuracy of her memory is qualified by Jane herself, and these examples only refer to her evidence about the 'Meningie incident'. It is reasonable to conclude that her memory is, in fact, unreliable, and it is quite illogical to conclude that her memory is to be trusted.

Extend this to the other two issues (beach at Brighton and St Mark's), then basing a case on Jane's memory is both unreasonable and illogical. Contrast that with the reasonable consistency of the evidence of the plaintiff and Alison Fleming. How Justice Gray was minded conclusively to regard Jane's evidence as "compelling" is, on any reading of the evidence, astounding. His dismissal of the evidence of both the plaintiff and Alison Fleming on what can be argued as utterly spurious

---

172 *Transcript of evidence given in Court* at page 1603 line 27 to page 1604 line 10.

grounds is alarming. Even more concerning is that Justices Vanstone, Nicholson, and Bampton utterly failed to pick up the errors in logic, and Justice Gray's inaccurate account of what the evidence actually said.

Chapter Six

Ten Reasons to Mistrust Gray's Findings Concerning Meningie

It should be said, straight away, that Jane provided three different stories about the Meningie incident to three different persons. The stories are different as to act and to place. The stories were these:

1. To Anglican cleric David Richardson, Jane alleged, in the early 2000s, that the plaintiff had at some unstated place, "shown her his penis and expected her to admire it".
2. To Anglican cleric John Stephenson, the incident described to him was fellatio and it took place on the beach in the Coorong district.
3. To the Police and to the Court, it was touching a penis in the context of a threesome and in a house at Meningie.

In addition, multiple logical errors in Justice Gray's judgement will be exposed with all their implications for injustice to be visited upon Dr Fleming.

First reason to mistrust

Justice Gray finds Jane's accusations proved before considering the evidence of the eyewitness and the memory expert

The trial judge made his "Meningie incident" finding based on a consideration of Jane's evidence in isolation from the evidence of the third person she said was present, the then Alison McNicol. Dr Fleming and Mrs Fleming both denied that they slept in the same room and that the alleged incident took place. Justice Gray reached his conclusion that the "Meningie incident" (version 3) occurred as described by Jane **before** he considered the evidence of Mrs Fleming and Dr Arnold (the independent expert on memory), and without reference to it.

As noted above, when discussing the Meningie incident, Justice Gray found **at paragraph [J392]** that Jane's evidence was "inherently credible and compelling. I am satisfied on the balance of probabilities that it is an event that in fact took place. I have regard to the caution I must exercise in acting on this allegation which involves the commission of a serious criminal offence." Then, **in the very next paragraph [J393]**, he says he must "**now** deal with the denial by Alison Fleming… that any such incident occurred". What we have is Gray's judgement that Jane's evidence is to be relied on, a judgement in which he makes no reference to other evidence contrary to her assertions and does not even consider that evidence before simply accepting the accusations of the female accuser.

Still, even later, at paragraph [J400] he deals with the expert evidence of Dr Arnold that casts serious

doubt on the reliability of Jane's recollections. Justice Gray's claim that he had "regard to the caution he must exercise in acting on this allegation which involves the commission of a serious criminal offence" is plainly ludicrous. He threw caution to the wind, so anxious was he to find in favour of Jane's story. On his own admission, he made his finding without considering any of the evidence to the contrary. He was exercising unfettered bias.

That Justice Gray came to his conclusion that the event as described by Jane was true **before** he had considered the evidence of the third person said to have been present and the expert witness on cognitive memory with respect to Jane raises serious doubts about Justice Gray's sense of how to evaluate evidence before making a conclusion, his sense of logic, and even his impartiality.

Moreover, the learned trial judge erred in not considering the Jane allegations before the Peter Kay allegations (about which the plaintiff was not suing).

Between [J62] to [J325], the learned trial judge allowed himself to act upon irrelevant considerations (eg the luncheon meeting at which the Flemings and Sue Kay were the participants) when he came to consider and determine whether the defendants have proved a serious criminal act to the required civil standard, bearing in mind the principles of *Briginshaw*.

Consequently, Justice Gray erred by using his conclusions at [J322] to [J325] concerning whether the plaintiff had certain separate conversations with Peter Kay and Mrs Kay and deciding that "is a finding which seriously affects the plaintiff's credibility and the reliance that I can place on his evidence generally". The judge accepted that Peter Kay gave "a compelling account" of his non-criminal allegations and that he was "a witness of truth". But it is impermissible for the learned trial judge to use those findings and put them in the scales to weigh Jane's account of the plaintiff having engaged in serious criminal behaviour. Put another way, Justice Gray erred, as a matter of law, in bringing his adverse findings concerning Peter Kay into account when considering whether the defendants had established the *Briginshaw* onus concerning Jane. In particular he erred in law in using findings based on the plaintiff's answers in cross-examination in his own case to make out the defendant's case.

Having done so, the trial judge fell into an error of principle. He may have fallen into error due to the amendment to the pleadings that he granted on the last day of the trial (which was an amendment the plaintiff sought on the morning of the first day of trial but which the trial judge refused). Having made the pleading amendment, it operated *nunc pro tunc,* that the new court order is to have effect from a date earlier than that upon which it is made. A judgment is entered, or a document enrolled so as to have the same legal force and effect as if it had been entered or enrolled on an earlier day, in this case at the beginning of the trial.[173]

Consequently, the problem set out at [J428] and [J430] concerning Diana Lynch was one of the judge's own making. At [428] he says, "My conclusion that the

173 Cf *Emanuele v ASC* (1997) 188 CLR 114; *Bingham v Beresi* [1994] Full Court WA SC lib 960152A.

defendants succeed in their defence of justification strictly makes it unnecessary to further consider the defendants' contextual truth defence and, in particular, whether the defendants have proved the allegations upon which they rely concerning Dianne Lynch." And then at [430] he says, "I have earlier noted that whilst the particulars given by the defendants in their plea of contextual truth alleged the commission of a criminal offence involving Ms Lynch if the occasion which was alleged to constitute the offence took place before Ms Lynch's seventeenth birthday, that plea is not maintained in the defendants' plea of justification to the imputation adopted by the plaintiff. Nevertheless, the allegation made by Ms Lynch was the subject of evidence and fully argued. I consider that I should record my finding in respect of it."

The trial judge not only should not have considered the evidence given by Ms Lynch, but he should also not have intruded any findings about Peter Kay into his findings concerning Jane. The respondent effectively conceded as much in its Written Submission to the trial judge:

> **As to the central allegations of sexual abuse the Defendants' case rests solely on the evidence of [Jane]. [232].**

The same was consistent with their plea in the Eighth Defence: refer Reasons [72].

Notwithstanding what was in the Written Submission from the defendant, Justice Gray used evidence from the Peter Kay matter to prove the Jane accusations as true. Which error in law was specifically referred to in the appellant's application for leave to appeal to the High Court.

> **When applying the Briginshaw standard to serious criminality it is not appropriate to rely upon evidence relating to non-criminal conduct which could only have been admissible consequent upon a ruling, subsequently reversed, that the applicant not have leave to adopt the respondent's contextual truth imputation of general criminality.**[174]

Second reason to mistrust

The need to set aside the evidence of the Reverend John Stephenson

To justify his judgement that he need not take into further account the two other versions Jane had given on earlier dates of what she claimed was a sexual assault, Justice Gray needed to deal with the evidence before the Court given by the Reverends John Stephenson and David Richardson.

In the early 2000s, Jane had given a completely different account of what happened at Meningie to family friend and cleric/counsellor the Reverend John Stephenson[175] than that given in evidence at the trial. In the first account, Jane named a different sexual act which took place in a different location, the Coorong beach, not

174 See Appendix B, n. 37.

175 Stephenson practiced TA., ie Transactional Analysis.

in a house in Meningie. This account was to the effect that concerning Meningie "she was juvenile when [Dr Fleming] got her to perform oral sex on the beach". Jane told Mr Stephenson that "this occurred at the country location in the South East. After the incident, they rejoined the McNicol family further down the beach".[176]

The trial judge was "inclined to accept [Jane's] explanation for the apparent inconsistency", namely that Stephenson had conflated the allegations of events at Meningie with those said to have occurred at St Mark's College (acts of fellatio) which will be dealt with later. Jane subsequently abandoned her allegation of fellatio at the beach. Jane's massive inconsistencies are simply to be wished away by this judge.

But Stephenson was present when Jane was interviewed by the Anglican investigator.[177] He would have heard her answers to those questions. Illogically, it is argued that because he could have conflated separate events, he therefore did. Hence, the benefit of the doubt goes to Jane to whom, in any case, he had already shown bias

Justice Gray gave the benefit of the doubt to Jane rather than suggesting that the inconsistencies raised questions about the credibility of Jane. Justice Gray acknowledged that the Reverend Stephenson's statement to the police "was admitted into evidence" but held he was "not prepared" to include it in his considerations despite the fact that Jane's story was inconsistent

176 Exhibit P71: Stephenson statement to police. *Jane's* cross examination on this appears in the Transcript at page 1738, lines 6-26.

177 Justice Gray *judgement* at paragraph 374.

with what the Reverend Stephenson had said she told him because he was no longer alive and so unable to be further questioned on his recall.[178] But since that evidence created problems for Jane's narrative when giving evidence before the Court, Justice Gray decided to disregard all of Stephenson's evidence. This he does by mere assertion, there being no logic involved here. He says he is "not prepared", that is to say, he just won't take serious account of the fact that Jane's story is inconsistent with what Stephenson said she told him because Stephenson was no longer alive and so unable to be further questioned on his recall.

> I am also not prepared to regard other aspects of the statement of Father Stephenson to which the plaintiff refers in his written submissions as necessarily inconsistent with Jane's evidence without the elaboration that might have been provided had Father Stephenson been able to give evidence.[179]

But really, there were no relevant allegations to conflate. Jane never gave evidence to anyone else of any incident involving oral sex on a beach at the Coorong, and she never gave evidence of any incident after which either she or they "rejoined the McNicol family further down the beach". This story contains remarkable details for Mr Stephenson to be mistaken about. And the particulars of the Defence (*The Advertiser*) do not refer to anything like that.

Unfortunately, by the time of trial, the Reverend

178 Justice Gray *judgement* at page 101 paragraph 357.

179 Justice Gray *judgement* at page 104 paragraph 375.

Stephenson had died and accordingly was not a witness in Court. Who was to have to bear the prejudice involved in Mr Stephenson not being available to testify and clarify further what Jane had told him? Dr Fleming. Of course! Also not able through death to give evidence about the sleeping arrangements at Meningie and the so-called incident on the beach, were the McNicol parents and their youngest son. The inability of these witnesses to appear formed a significant gap in the ability of the plaintiff to be awarded a fair trial, emphasising the difficulties faced by those such as Dr Fleming when the media publish stories about incidents that allegedly happened decades ago. The likelihood of witnesses having died in the interim is high and thus jeopardises the opportunity of a fair hearing for a plaintiff.

This is a further example of Dr Fleming being denied the opportunity to fully test Jane's evidence in the context of the evidence of other witnesses because of *The Advertiser*'s decision to publish, in a partisan manner, events which allegedly had taken place nearly forty years previously. It is also an example of the prejudice associated with the death of witnesses being visited upon the plaintiff (Dr Fleming) rather than the media defendants (*The Advertiser*).

This is intolerable, unjust, and contrary to any suggestion of fair process.

The absurdity of a man having oral sex with an under-aged girl at the beach when her guardians (the McNicol family) were nearby stretches credulity to breaking point.

Third reason to mistrust

The need to set aside the Reverend David Richardson's evidence

Another version of the Meningie incident was given by Anglican minister, the Reverend David Richardson, a witness called by the defendant. Jane had told Mr Richardson in the early 2000s that the plaintiff had "shown her his penis and expected her to admire it" which was "the extent of her cause for anger at John Fleming".[180]

Jane first made these allegations some thirty years after the alleged events.[181] In the face of this evidence Justice Gray says this:

> **To my mind there is considerable force in the fact that Jane has steadfastly persisted in her account of this incident** with an embellishment of a fact so readily liable to be rebutted. I am satisfied that the incident took place as Jane has described.[182]

This statement on Justice Gray's part is almost entirely incomprehensible.

Firstly, Justice Gray's claim that Jane was steadfast in her account of "this incident" is highly disputable given the evidence given by the Reverends Richardson and Stephenson.

---

180 *Transcript of evidence given in Court* at page 2001, lines 31-38. His evidence was given after Jane's evidence had concluded and there was no application to recall her.

181 Justice Gray *judgement,* paragraph 356.

182 Justice Gray *judgement,* paragraph 396.

Further, Jane did significantly more than "embellish" the account. She gave entirely different accounts to Mr Richardson, Mr Stephenson and to the Court. Jane alleged to Mr Richardson that the plaintiff had "shown her his penis and expected her to admire it". Mr Stephenson reported the incident described to him as fellatio and on the beach. To the Court, it was her touching his penis in a house at Meningie. The trial judge excused this inconsistency by characterising Mr Richardson's evidence that the allegation was "something of that sort"[183] as being an "indefinite response"[184] that did not necessarily reflect adversely upon Jane's account of the evidence. Looking at the full context of Mr Richardson's evidence on this point does not allow the description of that evidence to be an "indefinite response".

> Heywood-Smith: Did she say something along the lines that he had shown her his penis and expected her to admire it?
>
> Richardson: I think something of that sort, yes.
>
> Heywood-Smith: Was that all that she said to you on that topic?
>
> Richardson: Yes.
>
> Heywood-Smith: Your recollection now is that was the extent of her cause for anger at John Fleming?
>
> Richardson: Yes.[185]

183 Transcript of evidence given in Court at page 2001 lines 31-38.

184 Justice Gray *judgement* at paragraph 377.

185 Transcript at page 2001 lines 31-38.

While Justice Gray noted that Jane accepted that she may have said that to Mr Richardson, he made no comment as to what account might be taken of what was a very significant concession in respect of her credibility or her reliability. Further, Justice Gray made no reference at all to the most important aspect of this evidence, namely that Mr Richardson agreed that this represented "the extent" of Jane's allegation as made to him.

Justice Gray acknowledged that Jane's evidence was "readily liable to be rebutted".[186] He then concluded that he was satisfied that the incident took place as Jane described. But Jane had given at least three totally different accounts of the Meningie event. What was the basis for him selecting one of the three versions? Justice Gray doesn't precisely say. The reasons he proffered for holding Jane's allegations to be true, rather than admitting that questions were raised by the evidence of the Reverends John Stephenson and David Richardson, are inadequate.

It is not possible to describe these three different accounts as just "inconsistencies". **They are mutually exclusive, totally different accounts of an alleged event.**

In considering the quality or strength of Jane's evidence, Justice Gray attached no significance to these prior statements concerning Meningie and how much they varied from the evidence that Jane gave in Court.

Extraordinarily, and damningly, is the fact that none of this evidence was addressed by the Full Court when it dismissed Dr Fleming's appeal.[187]

---

186 Gray's judgement at paragraph 396.

187 Judgement of the Full Court of the Supreme Court at paragraphs 138-140.

The requirements of the *Briginshaw* rule were neither applied nor met, that is, **"in such matters 'reasonable satisfaction' should not be produced by inexact proofs, indefinite testimony or indirect inferences."**[188]

Fourth reason to mistrust

The need to set aside Jane's multiple contradictions and inconsistencies

As has been discussed, Jane gave two differing accounts of the alleged Meningie incident to two Anglican clerics and a third to the police and the Court. Justice Gray was aware that statements were made to various persons. In a short section of his judgement labelled "Statements made by Jane"[189] he simply noted their existence but explored no detail in those varying accounts. He then, dismissively, stated:

> All these documents form the foundation for an extensive cross-examination of Jane for the purpose of demonstrating inconsistent or conflicting statements made by her and otherwise seeking to cast doubt on the reliability of her evidence.[190]

Of course, Jane was cross-examined on the multitude of inconsistencies and contradictions offered by her at different times. However, Justice Gray apparently did not consider any of these inconsistencies and contradictions

188 *Briginshaw v Briginshaw*, [1938] HCA 34, 60 CLR 336 at p 362, Dixon J.

189 Justice Gray *judgement* at paragraphs 355-363.

190 Justice Gray judgement, paragraph 363.

serious enough to challenge his belief in the truth of what Jane said: "To my mind there is considerable force in the fact that Jane has steadfastly persisted in her account of this incident."[191] He described the plaintiff's case as one "seeking to cast doubt on the reliability of her evidence", which, after all, is hardly surprising given the plaintiff is arguing a case of defamation concerning these allegations. That one should doubt what Jane said when she gave three totally different accounts of the Meningie incident would appear entirely reasonable. The plaintiff did not need to seek to cast doubt, as the inconsistencies and contradictions in evidence were obvious.

Fifth reason to mistrust

The need to set aside evidence which challenged the allegation of the Meningie house incident

In considering the requisite strength of the evidence to determine whether a sexual assault had taken place at Meningie in the terms asserted to the police and the Court, ie Jane touched Dr Fleming's penis in a bedroom in the Rectory at Meningie, Justice Gray did not give proper regard to:

a) the fact that Alison's parents and youngest brother, but for the fact they were already dead at the time of the trial, could have given evidence that the girls did not sleep in Dr Fleming's bedroom; and
b) the evidence given by Alison's surviving younger brother that, while he could not recall the sleeping

191 Justice Gray *judgement*, 109 paragraph 396.

> arrangements at Meningie, their "mum was really conservative and dad was very protective".[192]

It is difficult to imagine a "very conservative" mother and a "very protective" father agreeing to their young daughter and Jane (for whom they were acting *in loco parentis*) sleeping unsupervised in the same room as a 27-year-old man.

Sixth reason to mistrust

Why Justice Gray decided that Mrs Alison Fleming was not to be believed

In her evidence Alison Fleming clearly contradicted Jane's account of what happened when they were holidaying at the Anglican Rectory at Meningie. She unequivocally rejected any suggestion that she and Jane had shared a bedroom with Dr Fleming, that any immoral actions took place of the kind Jane described, and that she had never made a pact with Jane to 'seduce' Dr Fleming. She was the eyewitness said by Jane to have been present when what she alleged happened.

Essentially, Justice Gray gave two reasons why he considered Mrs Fleming as a witness of no credit.

Firstly, as discussed above, Justice Gray apparently considered Alison Fleming's evidence in relation to the allegation by Peter Kay, namely that her recollections of a conversation with Ms Kay some 21 years earlier was not the same on one or two points as the recollections of Ms Kay. [see Chapter Four for detail.] It is suggested Justice Gray was wrong to judge one person unreliable and a liar because of differences on some points of an

192 *Transcript of evidence given in Court* at page 2474 lines 28-32.

unrecorded conversation held some 21 years earlier. Such a conclusion is illogical, could reasonably be deemed unjust, and that the evidence does not support that conclusion. A better appraisal would surely be that the two women had slightly different accounts based upon their memory.

High Court Justices Gaudron, Gummow and Kirby addressed this distinction in another case:

> But honest mistake, inadvertence, carelessness or misunderstanding leading to evidence shown to be false will not constitute perjury for which a criminal intention must always be proved. In R v Dickson it was rightly said:
>
> > [I]t is essential to distinguish between honesty and accuracy and not assume the latter because of belief in the former.[193]

As discussed previously in Chapter Four, Justice Gray not only embraces the logical fallacy of "the excluded middle" to justify his discrediting of Alison Fleming, but he seems to accept Harris's theory as a proved fact that "Mrs Fleming is a 'loyal protectionist' of her family unit and that she can rationalise the incident because of what has later become of her life".[194] No evidence was brought before the Court to justify this theory.

In effect, Justice Gray defamed Alison Fleming by holding her out to be the kind of person who would lie to protect her husband even though there was never any

193 *Mackenzie v R* [1996] HCA 35; (1996) 190 CLR 348; (1996) 141 ALR 70; (1996) 71 ALJR 91 (3 December 1996).

194 Justice Gray *judgement*, at paragraph 394.

evidence to support such an assertion, but nonetheless it is shameful, damaging, hurtful, and prejudicial.

Justice Gray's rejection of Alison Fleming's evidence was without sound foundation. His dismissal of her evidence sets at nought the value of her evidence on the sexist basis that she is married to the plaintiff and that her recall of a conversation 21 years earlier was not exactly the same as one of the other parties to the conversation. There was no evidentiary basis for Justice Gray to reject her as a witness of credit. His conclusion seems to have been based only on his partiality for witnesses for the defence.

Justice Gray had already rejected Dr Fleming as a witness of credit prior to his consideration of Jane's evidence. There was no rational basis for him to do this either. Justice Gray had settled on his narrative, the onus of proof was reversed, and to make sure his narrative succeeded he unfairly and illogically pronounced both Flemings and Dr Arnold to be untrustworthy witnesses. So much for truth and justice. And so much for the proper application of the doctrine of where lies the burden of proof (*onus probandi*).[195]

Seventh reason to mistrust Justice Gray's findings concerning Meningie

Jane falsely reconstructs evidence to fit in with her narrative

It is an incontrovertible fact, proved through Church records, that just as he testified, in January 1971

195 *Onus probandi incumbit ei qui dicit, non ei qui negat*: the burden of the proof lies upon he who affirms, not he who denies.

Dr Fleming was the locum for about a week at the Anglican Parish of Meningie/Tailem Bend. In Court, Jane steadfastly maintained that the Meningie incident was the first sexual contact she had with Dr Fleming. Jane, however, had also alleged sexual encounters in Dr Fleming's "rice bubble" car which, the evidence revealed, was disposed of in 1969. The year 1969 was a year when Dr Fleming was the curate at St. Jude's and Jane certainly knew him through the McNicol family. Here, she has clearly constructed a story in her mind which is at variance with, and contradicts, her other evidence about the "Meningie incident". Of this discrepancy, Justice Gray seems to have taken no account.

Witnesses for the defence, Bronte Koop and Candice Hyde

In opening the case at trial, counsel for the defendant, Andrew Harris, described to Justice Gray two witnesses he intended to call, Bronte Koop and Candice Hyde, in these terms:

> Bronte Koop was a friend of [Jane] in her late teens. They went out together. He will tell the Court that in the 1970s she confided in him about the fact of the sexual relationship she had had with the plaintiff. We will also call a person by the name Candice Hyde, who will also tell the Court that the witness Jane confided in her about her relationship with the plaintiff. I can't give you the precise date but it was the late 1970s they shared a house together.[196]

196 *Transcript of evidence given in Court* at page 718 lines 14 – 23.

During the trial, Harris dropped further reference to Candice Hyde, but reiterated his intention to call Bronte Koop as a witness when he told Justice Gray:

> He [Bronte Koop] is a witness from whom I propose to lead evidence of complaint being made or evidence of the fact that [Jane] in conversations with Bronte Koop while they were going out, so in the period sometime around the middle of 1972 to sometime in 1973, which was the duration of when they were boyfriend and girlfriend, that she told Bronte Koop about the fact of having had a sexual relationship with the plaintiff.[197]

In the event neither Koop nor Hyde were called to give evidence and counsel for the defendant offered no explanation for his failure to call them. It can only be surmised why this was the case. Counsel for the plaintiff, Paul Heywood-Smith KC, submitted at trial that an adverse inference ought to be drawn. However, Justice Gray made no reference to either Koop or Hyde. Neither did the Full Court refer to this matter when considering the appeal.

Evidence of expert witness

The issue as to whether Jane's memory could be trusted to give a faithful and accurate account of the events she describes was addressed by an expert witness, Dr Michelle Arnold, whose doctorate was in cognitive psychology. At the time of the trial, Dr Arnold was a lecturer and researcher in the field of human memory

---

197 *Transcript of evidence given in Court* at page 1422 lines 3 – 10.

and cognition at Flinders University. Dr Arnold was an expert witness called by Dr Fleming, the only expert witness to be called in the entire trial, but she was not deemed important enough by Justice Gray for her to be listed in his pantheon of "principal witnesses".

Dr Arnold made these important observations:

1. There is a great deal of research which shows that the beliefs a counsellor holds can have a significant impact on a client's memory and feelings regarding long-ago events. Counsellor, the Rev John Stephenson, had such an impact.
2. There are indications that Jane's belief as to how memory works has had a significant impact on her own memory of long-ago events.
3. There is a problem when counsellors have either taken no notes of counselling sessions or have discarded them as is the case with Jane.
4. After reading the evidence Jane gave at trial Dr Arnold said: "Given the provided transcripts, the opinions I expressed in my report have not altered but have been reinforced. I provide specifics regarding this reinforcement below."[198]

This matter will be dealt with in detail in Chapter Eight. It is sufficient for now to note that Justice Gray dismissed the evidence of the expert witness on memory, Dr Michelle Arnold, saying that her evidence did not "assist" him. As will be made clear there were no reasonable or cogent grounds upon which to so

198 P 85. Dr Michelle Arnold, Addendum to Report Prepared in the Matter of Fleming v The Advertiser Publishing Co P/L & ANOR, 19 January 2015.

summarily dismiss someone who knew a lot more about the science of memory.

Justice Gray made a further brief and contentious reference to Dr Arnold's evidence when he considered Mr Stephenson's account of his dealings with Jane. Justice Gray provided no reasons for rejecting Dr Arnold's evidence about the likely influence on Jane's memory of a counsellor like the Reverend John Stephenson, except to say that "her assumptions in that regard were strongly challenged in cross-examination".[199] It is the nature of our adversarial judicial system that much of importance is "strongly challenged" and does not constitute a reason for disregarding Dr Arnold's evidence on this matter.

Even more remarkably where Mr Stephenson's evidence is concerned, in Justice Gray's view, Dr Arnold's assumption that the location of the first incident was at a house in Meningie could not be relied upon. Justice Gray argued this on the basis that "Jane's evidence to this Court did not seek to assert the location of the first incident as anywhere other than a place in the Coorong."[200] The footnote provided by Justice Gray for this assertion is from the transcript of the evidence given in Court.

> Jane: I am not sure where it was but it was, it was at the Coorong.
>
> Harris: The Coorong.[201]

However, just a few lines on Jane says, "When I spoke to the police, they told me that it was, that it was Meningie". And a few more lines on she states:

---

199 Justice Gray *judgement* at paragraph 381.

200 *Ibid.*

201 Transcript of evidence given in Court at page 1368 lines 13-15.

> Harris: Do you recall arriving at the location you now know to be Meningie?
>
> Jane: I'm not sure it was Meningie, it was in that district.
>
> Harris: Well, if we work on the basis that the location that you went to I'm going to refer to as 'Meningie'.
>
> Jane: Okay.
>
> Harris: You've given your answer as to your understanding of where it was, and do you recall where you stayed?
>
> Jane: It was, it was a, a, a house. It was an old, older-style house.

It should be obvious to anyone that a house is not a beach. Jane's account to Mr Stephenson was that it was at the beach in the Coorong that the first incident took place. But her account to the Court was that it was in a house in the township of Meningie. Dr Arnold was correct, and Justice Gray was clearly wrong.

Jane's "attitude"

In the section of his judgement labelled "Jane's attitude",[202] Justice Gray disclosed the subjective nature of his judgement when he justified Jane's "exaggeration" and "paranoia". Justice Gray seemed unable to brook any questioning of Jane's evidence, stability, or character. He just "knows" that what Jane is saying is true and again indulges in a circular argument.

---

202 Justice Gray *judgement* at paragraphs 364-369.

> **There is every justification for Jane to feel wounded, vulnerable and resentful as a result of what she says was her experience with the plaintiff.** Those emotions come out in her interview with the journalist Nigel Hunt. The plaintiff refers to that interview to submit that it demonstrates a level of irrational malice towards the plaintiff. In particular in that interview Jane makes reference to a website photo of the plaintiff "looking like ·a paedophile"[203] and describes to Mr Hunt her perceptions of the plaintiff's effect on her life. None of the matters referred to by the plaintiff persuade me that Jane's feelings towards the plaintiff are other than what one might expect if they reflect her experience with the plaintiff. More particularly I do not accept that they, or any of the matters referred to by the plaintiff, demonstrate any loss of her sense of reality for me to doubt her reliability as a witness.[204]

Justice Gray's argument apparently was:

1. If Jane had experienced sexual abuse at the hands of Dr Fleming, then one would expect Jane "to feel wounded, vulnerable, and resentful".[205]

---

203 It was deeply concerning that Justice Gray seems to accept as evidence that someone is said to look like a paedophile. The same judge refused to accept photographic evidence of *Peter Kay*, dressed in nothing but a loin cloth with a dog's collar around his neck and the leash held by another man. *Kay* was on all fours like a dog. They were appearing in the gay Mardi Gras. The photograph was obtained from *Kay's* Facebook site where he had posted it.

204 Justice Gray *judgement* at paragraph 368.

205 Justice Gray *judgement* at paragraph 368.

2. Jane appears "to feel wounded, vulnerable, and resentful".
3. Therefore, Jane was sexually abused by Dr Fleming.

This is risible. Accepting premiss 2, that Jane felt "wounded, vulnerable, and resentful", one cannot assume that it is because she was sexually abused by Dr Fleming. This circular argument employed by Justice Gray does him no credit, and the failure of Justices Vanstone, Nicholson, and Bampton to see that it is a circular argument does them no credit either.

There was no serious attempt by Justice Gray to look at the evidence before him to see what other motives might be at play where Jane was concerned, just a willingness to believe bad faith on the part of Dr Fleming and his wife, while dismissing the evidence of any other witnesses that did not make his list of "principal witnesses". Their evidence is at best an inconvenience to be explained away.

In evidence, also, was a letter from Dr Fleming to the Professional Standards Director of the Anglican Diocese of Adelaide, Peter Caporaso, in which Dr Fleming said this:

> **In the early 1980s [*Jane*] told me that she had had sexual dealings with a prominent Adelaide politician when she was fourteen years of age. At the same time, she told me that a recently widowed man, and a good friend of ours, was a notorious homosexual who had given his wife a lot of grief by his behaviour. I asked her how she knew**

> **this, what evidence she had? She said she "just knew". I told her that she couldn't "just know" anything and warned her not to repeat such unsubstantiated allegations to anyone. In the case of the politician, I simply did not believe her because of what she said about my friend.**[206]

Speaking about her marriage to her first husband at the Catholic Church inquiry, Jane told Michael Abbott KC that her first husband

> ... was gay actually. It's sort of like one of those stories that you don't like to hear. It lasted a year. He was married three more times. Hasn't come out of the closet yet but there we are. Life goes on.[207]

That, too, was a most unlikely allegation about this many-times-married man. Jane gave no reasons to support her belief about her first husband.

All this evidence was available to Justice Gray and might have encouraged him to be more sceptical of Jane's credibility and reliability had he noted it. After all, he took more than 12 months to consider all the evidence before him. Or is this further evidence that Justice Gray wrote his judgement under pressure in the last 46 days of the 12 months adjournment? After all, the longer a judge leaves bringing down his judgement the more he loses his advantage of having just heard the evidence and

206 D12: Confidential letter from Dr Fleming to Exhibit Peter Caporaso, 31st of January 2011.

207 Exhibit P48: *Transcript of interview conducted by Mr Abbott KC with Jane*, 24th February 2009.

mistakes are more easily made. Justice Gray had form on this and was subject to fierce criticism by the High Court for his dilatoriness in another matter.

Eighth reason to mistrust Gray's findings concerning Meningie

One of the most incredible aspects of Jane's account of the Meningie allegation relates to the events that immediately followed. Jane had told an Anglican Church inquiry that it was her and Alison McNicol's goal to "seduce" the appellant. In cross-examination, Jane confirmed that was a goal she had discussed with Alison.[208] In his submission to Justice Gray, Mr Heywood-Smith pointed to the evidence that showed Jane saying that she and Alison never discussed the events of Meningie on the night that it occurred or at any time thereafter. In the circumstances, that they should never discuss their success defies credulity. If indeed the two girls were given to devising such an unseemly and vile plot, they would have had no problem in celebrating their 'success'. That Mrs Fleming agreed with Jane that they never discussed the alleged event is not surprising if no such event had ever occurred. While that submission was made at trial, it was not referred to by Justice Gray in his judgement.

The "Meningie incident" - a construction and fabrication?

If Jane's evidence is followed from her first claim until the defamation trial what we find is this:

---

208 *Transcript of evidence given in Court* at page 1623 lines 13-17.

1. Jane abandoned her first two claims made to Reverends Stephenson and Richardson, and settled on a third account, namely the 'threesome' alleged to have taken place in the house in Meningie.
2. Jane claimed that there was an incident in a house at Meningie where Dr Fleming slept in the same room as two fourteen-year-old girls, notwithstanding the presence in the house of the McNicol parents and their two sons.
3. Jane needed to provide motive and so claimed that she had entered into a pact with her friend to seduce Dr Fleming.
4. At some time in the room in which she claims to have slept with Dr Fleming and Alison McNicol, Jane claimed that the two girls approached Dr Fleming's bed, that one girl had kissed Dr Fleming while Jane herself says that she touched Dr Fleming's penis and without his invitation to do so.

It is strongly argued that the alleged seduction plot was a figment of Jane's imagination since the one with whom she says she plotted denied any such conversation occurred. Moreover Jane, by her own admission, never discussed with her alleged fellow plotter the success of their plot, an unlikely outcome if the plot really had been planned and succeeded as she alleges. The incident was comprehensively denied by Dr Fleming and Alison Fleming.

It seems reasonable to conclude based on the evidence (as compared to Justice Gray's emotional response to Jane) that Jane constructed the memory of an event that never happened. There is no evidence in the two judgements that any of these judges had seriously looked at what was a clearly constructed account of an event that never happened. Justice Gray did not question the credibility of the account provided by Jane and, by ignoring the advice of the expert on memory, Dr Michelle Arnold, allowed himself to be persuaded into believing this highly unlikely account of what Jane claims happened in Meningie.

Nineth reason to mistrust Gray's findings concerning Meningie

Following the Meningie pattern, the allegations of sexual misbehaviour said by Jane to have occurred over the next 18 months are, too, obviously examples of reconstructed (confected?) memory such that her reliability in relation to all her stories is further undermined. Those post-Meningie allegations will be fully discussed in the next chapter.

Tenth reason to mistrust Justice Gray's findings concerning Meningie

The corrupting power of money

At the time of the trial two of the three persons making allegations against Dr Fleming, had already received substantial compensation monies from the Anglican Church in Adelaide, South Australia, namely Jane and Dianne Lynch. The third person, Peter Kay, had not received compensation from the Anglican Church at the time of the trial but said he had not ruled out the possibility of pursuing that in due course.

This compensation had been provided by the Anglican Church even though it had never conducted any process to establish whether the allegations were true. Instead, assuming that the allegations were true, the Anglican Church provided significant financial compensation to these two women, and, in Jane's case, with more to come. It is suggested that these two women had a financial incentive to continue with their allegations in the Supreme Court, either to prevent the possibility of the Anglican Church taking action to reclaim the compensation that had been awarded for something that never happened, or in the hope that more compensation might be forthcoming.

It does not seem to have occurred to Justice Gray that Jane might be encouraged to continue with her story because she was already in receipt of ongoing compensation monies from the Anglican Church. Where Diane Lynch was concerned, Justice Gray dismissed her evidence.

The assumption that Jane was telling the truth was revealed in the evidence before the Court. Helen Carrig, the then Professional Standards Director for the Diocese of Adelaide, in a letter to Jane on 28 June 2005, some three years before the matter became public, and three years before Dr Fleming knew that she was making such an allegation, wrote:

> As I said in my letter the Professional Standards Committee considered your request and understood that **what happened to you as a teenager has had an impact.**[209]

209 Exhibit P52, at page 10.

Subsequently, in February 2008, Jane received $7,570 for reimbursement of past counselling fees, and fifteen further sessions of therapy at $140 per session.[210] On 6 November 2008 Jane wrote to the then Professional Standards Director, Peter Caporaso, to remind him that the Anglican Church had agreed to pay her Art School fees as well.[211]

On 9 April 2009 Archbishop Driver wrote to Jane agreeing to pay her a further $2080 provided she understood that **this would be part of her final compensation package**. And finally, there is the letter from Keith Stephens of the Adelaide Anglican Diocese of 9 March 2011 agreeing to pay for Jane's "cost of art supplies".[212]

So, without any process to decide factual truth, the Anglicans provided Jane with a financial incentive and the promise of more money to come, to continue with her allegations.

Where Dianne Lynch is concerned, the Anglican Church determined not to proceed any further with her allegations, although that did not stop them providing her with substantial compensation. Pursuant to a Deed of Release dated 21 August 2009,[213] she was given $61,000 and a cheque was sent to Medicare Australia for $6,800. These monies were paid to her to settle allegations that "she was unlawfully sexually assaulted or abused" by two Anglican clerics, one of whom was alleged to be

---

210 Exhibit P52 at page 30, Letter from Jeffrey Driver, then Archbishop of Adelaide, and dated the 27th of February 2008.

211 Exhibit P52, at page 38.

212 Exhibit P52, at page 41.

213 Made available by subpoena.

Dr Fleming. In return, the Anglican Diocese of Adelaide sought from Dianne Lynch an agreement that she accept that the Diocese was not liable at law.

In neither case was Dr Fleming subject to any inquiry or process to determine truth. The monies were paid, and in the case of Jane, the promise of further monies made.

These compensation monies had, as an indirect consequence, the potential to provide financial incentives for Jane and Dianne Lynch to maintain their allegations. The possible compromising of these two witnesses was raised by counsel for the plaintiff. Of this matter, Justice Gray took no account.

Conclusion

Jane's evidence regarding the "Meningie incident" was uncorroborated, contradicted by a witness Jane said was present, inconsistent in material respects with statements she had previously made, and inherently improbable. The variation in her accounts of the sexual act involved, and where it was meant to have occurred, should have given Justice Gray pause for thought and not an incentive to rationalise away, as he does, all the many difficulties with Jane's evidence.

Justice Gray was clearly mistaken to have accepted, as true, evidence which was so obviously internally contradictory, inconsistent, contrived, and contradicted by other witnesses, witnesses consistently overlooked or side-lined by him. Justice Gray was wrong to excuse, and in some cases entirely overlook, those many aspects of Jane's evidence which told against both her credibility and reliability.

Taken together, as they should have been, the difficulties with Jane's evidence tell of precisely the type of "uncertain proof" that, as referenced in Chapter One, *Briginshaw* warned against accepting in a case such as this.

> **But reasonable satisfaction is not a state of mind that is attained or established independently of the nature and consequence of the fact or facts to be proved. The seriousness of an allegation made, the inherent unlikelihood of an occurrence of a given description, or the gravity of the consequences flowing from a particular finding are considerations which must affect the answer to the question whether the issue has been proved to the reasonable satisfaction of the tribunal. In such matters "reasonable satisfaction" should not be produced by inexact proofs, indefinite testimony, or indirect inferences.**[214]

Justice Gray's entire argument in support of his conclusion that the "Meningie incident" occurred as Jane alleged is flawed. The logical flaw may be expressed in this way:

1. Jane alleged an event occurred involving the plaintiff
2. The plaintiff denies the event occurred as Jane alleged
3. The plaintiff's evidence is supported as true by an eyewitness (Alison Fleming) identified by Jane herself

214 Dixon J, *Briginshaw v Briginshaw*, [1938] HCA 34, 60 CLR 336 at p 362.

4. Alison Fleming (eyewitness) denies that the event ever occurred
5. Other relevant witnesses save one (Douglas McNicol) are deceased
6. Douglas McNicol has no recollection of the event occurring but throws significant doubt on circumstances that would allow the allegation to be true
7. Jane maintains that the event occurred

Conclusion: Therefore, the event occurred just as Jane alleged.

However, if statements 1 to 7 are true, the event has not been proved to have occurred. The conclusion simply does not follow from the list of premisses. It is a non sequitur.

Overwhelmingly the evidence points to the conclusion that the "Meningie event" (in any of the three different versions alleged) did not occur. Or, to put it more modestly, there was no proof that the "Meningie event" ever occurred. And if that was the case, then the rest of Jane's allegations might be thought to be very questionable indeed.

The exercise of right reason is foundational to the legal system allowing minds to move from evidence to truth. The great Roman legal philosopher, Cicero, reminds us all:

> **For there is but one essential justice which cements society, and one law which establishes this justice. This law is right reason, which is the true rule of all commandments and prohibitions.**

Whoever neglects this law, whether written or unwritten, is necessarily unjust and wicked.[215]

215 Cicero, *On the Laws*, (c. 52 B.C.), From CD Yonge, *The Treatises of MT Cicero*, London: Henry D Bohn, York Street, Covent Garden, MDCCCLIII, page 417.

Chapter Seven

The Meningie Finding Became the Prism Through Which Justice Gray Considered Other Allegations

Reasons are therefore essential to the common law judicial method. Moreover, those reasons must be so structured that they serve at least three purposes. First, they must permit the parties to see the extent to which their arguments have been understood and accepted. Lord MacMillan thought that the main object of a reasoned judgment "is not only to do but to seem to do justice." Second, they must be reasons that clearly explain the reasoning process and thereby further judicial accountability. Third, those reasons must declare and apply a principle or rule at a level of generality that transcends the facts of the case and enables other courts to decide other cases, identical in principle but not in detail, in the same way. It is necessary for a court to declare a rule or principle at this level of generality because, under the common law system of adjudication, courts not only resolve disputes but formulate rules and principles that can be used to decide comparable cases.[216]

216 The Hon Justice M H McHugh AC, "The Judicial Method", *The Australian Bar Association Conference, London, England,* 5 July 1998.

The "Brighton Beach incidents"

In addition to the allegation made about an incident at Meningie, Jane also made claims about sexual assignations said to have taken place at Brighton Beach and in the plaintiff's car. The plaintiff produced many witnesses which called into question the possibility of these occurrences. Nevertheless, Justice Gray, paid little or no regard to these witnesses and seemed to accept as true Jane's allegations of further incidents having occurred at Brighton Beach even though ultimately, he could not say that these claims had been proved. Having concluded that Jane's account of the incident at Meningie "took place as Jane has described",[217] Justice Gray stated:

> It is with the background of that finding that I consider Jane's evidence of the other incidents of sexual contact with the plaintiff.[218]

When Justice Gray stated that the "Meningie event" provided the "background" when considering further allegations, he meant the 'foundation' upon which he considered Jane's evidence of other sexual incidents. This statement suggested Justice Gray would consider Jane's evidence favourably, and presumably that of the plaintiff much less so.

> Premiss 1: Jane is always to be believed,
>
> Premiss 2: Dr Fleming is always to be disbelieved, and so,

217 Justice Gray *judgement* at paragraph 396. Justice Gray does not specify which of Jane's descriptions he accepts.

218 *Ibid.*, paragraph 397.

> **Conclusion: Dr Fleming is guilty of all the other incidents alleged against him by Jane. *Quod Erat Demonstratum.***

Circular reasoning *par excellence*! But then Justice Gray had already made such a logical absurdity much earlier in his judgement at paragraph 203 as discussed earlier.

The problems with Jane's set of allegations beyond Meningie is that they became more and more problematic in the light of what was said in evidence by witnesses for Dr Fleming. The problem for Dr Fleming was that Justice Gray's mind appeared to have been made up and the Full Court simply did not do its job properly in assessing the reliability of Jane's evidence.

Problems arose with Jane's evidence regarding her allegations of assignations with Dr Fleming at Brighton Beach, particularly as to how these secret assignations were organised, assignations which were alleged to have occurred during the 18 months after the Meningie incident.[219] According to Jane, the plaintiff constantly returned to the Brighton parish after his term as curate had expired at the end of 1970 and attended parish functions. At these functions, such as choir practice, the plaintiff would arrange secret assignations with Jane. The problems with this evidence are many, which should have raised serious questions for Justice Gray and should have convinced Justice Gray that this evidence by Jane was a fabrication.

---

219 Cf Justice Gray *judgement* paragraph 407 and the judgement of the Full Court at paragraph 144.

Jane claimed that between 1971 until halfway through 1972 Dr Fleming "frequently" attended Young Anglican Fellowship meetings at St Jude's on Saturday nights, and choir practices during the week even though he had left the parish.[220] In cross-examination she said:

> **When he was a curate he used to come and he was always around even when he left. He came regularly back to St Jude's. There were always, you know, there was never a long period when he wasn't around.**[221]

Jane claimed that there were multiple sexual incidents which occurred at Brighton after the so-called Meningie event. These assignations, Jane said, were arranged when she was at functions at church (St. Jude's) with the appellant during 1971 and 1972.[222]

However, evidence provided by other witnesses indicated that the plaintiff never attended Fellowship meetings after he left the parish which, in any case, were held on a Sunday night after Evensong not on Saturday nights.[223] Nor did he attend any church functions at St Jude's once he left the parish at the end of 1970. He never attended choir practice including even when he was a curate at St Jude's.

Jane had also told police that she saw the plaintiff at choir practice each week. However, when confronted in cross-examination with the fact that the plaintiff had by this time ceased his curacy at St Jude's parish, Jane claimed that she still saw the plaintiff at church functions.

---

220 *Transcript of evidence given in Court* at page 1409 lines 11-28.

221 *Transcript of evidence given in Court* at page 1488 lines 19-22.

222 *Transcript of evidence given in Court* at page 1393 line 38.

223 Exhibits D18 to D28 inclusive.

When pressed further, Jane claimed that the plaintiff "was always there. He didn't finish his curacy and then go. He still came back. He came back many times."[224]

> Heywood-Smith: You've used the phrase 'he was always there'. Do we understand from that that he was there then as much as he was when he was a curate?
>
> Jane: No, he wasn't there as much but he was there frequently.
>
> Heywood-Smith: Was he there once a week, once a fortnight, once a month?
>
> Jane: I don't recall.
>
> Heywood-Smith: What do you mean when you use the phrase 'always there'?
>
> Jane: I think I have just said that he was there frequently.
>
> Heywood-Smith: But are you able to say whether frequently means twice a week, once a week, once a fortnight, once a month?
>
> Jane: I can't say with any certainty.
>
> Heywood-Smith: You've got no idea at all.
>
> Jane: Frequently.

The claim that Dr Fleming continued to appear at church functions at Brighton "frequently" was controverted by every other witness from the St Jude's parish who was questioned on the topic. Dr Fleming's successor as curate at St Jude's and former Northern Territory policeman, the Reverend Russell Simmonds,

224 *Transcript of evidence given in Court* at page 1553 lines 19-21.

gave evidence that he had no recollection of the applicant's return to the parish whatsoever and that to do so was not an accepted or acceptable practice.

> Heywood-Smith: In the 14 months you were the assistant curate do you have any recollection of John Fleming coming back to St Jude's to participate in the life of the church?
>
> Rev Russell Simmonds: No. No.
>
> Heywood-Smith: Was there any practice about that in terms of –
>
> Rev Russell Simmonds: Well, the tradition basically once you left you left as a curate. I - if John came back I didn't know about it anyway, put it that way, no, it wasn't an accepted practice.
>
> Heywood-Smith: Do you have any recollection of inviting him back on any occasion?
>
> Rev Russell Simmonds: No, not to my knowledge.[225]

The suggestion that Dr Fleming ever attended choir practices at St Jude's was put to the witness Kirsty Henning (now a senior secondary school teacher) who was a member of that choir at the relevant time and so a contemporary of Jane.

> Heywood-Smith: Now in terms of the choir practice were you ever aware of - did John Fleming attend your choir practices?

225 *Transcript of evidence given in Court* at page 2578 lines 1-12.

> Kirsty Henning: No, not that I can recall at any stage.[226]

Kirsty Henning also gave evidence about whether Dr Fleming attended other Church functions.

> Heywood-Smith: After John Fleming left St Jude's, did you see him come back to St Jude's and participate in church activities?
>
> Kirsty Henning: Not at all, no.[227]

This evidence clearly raises serious doubts about Jane's reliability and was never adequately addressed by the trial judge who wrongly noted that "it is clear that the plaintiff maintained contact with the Brighton area and the McNicol family in particular."[228] There was no evidence that the plaintiff "maintained contact with the Brighton area" and nor was it put to Dr Fleming that he was ever there after he had completed his curacy. Dr Fleming maintained contact only with the McNicol family who lived in Seacliff.

The clear evidence is that Dr Fleming did not attend functions at St. Jude's after he moved to St. Mark's College.[229] Jane's evidence that he was "always there" cannot be accepted. It was not put to the plaintiff in cross-examination that he was "always there" **or even asked whether he was ever there.**

Justice Gray disregarded the import of this evidence which was mistreated both by Justice Gray and the Full Court[230] and in much the same way. It is not to the

226 *Transcript of evidence given in Court* at page 2360 lines 15-17.

227 *Transcript of evidence given in Court* at page 2361 lines 4-6.

228 Justice Gray *judgement* at paragraph 408.

229 *Transcript of evidence given in Court* at page 599 lines 9-12.

230 Full Court *judgement* at paragraphs 144-149.

point that Dr Fleming was "rarely in Brighton and its environs". Jane did not assert 'chance' meetings. There was no suggestion by her of meetings being arranged by phone or letter.[231] Her evidence was that meetings occurred at "church functions" and that the plaintiff was "always there". There were no such "church functions" at which the plaintiff was present.

Justice Gray in the end came to accept the reality that Jane's claims were not established.

> That means that I must take into account the unlikelihood of there being an occasion involving a church function that the plaintiff had attended that would set the scene for the encounters in the Brighton area that Jane described.[232]

The Full Court[233] simply ignored a fundamental flaw in Jane's allegations going to the reliability of her story and, indeed, of all her stories. Like Justice Gray, the Full Court seemed to accept the reverse onus of proof, that it was Dr Fleming who had to prove he didn't do certain things, wasn't at certain places, while the presupposition was always that Jane, as alleged victim, must always be believed.

Then there is the evidence Jane gave the police where she is caught out contradicting herself:

> **Jane: And he, we were parked, it would've been at the end of Shoreham Road, and**

231 There was no email at that time, no mobile or cell phones, and nor were there answering machines for the telephone.

232 Justice Gray *judgement* at paragraph 408.

233 *Ibid.*, 148.

um, we were walking along holding hands and I was feeling as if I was the chosen one, you know, like I was his girlfriend, like there was, it was a definite feeling, and um, Fleming told me then that he was gonna marry Alison, like he was-, and still holding my hand, and I thought at the time that that was because she was the pure one, you know, that she was the one who just kissed, 'cos you only kiss before you get married, and I was the one who did the dirty stuff, you know.

Police: And what dirty stuff are you referring to?

Jane: Um, the masturbation, basically, masturbation. I don't remember him ever kissing me passionately.

Police: You said you, you didn't masturbate him.

Jane: I don't remember him, I don't remember masturbating him in the car, I don't remember.

Police: Then what-

Jane: But I don't, I don't- I believe that it happened, I just don't remember how.

Police: All right.[234]

---

234 Exhibit P5O: *Transcript of police Interview with Dr [JANE] by Senior Constable 1st Class Sonni Hamden-Victim Management Section*, 10 October 2007, at page 17.

And …

> **Yeah, it. doesn't make sense does it, but I just, I don't, yeah, I don't, I don't remember, I don't remember how, but I know that I, I know that I'd touched, I know that I had at least touched him. I never, I don't remember ejaculation. I don't, I don't, and I-, but I do, I, I, I know that when I was walking along the beach with him that I had just done something that involved his penis, put it that way. I don't remember masturbating per se, but I know that I had just touched his penis.**[235]

Even Justice Gray had to admit that, in the end, the allegations at Brighton Beach could not be proved to support the defence of justification.[236] One can legitimately ask why then did Justice Gray not see that this seriously damaged the credibility of Jane. And further, why did that not become the background against which Justice Gray "consider[ed] Jane's evidence of the other incidents of sexual contact with the plaintiff." After all she was alleging a series of criminal acts and *The Advertiser* was not able to prove them true at any level.

The "St Mark's College" incident

Jane testified that she would attend St Mark's College on Saturday afternoons in the football season between 1971 and mid-1972 and perform oral sex on the plaintiff.

---

235 *Ibid.*, at page 18.

236 Justice Gray *judgement* at page 114 paragraph 411.

Dr Fleming denied that this occurred and testified that he had never engaged in fellatio in his life with any person at any time. And as we shall see in Chapter Thirteen, the 'lie detector' test he underwent showed that he was not lying when he said this. The first time Dr Fleming heard of such an allegation was in a letter he received from Archbishop Wilson reporting the findings of Michael Abbott KC who had been commissioned by the Catholic Archdiocese of Adelaide to consider how the Church had handled Jane's allegations.

> Having said this, one important finding, which was also made is that the nature of the allegations made by one of the complainants, "Jane", to Mr Abbott was significantly more serious than the allegations which had been raised by her in 2001, when she first came forward. The fresh allegations concern an act of fellatio alleged to have been performed with Fr Fleming when "Jane" was under sixteen years of age. Despite this, as **Mr Abbott has found, she was never willing to engage the Towards Healing process and accordingly the complaint raised by her (which at the time did not include the allegation of fellatio) was dismissed. I point out that I am aware that the police have determined not to proceed with this (or any other) allegation.**[237]

Jane's story grew in the telling. At first there was no mention of fellatio. Then there was one instance of

237 Archbishop Philip Wilson, letter to Dr John Doherty PP DCL (Dr Fleming's canon lawyer), page 2.

fellatio alleged. Then there were multiple incidents of fellatio said to have occurred at Dr Fleming's flat, from 1969 until the middle of 1975. At trial, however, Jane's evidence was that these incidents only occurred within the much-reduced time frame of between 1971 and early 1972.

In the Catholic Church inquiry, Jane told Michael Abbott KC that the last incident at St Mark's occurred when she was 18, just before the plaintiff married.[238] Jane turned 18 in November 1974 and Dr Fleming married in January 1975, some two and a half years after the last incident Jane described in evidence before the Court. And Alison Fleming could not have been "at the football" since the football season ended in September.

This is a very significant inconsistency. There is a substantial difference between an allegation of sexual activity lasting a period of about 18 months when Jane was aged 14 and 15 and an allegation of that period lasting about 4 years until after Jane's 18th birthday and Dr Flemings' engagement. The same inconsistent account was included in *The Advertiser*'s pleadings before trial, that is that the acts of oral sex continued after Jane's 17th birthday.[239]

Such inconsistency cannot simply be dismissed as Jane somehow "getting the dates wrong". It is a telling indictment of Jane's unreliability and should have been commented on by Justice Gray if it was to be disregarded. That Justice Gray failed to comment on this aspect of the evidence is a grievous error on his part, and one that very much disadvantaged the plaintiff. An inconsistency

238 Exhibit P46 at pp. 4 and 9.

239 Eighth Defence at [11.4.1] and [11.4.7].

of such proportion and import ought not to have been, and cannot now be, disregarded.

It is not at all unreasonable to suppose that this major error, and all the others, may well be a consequence of Justice Gray's "deplorable" delay in bringing down a judgement in this matter.

When recounting her allegation of oral sex, the specific incident recalled by Jane, and accepted by Justice Gray as having occurred, was an incident said to be the last occasion on which Jane attended St Mark's and performed oral sex upon the plaintiff. Jane testified that on this occasion the plaintiff was wearing red tracksuit pants with a white stripe.

But there is a problem with the red track suit pants detail. The plaintiff asserted he had never owned such an item and he was supported in this by other witnesses who regularly saw the plaintiff at that time. Three examples will suffice.

Kirsty Henning:[240]

> Heywood-Smith: Do you recall whether you ever saw John Fleming wearing a red tracksuit?
>
> Kirsty Henning: Certainly not.
>
> Heywood-Smith: Why do you say that?
>
> Kirsty Henning: Well, I can't imagine John in a red tracksuit, sorry.[241]

240 School Teacher with the Department of Education (SA). Music degree (1975). Postgraduate teaching qualification (1976).

241 *Transcript of evidence given in Court* at page 2368 lines 32-36.

Arlene Macdonald:[242]

> Heywood-Smith: In those years, prior to John Fleming's marriage, are you able to comment upon his usual attire, his dress?
>
> Arlene Macdonald: He almost always wore his clerical attire including his collar. He was very formal and even at events that you would think were totally social he nearly always wore it. Possibly at a camp he may have worn a jumper and jeans or something but 95% of the time I saw him he was in his clerical attire.
>
> Heywood-Smith: Did you ever see him in tracksuit clothing?
>
> Arlene Macdonald: Never, never. No, when I saw him occasionally in casual clothes I think it was something like jeans and jumper or something like jeans and shirt. It was never that casual.

And Alison Fleming:

> Heywood-Smith: In the period that you knew John Fleming from the beginning of 1969 to the time when you married, can you indicate how John Fleming was generally dressed?

---

242 Miss Macdonald "practised as a solicitor in a small firm in Adelaide for a couple of years. Then I went to the Australian Taxation Office, then the Commonwealth Ombudsman Office and went to Sydney in the mid 80s, came back to the Australian Government Solicitor's Office in 1988 and went to the bar in 1996 and retired in the middle of 2013". Cf Transcript page 2370 line 37 to page 2371 line 5.

> Alison Fleming: Usually in a black suit in the wintertime, with a clerical collar. In the summer he would wear short-sleeved black clerical shirts and black shorts.
>
> Heywood-Smith: And what about casual clothing, did he.
>
> Alison Fleming: He would wear jeans, blue jeans, and T-shirts.
>
> Heywood-Smith: Did you ever know him to wear tracksuits?
>
> Alison Fleming: I recall him wearing a tracksuit on a very, very few occasions.
>
> Heywood-Smith: Do you recall the colour of the tracksuit.
>
> Alison Fleming: Blue.
>
> Heywood-Smith: Did you ever know him to own a red tracksuit?
>
> Alison Fleming: No.[243]

In addition, the fashionable wearing of track pants was not "in" until the late 1970s and the description of the plaintiff wearing red tracksuit pants with a white stripe is an invention on the part of Jane. The only tracksuit pants owned by the plaintiff at that time were a very old set of blue track pants (with matching top). All of this was corroborated by witnesses.

As with the Meningie allegations, Jane's evidence was uncorroborated, and inconsistent with prior statements

243 *Transcript of evidence given in Court* at page 1941 lines 2-16.

and other evidence. Jane previously had told police that the incident involving the red tracksuit pants was a separate event to what she described as the last occasion of sexual contact between her and the plaintiff.[244] Justice Gray again seems to have ignored both the factual errors and the inconsistency involved in the telling and retelling of this story.

A further element to Jane's evidence regarding her Saturday afternoon visits to St Mark's College for sexual assignations with the plaintiff, was that they took place when "Alison was at the football".[245] However, the undisputed evidence at trial was that Alison McNicol [later Mrs Fleming] never went to the football without the plaintiff,[246] and with him only very intermittently. The plaintiff, on the other hand, went to the football nearly every Saturday afternoon with his brother Peter throughout the South Australian National Football League season.[247]

> Heywood-Smith: Did you ever accompany your brother, John or did he ever accompany you to football games?
>
> Peter Fleming: Yes, yes. All games that we would attend, home games at Prospect, John came to those home games, as did my mother

---

244 Exhibit P47 at pages 19 and 21.

245 Exhibit P48: Interview with M Abbott KC (24 February 2009); Exhibit P49: Interview with G Cannons (5 May 2010); Exhibit P51: Witness statement of Jane (19/10/2010).

246 *Transcript of evidence given in Court* at page 2039 line 36 – page 2040 line 28.

247 Evidence of the appellant's brother Peter Fleming: in the *Transcript of evidence given in Court* at page 2478 lines 1-10.

and father and my son and we went to most of the away games. A couple of exceptions were Central Districts in (sic) Alberton where we found the supporters a bit vigorous for our liking.

Heywood-Smith: You mentioned your son. I think your son Richard was born in 1965?

Peter Fleming: Yes.

Heywood-Smith: Do you have a recollection of taking him to the football?

Peter Fleming: Yes, I think from about the age of six.

Heywood-Smith: Do you have any recollection of your brother John accompanying you with your son?

Peter Fleming: Yes.

Heywood-Smith: I think that Football Park opened in May 1974.

Peter Fleming: Yes.

Heywood-Smith: Were you an original member of Football Park?

Peter Fleming: I was, yes.

Heywood-Smith: Do you recall whether or not you attended football games in that year with your brother John?

Peter Fleming: Yes, my brother John and my father and mother and my son. We went to the

> first game at Football Park and were members from day 1 and attended every game there.
>
> Heywood-Smith: Did you have any recollection of after your brother became involved with Alison McNicol, of her ever attending football games with him?
>
> Peter Fleming: She always came to Prospect, to the home games.[248]

In addition to this evidence, further submissions were made by Dr Fleming at trial. None of this evidence, which corroborated evidence given in Court by the plaintiff, Peter Fleming, and Alison Fleming, was referred to by Justice Gray in respect of Jane's claims that she would attend St Mark's on a Saturday afternoon because she knew that Alison was at the football. The undisputed evidence at trial was that it was Dr Fleming himself who went to the football most weeks during the relevant period and that when Alison did go to the football, she (and her brother) would go with Dr Fleming.

Accordingly, Jane's assertion that she would visit the appellant when Alison was at the football, on the undisputed evidence, was glaringly improbable. Of this, Justice Gray took no account.

Further, Jane's allegation that the St Mark's incident occurred while Alison was at the football was also inconsistent with what she told Michael Abbott KC in the Catholic inquiry. According to that version of events, the St Mark's incident occurred between November 1974 and January 1975; well outside of the football season. Again, of this major inconsistency, Justice Gray took no account.

248 *Transcript of evidence given in Court* 2478 lines 3-32.

The Plaintiff's evidence and corroborating evidence in response to Jane's allegations

Subject	Corroborated by	Contradicted by	Could have corroborated but deceased
The plaintiff did not sleep in same room at Meningie as Jane and Alison.	Alison Fleming; Douglas McNicol impliedly	Jane	Tom, Jean, and Malcolm McNicol
There was no threesome.	Alison Fleming	Jane	Tom, Jean and Malcolm McNicol
The plaintiff was not always at his flat in Seacliff after school as Jane alleged.	Alison Fleming	Jane, but later she greatly modified her assertions on this matter.	In first year, Jean McNicol always at home. Thereafter, Tom and Jean McNicol, now school teachers, were home early.
The plaintiff was not always in Brighton Parish after his term as Curate finished. He was never there.	Alison Fleming, Kirsty Henning, Rev Russell Simmonds, and Rev Joan-Claring-Bould	Jane	
The plaintiff did not attend choir practices at St Jude's.	Alison Fleming, Kirsty Henning, Rev Russell Simmonds, Rev Joan Claring-Bould. D Munro did not say he was ever at choir practice and she was "in charge of the girls' choir".[249]	Jane	
The plaintiff at football every Saturday during the winter	Peter Fleming, Alison Fleming		
The plaintiff never owned or wore red "trackies" and dressed clerically nearly all the time	Arlene Macdonald, Rev Joan Claring-Bould, Kirsty Henning, Alison Fleming	Jane claims to have seen The plaintiff wearing such "trackies"	
The plaintiff's reference to a ménage à trois to Mons Cappo was not a reference to Meningie	Arlene Macdonald, Alison Fleming, Monsignor Cappo		
The plaintiff's evidence re a rumour involving an SA MP	Mark Brindal		

249 *Transcript of evidence given in Court* at page 1785 line 22.

Sketches of Fleming's flat by witnesses

At trial, Jane was asked to draw a sketch of Dr Fleming's flat, the flat she claimed to have attended on many, many occasions. This was the sketch[250] she provided during the trial:

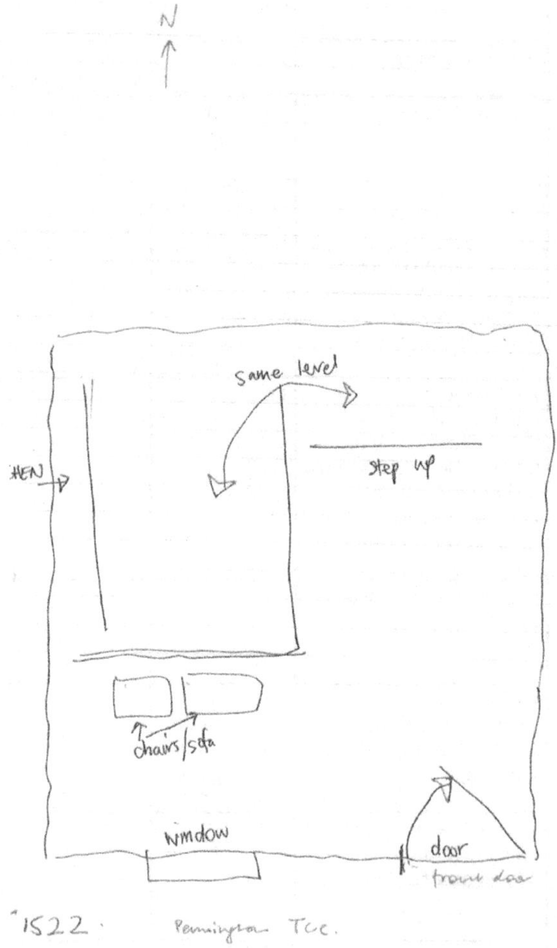

P45 Sketch of flat at St Mark's by Jane in Court.

250 Exhibit P45: Sketch of flat at St Mark's by Jane in Court

Having completed her sketch, the trial resumed, and Jane provided details of the meaning of her sketch. Significantly, she said that there was a raised section where there was a kitchen.

> **Jane: It was, it provided a, it was not quite a mezzanine, so it was just raised so that I'm trying to think whether the chair was above or below the height of the, of the floor of the (INDICATES) kitchen area. I never went up to that level so I can't, I can't visualise how because I never went up there. I know it was higher up.**[251]

The fact is that there was no mezzanine floor, no raised area, and no kitchen or kitchenette in the flat. If Jane frequented the flat as she claimed, no such mistake could possibly have been made. Jane does not even identify that there was a bedroom in this flat. Peter Kay gave a much more accurate sketch of the flat (although not perfect in all respects). It was acknowledged by all witnesses in a position to know that Kay visited the flat at all Anglican society events and on some other occasions as well. Kay's sketch[252] and Dr Fleming's sketch of how his flat looked when he occupied it in the early 1970s[253] are on the next page.

The sketches by the plaintiff and the witness Peter Kay substantially agree, while that by Jane strongly suggests she was never there, and certainly not with the frequency she alleged in Court. Nevertheless, Justice

251 *Transcript of evidence given in Court* at page 1521 lines 5-10.

252 Exhibit P69 dated 8th of May 2008.

253 Exhibit P74, Hand-drawn floor plan of flat, Hawker House.

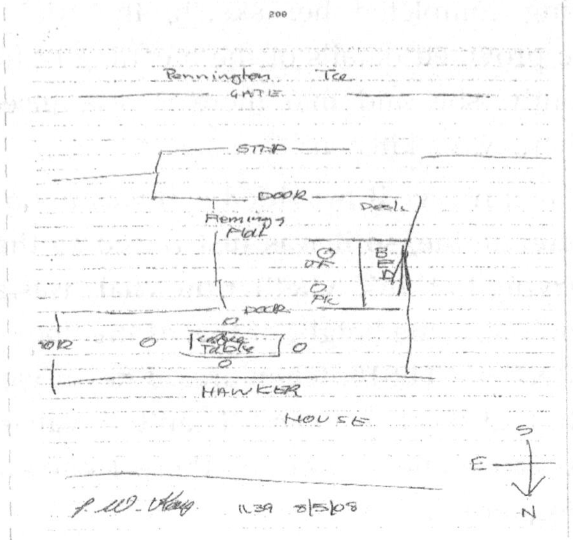

Kay's sketch.

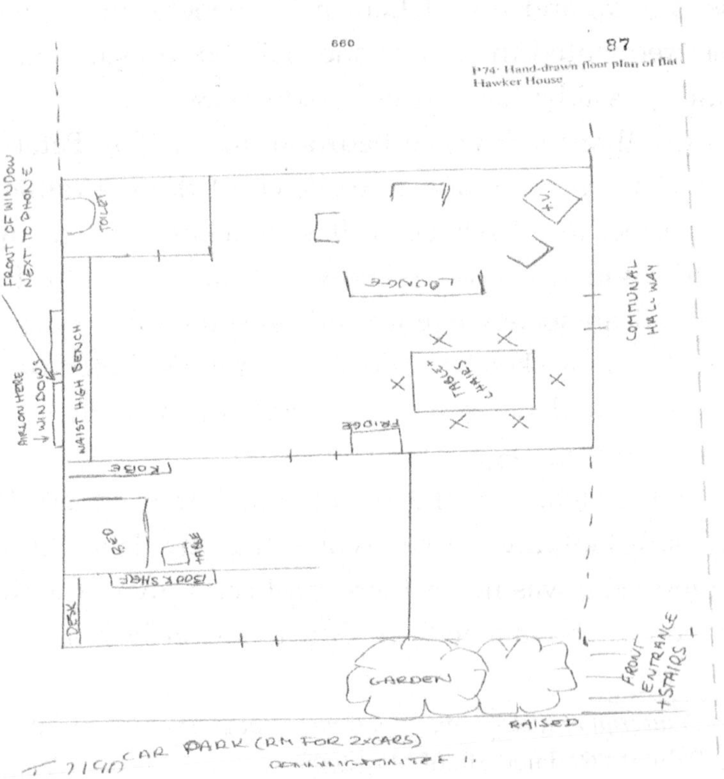

Dr Fleming's sketch.

Gray, against all the evidence, found:

> It is possible that what Jane is describing as the living area is the study area described by the plaintiff. In her police statement Jane said that she never went anywhere else in the flat. **There is not enough in the detail given by Jane of her description of the flat for me to conclude that she had never attended it.**[254]

It is suggested, however, that it was not possible for Jane to be describing the flat as her sketches make no provision at all for a study. Both Dr Fleming and Peter Kay made provision for a very small study in the same place in their layout of the flat. Further, Justice Gray acknowledges that Jane never went anywhere else in the flat although she does make provision for a mezzanine floor kitchen which never existed!

> **Harris: I want to suggest to you that she visited your flat at St Mark's College on multiple occasions.**
>
> **Dr Fleming: That is not true.**
>
> **Harris: Did she ever come to your flat at St Mark's?**
>
> **Dr Fleming: I believe that she did in company with others on one occasion. I've been told that. I don't recall the incident myself.**[255]

254 Justice Gray *judgement* at paragraph 420.

255 *Transcript of evidence given in Court* at page 643 lines 1-7.

The issue was not that "she had never attended" the St Mark's flat. Dr Fleming, for example, said that he thought she may have visited the flat on one occasion with the McNicols to see his new accommodation. The issue was that Jane's sketch lacked any detail to indicate familiarity with the plaintiff's flat and moreover described a mezzanine floor and a kitchen which did not exist.

Rather than "there is not enough in the detail given by Jane of her description of the flat for me to conclude that she had never attended it" it is suggested that Justice Gray should have concluded:

> **there is not enough in the detail given by Jane of her description of the flat for me to conclude that she had ever attended it.**

The reversal of onus of proof is again noted.

What can be said, however, is that while Jane claimed to have been there frequently for sexual liaisons, her sketch of the flat does not match that claim. Her sketch is consistent with the plaintiff's evidence that she may have attended on one occasion only and in company with others. Jane's sketch does not provide proof that she was often in the flat, as she seems to have no idea of its layout. The suggestion that Justice Gray was of the view that Jane was always to be believed[256] is reinforced.

It would seem that Justice Gray's treatment of what was said to have happened in Dr Fleming's flat at St Mark's was superficial and tendentious. Justice Gray devotes thirteen paragraphs to finding that the alleged event of fellatio occurred, eight of which discuss what

256 *Ibid.*

Justice Gray seemed to think was a relatively benign criticism of Jane's evidence that she was unable to properly describe the layout of the flat at St Mark's.

Jane's memory – reliable?

The substantial inconsistencies, improbabilities, and impossibilities in Jane's evidence about alleged events at St Mark's College are ignored entirely by Justice Gray. In one paragraph, he refuses to accept the scientific evidence as to how memory works provided by the expert witness Dr Arnold, preferring instead his own personal and inexpert opinion.

In Court, Jane seemed unable to recall accurately statements she made to the police but could recall events she had not recounted to the police at interview. Moreover, she signed the police statement some eight months after it was given to her to check for accuracy. Her rationalisation for these inconsistencies was remarkable.

Jane referred to the interview in her cross-examination where she said:

> When I read it for accuracy I was reading it for what was written, what was written accurate, not that, I mean I don't remember what I, what I wrote but I know that during the interview I didn't give, I refused to give details of, of the oral contact because it made me, made me dry retch and I said I didn't want to talk about it anymore, I didn't want - it was enough, I kept repeating the mantra of my psychologist who said I didn't have to think about it, I didn't have to talk about it,

> it was enough to remember the first incident - remember, yeah, didn't have to think about it, didn't have to talk about, different from-[257]

Justice Gray swallowed this rationalisation hook, line, and sinker. In doing so he needed, of course, to find a reason, any reason, to repudiate expert evidence given by Dr Arnold.

> **The plaintiff specifically refers to this passage and, in particular, the opinion of Dr Arnold in respect of it, for the proposition that "there is no scientific evidence that links bodily expression of memory (that is, in the absence of conscious memory) to specific past events". I do not accept Dr Arnold's criticism that that is what is taking place in the passage of evidence that I have quoted. I take the passage as Jane saying that she does have a conscious memory but that she is not going to talk about it. I regard the passage as consistent with her memory causing the physical reaction that she describes not the physical reaction providing the memory.**[258]

Here, Justice Gray misrepresented the evidence. The evidence used by Dr Arnold clearly shows that what Jane is saying is that her body remembers and reacts even though *she actually has no memory of the details.*

No reasons are provided as to why Dr Arnold's expert evidence is to be rejected. Any benefit of any doubt must go to the "principal witnesses". So, on the

257 *Transcript of evidence given in Court* at page 1525 lines 1-13.

258 Justice Gray *judgement* at paragraph 423

basis that he knows better than the expert, Justice Gray goes on to say, in the next paragraph,

> I regard Jane's evidence recounting clear and explicit details of the nature of the sexual contact in this incident as compelling. I do not regard her evidence as affected by an uncertainty of recollection of the incident itself and certainly not an uncertainty that has caused me to not be satisfied of the detail of the sexual contact between Jane and the plaintiff.[259]

It seems that, for Justice Gray, the presumption of guilt was applied to Dr Fleming, and that nothing he or his witnesses could say would really count as evidence that this Catholic priest didn't do what he was accused of. Moreover, of all the acts of fellatio alleged to have occurred over eighteen months, Justice Gray finds that only one of these acts occurred, although he does not say which one. Jane's allegations were of multiple incidents over an extended period (of greater or lesser span depending upon to whom she was talking). How does Justice Gray pick just one event and then without any specification as to which event and when?

How Justice Gray could find as he did on a proper application of the principles espoused in *Briginshaw*, is mystifying. Considering the unreliable nature of Jane's evidence, this Court ought to have found that the respondents did not discharge their onus of proving the truth of the allegation of sexual contact at St Mark's to the *Briginshaw* level.

259 Justice Gray *judgement* at paragraph 424.

Did Jane confuse her sexual experiences with her infatuation with Dr Fleming?

In evidence Jane gave to Greg Cannons who was an investigator acting on behalf of the Anglican Church (Diocese of Adelaide) she suggested she was the subject of unwanted sexual advances by her uncle.

> **I was good at keeping secrets and I'd better tell you this and I'm gonna tell the, the um, the lawyers this because I don't know if I told Fleming he might maintain that I was already . .. well I said I was vulnerable but, you my ... so I vaguely knew about older men making inappropriate advances. My uncle had, you know, tried to kiss me passionately before that time so · may have told Fleming but ... so I knew ... I would have ... and I, and I dealt with that, that particular incident by cutting off all contact with my uncle. He left lived in Sydney and I was just...just refused to have anything to do with him. I just...just refused to have anything to do with him. I think I would have known that it was wrong and I wanted to get away but, also not have wanted to say anything because I was already, I was um under John's spell.**[260]

260 Exhibit P49: *Transcript of interview by Mr Cannons of [JANE]*, 5th May 2010, questions 399

Note that Jane claims that this uncle incident occurred before Dr Fleming, and then contemporaneously with Dr Fleming.

In evidence to Greg Cannons, she also claimed to have been sexually active when underage. In that evidence, which was before the Court, Jane voluntarily spoke of two sexual episodes with named men while she was about 14 to 15 years of age, episodes which she claimed to have instigated.

> **Jane: It was a dick, it's just a dick but that was playing with my mind and set .. set me up to not understand the difference between right and wrong. But the very next thing that I did was to go and find someone to lose my virginity with. I was 15 - I mean so it must have been closer to when I was 15 - and I found a 26 year old bloke called Claus Schumann actually who lived in the next street from me ... Yarmouth then the next one going towards the city and ...**
>
> **Jane: And um, I remember I went to his house and I was clinical. It was completely clinical. I just wanted to see what it was, you know, like, and you know, it was downhill from there for me. (laugh)**
>
> **Cannons: But you obviously ... but you obviously knew this person though?**
>
> **Jane: Yeah, I met him on the beach. So ...**
>
> **Cannons: Mm. On that day, on that day?**

Jane: No, no, no, no, no, no, no, no I think it took a while but then I kind of must have ... I mean, you know, I was a slut so I gotta find out what slutdom actually means, you know.

Cannons: Mm. All right. Did you tell anyone about what happened on ...

Jane: No.

Cannons: on that day on the beach?

Jane: No. No, because I didn't want to be talked about because remember that, you know, um, I was a slut, did l want everybody to know that I was a slut? But he didn't make it. .. I mean he never said that or whatever, it's all by implication.[261]

So, in this part of the interview, Jane named a twenty-six-year-old man with whom she claimed to have had vaginal sexual intercourse "to see what it was like". No evidence was provided to prove that this claim was true. Jane then went on to name another man with whom she claimed she had penile sexual intercourse and fellatio.

Cannons: Now [Jane] you wanted to just add something in connection with what we were talking about before obviously?

Jane: Yeah um, the rea ... the other reason I'm absolutely sure that I did perform oral sex on numerous occasions is that um, I, I ...

261 Exhibit P49: *Transcript of interview by Mr Cannons of* [JANE], 5th May 2010, questions 501-508 and their answers.

my second major boyfriend - his name was Wally Vladimir - he was Russian. Anyway whatever ...

Cannons: Wally, I'm gonna need some sort of ...

Jane: … he was terribly ...

Cannons: ... spelling on that. So Vlad ... Vlad ...

Jane: I couldn't remember. I, I... apparently if you raise your left eyebrow you'll remember. Somebody just told me that yesterday but it hasn't worked yet. (laugh)

Cannons: So I'll have to ...

Jane: Chicknaiken ... it did work, I did, it did work, Chicknaiken was his name.

Jane: Um, he was terribly jealous and not... whatever and I.. . and I remember very, very vividly 'cause he used to ... he's say, you know, you know, he wanted to know everybody I'd ever kind of kissed and whatever it was ... and I never told him about Fleming. And I remember being resentful... not resentful but thinking ... like I remember engaging in oral ... in oral sex with him and thinking well you wouldn't be complaining er, you know, I know how to do this and I. .. because I'd never told him about Fleming and it was like.

Cannons: Right, mm.

> **Jane: … you know, the reason I can do this is 'cause I've had experience and I'm not gonna tell you about that one, you know, but you know ...**
>
> **Cannons: Yeah, you were ...**
>
> **Jane: you're angry with me for ... 'cause I did tell him about losing my virginity and he'd given me such a hard time about it and I remember thinking well you wouldn't be ... you're not complaining now are you kind of thing, you know. (laugh)**
>
> **Cannons: Yep, all right, okay.**
>
> **Jane: So ... which is a terrible thing, it sounds disgusting that!. .. anyway it's how it was.**[262]

Clearly, Jane claims to have had experience of fellatio with another named man who also seems to have been an adult. No evidence was provided to prove that claim was true.

The description quoted above of Jane's claimed fellatio involvement with Walter Chicknaiken is entwined with the fellatio she claims to have experienced with Dr Fleming.

From the evidence provided to Cannons, it is not unreasonable to conclude that Jane's memories of these incidents, including the memory of her uncle's inappropriate advances, and assuming they are accurate (for which no evidence was provided), have become

262 Exhibit P49: *Transcript of interview by Mr Cannons of [*JANE*],* 5th May 2010, questions 572-583 and their answers. *Cannons* was the investigator acting on behalf of the Anglican Church.

mixed up with Dr Fleming, the one upon whom, it seems, that she was fixated, the one she claims to have plotted to "seduce".[263]

Support for this interpretation of Jane's evidence will be readily seen in the expert evidence of Dr Arnold as set out in her report, which will be fully discussed in the next chapter. In her report, Dr Arnold says:

> **remembering an event involves a reconstructive process of putting together traces, which can include unique bits of an original experience, but also assumptions about how things are or were, and new information we have learned since the event took place.**[264]

263 *Transcript of evidence given in Court* at page 1623 lines 13-17.

264 Exhibit P85 at page 3.

Chapter Eight

Dr Michelle Arnold: Expert Witness

Cognitive psychology tells us that the unaided human mind is vulnerable to many fallacies and illusions because of its reliance on its memory for vivid anecdotes rather than systematic statistics.[265]

The treatment of Dr Michelle Arnold (scientific expert in memory who appeared as a witness for the plaintiff) by the judges in both the trial and at appeal is of considerable concern when considering the case of *Fleming v The Advertiser.*

The dismissal of the evidence of Dr Arnold, a respected scholar, and the terms in which she was described was unreasonable and unprofessional.

First, who is an expert?

> **An expert, in the legal sense, is one who by reason of special qualifications is able to express informed opinions on some subject requiring special knowledge or understanding.**[266]

---

265 Steven Pinker, Johnstone Family Professor in the Department of Psychology at Harvard University.

266 Australian Law Reform Commission, "Who is an Expert?", 2010, https://www.alrc.gov.au/publication/recognition-of-aboriginal-customary-laws-alrc-report-31/24-the-proof-of-aboriginal-customary-laws/who-is-an-expert/

Who determines who is an expert?

> **Ultimately it is up to the judge to determine who is or is not qualified as an expert witness.**[267]

It was never suggested by the judge or by the defendants that Dr Arnold was not an expert on memory.

> **The British Psychological Society (*British Psychological Society,* 2008, 2010) has proposed that a memory expert witness for the court is someone whose expertise is recognised by the research community. This recognition is typically demonstrated in the form of outputs that are publicly verifiable – most importantly, peer-reviewed publications. In our view, courts should require putative memory expert witnesses to provide evidence of their expertise in human memory, and this evidence must be available to all parties. At a minimum these experts will have earned a PhD in psychology or a related discipline, hold a position at a research institution, and have published a significant number of empirical papers in internationally recognised peer-reviewed journals (for the most part, conference presentations or**

267 Rachel Zajac, Maryanne Garry, Kamala London, Felicity Goodyear-Smith & Harlene Hayne (2013) "Misconceptions about childhood sexual abuse and child witnesses: Implications for psychological experts in the courtroom", *Memory,* 21:5, 615, DOI:10.1080/09658211.2013.77827

> **posters are no substitute for peer-reviewed publications).**[268]

Dr Michelle Arnold: Qualification as an expert on "memory"

At the beginning of her Report, Dr Arnold described her qualifications as an expert especially in human memory and cognition.

> **I completed a BA degree in Psychology (with Distinction) from the University of Lethbridge (Canada) in 1997. Subsequently, I went on to complete rigorous research and teaching training in the area of human memory and cognition at the University of Victoria (Canada). Specifically, I received my MSc in Cognitive Psychology in 2001, and my PhD in Cognitive Psychology in 2005. I then undertook further research experience and training through a postdoctoral position as a Research Fellow in Psychology at Southampton University (UK) from 2005-2007.**
>
> **I have been a lecturer in Psychology at Flinders University since May 2011, where I teach courses, supervise honours and PhD students, and conduct research in the field of human memory and cognition. Previously, I was employed as a lecturer**

268 *Ibid*.

> **from 2007-2011 in Psychology at St Andrews University (Scotland), where I also taught and conducted research in memory and cognition. My teaching and research encompass both basic memory questions (e.g., how memory in general works) and applied memory issues (e.g., underlying mechanisms of recovered memories for abuse). I have published scientific papers regarding the topic of human memory in peer-reviewed psychology journals, and I regularly present the results of my research at scientific conferences both nationally and internationally. I have also served as an ad hoc reviewer for prestigious psychology journals and for large-scale research funding bodies. I also am a member of professional scientific organisations, such as the Society for Applied Research in Memory and Cognition, (SARMAC) and the Psychonomic Society.**[269]

In her curriculum vitae, Dr Arnold listed 14 publications in peer-reviewed journals and 4 more currently under review for publication. In addition, she had made nearly 40 presentations at academic conferences from 1999-2014 and received 10 scholarships and other awards. This is an academic with an impressive history in research and publications. She is an expert in her field and at no time in the trial were her credentials

269 Michelle M. Arnold, PhD, "Report Prepared in the Matter of Fleming v The Ad Weekend Publishing Co P/L & Ai", 7th July 2014, Exhibit P84.

called into question. Nor indeed was the scientific evidence, upon which she relied, contradicted.

The assumptions provided to Dr Arnold by counsel for Dr Fleming

In her letter of appointment to Dr Arnold, solicitors for Dr Fleming requested Dr Arnold to give her "expert opinion on the following issues".

1. How does an individual remember an event? How does an individual judge an event as real?
2. What is the mechanism of repression of memory for long-ago abusive events?
3. According to the research, what impact, if any, does a counsellor's personal beliefs have on the client's memory of long-ago events? What impact, if any, would a counsellor such as JS have on the memory of "Jane" and the reliability of her memory of long-ago events in respect of Father Fleming?
4. What dangers, if any, do professional psychologists recognise in persons who attempt to recollect long-ago abusive events? From the material provided to you, what, if any, of those dangers are present in respect of "Jane"?
5. What is "body memory"? What does the research say on body memory as to its accuracy? From the material provided to you, is "Jane" articulating what some therapists may label a body memory?
6. What impact, if any, does a person's belief as to how memory works, such as repression of memory or body memory, influence that person's

memory for long-ago abusive events? From the material provided to you, is there any indication that Jane's belief as to how memory works has impacted on her own memory of long-ago events?

7. Is it important for a counsellor to take and retain notes of each counselling session with a person who presents at counselling without a clear memory of a long-ago abusive event? If yes, why?[270]

In her report back to solicitors for Dr Fleming, Dr Arnold set out her working assumptions upon which she would rely. These were:

1. "Jane" has received counselling on and off since at least her early twenties.
2. "Jane" received counselling from an Anglican priest, JS.[271]
3. "Jane" had taught piano to the children of JS and that she has kept in touch with those children.
4. JS [John Stephenson] personally knew Fr Fleming.
5. JS may have had an antagonism towards Fr Fleming.
6. JS was the first person to whom "Jane" reported her allegations concerning Fr Fleming.
7. In relation to the alleged incident at Meningie, it was JS who told "Jane" that the Meningie church was vacant as there was not a parish priest there between 1969 and 1970.
8. That on May 5 2010, after the newspaper publications, the Anglican Church Professional

270 *Ibid.*

271 The Reverend John Stephenson.

Standards Office interviewed "Jane" in the house of JS, who acted as a support person for "Jane" and JS was present when she was interviewed.

9. That "Jane" told the Anglican Church Professional Standards Office investigator that JS had extended his pastoral care to her "when he really didn't have to" and that JS and his wife had included her in their family, which "made a big difference" and "I wouldn't be here but for these two people".
10. That four days prior to the first publication in The Sunday Mail, JS telephoned "L"[272] to say that there was going to be an article published in The Sunday Mail concerning sexual accusations against Fr Fleming.
11. That JS told "L" that "Jane" was an accuser and JS asked "L" if she had been abused by Fr Fleming.
12. The solicitors for *The Sunday Mail* took instructions from "Jane" that were to the effect that 'neither she nor her counsellors from time to time have retained any notes of counselling sessions' and, in addition, that her counsellors were/are 'qualified'.[273]

Dr Arnold's expertise was unchallenged. Her evidence as to how memory works was unchallenged. Her evidence was that it does not function like a video recorder and that there is no scientific evidence that links bodily expressions of memory to specific past events. The unchallenged expert evidence was that one of the

272 Unidentified

273 Exhibit P84: *Report of Dr Michelle M. Arnold, Ph.D. Lecturer in Psychology Flinders University*, 7th of July 2014

dangers for a person attempting to recollect long-ago abusive events "is the potential for reinterpretation of the long-ago events. Specifically, reinterpretation involves a person – consciously or unconsciously – distorting a past event in a way that becomes consistent with that person's current beliefs." Dr Arnold could see "clear examples of reinterpretation across Jane's own statements". The learned trial judge made no reference to this evidence.

The "strong challenge" to Dr Arnold's assumptions

In his judgement, Justice Gray referred to Dr Arnold's assumptions as having been "strongly challenged". More accurately, two of the assumptions provided to Dr Arnold by counsel for the plaintiff were strongly challenged. That these assumptions were "strongly" challenged adds nothing to an assessment of whether the challenge was effective. The strongest aspect of the challenge went to the accuracy of the assumption that:

> **JS [Stephenson] was the first person to whom "Jane" reported her allegations concerning Fr Fleming.**

In cross-examination Junior Counsel for the defendant, Barnett, put it to Dr Arnold that this assumption was wrong and was known by Dr Arnold to be wrong. Barnett pointed to document number 6 in the list of documents provided to Dr Arnold by counsel for the plaintiff and to which Dr Arnold referred in her report. This document is a statement given to the police by Bronte Koop who said that Jane had told him about the abuse sometime in 1972. From Barnett's line of questioning, it would appear that she was asserting that, if Dr Arnold was an independent expert, she (Dr Arnold) should have stated that this assumption was incorrect. Moreover, it might well mean that there was a continuous trail of evidence of Jane's abuse from as early as 1972.[274]

It is not clear why Barnett was pushing this line of questioning given the following:

- In 2002 Jane told Dr Tanya Black of the Anglican Church that "this was the first time … [she] had talked about it in any detail, though she says that she had told David Richardson something of it a few years ago".[275] In saying this she did not refer to a conversation with Bronte Koop.
- Jane sought out Bronte Koop to provide evidence for her. They maintained email correspondence at least up until the time when Koop gave his police statement, dated 11 February 2008. How much Jane influenced Koop in his memory recall is not known since his evidence was never tested in Court. In his police statement Koop said that Jane had told him that she had had a sexual relationship with Dr Fleming before he and Jane were going out together. Koop's statement appears to date their relationship as beginning in 1971 or 1972, when he was 16 years old.[276] The alleged "Meningie incident" was dated January 1971. Elsewhere, Jane had claimed in evidence

274 Cf *Transcript of evidence given in Court* page 2666 line 12 – page 2670 line 28.

275 Dr Tanya Black, "Additional Report and information following report dated 6 March 2002", and provided to SAPOL.

276 *Ibid.*

that she "started going out with Bronte in about the middle of 1972".[277] Koop said he got married in 1974.[278] He also said he couldn't recall Jane "going into any specifics in regards (*sic*) to the sexual acts".[279]

- In reference to the relevance of evidence to be given by Koop, Justice Gray ruled: "The fact she [Jane] spoke of it to another person, that seemed to me to be as far as you need to go in your examination of that because what she said to another person is not evidence of it but it is a relevant fact, if you want, to rebut any suggestion of recent invention or to explain that there was at least someone who was spoken to about it, it seems to me to be unexceptional."[280]
- However, Harris elected not to call Bronte Koop as a witness and therefore his written statement was not subject to cross-examination. The prejudice for this must count against the defendant who asserted that Koop would appear but never in fact called him. Given that Koop could not be cross-examined and the lack of detail in Koop's police statement, and the failure of the defendant to call him, **it is difficult to know exactly what was said to him and when.**

As Koop was not called to give evidence, and his evidence, even if accurate, proved nothing about whether

277 *Transcript of evidence given in Court* at page 1359 line 25-26.

278 Statement of Bronte Malcolm Koop to the SA Police, 11th of February 2008.

279 *Ibid.*

280 *Transcript of evidence given in Court* at page 1425 lines 12-19.

any of Jane's allegations were true, it is difficult to understand why Justice Gray chose this as an example of a "strong challenge" to Dr Arnold's assumptions. Strong challenge is the very nature of Australia's adversarial court system. Justice Gray does mention it but only in relation to one witness, one who, despite her admirable qualifications, could not gain admission into Justice Gray's pantheon of "principal witnesses" or the Full Court's "main witnesses".

Further, Justice Gray stated in his judgement concerning the written evidence of The Reverend John Stephenson that he was not available to elaborate further on it:

> **I am also not prepared to regard other aspects of the statement of Father Stephenson to which the plaintiff refers in his written submissions as necessarily inconsistent with Jane's evidence without the elaboration that might have been provided had Father Stephenson been able to give evidence.**[281]

Justice Gray seems to apply different rules to similar issues. He implies a "strong challenge" is evidence that one of the assumptions provided[282] to Dr Arnold to work with was, at least to some extent, questionable. At the same time, a strong challenge to Jane's evidence based upon Stephenson's detailed report to the police can't be considered because he (Stephenson) was not

281 Justice Gray *judgement* at paragraph 375.

282 It must be remembered that the assumptions were not assumptions made up by Dr Arnold, but assumptions upon which she was instructed to proceed.

able (through death) to appear in Court to be questioned about it. On the other hand, Bronte Koop was available to give his evidence and be questioned about it, but the defendant failed to honour its promise to call him as a witness.

Neither Koop nor Stephenson gave evidence in Court, but Koop's evidence was used while Stephenson's was not.

Moreover, when Dr Arnold addressed a question put to her by the counsel for the plaintiff after Jane had given evidence, Dr Arnold made no specific comment on the Stephenson influence but said:

> **Given the provided transcripts, the opinions I expressed in my report have not altered but they have been reinforced. I provide specifics regarding this reinforcement below.**

In the addendum to her report, Dr Arnold had no reason to specifically refer to the influence of Mr Stephenson because his influence on Jane was well established before the trial began and because Mr Stephenson was no longer alive and could therefore not give evidence in Court. Moreover, the fact that the police told Jane that Dr Fleming had volunteered to the police he had been in Meningie also influenced Jane in her later recall of the version of events.

Justice Gray when referring to the addendum to the report stated that Dr Arnold had "noted that memory of an event may have both positive and negative aspects, those aspects are not occurring in isolation". He then quoted from Dr Arnold's addendum:

> **Thus, the way she [Jane] refers to blocking out one aspect of the event, while being**

> **willing to maintain details about other aspects of that event, does not correspond with the predominant scientific research and understanding of memory. Because remembering an event is not simply a matter of verbatim playback, but rather is reconstructive, the predominant scientific view is that we are not able to so neatly and cleanly control our memories in the way described by Jane.**[283]

That statement is left hanging in the air, so to speak. Justice Gray does not apply Dr Arnold's description of the reconstructive nature of memory either to Jane's memory claims, or to his own amateur diagnosis when he opines: "I do not regard her evidence as affected by an uncertainty of recollection of the incident itself and certainly not an uncertainty that has caused me to not be satisfied of the detail of the sexual contact between Jane and the plaintiff".[284]

Dr Arnold's evidence

How does memory function?

Firstly, Dr Arnold described what memory is, and what it isn't, in terms of function.

> Although there is an intuitive appeal to think that our memory functions like a video recorder, we know through years of

283 Exhibit P85 at page 2. Cited in Justice Gray *judgement* at paragraph 400.

284 Justice Gray *judgement* at paragraph 424.

> research that this metaphor is not an accurate representation of how people remember events. Specifically, memory involves more than just taking in information and storing it; for example we cannot simply pinpoint a particular point in time and play it back unedited. Instead, **remembering an event involves a reconstructive process of putting together traces, which can include unique bits of an original experience, but also assumptions about how things are or were, and new information we have learned since the event took place** (Bodner & Lindsay, 2003; Lindsay & Read, 1994; Loftus, 2005).[285]

Dr Arnold then made three important points:

a) Since remembering an event is a reconstructive process, rather than a verbatim playback, it can be susceptible to error.
b) Real-life cases involving people who have later retracted their accusations illustrate that suggestive influences, such as suggestive therapeutic techniques by counsellors, can lead people to falsely remember sexual abuse incidents that never actually happened *(e.g., Loftus* & Ketcham, 1994).
c) Research suggests that true memories can be very difficult to distinguish from false memories (Laney & Loftus, 2008). For instance, people can be as equally confident in their true memories as

285 Exhibit P84, Michelle M. Arnold, PhD, "Report Prepared in the Matter of FLEMING v THE AD WEEKEND PUBLISHING CO P/L & Ai", 7th July 2014, at page 3.

> their false memories, and they tend to describe both true and false memories with detail and emotion. **However, it is important to point out that developing a false memory (e.g., incorrectly classifying an imagined event as real) is different from deliberate deception or lying: People with a false memory come to genuinely believe that the critical event did in fact happen.**

Some of the principal issues raised by Dr Arnold in her report and which call into serious question Jane's reliability in her memory recall of events need to be discussed more closely.

What is the mechanism of repression of memory of long-ago abusive events?

The concept of repressed memory

Dr Arnold commenced her report with a discussion of repressed memory, a concept that has been used in such cases as alleged historic abuse.

> The concept of "repressed memory" was made popular with the work of Sigmund Freud, and it refers to the idea that painful and traumatic experiences - such as childhood maltreatment and sexual abuse can be barred from our conscious awareness (Loftus, 1993).
>
> Some therapists believe that psychological maladjustment in adulthood is caused by repressed memories of trauma and/or abuse (Bass & Davis, 1988; Blume; 1990; Fredrickson,

> J 1992). **However, despite this belief, there is no credible or reliable scientific support for the mechanism of repression** (Holmes, 1995). Indeed, reviews of the evidence for the mechanism of repression from psychology research, medical literature, and nonmedical literature strongly indicate that **the idea of repression is a "social construction" that dates from the nineteenth century** (McNally, 2007; Pope, Poliakoff, Parker, & Hudson, 2007).[286]

To reiterate, it was Dr Arnold's considered argument there is no credible, scientific support for the concept of repressed memory.

What is "body memory"? What does the research say on body memory as to its accuracy? From the material provided to you, is "Jane" articulating what some therapists may label as a body memory?

Body memory

Jane frequently referred to her physical feelings when certain subjects were broached. This is referred to as "body memory". Dr Arnold explained the concept as:

> …the idea that victims of abuse may lack a conscious memory of their abuse (e.g., they cannot provide conscious details of what

286 *Ibid.*, at page 4.

> happened), but their bodies remember the abuse. In other words, even if a person cannot consciously recollect an abusive event, her/his body will "keep the score" and thus the person may experience bodily expressions of the abuse memory (McNally, 2005; van der Kolk, 1994). Although some therapists believe in this idea, physical symptoms that manifest as "body memories" cannot be reliably linked to a particular past experience (Loftus & Ketcham, 1994; Spanos, 1996). **However unpleasant, physical experiences may be misinterpreted as a body memory and consequently be inaccurately attributed to a past abusive event** (McNally, 2005).[287]

Applying all of this to the evidence before her, Dr Arnold raised another red flag concerning the reliability of Jane's memory. She refers explicitly to what Jane says she experiences physically, and sees it in this way:

> From the material I have been provided for Jane, there is evidence in both the written and audio documents that she is articulating what some therapists would label as a body memory. For example, in written document #6 she talks about an abuse incident where she saw his penis, but describes it as "At the time I saw his penis but I can't connect to the memory. I know it was in my mouth because I can feel it there but I don't have clear memory of actually looking at it" (pg 20).

287 *Ibid.*, at page 7.

> Further, in audio document #12 (003_C_001, starting around the 20:25 mark) she describes talking to the police and "not wanting to go there" with details, and that she started gagging and had to leave the room to "puke". She then follows up this statement by saying that " ... but I do know that it happened I just can't remember the details ... ". Finally, she also makes reference to oral sex in written document #66 (pgs 8-9), and states she "thoroughly repressed these memories" but while being interviewed by the police in 2007 about these particular events she "began gagging and vomiting".[288]

Dr Arnold's evidence about body memory is applied to Jane who, in her own words says she knows something happened because her body tells her so even though she "can't remember the details".

To summarise, the uncontradicted scientific evidence provided by Dr Arnold argues:

1. There is "no credible or reliable scientific support for the mechanism of repression"[289]; and
2. There is "no scientific evidence... that links bodily expression of memory (i.e. in the absence of conscious memory) to specific past events."[290]

It is suggested that one can therefore conclude that any attempt by the defendant or by Jane herself to explain

288 *Ibid.*

289 Exhibit P84, Dr Arnold's First Report at page 4

290 Exhibit P85, Dr Arnold's Supplementary Report, at page 1

away inconsistencies in Jane's evidence by reference to a conscious effort on her part not to remember certain details of incidents (ie repressed memory) should be rejected as being contrary to scientifically established knowledge of the process by which human memory works. Put another way, a traumatic event continues to plague the victim of that event and he or she cannot get rid of the memory. Similarly, any reference to "body memories" should be rejected as they cannot be linked to a particular experience, and further, unpleasant physical experiences can be misinterpreted as body memory and wrongly attributed to a past event.

According to the research. what impact, if any, does a counsellor's personal beliefs have on the client's memory of long-ago events? What impact, if any, would a counsellor such as JS [the Rev John Stephenson] have on the memory of "Jane" and the reliability of her memory of long-ago events in respect of Father Fleming?

Potential impact of a counsellor's personal beliefs

In answer to the question from plaintiff's counsel, "According to the research, what impact, if any, does a counsellor's personal beliefs have on the client's memory of long-ago events", Dr Arnold made this very important observation based upon scientific evidence, not upon her opinion or an individual judge's personal experience.

> **There is a great deal of research that shows that the beliefs a counsellor holds can have a significant impact on a client's memory and feelings regarding long-ago events.** For example, counsellors sometimes interpret client information, and interview or diagnose clients, in a way that may reflect their existing belief(s) about the client's problems (Brainerd & Reyna, 2005; Haverkamp, 1993; Jackson & Nuttall, 1993). Holding an existing belief can lead to biased interviewing procedures, which can in turn lead to the client developing a distorted memory for her/his past (Ceci, Kulkofsky, Klemfuss, Sweeney, & Bruck, 2007; Hi11, Lynn, Payne, Krackow, & McCrea, 1999). Relatedly, **a substantial body of research has demonstrated that the information a person is exposed to after-the-fact can influence what s/he later recalls about an original event** (e.g., Loftus, 1996, 2005). Thus, for example, if a counsellor asks a client leading question about her/his abusive history, these questions could have an influence on what the client remembers about her/his past.[291]

Two principal factors emerged:

1. Clients can be influenced in memory and feeling through their interaction with a counsellor; and

291 Exhibit P84, Dr Arnold's First Report at page 4

2. A client's memory of the past can be influenced by what he or she has heard more recently, about a person who is an alleged abuser, about the surrounding details, about almost any relevant fact or opinion.

Applying the research to the documents supplied to her, Dr Arnold concluded that the Reverend John Stephenson "could have had a biasing impact and/or a negative influence on the accuracy and reliability of Jane's memory for long-ago events in respect to Father Fleming".[292] On the evidence before her, Dr Arnold remarked that "at a minimum, it appears that JS [Stephenson] was not a 'neutral' counsellor, and thus his beliefs could have biased Jane's memory and/or interpretations in regards (*sic*) to Father Fleming." Dr Arnold stated:

> There also is evidence that JS may have provided Jane with information that influenced her subsequent recollections and statements of the long-ago events in regards (*sic*) to Father Fleming. For example, in relation to the alleged first abuse event in Meningie, JS informed Jane that the Meningie church was vacant between 1969 and 1970. This is important because in the earliest document from 2003 (#57, pg 2), Jane only refers to the first event as happening "in the country". In the following document from 2007 (#6, pgs 8-9), Jane again refers to the first event as happening in the country, but then explicitly states she is "unsure of the name of

292 *Ibid.*, at pages 4-5

> the town". It is not until the document from 2009 (#36, pg 2), that she refers to the place as starting with M, and then agreeing with the interviewer when he volunteers Meningie. By the final document in 2010 (#66, pg 5) she appears to freely volunteer for the first alleged abuse event that she "travelled to a country town [she believes] to be Meningie". Thus, taken together, Jane appears to have changed over the years from being unable to provide any memory of the town to volunteering without prompting that she believes it was Meningie.[293]

In addition to all of this, Dr Arnold noted the very close personal relationship that had existed over a long period of time between Jane and the Stephenson family. Jane felt included in their family by Stephenson and his wife such that Jane could say that "[she] wouldn't be here but for these two people". Hence, Dr Arnold suggested:

> …the information provided by JS likely carried a lot of weight with Jane. Specifically, people are more likely to incorporate information whether it be accurate, biasing, or misinformation (i.e., distorted/inaccurate information) into their own memories when the source of that information is trusted, or considered to be highly credible, powerful or likeable (Dodd & Bradshaw, 1980; Vornik, Shannan, & Garry, 2003; French, Garry, & Mori, 2009).[294]

---

293 *Ibid.*, at page 5.

294 *Ibid.*

What impact, if any, does a person's belief as to how memory works, such as repression of memory or body memory, influence that person's memory for long-ago abusive events? From the material presented to you, is there any indication that "Jane's" belief as to how memory works has impacted on her own memory of long-ago events?

The influence on memory of a person's belief in how memory works

Dr Arnold's short answer to the question "What impact, if any, does a person's belief as to how memory works, such as repression of memory or body memory, influence that person's memory for long-ago abusive events? was "yes", there is an impact. Dr Arnold provided research findings to back up the statement that "a person's belief about memory can influence the inferences they make about their own memory" and applied findings to Jane's evidence.

> From the material provided, there is evidence to suggest that Jane's beliefs about memory may have impacted her memory of long-ago events. As already mentioned in my answer to question #5, Jane does appear to articulate what some counsellors would label as a body memory (i.e., gagging and vomiting). Further, as discussed in that answer, she does seem

willing to rely on these body memories, in the absence of specific details, as evidence of long-ago abusive events.

In terms of other memory beliefs, in document #6 Jane claims she has no memory for most of the alleged abuse events because of how she explains memory works for repeated events. Specifically, she states that "The reason it's not clear is because it happened multiple times. So they don't stay in your memory because it's not a vivid event. It's just like trying to remember eating dinner when you were 16 years old. The memory is not there because it happened so often." (pg 23). However, in document #66 Jane's explanation for her lack of details at that time is that the memory has been "blocked." For example, at one point she states "Because I have blocked the memory, I cannot describe what occurred when we were sitting in the car ... " (pg 8), and then later goes on to state "I know definitely that I engaged in both masturbation and oral sex with John Fleming but I have completely blocked the memory of it." (pg 8). Thus, it appears that Jane uses contradictory beliefs about memory at different points to explain why she does not have specific details for the long-ago abusive events; that is, at certain points it is because she never encoded them into memory (i.e., they were never "recorded" in the first place), versus other points it is because she has blocked the memories

> completely from consciousness (i.e., similar to repression).[295]

This analysis also answered the question put to Dr Arnold, "From the material presented to you, is there any indication that Jane's belief as to how memory works has impacted on her own memory of long-ago events", again in the affirmative. There are indications that Jane's belief as to how memory works has had a significant impact on her own memory of long-ago events. It should be noted that Dr Arnold was not provided with the transcript of the evidence Jane gave to Greg Cannons, of the Anglican Church. If she had, her conclusions would have been further strengthened. (That evidence is discussed in Chapter Six.)

Is it important for a counsellor to take and retain notes of each counselling session with a person who presents at counselling without a clear memory of a long-ago abusive event? If yes, why?

Dr Arnold also addressed the matter of how much importance should be attached to the fact that none of Jane's counsellors took contemporaneous notes of their counselling sessions with Jane. In her answer to the question "Is it important for a counsellor to take and retain notes of each counselling session with a person who presents at counselling without a clear memory of a long-ago abusive event", this was Dr Arnold's written evidence.

295 *Ibid.*, at page 8

When a person presents at counselling without a clear memory of a long-ago abusive event(s) it is important for the counsellor to both take and retain notes for each session. One of the main reasons this is important is because the counsellor needs to be able to review the progress of a client's recollection of the alleged abusive event(s). Specifically, because memory is not like a video camera, but rather is reconstructive, it is important for the counsellor to always be focussed on examining the likelihood that the details/ memories the client provides as a consequence of trying to recollect long-ago abuse are likely to be accurate. In other words, it is important that counsellors both identify and challenge any distilled memories or thoughts about the long-ago abusive events (e.g., Australian Guidelines for the Treatment of Acute Stress Disorder and Posttraumatic Stress Disorder, 2013), and to do so they need to engage in good record-keeping of each session. In the case of a person who presents without a clear memory of long-ago abuse, it also is important to take and retain notes so that, if necessary, it can be determined whether any suggestive information was introduced, or whether any suggestive techniques were used by the counsellor. Indeed, even when counsellors are deliberately trying to refrain from introducing any source of bias or suggestion, they may inadvertently use leading and suggestive questioning with their clients (Lindsay & Read, 1995). Thus, taking and retaining notes allows both the counsellor(s) and any other individuals (e.g., other counsellors or investigators) to better gauge the probable accuracy of the client's recollections of long-ago abuse.

It should be noted that it is the Australian Psychological Society (APS) that recommends psychologists adhere to the Australian Guidelines for the Treatment of Acute Stress Disorder and Posttraumatic Stress Disorder (2013) that I referenced in the above paragraph. Further, the APS adopted a Code of Ethics in 1997, which it periodically updates, with the express purpose that it "articulates and promotes ethical principles, and sets specific standards to guide both psychologists and members of the public to a clear understanding and expectation of what is considered ethical professional conduct by psychologists" (Code of Ethics, 2007; pg 6). **In line with the opinion I expressed above regarding record-keeping, standard B.2.1. of the Code of Ethics (2007) states the expectation "Psychologists make and keep adequate records", and standard B.2.2. states the expectation "Psychologists keep records for a minimum of seven years since last client contact unless legal or**

> **their organisational requirements specify otherwise".**[296]

There is a problem when counsellors have either taken no notes of counselling sessions or have discarded them as is the case with Jane. If the counsellor later wishes to establish just what was going with this person's memory and who or what may have been influencing factors, she needs to have records which would stand as evidence.

Justice Gray's assertion that he does not see how the report by Dr Arnold assisted him is extraordinary. Dr Arnold specifically identifies all the red flags that should be applied before seemingly blindly accepting what Jane says is in all respects as being accurate, reliable, and "compelling". It could be suggested that either Justice Gray did not read the report, read the report and did not understand it, or read the report and did not want to let Dr Arnold's compelling and uncontradicted expert opinion influence him given his preconceived commitment to the idea that adult persons recalling long past events are to be completely believed where allegations of sex abuse are concerned.

It seems that Justices Vanstone, Nicholson, and Bampton were only too pleased to go along with Justice Gray's unjustified and simplistic assumptions in this matter. However, unlike Justice Gray's apparent position, there are judges who are up to date with the literature on memory and recognise the difficulty of simply accepting witness statements at face value. One such judge is Judge Penelope Wass SC.

---

296 *Ibid.*, at pages 8-9.

Lecture by Judge Penelope Wass (2016)

Judge Penelope Wass SC was sworn in as a judge of the District Court in New South Wales in June 2016. In a State Government media release the Attorney General noted that "Ms Wass has a quarter of a century of experience in law, including nine years as a Commonwealth prosecutor and 16 years as a barrister … [and] … has maintained a diverse civil and criminal practice, appearing regularly in the District Court, Supreme Court, and the state's highest appeal Courts. She also has taken matters to the Federal Court and High Court."[297]

In June 2016 Judge Wass presented a very important paper to the *Legal Aid Conference,* entitled "Would I lie to you? (an examination of eyewitness testimony in a criminal trial)". Her opening sentence on memory sets the scene:

> **Notwithstanding what the Courts have said since before Federation, one of the greatest misconceptions we continue to have about memory is that it is largely an accurate recorder, faithfully transposing into our brain events as they occur. From a witness' point of view, it is important to remember that whilst we often doubt the memories of others, we rarely question our own. However, all witnesses, no matter how seemingly reliable and honest, are accessing changing or changeable data. The process**

297 http://www.justice.nsw.gov.au/ExhibitPages/media-news/media-releases/2016/New-District-Court-.aspx

> **of experiencing or acquiring, laying down or storing memory and then reproducing an account, all of which is involved in "recalling" or "remembering", and therefore giving evidence in a criminal trial, is disconcertingly malleable. It is at best, almost always, a rough reconstruction with inaccuracies and distortions.[298] [emphasis added]**

Here Judge Wass was stating in her own words what Dr Arnold wrote about memory in her report to the Court. Moreover, Judge Wass discussed where she saw the understanding of memory today. Although her discussion of memory was in the context of the reliability of witness testimony in criminal trials, what she said was also true of what witnesses say in civil proceedings such as a defamation case.

> **Where it is said by a witness to have "remembered" those kinds of details, a level of reconstruction rather than recall is likely to be coming.[299]**

How reconstruction of memory may work is evidenced by this example from Judge Wass:

> **In an inquest I observed a nurse, honestly and sincerely, firmly and convincingly, give evidence that she gave a patient a 4ml/h dose of Fentanyl. All of the other evidence,**

298 Judge Penelope Wass SC, "Would I lie to you? (an examination of eyewitness testimony in a criminal trial)", paper delivered to *Legal Aid Conference*, June 2016, 2.

299 *Ibid.*, 5.

> **from other witnesses and including the log of the machine that administered it, showed overwhelmingly that she administered a fatal 200ml/h dose. No doubt, she was supposed to and at the time wanted to administer 4ml/h, she thought she had so administered it, she now wishes she had administered it. But overwhelmingly the evidence was that she did not. Now, question the outcome of that case, had she been the only witness to the event. Add to that a consideration of memory when extraordinary things occur, where people die or are seriously injured, and ask yourself how reliable that memory is likely to be. And how reliable is that memory likely to be some time after the event and where the witness may feel at fault, or where they feel that others are at fault?**[300]

The issue of the impact of the passage of time on memory, clearly relevant in the matter of *Fleming v The Advertiser*, is referred to by Judge Wass in these terms:

> **Obviously, the passage of time is going to affect the accuracy of an eyewitness account. Even the law has to some extent caught up with this scientific fact. Events, such as historical child abuse allegations, that took place years ago are more likely to be challenged as being inaccurate. We know this to be true when we try to recall**

300 *Ibid.*, 7.

> **day-to-day events from childhood. However, the length of time before memory begins to decay is quite short. The rate of memory decay is not linear but it does decay quickly. A time-span of even few hours between the observation and the first viewing of a photo board or a line-up, or the first statement to police, or to a solicitor or friend, may be significantly unreliable.**[301]

While Judge Wass suggested that "even the law has to some extent caught up with this scientific fact", that certainly did not appear to be the case where the four judges of the Supreme Court in South Australia are concerned. Apparently, any confusion, inconsistencies or vagueness in the evidence being given by one side's witnesses (in this case witnesses for the defendant) was simply to be rationalised, or otherwise overlooked.

Wass and Legal Authorities Regarding Memory Reliability

In this section of her paper, Judge Wass also addressed the history of the case law on memory reliability. Attention is drawn to the most recent authorities which are cited here precisely as Judge Wass stated them to be.

> **The difficulties in extracting truth from memory, after time has taken its toll, were exposed by Street CJ. in the Report of the Royal Commission of Inquiry into Certain Committal Proceedings Against K E**

---

301 *Ibid.*, 15-16

Humphreys (July 1983). His Honour said (at 9-10):

"In the intervening five or six years, rumours waxed and waned. In some cases suspicion underwent subtle change to belief, which itself progressed to reconstruction, which in turn escalated to recollection. No presently stated recollection could be safely assumed not to have progressed upwards and not to be the product of one of these earlier stages. The sheer frailty of human memory of necessity required a most anxious and critical appraisal of the evidence of the witnesses, no matter how credit-worthy they might be. It became apparent that in the years since August 1977 the recollections even of those with undoubted first-hand knowledge have in some instances faded, in some instances fermented, and in some instances expanded. Moreover, in many cases the realisation of the significance - indeed, the enormity - of what had occurred has tended to transmute into a more or less cynical acceptance of what had, or was believed or rumoured to have, taken place."

In *Watson v Foxman* (1995) 49 NSWLR 315 at 318-319, McClelland CJ in Eq said, in the context of allegations of misleading and deceptive conduct:

> "In many cases (but not all) the question whether spoken words were misleading may depend upon what, if examined

> at the time, may have been seen to be relatively subtle nuances flowing from the use of one word, phrase or grammatical construction rather than another, or the presence or absence of some qualifying word or phrase, or condition. Furthermore, human memory of what was said in a conversation is fallible for a variety of reasons, and ordinarily the degree of fallibility increases with the passage of time, particularly where disputes or litigation intervene, and the processes of memory are overlaid, often subconsciously, by perceptions or self-interest as well as conscious consideration of what should have been said or could have been said. All too often what is actually remembered is little more than an impression from which plausible details are then, again often subconsciously, constructed. All this is a matter of ordinary human experience."[302]

The two problems associated with memory identified in these passages, namely reliability over time and the fallibility of recollection of conversations increasing over time, seemingly eluded Justice Gray, notwithstanding that Dr Arnold provided sound scientific evidence for him to improve his understanding and awareness of the difficulties. On the other hand, Judge Wass, and the legal authorities she cites, seem to have no difficulty in seeing how expert evidence around memory "assists" them.

---

302 *Ibid.*, 22.

Other legal authorities

Counsel for the plaintiff had already provided authorities to the Court in their *Plaintiff's Outline of Submissions* dated 5 February 2015. Counsel for Dr Fleming asked Justice Gray to have regard to the following authorities:

In *Crouch v Hooper* (1852) 16 Beav. 182 at 184-5: 51 ER 747 at 748 Sir John Romilly MR said:

> **It is a matter of frequent observation that persons dwelling for a long time on facts, which they believe must have occurred, and trying to remember whether they did so or not, come at last to persuade themselves that they do actually recollect the occurrence of circumstances which, at first, they only begin by believing must have happened. What was originally the result of imagination becomes in time the result of recollection.**

In *Watson v Foxman* (1995) 49 NSWLR 315 at 319, McLelland CJ in Eq said:

> **Human memory of what was said in a conversation is fallible for a variety of reasons, and ordinarily the degree of fallibility increases with the passage of time, particularly where disputes or litigation intervene, and the processes of memory are overlaid, often subconsciously, by perceptions of self interest as well as conscious considerations of what would have been said or could have been said. All too often what is actually remembered**

> **is little more than an impression from which plausible details are then, again subconsciously, constructed. All this is a matter of ordinary human experience.**

Counsel for the plaintiff observed:

> **No clearer instances of the observation of Sir John Romilly could be imagined than the case of [JANE] re the Meningie allegation, Brighton beach incident, and red track suit pants incident; and the case of Lynch re the one allegation she makes.**

It is astonishing that Justice Gray did not address these cases when it came time to deal with the memory issues of Jane. Justice Gray chose not to be "assisted" by anyone else's opinion on these matters other than his own. And nor, did it seem, that Justices Vanstone, Nicholson, and Bampton considered it necessary to review these cases when they were meant to be reviewing Justice Gray's judgement.

The significance of reliance on witness demeanour

Justice Gray was impressed by witness demeanour, or at the least, claimed that witness demeanour led to his findings of credit where his "principal witnesses" were concerned. For Judge Wass, however, this is a problematic approach in face of the scientific evidence:

> **Often, much is made in litigation of the demeanour of a witness in the witness box and it is well known that successfully asking**

> **an appeal Court to overturn a finding where the evidence of the respondent was accepted by the trial judge, partly on findings of credit based on demeanour, is notoriously difficult.**
>
> **However, in recent years, judges have become more aware of scientific research that has cast doubt on the ability of judges (or anyone else) to tell truth from falsehood accurately on the basis of such appearances. Considerations such as these have encouraged judges, both at trial and on appeal, to limit their reliance on the appearances of witnesses and to reason to their conclusions, as far as possible, on the basis of contemporary materials, objectively established facts and the apparent logic of events. This does not eliminate the established principles about witness credibility; but it tends to reduce the occasions where those principles are seen as critical.**[303]

Judge Wass made a number of points which are singularly relevant to the case of *Fleming v The Advertiser*, points concerning not only the demeanour of witnesses, the ability of judges to discern the truth, but also unacknowledged judicial prejudice.

> **A test of "glaring improbability", "incontrovertible error" or "palpable misuse of an advantage" pays, I am inclined**

303 *Ibid.*, 26

to think, altogether too much deference to a trial judge's view of the facts and advantages, both actual and supposed. This is not to deny, however, that deference should be paid to first instance findings of credit. It is simply to prefer that a test of wrongness on any appeal to be guided by, rather than bound by, findings on credit, or on the basis of demeanour.

Judges have become more aware of the scientific research that has cast doubt on the ability of judges (or anyone else) to tell the truth from falsehood accurately on the basis of such appearances [See material cited by Samuels JA in *Trawl Industries of Australia Pty Ltd v Effem Foods Pty Ltd* (1992) 27 NSWLR 326 at 348 and noted in SRA (1999) 73 ALJR 306 at 329; 160 ALR 588 at 617-618].

Mason P, in *Unconscious Judicial Prejudice* (2001) 75 ALJ 676, discussed cognitive illusions revealed by psychological studies. His Honour pointed out that these illusions can lead to systematic error or bias when making factual findings (at 684 - 685). See also *SRA (NSW) v Earthline Constructions Pty Limited* per Kirby J at 329.

The statements in *Fox v Percy* (2003) 214 CLR 118 by Gleeson CJ, Gummow and Kirby JJ at 128 -129, [30] - [31] were thought at the time to be somewhat of a watershed. Their honours observed:

> **It is true, as McHugh J has pointed out, that for a very long time judges in appellate courts have given as a reason for appellate deference to the decision of a trial judge, the assessment of the appearance of witnesses as they give their testimony that is possible at trial and normally impossible in an appellate court. However, it is equally true that, for almost as long, other judges have cautioned against the dangers of too readily drawing conclusions about truthfulness and reliability solely or mainly from the appearance of witnesses [eg Trawl Industries of *Australia Pty Ltd v Effem Foods Pty Ltd* (1992) 27 NSWLR 326 at 348, per Samuels JA.] Thus, in 1924 Atkin LJ observed in *Société d'Avances Commerciales (Société Anonyme Egyptienne) v Merchants' Marine Insurance Co (The "Palitana")* [(1924) 20 Ll L Rep 140 at 152].**[304]

For Judge Wass:

> **A trial judge ought not misuse his or her advantage of assessing a witness in the witness box. It is necessary to critically analyse the content of the witness' evidence. Judges ought not act on demeanour and accept evidence which is inconsistent with facts established by the evidence of others and the contemporaneous documents and which was otherwise glaringly improbable:**

304 *Ibid.*, 29-30.

> **see also *Devries v Australian National Railways Commission* (1993) 177 CLR 472 at 479 per Brennan, Gaudron, and McHugh JJ."**

Would that Justice Gray, Vanstone, Nicholson, and Bampton had heeded this advice. Despite having access to the uncontradicted evidence of expert witness Dr Michelle Arnold, Justice Gray chose not to use it and, even worse, chose to set it aside on the spurious basis that Dr Arnold was biased, and that her evidence did not "assist" him.

Justice Gray's general assessment of the Dr Arnold evidence

We should remind ourselves what Justice Gray had to say about Dr Arnold's evidence and then look at the evidence itself to see if his dismissal of her evidence can be justified.

Dr Arnold had provided, as evidence, a document she generated to remind herself of what details she needed to check before giving her second opinion in the light of the evidence Jane had given in Court. The defendant said that this document was evidence that Dr Arnold was biased, that she was a "hired hand". Justice Gray appeared to accept that opinion. But it is simply unreasonable to deduce that Dr Arnold compromised her independence by preparing this document. An expert, meticulously trying to get the facts right before writing a second report by reminding herself of what elements she needed to recheck, is evidence of professionalism. Justice Gray concedes that Dr Arnold "was not providing the questions to" the plaintiff's solicitors yet still rejected her application of the scientific evidence (uncontradicted) to the evidence given by Jane.

There are other very good reasons why Justice Gray's assessment of Dr Arnold's evidence should be called into question. But first, three important preliminary points should be noted here:

1. Why would Dr Arnold be biased towards Dr Fleming? Dr Fleming had had no contact of any kind with Dr Arnold before the trial, meeting her for the first time when she came to Court to give her evidence. No evidence was presented which in any way suggested that the experienced Dr Arnold had ever been a 'hired gun'.
2. *The Advertiser* had her report in plenty of time before the trial. It was open to them to get another opinion. If *The Advertiser* really believed that Dr Arnold was biased, why didn't its solicitors do that? They were not troubled by money problems as was Dr Fleming. So, they could easily afford it. Did they do it and not like what they found? Or did they not do that because they knew that the Dr Arnold Report was very well argued and used the most up-to-date findings from the literature?
3. Dr Arnold's scientific evidence was uncontested.

Justice Gray's catastrophic errors in his assessment of Dr Arnold's evidence

In evidence before the Court were two documents prepared by Dr Arnold, the report and the addendum to this report. The first report was written prior to the case being heard in Court. Within the report, Dr Arnold listed the documents which she had in front of her and upon which she had relied.

The addendum was written after Jane had given her evidence in Court. At the beginning of the addendum, Dr Arnold addressed this question:

> Having been provided with the Court *Transcript of evidence given in Court* of [Jane] given 28 October to 31 October (inclusive) and from 17 November to 18 November 2014, has any opinion expressed in your Report dated 7 July 2014 changed or altered in any way?[305]

Her response is clear and unequivocal:

> **Given the provided transcripts, the opinions I expressed in my report have not altered but they have been reinforced.** I provide specifics regarding this reinforcement below.[306]

Justice Gray seemingly misunderstood the sequence of the two documents when he wrote:

> A significant proportion of her opinion was directed towards her views concerning the influence of therapists or suggestive therapeutic techniques in leading to false or recovered memories. In that regard Dr Arnold expressed an opinion as to the impact that she thought Father Stephenson, as a counsellor, may have had on the accuracy

305 Exhibit P85: *Addendum to report of* Dr Dr Arnold.

306 *Ibid.*

> and reliability of Jane's memory. Her assumptions in that regard were strongly challenged in cross-examination however, the example given by Dr Arnold of what was said to be Father Stephenson's influence on Jane's memory related to what was said to be Jane's assertion that the first event occurred at Meningie. **In fact it is clear that, contrary to Dr Arnold's view, Jane's evidence to this Court did not seek to assert the location of the first incident as anywhere other than a place in the Coorong.** Jane says that after the police interviewed the plaintiff, the plaintiff had identified Meningie and that the police had told her of that. References by Jane in subsequent statements to which Dr Arnold refers which identify Meningie as the location were made after that time. Those references provide no support for Dr Arnold's hypothesis that Father Stephenson influenced Jane's memory in that or any other respect.[307]

Justice Gray said that Jane's new evidence about the Coorong given in Court after 8 October 2014 was not considered by Dr Arnold in her report dated 7 July 2014. But how could it have been? Dr Arnold was referring to all the statements Jane made **before the trial**.

When Justice Gray said that "Jane's evidence to this Court did not seek to assert the location of the first incident as anywhere other than a place in the Coorong"', that was not correct either. Throughout the trial reference

307 Justice Gray *judgement* at Paragraph 381.

was made to the "Meningie incident". Meningie is a town, the Coorong is a district. Moreover, Jane, at trial, accepted that as fact in her evidence:

> **Harris: Do you recall arriving at the location you now know to be Meningie?**
>
> **Jane: I'm not sure it was Meningie, it was in that district.**
>
> **Harris: Well, if we work on the basis that the location that you went to I'm going to refer to as 'Meningie'.**
>
> **Jane: Okay.**[308]

Moreover, Justice Gray asserts that the references provided by Dr Arnold provide "no support for Dr Arnold's hypothesis that Father Stephenson influenced Jane's memory in that or any other respect".

Justice Gray is totally wrong when he says this. Firstly, Heywood-Smith, counsel for the plaintiff, had already drawn to Justice Gray's attention the fact that Jane had told the police that Stephenson had influenced her memory about *Meningie* being the town. Heywood-Smith stated:

> Then on p.28, the middle paragraph, with reference to a 'John Stephenson' in that paragraph, it would appear that Mr Stephenson assisted in the identification of the South-East town or Coorong town of Meningie. That's all of significance in that statement.[309]

308 *Transcript of evidence given in Court* at page 1369 lines 31-36.

309 *Transcript of evidence given in Court* at page 62 lines 9-16.

The page 28 reference was to the police witness statement in which Jane says:

> John STEPHENSON was the priest at Saint Jude's about ten years after FLEMING left. He was the first person I reported this to. He was also on the Professional Standards Committee in 2001, but I also knew him in my early twenties. I taught his children piano. I've kept in touch with the children. In relation to the country place that we went to, STEPHENSON told me that the MENINGIE church was vacant at the time[310] **and there wasn't a parish priest there between 1969 and 1970. So that's possibly the church that FLEMING went to. He would have gone there or somewhere like that because the place didn't have a priest. They probably let everyone have a go there.**[311]

This statement was made to the police on 10 October 2007 and signed by Jane on 30 July 2008. So, she made that statement to the police more than 12 months before Dr Fleming was interviewed by the police (November 2008), the interview when Dr Fleming volunteered that he had been in Meningie at the relevant time.

Second, Dr Arnold not only included that police statement in her list of the documents upon which she relied, but clearly referred to it and much more besides. Jane goes from not knowing the name of the country

---

310 Actually, Stephenson was wrong about that. The parish priest was the Reverence George Gatenby who asked Father Fleming to be the *locum tenens* for the first ten days of January.

311 Exhibit P47: *Statement of [JANE] to South Australia Police,* 30th July 2008

town in 2003 and 2007, to saying it was a town beginning with "M", and by 2010 confidently stating it was Meningie. Dr Arnold discussed the evidence before her:

> There also is evidence that JS [Stephenson] may have provided Jane with information that influenced her subsequent recollections and statements of the long-ago events in regards to Father Fleming. For example, in relation to the alleged first abuse event in Meningie, JS informed Jane that the Meningie church was vacant between 1969 and 1970. This is important because in the earliest document from 2003 (#57, pg 2), Jane only refers to the first event as happening "in the country". In the following document from 2007 (#6, pgs 8-9), Jane again refers to the first event as happening in the country, but then explicitly states she is "unsure of the name of the town". It is not until the document from 2009 (#36, pg 2), that she refers to the place as starting with M, and then agreeing with the interviewer when he volunteers Meningie. By the final document in 2010 (#66, pg 5) she appears to freely volunteer for the first alleged abuse event that she "travelled to a country town [she believes] to be Meningie". Thus, taken together, Jane appears to have changed over the years from being unable to provide any memory of the town to volunteering without prompting that she believes it was Meningie.[312]

312 Exhibit P84 Report of Dr Arnold 7th of July 2014.

Now document number 66 referred to by Dr Arnold is a further statement to the police made on 19 October 2010 and was Exhibit P51 in evidence. In that document, Jane says:

1. My understanding is that John Fleming was going to Meningie on church business and asked the McNicol's (*sic*) to go along with him …
2. Sometime before travelling to Meningie, I remember …
3. John Fleming travelled separately to Meningie …
4. Since then the police have told me that John Fleming, in an interview with them, volunteered that he travelled to Meningie church at around this time, …
5. Since then I have concluded that it is the Meningie church where this occurred. **Prior to John Fleming's police interview, I described the rectory to John Stephenson who confirmed that my description matched the church and rectory at Meningie** …
6. I can't clearly recollect whether the house at Meningie had two or three bedrooms …
7. I believe that John Fleming and the McNicol family stayed more than one night at Meningie …[313]

All that Dr Arnold said in her report was justified by the evidence, evidence which Justice Gray had been unable to marshal. And no doubt it was because of what Jane had already claimed in police statements that counsel for *The Advertiser*, Harris, framed his questions

313 Exhibit P 51: *Witness Statement of [*JANE*]*, 19th of October 2010.

in relation to Meningie. All the references provided by Dr Arnold, taken together, provide ample support for Dr Arnold's conclusion that Mr Stephenson influenced Jane's memory in that and in other respects.

In addition to this apparently inexplicable misinterpretation of Dr Arnold's report, Justice Gray then traduces the professionalism of Dr Arnold, thereby undermining her evidence and allowing him to dismiss what she has to say. What was Justice Gray doing for 12 months that he couldn't get the facts right?

Justice Gray's claim to superior knowledge about cognitive memory

Having cited the expert witness on the science of cognitive memory, Justice Gray claimed that from his expertise on memory (which is hardly comparable to an expert) that he did not agree with Dr Arnold and presumably with the "dominant scientific research and understanding of memory" upon which she relied.

> **While I do not regard Jane as seeking to control her memory as opined by Dr Arnold I take Jane to be trying to give an honest if imprecise account of her thought processes. ... This, I accept, as a response to Jane not wishing to think about what she regards as an extremely upsetting experience. However, it does leave open the reliance that I might place on her evidence as to the specific nature of the sexual activity that took place on that occasion.**[314]

314 Justice Gray *judgement* at paragraph 401.

Contrary to Dr Arnold and based upon nothing but his unsubstantiated opinion of what he imagines the evidence on cognitive memory to mean, Justice Gray, yet again, finds for Jane. The plaintiff had no way forward in dealing with a judge who asserted the sovereignty of his personal opinion based on his personal experience as superior to the scientifically well-founded opinion of an expert on cognitive memory.

Justice Gray next discusses Dr Arnold's opinion on "body memory". He begins by citing Jane's evidence:

> **Later, again in the interview, Jane said:**
>
> **... I think I remember, I think that's why I was choking before, because I, I think that he did ejaculate, and I think it was in my mouth, and um, and that's, that's really revolting.[315]**
>
> **But- Jane referred to the interview in her cross-examination where she said:**
>
> **... during the interview I didn't give, I refused to give details of, of the oral contact because it made me, made me dry retch and I said I didn't want to talk about it anymore, I didn't want - it was enough, I kept repeating the mantra of my psychologist who said I didn't have to think about it, I didn't have to talk about it, it was enough to remember the first incident - remember, yeah, didn't have to think about it, didn't have to talk about, different from- [316]**

315 Exhibit P5O, p 24.

316 *Transcript of evidence given in Court* at page 1525 lines 4-13.

The plaintiff specifically referred to this passage and, in particular, the opinion of Dr Arnold in respect of it, for the proposition that "there is no scientific evidence that links bodily expression of memory (that is i.e. in the absence of conscious memory) to specific past events". However, Justice Gray does not accept the scientific evidence provided by Dr Arnold as she applied it to Jane.

> **I do not accept Dr Arnold's criticism that that is what is taking place in the passage of evidence that I have quoted. I take the passage as Jane saying that she does have a conscious memory but that she is not going to talk about it. I regard the passage as consistent with her memory causing the physical reaction that she describes not the physical reaction providing the memory.**[317]

But let us look again at what *Dr Arnold* said in full context.

> **In regards to my answer to question #5 in my report, I provided examples of how Jane is articulating what some therapists would label as a body memory. I noted one example that involved her talking to the police, and she reiterated this example in her testimony. Specifically, in the transcripts she states "I know that during the interview I didn't give, I refused to give details of, of the oral contact because it made me, made me dry retch and I said I didn't want to talk about it anymore, I didn't want to - it was enough, I kept**

317 Justice Gray *judgement* at paragraph 423.

> **repeating the mantra of my psychologist who said I didn't have to think about it, I didn't have to talk about it, it was enough to remember the first incident..." (pg 1525, lines 3-10). Thus, consistent with document #66, she is recounting an event in which she does not provide specific details, but seems to be taking her physical reaction (i.e., retching) as evidence that this particular event occurred. There is no scientific evidence, though, that links bodily expressions of memory (i.e.; in the absence of conscious memory) to specific past events.**[318]

Unlike Justice Gray, Dr Arnold did not cherry-pick the data upon which her opinion relied. It is not just what Jane said at trial. In her report, Dr Arnold listed all the documents which she had before her, and which were in evidence. Among these was document #66, which was a witness statement signed by Jane on 19 October 2010 (some two years after the first publications by *The Advertiser*) and witnessed by Judith Perreall. Dr Arnold pointed out that Jane's statement at trial was "consistent with document #66" which contained her statements pre-trial.

Justice Gray made no reference to what was in 'document #66', the basis upon which Dr Arnold first concluded that Jane was appealing to 'body memory'. He merely contented himself with what he thought was the case in reference only to what Jane said in Court. No doubt the long delay of more than 12 months affected Justice Gray's recall of what evidence was available to

318 Exhibit P85: *Addendum to report of* Dr Arnold.

him to consider. It should also be noted that Justice Gray gave no indication that he was in any position to state that Dr Arnold misapplied the scientific evidence which was uncontradicted evidence.

Justice Gray's final (and patronising) assault on Dr Arnold's expertise

As discussed above, Justice Gray appeared to have supported the questioning of Dr Arnold's reputation as an independent expert. The scientific evidence of Dr Arnold was uncontested, and Justice Gray gave no explanation as to why he considered himself qualified to argue that Dr Arnold did not act independently in her role as an expert witness.

Dr Arnold was engaged as an expert in the most professional manner by Ms Amy Sobels from Sykes Bidstrup, solicitors for the plaintiff, as may be seen from the letter of engagement.[319] Nowhere in that letter or in subsequent communications is Dr Arnold requested to be a 'hired gun' for Dr Fleming. Indeed, The letter of instruction makes it clear that Dr Arnold must comply with the rules of the Court which say:

> **Please ensure that your report complies with Rule 160 and Practice Direction 5.4.**
>
> **In particular, we draw your attention to the following matters in the Practice Direction:**
>
> - **An expert witness has an overriding duty to assist the Court on matters relevant to the expert's area of expertise.**

319 D55: *Letter of instruction to* Dr Arnold, 2 July 2014.

- **An expert witness is not an advocate for a party.**

There was nothing to suggest that Dr Arnold was doing anything other than acting professionally. She had no contact with Dr Fleming. She presented as a disinterested party and no evidence was provided to indicate that Dr Arnold would abuse her professional standing to act as a 'hired gun'.

Dr Arnold framed her report in accordance with the instructions given her which included instructions to abide by the Court's requirements.

> **Practice**
>
> **Direction 5.4 entitled 'Guidelines for Expert Witnesses In Proceedings in the Supreme Court of South Australia'. We also enclose* a copy of rule 160.**[320]

Dr Arnold's report was duly prepared and delivered to Ms Sobels,[321] well before the commencement of proceedings thereby more than meeting the requirement that "expert reports must be served early in the proceeding".[322]

Subsequently, Ms Sobels emailed Dr Arnold:

> **I am writing to touch base in relation to Father Fleming's defamation trial. As you are aware, the trial took place over 4 weeks in October. Unfortunately, the evidence did not conclude in that time and accordingly**

320 *Ibid.*

321 Exhibit P84: Report of Dr Arnold *Report Prepared in the Matter of DR FLEMING v THE AD WEEKEND PUBLISHING CO P/L & A1*, 7 July 2014.

322 Chapter on "Evidence" in *Australian Civil Procedure*.

the Court has set aside a further 3 weeks. The following are the dates upon which the trial is set to resume:

- **17 November 2014 - 21 November 2014; and**
- **12 January 2015 - 23 January 2015.**

We expect that the Defendants will require most of the week of 17 November in order to complete their case.

Accordingly, we do not anticipate requiring you to give evidence until January. Could you kindly let me know as a matter of urgency if you are unavailable on those dates in January?

I would also be grateful for an opportunity to discuss evidence which has come to light over the course of the Trial. Is there a convenient time for you to speak over the phone? (I know it is a very busy time of year with exams and assessment.)

Many thanks for your ongoing assistance, it is greatly appreciated.[323]

Three days later, Ms Sobels followed up with another email:

Dear Michelle

Please find attached hereto transcript of Jane's evidence to date.

323 D56: *Email correspondence between Ms Sobels and* Dr Arnold, 7 November 2014.

> **I look forward to speaking with you on Thursday at 1pm. Please let me know if you have any difficulties reading through the transcript before this time. (There are some extensive evidentiary arguments on 28 and 29 October so the bulk of the evidence is in the transcript on 30 and 31 October.)**
>
> **If you feel it would be of assistance to view the exhibits, I can arrange for these to be scanned and emailed to you.**[324]

Prior to the conversation with *Ms Sobels,* Dr Arnold read the materials provided to her and prepared a document titled 'Potential questions for Jane'.[325] This document was generated by Dr Arnold for her use alone as an aide memoir, comprising a list of matters she needed to check for her forthcoming discussion with counsel for the plaintiff in case some matters of fact needed clarification. Dr Arnold then prepared an addendum to her original report[326]. In the addendum, Dr Arnold stated:

> **Given the provided transcripts, the opinions I expressed in my report have not altered but they have been reinforced.**[327]

Junior Counsel for the defendant, Barnett, argued that the title of this document "Potential Questions for Jane" implied that Dr Arnold was biased.

324 D57: *Email correspondence from Amy Sobels to* Dr Arnold, 10 November 2014.

325 D58: *Potential questions* for Jane.

326 Exhibit P85: *Addendum to Report Prepared in the Matter of DR FLEMING v THE ADVERTISER PUBLISHING CO P/L & ANOR,* January 19, 2015.

327 *Ibid.*

In the light of the correspondence and the very objective and professional way Dr Arnold complied with her instructions, how could Justice Gray have been convinced by a proposition with no foundation in fact? How could he possibly say that a document prepared for her own personal use and for which there is a very reasonable explanation, count as evidence to call into question Dr Arnold's "independence" as an expert. Dr Arnold was clear in explaining why she drew up the list of questions and issues and for whom that document was intended. Justice Gray's acceptance of the defendant's argument does him no credit particularly when he used the defendant's theory of 'bias' to traduce Dr Arnold's professionalism.

Justice Gray's refusal to engage with Dr Arnold's expert evidence on memory. It seems that Justice Gray did not address thc details of Dr Arnold's evidence because he had already discounted her conclusions. Justice Gray preferred to be guided by his impressions and prejudices which is why Dr Arnold's expert opinions did not "assist" him.

For Justice Gray:

1. Counsel for *The Advertiser* submitted that Dr Arnold is biased.
2. There is a problem about Dr Arnold labelling a document "Potential Questions for Jane" even though Dr Arnold assures the Court of how the document was meant to be used and was in fact used.
3. Dr Arnold discussed this document with Ms Sobels, solicitor for Dr Fleming.
4. I should therefore be "cautious" about accepting Dr Arnold's views.

5. "In any event" Dr Arnold's opinions do not "assist" me.
6. Considering Dr Arnold's precise views on all substantive matters, I don't agree with her.
7. Therefore, Dr Arnold's evidence can be rejected in every important particular.

Justice Gray's account of the procedural matter of how a document is labelled allows him to find a procedural way not to give that evidence the respect it deserves and even though the document to which objection had been drawn by the Respondents was not written until well after the main Report had been written and well after Jane had been examined and cross-examined. The questions could not possibly be asked of Jane. In the context of why this document was assembled, the title, "Potential Questions for Jane", means no more than the issues Dr Arnold would need to consider and get right before she committed herself in a second written report which was an *addendum* to her first report. Is Justice Gray really implying that this expert, a person internationally known for her expertise and independence of mind, is lying to him when she states precisely how her document was assembled and for what purpose? But in case his arguments fail (really mere assertions of his personal opinion as to how memory works), he then hides behind a judge's lofty way of saying either he doesn't understand what is being put to him, or he does but fears where that might take him. "I do not think I am assisted by them [Dr Arnold's views]." As shown earlier in this book, the procedural issue of how an academic formulates a title for a paper for her own personal use, (and remember that Justice Gray is no academic), is entirely a matter of opinion. Moreover, it is of minor importance and certainly not enough to question Dr Arnold's independence, objectivity, honesty, and expertise.

And finally, just to make sure Dr Arnold knows her place, Justice Gray gratuitously insults her by referring to what he considers to be her "naivety or inexperience". And yet it is Dr Arnold who shows that she is the one who has not only the expert knowledge about memory and the way that the scientific evidence should be applied, but also a much surer grasp of the evidence than Justice Gray.

Conclusion

There is something very much askew with a judicial system where judges do not confine themselves to be finders of objective fact. It is a gross imposture to pontificate in areas of knowledge in which one is not an expert.

Dr Arnold charged a very fair and modest fee for her work. Despite the attempts to undermine her credibility, she was an independent expert in an important area of scientific knowledge and was dismissed in the most patronising terms possible. Justice Gray appeared to be attacking Dr Arnold's character in accepting the defendant's claim that Dr Arnold was biased. No suggestion was given to explain what incentive Dr Arnold had to be biased. She earned little money from the project and had never met the plaintiff. Rather, it can be argued that Dr Arnold had more to lose when Justice Gray made disparaging comments about her character as a professional academic.

Chapter Nine

Justice Gray's Misapplication of the *Briginshaw* Rule

At [J178] – [J188] the learned trial Judge addressed the standard of proof. At [J181], his Honour (mis) quoted a passage from Neat Holdings v Karajan Pty Ltd. His Honour then refers to the defendants' submission. At [J182] his Honour does not accept that submission if it is "directed to the clarity and cogency of the evidence required to prove the criminal behaviour alleged in the present case..." His Honour did not accept that submission at [J183] because "A direction for the need for clear, cogent or strict proof was not required in Neat Holdings because in that case the contest was between evidence given by both the plaintiff and the defendant that the other had been guilty of deliberate falsification of its records of takings."

His Honour had fallen into error at [J183] in misapplying Neat Holdings. The judge has wrongly equated the issue he is to decide as being of the same type of issue the trial judge in Neat Holdings had to decide.

In Neat Holdings there was an established incontrovertible fact – there were two sets of weekly takings books. Both sets of books could not be genuine. A choice had to be made as to which set of books was false. However, in the present case, in the context of Jane's allegations of criminal activity at Meningie and St Mark's College, there was no existing incontrovertible fact.

At [J184] his Honour's error is exposed: "I do not take the Court in Neat Holdings as detracting from the remarks concerning the requirement for clear or cogent or strict proof in appropriate cases, of which I regard this as one" [but then he qualifies that by saying] **"dependent, as it is, upon the acceptance or otherwise of the direct evidence of particular witnesses."**

Unlike Neat Holdings, the fact that the alleged incidents ever occurred was in dispute. See judgment of Peek J in *Stanberg Pty Ltd v Tabibi* [2012] SASC 187 at [101] – [118], in particular at [109]:

> Thus, far from suggesting that there was no such requirement in relation to the proof of a grave matter in the confines of a civil case, the [Neat Holdings] Court proceeded on the basis that such would normally be required but that such requirement had little work to do where the parties did not contest the fact that deliberated falsification of records had in fact occurred by one of the two parties.

The learned trial judge fell into error by misdirecting himself at [J183] that he had to make "a choice between competing and mutually inconsistent allegations of [criminal] conduct". In the present case, the application of the *Briginshaw* principles did not require his Honour to choose between Jane's statement that criminal acts occurred and the plaintiff's denial that such acts occurred. The law does not require the judge to balance probabilities and say which way they incline.[328]

At [J185], the learned trial judge referred to Rejfek v McElroy and set out a passage from that judgment. His Honour omitted the important first part of that passage. The passage cited by His Honour refers to a footnote reference to Helton v Allen per Starke J at 701. The learned trial judge made no reference to the 'presumption of innocence'.

At [J191] the judge repeated his formulaic recitation of "the need for clear and cogent evidence" (citing Reifek v McElroy) but he failed to mention the requirement of "a greater strictness of proof". Furthermore, the judge erred in coming to his finding at [J232] that the Meningie incident "is an event that in fact took place" before considering:

- the evidence of the other person (other than the plaintiff), and
- the expert evidence as regards remembering events said to have occurred more than 40 years ago.

When discussing the Meningie incident, his Honour found at [J392] that Jane's evidence was "inherently credible and compelling. I am satisfied on the balance of probabilities that it is an event that in fact took place. I have regard to the caution I must exercise in acting on this allegation which involves the commission of a serious criminal offence." Then, in the next paragraph [J393], he says he must now "deal with the denial by Alison Fleming… that any such incident occurred".

328 Gageler J, *Henderson v Queensland* [2014] HCA 52 at [87], [88].

Then at [J400] he comes to deal with the expert evidence of Dr Arnold that casts doubt on the reliability of Jane's recollection.

Furthermore, the Reverend John Stephenson's sworn statement to the police in May 2008 details what Jane had told him. Mr Stephenson said that Jane had told him "that the plaintiff got her to perform oral sex on the beach. This occurred at the country location in the South East. After the incident they rejoined the McNicol family further down the beach."

The trial judge wrongly accepted Jane's oral evidence that "Father Stephenson may have conflated all of the incidents that she had told him about. There is some reason for thinking that this may be the case. I am inclined to accept Jane's response as the explanation for the apparent inconsistency". That is mere conjecture or speculation. A distinction is to be made between inferences that may properly be drawn from the facts and mere conjecture or speculation, which is not permissible.[329] The judge's statement - "I am inclined to accept..." - gives no weight to the presumption of innocence. It takes no account of the need for clear, cogent, or strict proof of the Meningie incident. It is not evidence that is "clear and cogent such as to induce, on a balance of probabilities, an actual persuasion of the mind as to the existence of the" crime.

It is apparent from the reasons of judgment, read as a whole, that the finding in respect of the "ménage à trois" (see section below in "Use of Credit findings") was critical to the decision that the appellant was lying

329 *Holloway v McFeeters* (1956) 94 CLR 470 at 484.

in his denials about the Meningie and St Mark's College allegations. But in engaging in speculation to explain away Fr Stephenson's inconsistent statement and making a finding on the Meningie incident before he had considered Alison Fleming's evidence or Dr Arnold's evidence, meant the trial judge did not turn his mind sufficiently to the steps to be taken in order to reach the seriousness of his conclusion.

Not only did he not direct his attention to the degree of proof required but his Honour allowed the "ménage à trois" statement to assume a quite unwarranted significance in the conclusions he reached. That issue seems to have diverted his Honour's attention from what was necessary to justify a finding that the Meningie incident and the St Mark's incident both occurred as a matter of fact as described by Jane in the witness box. The Defence case on the "ménage à trois" issue was a criticism of how a witness (the plaintiff) was forced to struggle with his memory of what he said in a conversation more than 20 years earlier. The defendant's attack that the conversation was evidence of "esoteric knowledge" of the Meningie incident completely collapsed. The plaintiff's explanation was supported by other evidence.

The dominant role that the "ménage à trois" issue played in his Honour's mind and the absence of any real analysis of the evidence [only that the evidence strongly tells "against any confidence that I might have in accepting or giving weight to his emphatic and positive denials in other aspects of his evidence"] lead inevitably to the conclusion that the judge did not adequately deal with the evidence in the light of *Briginshaw*.

Chapter Ten

Appeal to the Full Court of the Supreme Court in South Australia

Wise men are instructed by reason; men of less understanding, by experience.[330]

It is fair to say that many people were shocked by Justice Gray's judgement, including some who are well versed in the law. Even more dishearteningly, even before the appeal was heard was it suggested that an appeal court would be very unlikely to overturn the judge of first instance. That appeals tend to favour the trial judge is not an uncommon view including, for example, that of Glenn McGowan KC:

> **Despite decades of efforts to impose an obligation on appellate courts to conduct a real 'rehearing',[331] it remains the case that appeals from factual findings are difficult and parties must regard the trial as the best,**

330 Cicero, *Letters to Atticus.*

331 *CSR Ltd v Della Maddalena* (2006) 80 ALJR 458 at 466 [21] per Kirby J (Gleeson CJ agreeing at 462 [1]), at 492 [180] per Callinan and Heydon JJ; *Fox v Percy* (2003) 214 CLR 118 at 128 [29] per Gleeson CJ, Gummow and Kirby JJ; *State Rail Authority (NSW) v Earthline Constructions Pty Ltd (in Liq)* (1999) 73 ALJR 306.

> **and sometimes only, real opportunity to get it right.**[332]

McGowan went on to say:

> **There are many reasons why this is so. However, mere respect for the trial judge is not one of them. It has been recognised for many years now that a trial judge's assessment of credibility of witnesses on the basis of demeanour is not reliable.**[333] **Rather, the modern principle of restraint on appellate factual review is based on finality and limited judicial resources.**[334] **These bases are really no more than certainty and economics by other names. Those arguments do not impress progressive thinkers such as Hon David Ipp AO, KC**[335] **and Professor Luntz**[336] **who do not see any justification for letting any error through the reviewing net. They would echo another Australian, Lord Atkin's, 1933 aphorism "[f]inality is a good thing, but justice is a better."**

---

332 http://www.gadens.com/publications/Exhibit Pages/Limits-on-appeals-from-factual-findings.aspx

333 Bell, Hon Justice V., "Appellate Review of the Facts" *Sir Maurice Byers Lecture* 20 August 2014 reprinted in NSW Bar News Summer 201415 p.26.

334 See e.g. the Woolf Review in England 1996; Bingham, "The Judge as Juror: The Judicial Determination of Factual Issues" (1985) 38 *Current Legal Problems* 1 at 11.

335 Ipp, "Problems with FactFinding" (2006) 80 *Australian Law Journal* 667.

336 Luntz, "RoundUp of Cases in the High Court of Australia in 2003" (2004) 12 *Torts Law Journal* 1.

Despite this concern, Dr Fleming decided to appeal the decision based on the legal advice he received regarding the flawed nature of Justice Gray's judgement. It was felt, following *Fox v Percy*,[337] almost any group of judges would feel obliged to uphold the appeal. In *Fox v Percy* the court was unanimous in upholding the overturning of the trial judge's decision based upon his finding of fact.

The Advertiser first tried to block the appeal being heard, requesting a Supreme Court order be made to require Dr Fleming to put up a large sum of money in advance to ensure their costs were covered if the appeal failed. Given Dr Fleming's impecunious state he would have been unable to find such a sum. Supreme Court Judge Stanley ruled that it would be unjust for Dr Fleming to be prevented from having an appeal heard on these grounds and found in his favour.

A great deal of time was spent examining Justice Gray's judgement and preparing the grounds of the appeal. A clear timeline of crucial events was prepared, a copy of which is provided in *Appendix A*. It was hoped that the three judges appointed, Justices Vanstone, Nicholson, and Bampton would bring fresh and clear minds to what was being put to them.

Prejudice in favour of the "principal witnesses"

Just as Justice Gray had arbitrarily designated witnesses for the defence as "principal witnesses", so too did

337 (2003) 214 CLR 118.

Justices Vanstone, Nicholson, and Bampton. Their term, "main witnesses", referred to the same persons contained in Justice Gray's list of "principal witnesses". Consideration of the appeal was apparently to be framed through the lenses of these individuals, with Dr Fleming (the appellant) left to prove his case without any of his witnesses being deemed sufficiently important to be considered a "main" witness, including two who had provided crucial evidence, Alison Fleming and Dr Arnold. The appeal judges stated:

> **Evidence relating to justification**
>
> **Before extracting the appellant's specific complaints about the Judge's evaluation of the evidence on the principal issue in the appeal, justification, we shall briefly summarise the evidence of the main witnesses.**[338]

To recap, the main witnesses were Jane, Peter Kay, Sue Kay, Dianne Lynch, and Alan Courtney, whereas the appellant, Alison Fleming, Dr Arnold and all other witnesses for the appellant were omitted from this list.

The Appeal Judges uncritically followed the same approach taken by Justice Gray, with foreseeable results. As already discussed, this approach inverted the onus of proof and arbitrarily privileged one side over the other. It was only after the evidence of the "main witnesses" has

338 Fleming *v Advertiser-News Weekend Publishing Company Pty Ltd & ANOR* [2016] SASCFC 109 (29 September 2016) Last Updated: 29 September 2016 Supreme Court of South Australia (Full Court: Civil), at paragraph 55. Hereinafter this judgement will be referred to as Justices Vanstone, Nicholson, and Bampton judgement.

been uncritically outlined that the main points of appeal were considered.

Further, it was not until the end of their judgement that Justices Vanstone, Nicholson, and Bampton dealt with the ground of appeal in regard to how Justice Gray reached his finding that the appellant's credibility was questionable. This could well be argued to be unfair to the appellant.

Evaluation of the appellant's credibility[339]

Justices Vanstone, Nicholson, and Bampton dealt with the question of the appellant's credibility by simply repeating what Justice Gray had argued.[340] No serious account was taken of the arguments provided by the appellant to show how deeply flawed was this approach. The very serious allegation of bias can be made given what the three judges said in relation to the use of the ménage à trois:

> **In our view, the Judge was entitled to take a dim view of the appellant's evidence on the topic of the ménage à trois. Plainly, the appellant saw the appearance of the expression in Monsignor Cappo's report to Archbishop Faulkner as an embarrassment to him. He was prepared to pit his credibility against that of Monsignor Cappo and to**

339 Justices Vanstone, Nicholson, and Bampton *judgement* at paragraphs 162-169.

340 *Ibid.*, at paragraphs 162-167.

> **assert that Monsignor Cappo had engaged in "creative" writing, plainly not recalling that Monsignor Cappo had been taking notes at the time of the interview. When the notes were produced and the evidence of Monsignor Cappo given, the appellant appeared to recall his use of that term to Monsignor Cappo in a different context. However, the Judge was entitled to the view that the damage was done.**[341]

This is deeply concerning on every point. The statement that the appellant "was prepared to pit his credibility against that of Monsignor Cappo" was highly suggestive and speculative and for which there was no evidence. Credibility and memory recall are not the same thing. What was put to the appellant at trial was that he had surreptitiously adverted to the version of the "Meningie incident" known as the ménage à trois to Monsignor Cappo. Since that incident never occurred, the appellant was right to say that he never said that.

Moreover, the appellant did not merely **appear to recall** his use of the term ménage à trois. He accurately recalled an event that happened, and his recollection of that event was corroborated by two witnesses. He told the truth.

Justices Vanstone, Nicholson, and Bampton seemingly did not examine closely what was argued in the appellant's submission or the evidence upon which this was based.

The ruling by the appeal judges that Justice Gray was "entitled to the view that the damage was done"

341 *Ibid.*, at paragraph 167.

trivialises the legal process. A court of law is expected to be dedicated to finding the truth. A mistake in the appellant's recollection should not affect the outcome of a search for truth.

Justices Vanstone, Nicholson, and Bampton held:

> **There can be no question that all aspects of the appellant's presentation as a witness were available to the Judge as a basis to assess credibility. The appellant gave evidence which was in conflict with that of a number of other witnesses. The Judge had a good deal of material on the basis of which to assess the appellant's honesty and reliability. His reasons demonstrate that he did so in a dispassionate and measured way.**[342]

However, the appellant's evidence was, in fact, supported by several witnesses who were in a position to know objectively what happened. In contrast, much of the evidence that was at variance with the appellant's was based on hearsay, what either Peter Kay or Jane told, Sue Kay, the Reverend Alan Courtney, and the Reverend David Richardson. The witnesses who supported the appellant's account were there at the time. Their evidence was not based on what someone else had told them. Justices Vanstone, Nicholson, and Bampton seemingly overlooked the fact that the appellant was not wrong in the one matter upon which Justice Gray apparently based his decision about Fleming's credibility.

Secondly, the appeal judges held that "The appellant gave evidence which was in conflict with that of a

342 *Ibid.*, at paragraph 168.

number of other witnesses". Using this as evidence to support the questioning of the appellant's credibility contrasts most unfavourably when compared with the view taken of conflicting evidence given by witnesses for the defence. For example, Peter Kay's evidence conflicted not only with the appellant, but also Alan Courtney (on two crucial matters), Alison Fleming, Arlene Macdonald, Kirsty Henning, and the Reverend Joan Claring-Bould. Why should it not follow, using that logic, that Peter Kay should be disbelieved?

Simply asserting that "The Judge had a good deal of material on the basis of which to assess the appellant's honesty and reliability" does not in itself demonstrate that Justice Gray did so "in a dispassionate and measured way." Evidence for such a "dispassionate and measured" assessment appears to have been lacking as Justices Vanstone, Nicholson, and Bampton did not reference any evidence of it. The fact of the matter is that Justice Gray made his finding based on what he unfairly judged to be Dr Fleming's lack of credibility before he had heard any other witness, and on the single issue of the ménage à trois brouhaha.

One is left with the ineluctable conclusion that the writer or writers of this judgement just didn't do their homework and were wanting to dismiss the appeal and uphold the judicial rectitude of Justice Gray.

When one reads the Gray judgement and the subsequent judgement of the Full Court to which Fleming had appealed one is left to wonder why Justice Gray (with Justices Vanstone, Nicholson, and Bampton accepting on appeal) was so willing to accept that the two Catholic principals, Alison Fleming and Dr Fleming, were likely to be liars and to find, on no basis of fact, that they were not to be trusted?

Jane's statement

As discussed in detail in Chapter 5, Jane stated unequivocally that, based upon her memory, the plaintiff engaged in criminal sexual abuse with her at Meningie. There were no corroborating witnesses to this claim, whereas a witness said to be there at the time of the alleged event corroborated the plaintiff's denial. Despite this, the appeal judges agreed with Justice Gray that this was sufficient to establish the historical allegation as fact.

Even more concerning was that Justices Vanstone, Nicholson, and Bampton utterly failed to question or analyse Justice Gray's acceptance of uncorroborated evidence from Jane.

Judicial prejudice and the Church

While one had an uneasy sense of anti-Catholic hostility throughout these proceedings, nowhere was this clearer than in the judgement of Justices Vanstone, Nicholson, and Bampton. As previously discussed, Peter Kay gave evidence that he had made allegations of homosexual conduct involving Dr Fleming to Archbishop Leonard Faulkner just before Dr Fleming was ordained as a Catholic priest. Archbishop Faulkner investigated the matter, found no reason why Fleming should not be ordained, and the ordination went ahead.

At trial, it was pointed out that Archbishop Faulkner could not have gone ahead with the ordination of

Dr Fleming if he had found evidence of scandalous behaviour on the part of the candidate. The Archbishop was unable to give evidence because of his mental and physical frailty. Justices Vanstone, Nicholson, and Bampton concluded that it would not have made any difference one way or the other in establishing the credibility of Kay's accusations:

> **Furthermore, that the Archbishop allowed the appellant's ordination to proceed in the face of Peter's allegations is, for two reasons, colourless. First, the response of church officials to complaints of sexual misconduct by church functionaries is, now notoriously, problematic. Secondly, whatever its flavour, the Archbishop's opinion of the situation regarding the appellant and his forthcoming ordination is plainly irrelevant.**[343]

First, what is "colourless" meant to convey in this context? Do they mean, as dictionaries define it, that the decision of Archbishop Faulkner is "uninteresting, dull, boring, tedious, monotonous, dry, drab, dreary, wearisome"? What is conveyed here is a deeply disturbing attitude/prejudice to the extremely serious decision of an Archbishop to ordain a man to the diaconate and priesthood of the Catholic Church.

Second, Justices Vanstone, Nicholson, and Bampton say: "the response of church officials to complaints of sexual misconduct by church functionaries is, now notoriously, problematic". This is seriously wrong

343 Justices Vanstone, Nicholson, and Bampton judgement at paragraph 120.

on two counts. Judges have no business appealing to popular prejudice ("notoriously") to justify the position they want to adopt, and it is logically impermissible for anyone, including judges, to argue from the general to the specific in the way that they do. For example, from the observation that Australians are generally known to be peaceful, it does not follow that this man or woman in front of me must be peaceful. And nor does it follow from what could be described as a prejudiced assertion "that the response of church officials to complaints of sexual misconduct by church functionaries is, now notoriously, problematic", that the particular response of this Archbishop in this case was problematic.

Third, they simply state, without reason, that the Archbishop's investigations and conclusions are "plainly irrelevant". Why would they not be relevant? No reason is given. The Archbishop's investigations and conclusions would certainly have assisted the appellant. One could argue that would be reason enough for them to be considered. More importantly, the Archbishop's conclusions would have assisted the discovery of the truth about what really happened. Is the truth to be regarded as "uninteresting, dull, boring, tedious, monotonous, dry, drab, dreary, wearisome" where a religious figure is concerned? The question must then be raised that if so, why were the findings of the Anglican clerics, the Reverends Courtney and Richardson not also depicted as colourless and irrelevant?

Justices Vanstone, Nicholson, and Bampton argued from the universal presumption that all Catholic clergy fail in governance, to form the particular judgment that as Archbishop Faulkner was a member of the

Catholic clergy, he therefore must have failed in regard to governance matters involving Dr Fleming. Such a view can be argued to be based on nothing other than an ill informed and biased view of the Catholic Church. Evidence given at the *Royal Commission into Institutional Responses into Child Sexual Abuse*[344] (the Royal Commission) indicated that the Archdiocese of Adelaide positively stood out among the other dioceses in Australia in its practices and outcomes. Here is a clear indication of the danger of allowing ill-informed prejudice to influence reasoning, particularly when holding such an important role as a judge. Unfortunately, the findings of the Royal Commission were not available to Justices Vanstone, Nicholson, and Bampton, but that does nothing to lessen the egregious nature of their prejudice and the impact on their judgement of this case.

On the morning of the seventh of February 2017, four expert witnesses gave evidence to the Royal Commission, two of whom were Professors Ormerod and Moloney. Neither were strangers to the problematic way some bishops and religious congregations dealt with complaints of child sexual abuse.

Professor Neil Ormerod was an academic mathematician but is now a Professor of Theology at the Australian Catholic University. He is a layman and married. In his evidence Professor Ormerod said this:

> **There were a number of us who were sort of living in a communal sort of setting. I met**

---

344 Transcript of the Royal Commission into Institutional Responses to Child Sexual Abuse, *Public Hearing - Case Study 50 (Day 243)*, the 7th of February 2017.

> **my wife in that setting, my future wife. We married. Some 12 years later, she revealed to me that the priest who was at the centre of that community had sexualised his relationship with her, and that set in train my interest in the issue of clergy sexual abuse.**[345]

As a married couple, Professor Ormerod and his wife, Thea, were able to assist other victims of sexual abuse, not only those who were abused as adults. Together with his wife, Professor Ormerod wrote "what's probably the first book on sexual abuse in the Australian context."[346] That book is titled, *When Ministers Sin,* and was published in 1995.[347]

During the course of his evidence Professor Ormerod made the following statement in relation to the Catholic Archdiocese of Adelaide and the leadership and governance carried out by Archbishop Leonard Faulkner and Archbishop Philip Wilson.

> **The other interesting thing, of course, is what was the *lowest diocese in Australia,* and that was Adelaide. Now, ask ourselves what is it that is special about Adelaide?**[348]

---

345 Transcript of the Royal Commission into Institutional Responses to Child Sexual Abuse, *Public Hearing - Case Study 50 (Day 243),* the 7th of February 2017, at page 24839.

346 *Ibid.,* at page 24840.

347 Neil and Thea Ormerod, *When Ministers Sin,* Morehouse Pub Co, New York.

348 Transcript of the Royal Commission into Institutional Responses to Child Sexual Abuse, *Public Hearing - Case Study 50 (Day 243),* the 7th of February 2017, at page 24854.

Here, Professor Ormerod is referring to a report published by the Royal Commission which, *inter alia,* deals with the numbers of complaints of child sexual abuse made in each Catholic Diocese. The Archdiocese of Adelaide has, by far and away, the smallest number of cases of allegations of child sexual abuse.[349]

Professor Ormerod goes on to consider why it might be that the record in the Archdiocese of Adelaide is so much better than any other diocese in the Catholic Church in Australia.

> **Why is Adelaide so different? Now, those of us who know the history somewhat of Adelaide know that when Leonard Faulkner was made Archbishop in 1985, he was asked whether he wanted an auxiliary bishop, and he said, no, he didn't want an auxiliary bishop, he didn't need an auxiliary bishop, but he set up a pastoral team around him as Bishop, as Archbishop, of that diocese, which included a number of women. So that became a team in ministry between himself and those women. That's a decision that he made. Now, the priests at the diocese at the time didn't like it, but I think you begin to see some of the effect of that if you look at the continuing practice of Philip Wilson, who is the current archbishop there. He continues to have women in**

---

349 Royal Commission into Institutional Responses to Child Sexual Abuse, *Analysis of Claims of Child Sexual Abuse Made with Respect to Catholic Church Institutions in Australia,* June 2017, SBN: 978-1-925622-22-5 Commonwealth of Australia 2017.

> **senior leadership roles within the diocese, and I think that's a significant factor of difference in that data from other dioceses in Australia.**[350]

Responding to questions put to him by the Chair of the Royal Commission as to why this innovative style of Episcopal governance was not popular with the clergy, Professor Ormerod said:

> **Well, you're talking about a very male culture, and suddenly to find that there are women in the diocese who have authority over them was not something that a lot of them appreciated. But the figures that you have bear out that there was a significant cultural difference in that diocese from every other diocese in Australia.**[351]

Professor Ormerod then went on to elaborate why such a move introduced by Archbishop Faulkner was extraordinary in the Catholic Church in Australia, the impact that it had had, and that his successor, Archbishop Wilson, had continued with this practice until his retirement.

In all this evidence given to the Royal Commission into Institutional Responses to Child Sexual Abuse, Professor Ormerod was supported by Professor Francis James Maloney. Professor Maloney was also highly experienced in matters of child sexual abuse having been

---

350 Transcript of the Royal Commission into Institutional Responses to Child Sexual Abuse, *Public Hearing - Case Study 50 (Day 243)*, the 7th of February 2017, at pages 24854 – 24855.

351 *Ibid.*, at page 24855.

given the job of sorting out the mess (in relation to child sexual abuse) in the Salesian Order of which he was a member and served as Provincial Superior (2006 – 2011).

Not only was Professor Maloney's evidence complimentary of Archbishop Faulkner and the way that he administered the Archdiocese of Adelaide, but he also commended Archbishop Wilson who continued this innovative approach to the Episcopal governance of the local Church.

It is suggested that it might be timely for a review to be conducted, examining the extent and nature of prejudice that is evident in court judgements. The question must be raised as to why it is apparently legitimate for judges to import public prejudice into the reasons they give for their judgements, prejudice with which they obviously agree, or they wouldn't be appealing to it. One trusts that it is not widespread but, in this case, for example, it was strongly evident, very disturbing, and ultimately detrimental to a fair hearing.

Assessment of Dr Arnold's evidence[352]

Justices Vanstone, Nicholson, and Bampton treated the grounds of appeal in relation to the expert Dr Arnold with what can only be described as contempt. They addressed the expert witness issues in twelve short paragraphs, nearly all of which are a reiteration of Justice Gray's conclusions. Nowhere do we find evidence that Justices Vanstone, Nicholson, and Bampton took

352 Justices Vanstone, Nicholson, and Bampton *judgement* at paragraphs 155-161.

any account whatsoever of the substantial problems associated with Justice Gray on this matter and which formed a crucial part of the grounds for appeal.

This is what the Full Court said about this matter in their judgement on the appeal against Justice Gray:

> ***We do not consider*** that one could sit as a Judge for more than a decade and yet be ignorant of the dangers of reconstructed memory, memory influenced by counsellors and other confidantes, selective memory and exaggeration. **The sorts of matters highlighted by Dr Arnold were the very things which the Judge would have been alive to** in any event. **Expert witnesses such as Dr Arnold are called**, not to assume the function of a judge, but **to assist the judge in his or her decision**. Particularly in circumstances where, perhaps through inexperience, Dr Arnold had **seemingly taken a partisan view** to the matter, we consider that no criticism can attach to the Judge in his finding that the expert evidence was not of assistance.[353]

The Full Court, Justices Vanstone, Nicholson, and Bampton, employ the same imperious tone as Justice Gray. Look at the language they employ. "We do not consider". The arrogance is breath-taking. Judges are not meant to be giving evidence. Their opinion or what they "consider" has nothing to do with "fact" but everything

353 Justices Vanstone, Nicholson, and Bampton *judgement* at paragraphs 155-161.

to do with their own personal attitudes, their ignorance of the science, and their need to support each other. It proves nothing to make a general statement about judges with experience of a decade or more and then conclude to the particular judges in this particular case. It has nothing to do with fact to say in general what a judge would "be alive to" and then conclude that the particular judge involved in this case was indeed "alive" to the issues involved, and especially where all the evidence points in a contrary direction.

This is an incorrect inductive argument. Inductive arguments differ from deductive arguments in that the arguer is asserting the truth of the conclusion as probable or probably true. Note that probability could be very low to very high.

The Full Court simply claimed that what they have said about judges in general is unquestionably true. In the absence of evidence, that cannot be said and so the probability of their conclusion may well be very low.

With deductive arguments, you can always add further premisses to make the conclusion even more certain. Not so with an inductive argument. Nothing can be added to make the inference more certain.

To make the kinds of conclusions that Justices Vanstone, Nicholson, and Bampton claim to make, one would need to have regard to the evidence in relation to the terms of the appeal as set out by counsel for Dr Fleming. The present writer is unable to conclude from the judgement of Justices Vanstone, Nicholas, and Bampton that that is certainly what those judges did. It was not shown by evidence that Dr Arnold was partisan and there is no evidence in the written judgement of the Full Court that Justices Vanstone, Nicholas, and Bampton did what they were meant to do, critically evaluate the evidence for that themselves.

Then we have the *tour de force* by these judges:

> **Expert witnesses such as Dr Arnold are called, not to assume the function of a judge, but to assist the judge in his or her decision.**

What on earth does this mean? The judge is there as a finder of fact. He is not there "to assume the function of" an expert! Judges do not know it all where facts outside of their area of expertise are concerned. The judge can only be assisted by an expert if he or she is prepared to listen carefully to what he or she is being told. In this case Justice Gray, and therefore the other three judges, Justices Vanstone, Nicholson, and Bampton were given uncontradicted evidence, richly referenced to the latest scientific literature. They chose not to listen. Instead, Justices Vanstone, Nicholas, and Bampton gave evidence which they are not entitled to do. You can't assist people who think they know what they don't know. That giant of human philosophy and wisdom, the great Socrates

> … concluded that he was better off than his fellow citizens because, while they thought they knew something and did not, he was aware of his own ignorance. The god who speaks through the oracle, he says, is truly wise, whereas human wisdom is worth little or nothing (Apology 23a).
>
> This awareness of one's own absence of knowledge is what is known as Socratic ignorance, and it is arguably the thing for which Socrates is most famous.

> Socratic ignorance is sometimes called simple ignorance, to be distinguished from the double ignorance of the citizens with whom Socrates spoke. **Simple ignorance is being aware of one's own ignorance, whereas double ignorance is not being aware of one's ignorance while thinking that one knows.** In showing many influential figures in Athens that they did not know what they thought they did, Socrates came to be despised in many circles.[354]

Of course, the judge is called upon to make final decisions and, where conflicting experts are concerned, evaluate which expert has the better claim to have a case. But this expert, Dr Arnold, presented an uncontradicted account of the science of memory, and drew the right and salient conclusions when applying the science to the evidence before her. She was accused of being a "partisan" on no basis of fact whatsoever as we shall see in the next section. "No one loves the messenger who brings bad news", [στέργει γὰρ οὐδεὶς ἄγγελον κακῶν ἐπῶν.][355]

A detailed submission was prepared by the appellant outlining the deficiencies of Justice Gray's treatment of Dr Arnold's evidence, as discussed in Chapter 7. For example, the central issue of whether Jane was influenced by her counsellor, Anglican cleric the Reverend

354 *Internet Encyclopedia of Philosophy: A Peer-Reviewed Academic Resource*, http://www.iep.utm.edu/socrates/

355 Sophocles, *The Antigone of Sophocles*, "Line 277". Edited with introduction and notes by Sir Richard Jebb. Cambridge University Press, 1891.

John Stephenson, was addressed in detail in written submissions made to the Full Court. As previously discussed, this was one of the main reasons why Justice Gray rejected Dr Arnold as a witness.

The trial judge said at [J380] that he was cautious about accepting Dr Arnold's views but "[i]n any event, I do not think that I am assisted by them". Dr Arnold's expertise was unchallenged. Her evidence as to how memory works was unchallenged. Her evidence was that it does not function like a video recorder and that there is no scientific evidence that links bodily expressions of memory to specific past events.

The unchallenged expert evidence was that one of the dangers regarding a person attempting to recollect long-ago abusive events "is the potential for reinterpretation of the long-ago events. Specifically, reinterpretation involves a person – consciously or unconsciously – distorting a past event in a way that becomes consistent with that person's current beliefs." Dr Arnold could see "clear examples of reinterpretation across Jane's own statements". Justice Gray made no reference to this evidence.[356]

At paragraph 381, in the context of the influence of therapists or suggestive therapeutic techniques leading to false or recovered memories, Justice Gray discussed Dr Arnold's opinion that the Reverend John Stephenson,

356 One such "clear example" was that Jane reinterpreted the significance of the plaintiff having kept a letter that she wrote to him at the time she was seeking to adopt a baby. It went from *"her strong desire for a child motivating her to write a person she deemed important enough to help her case, to reinterpreting the event as evidence of sinister motives on Father* Fleming*'s part and his desire to potentially harm her"*: Dr Arnold report at page 6.

as a counsellor, may have influenced the accuracy and reliability of Jane's memory. Justice Gray concluded that the references in Dr Arnold's report to Jane's earlier statements "provided no support for Dr Arnold's hypothesis that Father John Stephenson influenced Jane's memory in that or any other respect". The sole basis for Justice Gray's conclusion is that "Jane's evidence to this Court did not seek to assert the location of the first incident as anywhere other than a place in the Coorong". Jane says that after the police interviewed the plaintiff, the plaintiff had identified Meningie and that the police had told her of that". The judgment references transcript at page 1368 lines 13-15 and transcript at page 1641 lines 32-37.

Now, the transcript[357] reveals the following:

> **Harris: Where did you go with the McNicols?**
>
> **Jane: I am not sure where it was but it was, it was at the Coorong.**
>
> **Harris: The Coorong.**
>
> **Jane: Yes.**
>
> **Harris: I'll come back to that in a moment but who made the journey …**
>
> **Harris: In more recent times have you made inquiries to identify the location at which you went with the McNicols.**
>
> **Jane: The – when I spoke to the police they told me that it was, that it was Meningie and I –**

357 *Transcript of evidence given in Court* at page 1368 lines 13-32.

It is clear from reading the transcript of the cross-examination of Jane on this topic[358] and considering other evidence, that Jane is mistaken as to when and who assisted her.

The signed SAPOL statement of Mr Stephenson dated 7 May 2008,[359] was made some six months before SAPOL interviewed Dr Fleming.

Mr Stephenson's evidence is that Jane came to lunch in February 2008 [so only a few months before Mr Stephenson made his SAPOL statement]:

> **The purpose of the contact with me was to help her remember where an incident might have taken place with FLEMING. She said to me that she had gone down to one of the parishes in the South East with the McNICOL family and FLEMING. She said that she could remember the house description but not the church. She said that the house was a standard small country rectory. She described burnt limestone walls, double-fronted with the door in middle. I thought that the rectory was near the beach, but have since discovered that I was confusing this conversation with a previous one about FLEMING. I though (sic) it was likely to have been situated at MENINGIE or KINGSTON but I now think it was most probably MENINGIE. I have**

358 *Transcript of evidence given in Court* from page 1640 line 18 to page 1643 line7.

359 Exhibit P71 *Rev John Stephenson's statement to SAPOL,* 7th May 2008.

> **since asked the Bishop, Stuart SMITH, who is responsible for the Murray Lands, if he could check for me if FLEMING'S name is in the rectory for MENINGIE or KINGSTON. I believed the books have been archived or still in the church. I cannot remember the year I requested. I have not received an answer back yet from Bishop SMITH.**[360]

It is clear from that evidence that by 7 May 2008 Mr Stephenson thought that "it was most probably Meningie". Given that his SAPOL statement was signed only 3 months after his luncheon with Jane and given that the "purpose of the contact with me was to help her remember where an incident might have taken place", a fair inference is that Mr Stephenson is likely to have told Jane that he thought that "it was most probably Meningie".

Contrary to Jane's evidence,[361] it certainly is **not** the case that at her "first formal" police interview in September 2007 the police told her that Dr Fleming had identified Meningie. The police did not speak to Dr Fleming until more than a year later (November 2008). That Jane, at the very least, is confused about all of this is made apparent when she later says at Transcript page 1641 lines 32-37 (which evidence is referred to in footnote 395 of the Judgment) that it was not during the occasion of the police interview in September 2007 the police told her. It was on another occasion "they definitely told me

360 Exhibit P71, *Rev John Stephenson's statement to SAPOL*, 7th May 2008, Pages 3-4.

361 *Transcript of evidence given in Court* at page 1641 lines 1-10.

that it was – that Dr Fleming had said Meningie". As in truth bound to do, Dr Fleming did volunteer to police, during his interview in November 2008, that he had gone on a *locum* to Meningie at the end of his time as curate at the Brighton parish in January 1971. But in light of the evidence of Mr Stephenson, Jane is mistaken when she is asked this question and gave this answer:[362]

> ***Heywood-Smith*: Do I understand from that you had no assistance at all from John Stephenson of the identification of Meningie?**
>
> **Jane: None at all.**

Consequently, Justice Gray erred in finding at paragraph 381 of his judgement that there is "no support for Dr Arnold's hypothesis that Stephenson influenced Jane's memory in that or any other respect".

Dr Arnold's hypothesis (at p5 of her Report) is cross-referenced to various records of hearing:

> **In December 2003, Jane's Anglican Church interview (p2) refers only to the first event as happening "in the country";**
>
> **In October 2007, in Jane's SAPOL statement (p8-9) she refers to the first event as happening in the country, but then says she is "unsure of the name of the town";**
>
> **In February 2008, Jane has lunch with Fr Stephenson and the "purpose of the contact with me was to help her remember where an incident might have taken place";**[363]

362 *Transcript of evidence given in Court* at page 1641 lines 10-12.

363 Exhibit P71, *Stephenson's* SAPOL statement at page 3

By 7 May 2008, Fr Stephenson says he thinks "it was most probably Meningie" and he has asked the bishop to check for Fr Fleming's name in the records of the Kingston and Meningie parishes;

In November 2008, Fr Fleming has his first (and only) interview with SAPOL.

When cross-examined about these matters, Jane was asked these questions and gave these answers at transcript page 1642 lines 10-32:

Heywood-Smith: I will ask it again, on no occasion did you ever tell anybody that you had assistance from John Stephenson in identifying Meningie as the country, destination?

Jane: Once the police had told me that he [Fleming] had said Meningie, John Stephenson did go to the Anglican archives to look at the Meningie register. But, you know, your honour, can I explain why I'm getting upset? John Stephenson was one of the most…

Heywood-Smith: The question however had nothing to do with John Stephenson's integrity, the question was simply: did he assist you in identifying Meningie as the source, as the destination.

Jane: I'm sorry, I must be misinterpreting your tone of voice. I apologise.

> **Heywood-Smith: I understand from your answer that it was: no, he didn't other than after John Fleming had identified it.**
>
> **Jane: That's correct. I apologise.**

The evidence of the correct sequence of events is incontrovertible: after lunching with Jane in February 2008 and **before** the 7th of May 2008 when he gave his signed statement to SAPOL, the Reverend John Stephenson had asked Bishop Smith "if he could check for me if Fleming's name is in the rectory for Meningie or Kingston. I believed the books have been archived or still in the church."[364]

This incontrovertible fact demonstrates that the trial judge's conclusion at paragraph 381 of his judgement is erroneous when he avers that it was **only after** the police had spoken to Fleming was Meningie identified. Consequently, to use this finding as the basis for his dismissal of Dr Arnold's evidence was an error, and a serious one at that. Furthermore, the judge wrongly made a subtle change in Dr Arnold's opinion in his last sentence of paragraph 381 in that Dr Arnold's hypothesis has been mutated from "Fr Stephenson may have influenced" to "Fr Stephenson influenced". Dr Arnold always said that that there were two sources of

---

364 Thus, Jane's evidence to the Court is plainly wrong that *Stephenson* did not assist her about the identification of Meningie other than **after** Fleming had identified it to police in November 2008 and that "*once the police had told me that he had said Meningie, John Stephenson did go to the Anglican archives to look at the Meningie register*". It is incontrovertible that months **before** police spoke with Fr Fleming, *Stephenson* had asked the relevant bishop to consult the archives for Kingston and Meningie parishes to "*check for me if* Fleming'*s name is in the rectory for Meningie or Kingston*".

information as to the identification of Meningie.[365] Dr Arnold did not deny that there were other influences apart from Mr Stephenson[366] but she correctly stated that the plaintiff via the police "wasn't the original source".[367] Dismissing the possibility that Mr Stephenson may have "influenced Jane's memory in that or any other respect" means that the trial judge did not properly consider Dr Arnold's opinion on the possible impact a counsellor may have on the reliability of a person's memory of long-ago events. This Court "must not shrink from giving effect to" its own conclusions.[368]

Justice Gray got wrong a crucial piece of evidence in relation to Dr Arnold's evidence, an error that not only had major negative implications for Dr Arnold's credibility in Justice Gray's eyes, but for the entire case being brought by the appellant. There is no evidence that Justices Vanstone, Nicholson, and Bampton adequately checked the references in the submission prepared for them by the appellant which outlined where Justice Gray erred.

> **We do not consider that one could sit as a Judge for more than a decade and yet be ignorant of the dangers of reconstructed memory, memory influenced by counsellors and other confidantes, selective memory and exaggeration. The sorts of matters highlighted by Dr Arnold were the very**

365 Transcript of evidence given in Court at page 2683 line 31.

366 *Transcript of evidence given in Court* at page 2685, page 2688, and page 2718.

367 *Transcript of evidence given in Court* at page 2718 line 5.

368 *Fox v Percy* (2003) 214 CLR 118 at 28 [29].

> **things which the Judge would have been alive to in any event. Expert witnesses such as Dr Arnold are called, not to assume the function of a judge, but to assist the judge in his or her decision. Particularly in circumstances where, perhaps through inexperience, Dr Arnold had seemingly taken a partisan view to the matter, we consider that no criticism can attach to the Judge in his finding that the expert evidence was not of assistance.**[369]
>
> **This ground of appeal is not made out.**[370]

This reads more as a defence of the assumed superiority of judges, and apparently it was deemed not necessary to include any detailed reasoning for the dismissal of this ground of appeal. These are extraordinary assertions with no evidence provided to support them. Contrary to what Justices Vanstone, Nicholson, and Bampton asserted, there was no evidence that Justice Gray was "alive" to these things.

Imperiously Justices Vanstone, Nicholson, and Bampton held: "Expert witnesses such as Dr Arnold are called, not to assume the function of a judge, but to assist the judge in his or her decision." Well might others say:

> **Judges such as Justices Vanstone, Nicholson, and Bampton and Justice Gray are called, not to assume the function of experts, but to**

369 Justices Vanstone, Nicholson, and Bampton *judgement* paragraph 160.

370 *Ibid.*, paragraph 261.

> **accept the assistance that experts necessarily provide for them especially when their evidence is uncontroverted.**

Justice Gray was cautious about accepting Dr Arnold's views, but, and this is the gravamen of Justice Gray's opinions where Dr Arnold is concerned, "in any event I do not think that I am assisted by them". Justices Vanstone, Nicholson, and Bampton in their judgement simply parrot Justice Gray's views: "In any event, he said that he did not think that he was assisted by them."[371] One cannot assist people who don't know what they don't know and who seem impervious to the knowledge that would correct them.

In his judgement, Justice Gray held that Dr Arnold could not say that what Jane "was describing was a consequence of a false memory",[372] but as the appellant's counsel pointed out to Justices Vanstone, Nicholson, and Bampton, that was inconsequential in the required assessment of the evidence by the trial judge. Dr Arnold could not say definitively that Jane was, in fact, describing a false memory because Dr Arnold did not have access to certain material such as what Jane had sent to the Reverend John Stephenson[373] or to Jane's diaries. Dr Arnold stated she never saw this as a recovered memory.[374] That it is not a repressed or recovered memory did not change the "red flags of memory" Dr Arnold identified in respect of reliability.[375] "Regardless

371 *Ibid.*, paragraph 380.

372 Justice Gray *judgement* at 381.

373 Exhibit P71, *Stephenson* SAPOL statement, at page 2.

374 *Transcript of evidence given in Court* at page 2860 line 31.

375 *Transcript of evidence given in Court* at page 2662 line 34

of whether you call it repressed memory or not, actually doesn't matter. What you're looking at is the memory experience itself."[376] Dr Arnold's evidence was that Jane's description of her memories did not fit with what she argued was how memory works scientifically.

Justices Vanstone, Nicholson, and Bampton held:

> **Dr Arnold gave evidence about the way in which memory can be distorted and, in some cases, can be entirely false. She did not assert that Jane's memories were false, but identified what she called "red flags" in the material she had seen: t/s 2650.**[377]

This suggests that the appeal judges gave little consideration to this fundamental element of the appeal. There was no sign that these judges understood what was the reach, the scope, and the importance of the "red flags" identified by Dr Arnold in the light of the uncontroverted scientific evidence she made available to the Court.

Evaluation of Peter Kay's evidence

Much can be said about how Justices Vanstone, Nicholson, and Bampton responded to the appellant's concerns with how the Peter Kay allegations were dealt with at trial. For example, Peter Kay claimed that he had shared a room with the appellant on University Anglican Society camps (*plural*).

376 *Transcript of evidence given in Court* at page 2663 line 8.

377 Justices Vanstone, Nicholson, and Bampton *judgement* at paragraph 156.

As was the case with Jane's evidence, a similar pattern emerged when looking at the key pieces of evidence the plaintiff gave in Court, and elsewhere, in relation to Peter Kay. The plaintiff was corroborated in all that he said, whereas no corroboration was given in support of Peter Kay. The witnesses called by the defence repeated stories told to them by Peter Kay himself, and as has already been shown, they seem to have been told different stories about what was meant to be the same subject.

The Plaintiff's evidence and corroborating evidence re Peter Kay

Subject	Corroborated by	Contradicted by	Could have supported Fleming but dead or indisposed
The plaintiff did not share a room with Peter Kay at Anglican Society camps.	Arlene Macdonald, Rev A Courtney, Kirsty Henning, Rev Joan Claring-Bould	Peter Kay	
The plaintiff's evidence re Kay's sexual advance in Wheaton Road.	Peter Kay, Archbishop Faulkner in so far as he decided after investigation to ordain Fleming		Canon Russell Cameron was told about it by Dr Fleming at the time it occurred but deceased by time of trial. Archbishop Faulkner, but he was unable to give evidence because of mental defect.
Peter Kay did not stay behind in Dr Fleming's St Mark's flat after Anglican Society meetings.	Arlene Macdonald, Kirsty Henning, Rev Joan Claring-Bould	Peter Kay	
The plaintiff's evidence of conversation with Sue Kay re Dr Fleming's relationship with her husband.	Sue Kay		

The plaintiff's evidence of conversation with Alan Courtney re Dr Fleming's relationship with Kay	Alan Courtney (but with two important exceptions)		
The plaintiff's evidence that he made admissions to no one re Kay's allegations		Alan Courtney's evidence contradicted Fleming. On the one hand, he said he had never discussed specifics with Dr Fleming, but later said that Dr Fleming agreed he had been involved in mutual masturbation with Kay. There were no witnesses to this conversation and nor were notes made of it.	
The plaintiff's denial of sexual relationship with Kay as he, Kay, described it	Archbishop Faulkner in so far as he decided after investigation to ordain Fleming,	Peter Kay; Sue Kay and Alan Courtney told the court what they said Peter Kay had told them. Peter Kay had told each of them different stories.	Archbishop Faulkner could not give evidence due to loss of mental acuity. Canon Russell Cameron, deceased

The Anglican cleric Alan Courtney, the key and only possible corroborative witness in this matter, unambiguously contradicted Kay's allegations. Moreover, Kay's allegation was comprehensively rejected by other witnesses who also attended those camps. Justices Vanstone, Nicholson, and Bampton held:

> The respondents called Father Courtney in relation to another topic, but led no evidence from him about the camp at Mylor. However, in cross-examination, the appellant's counsel asked Father Courtney whether he had been asked to share a room with either Peter or

> the appellant, or both, at one of the camps he had attended, and he denied it. The appellant also called evidence from **several female church stalwarts**, who were involved in the organisation of the camp, to the effect that, at such camps, the appellant invariably slept alone in separate accommodation.[378]

Why the patronising reference to "several female Church stalwarts"?[379] In using such terms, it is suggested that Justices Vanstone, Nicholson, and Bampton were implying that these witnesses were unable to tell the truth because they were obsessively "loyal". But no evidence was presented to the Court to support such an implication. The question must be asked why Justices Vanstone, Nicholson, and Bampton used language which is inaccurate, patronising, and dismissive in tone, and perhaps more worryingly, why they thought that they had the right to do so. These were adult witnesses, students at the time of the alleged events, present at the camps referred to, had personal knowledge of the way these camps were organised, and are all now distinguished professional people. They deserved to be treated with respect. Next,

> The Judge referred to this topic at [243]–[246]. He noted that Father Courtney had given "**a bare denial**" of being invited to share a room with Peter or the appellant on any occasion. However, the Judge added that Father

378 *Ibid.*, at paragraph 122

379 Stalwart: "a loyal, reliable, and hard-working supporter of or participant in an organization or team".

> Courtney had not been fully cross-examined about that.[380]

The evidence was clear. Alan Courtney categorically denied Peter Kay's evidence. But if Justice Gray had considered more was needed, he could have asked for it himself and counsel could have further developed the matter in redirect. In any case, judges deal with the evidence before them, not what in their imagination they might think it might be. Alan Courtney's denial was backed up by other witnesses meaning that it was not a "bare denial". Either he was in the room or not and was invited to share with either or both Peter Kay and the appellant or he was not.

> The appellant argues that here was an occasion when the evidence of a third party might have given independent support to Peter's account of events, but fell short of doing so. **The appellant complains that the Judge should have, but did not find that Father Courtney's denial of any such invitation undermined Peter's credibility**. And it is put that, by referring to the limited cross-examination of Father Courtney, the Judge was effectively throwing the onus on the appellant to disprove the underlying allegation.[381]

As argued, Justice Gray **was** doing just that, and that was his general approach to the appellant throughout his

380 Justices Vanstone, Nicholson, and Bampton *judgement* at paragraph, 123.

381 *Ibid.*, at paragraph 124.

judgement, as has already been shown. The appellant stated that Alan Courtney's evidence **contradicted** that of Peter Kay on that point. It is difficult to understand why these judges could not deal properly with the evidence on this matter if it was not to continue to show preference to "principal witnesses" like Peter Kay and in the face of all the evidence which told against their account of the matter.

> **We find no force in these arguments**. Indeed, the ground, as it stands, suggests that there was some obligation upon the respondents to cover this topic when leading the evidence of Father Courtney. **That is a misconception**. In any event, Father Courtney's denial of there being such an occasion might or might not have any significance. He was looking back over events which occurred some 40 years ago. He could hardly be expected to recall a suggestion or invitation that he sleep at a particular place where it meant nothing to him. The Judge was entitled to the view that his denial added nothing.[382]

There is no argument here, just assertion. "We find no force in these arguments" but no explanation is proffered for this conclusion. A key point of Peter Kay's allegations was that he and the appellant shared a room not at just one camp, but at camps, plural. The appellant, although not required to, provided witnesses at trial to attest the event never happened. At trial, the onus was on the defendant to prove the event had occurred.

382 *Ibid.*, at paragraph 125.

Justices Vanstone, Nicholson, and Bampton, however, held:

> **In any event, Father Courtney's denial of there being such an occasion might or might not have any significance. He was looking back over events which occurred some 40 years ago. He could hardly be expected to recall a suggestion or invitation that he sleep at a particular place where it meant nothing to him. The Judge was entitled to the view that his denial added nothing.**[383]

This was the first time that the issue of memory being faulty based on recalling events of 40 years ago as in the case of Jane and more than 30 years ago in the case of Peter Kay was raised. The memory problems of events of many years ago were invoked solely to undermine the appellant's case. At no point was Dr Fleming allowed to have even the slightest problem with memory, no matter how minor, without being blamed for it.

There are several incidents which would have meant nothing to Dr Fleming at the time but for which he was held to be accountable for even the smallest error in remembering them. A slight difference with the recollections of Peter Kay or Sue Kay is a deliberate fault by either Dr Fleming or Alison Fleming. Jane was always excused problems with memory even when concerning memories which, if true, would have been of great significance to her. Considering this, it is difficult

383 *Ibid.*, at paragraph 125.

to comprehend that the appeal judges could conclude as they did.

> **We do not apprehend any issue in relation to the onus of proof. That other witnesses confirmed that the usual accommodation arrangements at such camps were that the appellant would have his own room could hardly determine the issue. Those witnesses faced the same difficulties as Father Courtney. In any event, even if that were the usual practice, those persons would hardly be in a position to know that it was followed invariably.**[384]

One must question how they could not "apprehend" any issue in relation to the onus of proof. Throughout the trial, the appellant had to prove his innocence, that is, that alleged incidents had *not* occurred, not the defendant having to prove they had. This approach seemingly was adopted at the appeal stage. Having excused Courtney's contradiction of Kay based on his memory of events 40 years ago, Justices Vanstone, Nicholson, and Bampton concluded that the other witnesses who said the same thing (Arlene Macdonald, Kirsty Henning and Joan Claring-Bould) must have been afflicted by the same memory problem. Apparently, Justices Vanstone, Nicholson, and Bampton and Justice Gray were entitled to simply set aside crucial evidence which was agreed upon by no less than four witnesses, one of whom was a favoured "principal or main witness". These witnesses concurred unambiguously with what the appellant stated

384 *Ibid.*, at paragraph 125

was his invariable practice, that he did not share sleeping quarters with students. Then, in a demonstration of what could be deemed as biased, if not malicious, Justices Vanstone, Nicholson, and Bampton held that even if all four witnesses were correct, namely that it was the 'usual' practice, they would hardly be able to know that it was followed "invariably".

The fact is that the four witnesses were there at the camps. Justices Vanstone, Nicholson, and Bampton were not at those camps. No one said anything other than this practice was always followed. All four were clear and definite about what was the "invariable" practice. Justices Vanstone, Nicholson, and Bampton, disgracefully, drew conclusions clearly contrary to the evidence provided to them.

Full Court's response to the grounds of appeal regarding Jane's evidence

The principal grounds of appeal that concerned Jane's evidence referred to glaring instances of inconsistency to the point of self-contradiction, to the non-availability of crucial witnesses due to death and incapacity (a function of the long delay between alleged events and the reporting of them), and to not only the lack of corroboration but the directly contrary evidence of the only person who could have corroborated Jane. Justices Vanstone, Nicholson, and Bampton commenced their consideration of the appeal with:

> **Ground 2 complains that the Judge's findings that the Meningie and St Mark's incidents were proved were "against the**

evidence and the weight of the evidence ...". We are prepared to treat that assertion as equivalent to a claim that it was not open to the Judge to make those findings in the face of deficiencies and weaknesses in Jane's evidence, as particularised. The principal argument made by the appellant rests on inconsistencies between what Jane told the Judge, as against what she had said in various interviews, not only with police, but also with a number of church personnel or agents over a period commencing in July 2002 and finishing with an interview with Mr Greg Cannons, instructed by the Anglican Church Professional Standards Committee on 5 May 2010. These had been recorded and committed to writing. In addition it is argued that inadequate reasons were given for discounting them.[385]

The purpose underlying those interviews is not always clear. The number of them and the manner in which they were conducted reflects no credit on the Anglican or Catholic Churches. Nonetheless, the appellant was entitled to crossexamine (*sic*) Jane on them and to highlight any inconsistencies as between her evidence and prior statements. There was a significant amount of such crossexamination (*sic*) and almost

385 Justices Vanstone, Nicholson, and Bampton *judgement* at paragraph 138.

> **invariably Jane acknowledged the prior statements put to her. Notwithstanding her acknowledgments, counsel for the appellant tendered all the statements and they were admitted without objection. This had the unfortunate result that, instead of being treated as merely documents which were the source of the contradictory statements put to Jane, they seemed to assume – at least in counsel's eyes – an undeserved status. If their tender meant that the appellant could rely on additional suggested inconsistencies appearing in the documents but not put to Jane, then these documents were also available to show that there was an underlying consistency in the essential account Jane gave of the course of events involving the appellant.**[386]

In the first instance it can be deemed more than somewhat puzzling that it was "not always clear" to Justices Vanstone, Nicholson, and Bampton what the purpose was of a range of interviews given by Jane that contained allegations of relevance to the appeal. Not only were the purposes of the interviews they conducted clear in the light of those Churches' obligation to take reports of sexual abuse seriously, but they were carried out professionally. Further, to question the number of interviews and how they were conducted, with no further elaboration, could be considered an unfounded and unnecessary attack on both Churches concerned.

386 *Ibid.*, at paragraph 139.

Justices Vanstone, Nicholson, and Bampton went on to assert that these documents assumed an undeserved status in the eyes of the appellant's counsel. No clarification or support of this assertion was provided. It was also suggested that if the documents could be used by the appellant to show inconsistency, they could equally stand as evidence for the other side showing consistency of an account. That might be possible if the inconsistencies were minor, but the material cited by the appeal judges showed evidence of critical inconsistencies, going to the heart of Jane's story. The judges did not demonstrate in what manner the evidence could also show a consistent account. The inconsistencies relied on in relation to the Meningie incident included that in evidence Jane said that when Alison was kissing the appellant she, Jane, was sitting on the bed with her hand on the appellant's penis; whereas she agreed she had told police (Exhibit P50 pp 11-12) that she was kneeling. **The Judge said that he did not consider that this demonstrated unreliability**: [386]. It was also put to Jane that she had been inconsistent as to which hand she had used to hold the appellant's penis. In evidence, she said it was her left hand, while to police she nominated her right hand. Then, to the Court, Jane said she could not recall the appellant touching his penis, and she could not recall telling Mr Abbott that he did. Next, in her evidence, Jane said that the following morning she used the excuse of "women's business" to explain why she wished to go home, but she had not previously volunteered the use of that excuse. Then, she was inconsistent at various times as to the identity and description of the man who had driven her home from Meningie. Complicating this issue was that Jane had made some inquiries of her own to try and ascertain the driver's identity. Outlining the contradictions on this topic, the Judge said there appeared to be "a degree of reconstruction" about the driver's identity: [390].[387]

Concerns such as these raised by the appellant in relation to Jane's evidence were not analysed by the appeal judges, beyond noting that Justice Gray did not consider the identified inconsistencies as indicating unreliability. Unfortunately, the criteria for "unreliability" were not defined by Justice Gray or by Justices Vanstone, Nicholson, and Bampton.

Possibly the most egregious error of all in this discussion, is that Justices Vanstone, Nicholson, and Bampton made no reference whatsoever to the most important of Jane's inconsistencies in her account of what she said happened at Meningie. Indeed, these were not just inconsistencies, they were contradictions as to place, who was there, and what act was said to have been done, namely whether the "incident" involved fellatio occurring at the beach at the Coorong, or the appellant showing Jane his penis at an unstated place, or one of touching when in a house at Meningie with a third party involved.

It is difficult to understand why these issues of inconsistency were not addressed by the appeal judges, other than to claim:

> **The Judge discussed these matters in a section of the reasons headed "The plaintiff's specific criticisms of Jane's evidence". It was**

387 *Ibid.*, at paragraph 140.

> **not as if he ignored them or overlooked them. It was for him to evaluate them. His Honour found that, taking them all into account, they did not detract from the force of Jane's account: [392]. The Judge was entitled to take that view. In our opinion, none of the inconsistencies is particularly significant when account is taken of the long period of time since the events, the age of Jane at that time, the obvious upset of being questioned on so many occasions about the events, and their inherently disturbing nature.**[388]

The slightest suggestion of a memory failure by the appellant was considered to be significant, whereas the multitude of errors, contradictions and inconsistencies in Jane's evidence are to be overlooked as insignificant because she was upset about being questioned on so many occasions about the events and their inherently disturbing nature. No consideration is given to the possibility that much of Jane's distress may have occurred because she was giving evidence about an incident that had never happened. **None of the four judges apparently considered even the possibility of the distress that the plaintiff may have been enduring in defending himself against, untrue and inconsistent allegations concerning embarrassingly salacious matters.** Judges are meant to be fair and impartial, guided by the evidence. Again, the reversal of onus of proof is clear:

388 *Ibid.*, at paragraph 141.

> **In respect of the Brighton beach incident, where Jane had in a police interview relied on her 'feeling' or 'assumption' that something sexual had happened, the Judge was unable to make a positive finding: [411]. This example demonstrates that, contrary to the assertion in ground 2.3, the Judge reflected that shortcoming in his findings.**[389]

It demonstrates nothing of the kind. What form of logic do Justices Vanstone, Nicholson, and Bampton use to arrive at a conclusion not present in the premisses?

> **Premiss 1: Jane alleges sexual events with Fleming at Brighton Beach.**
>
> **Premiss 2: In a police interview Jane says that the basis for her allegation is her 'feeling' or 'assumption' that something sexual had happened.**
>
> **Conclusion: Because Justice Gray mentioned premiss 2 and couldn't make a positive finding that the Brighton incidents occurred, he dealt with all other allegations (including Meningie and St Mark's) fairly and based upon objective fact.**

The conclusion simply does not follow. There is nothing in the two premisses about Meningie and St Mark's, so they cannot be part of the conclusion. It is simply impermissible for Justices Vanstone, Nicholson, and Bampton to conclude that Justice Gray was in any way entitled to his misinterpretation (to put it mildly)

389 *Ibid.*, at paragraph 142

of the evidence and favour *The Advertiser*. And speaking of misrepresentation, Justices Vanstone, Nicholson, and Bampton began with a misinterpretation of the appellant's submission:

> **The appellant complains in ground 2.4 that, in accepting Jane's evidence of the Meningie incident, the Judge "failed to consider" the contrary evidence of Mrs Alison Fleming to the effect that the two girls slept in a room separate from that occupied by the appellant, and that nothing occurred between them. In fact, his Honour did consider that evidence. He quoted Mrs Fleming as saying the allegation was "absolutely untrue": [393]. He referred to having earlier rejected her evidence where it was contrary to the evidence of Peter's wife: [305]. Although some years had passed since the conversation attested to involving Peter's wife, the appellant and Mrs Fleming (and longer since the Meningie incident), both incidents were of a nature to stay in the memory. His Honour accepted the evidence of Peter's wife over that of the appellant and Mrs Fleming. A finding that he could not accept Mrs Fleming's evidence in one context was bound to flow into other aspects of her evidence. If she was motivated to fashion her evidence to protect the appellant, then her evidence on other topics would be of little assistance. It was not a question of applying some sort of**

> **onus to her evidence, as suggested by Mr HeywoodSmith. The Judge was entitled to choose between the accounts and to take the view that her evidence could not prevent a finding that Jane's account was true. No further reason was required: R v Beard [2004] SASC 411.**[390]

Nowhere did the submissions claim that Justice Gray failed to consider Alison Fleming's evidence. What was submitted was that Justice Gray did not consider Alison Fleming's evidence "**before**" concluding that Jane's account of the alleged event was true.

That was a serious error by Justice Gray, an error compounded by Justices Vanstone, Nicholson, and Bampton who appeared to completely misunderstand this important ground of appeal. The appeal judges gave the impression of refuting an argument, while actually refuting an argument that was not in fact presented by the appellant.

The appellant's written submissions clearly stated:

> **Justice Gray "failed to consider the evidence of the third person involved in the Meningie incident before finding at [392] that Jane's allegation is true."**

In other words:

> **The judge erred in coming to his finding at [J232] that the Meningie incident "is an event that in fact took place" <u>before</u> considering:**

390 *Ibid.*, 143.

- The evidence of the other person (other than the plaintiff, ie Alison Fleming), and
- The expert evidence given by Dr Arnold regarding the memory of events said to have occurred more than 40 years ago. [The emphasis was contained in the original and not added here]

One can seriously question the suggestion by Justices Vanstone, Nicholson, and Bampton that Justice Gray was right to doubt Alison Fleming's credibility because she disagreed with a minor aspect of Sue Kay's memory of a conversation that had occurred 20 years earlier. Further, Justices Vanstone, Nicholson, and Bampton agreed with Justice Gray's view that one aspect of difference in memory of a conversation was firstly an error on Alison Fleming's part and that it was of such importance that it was reasonable to hold that Alison was generally unreliable as a witness. Disagreement on such a relatively trivial matter does not warrant questioning the credibility of either party.

With no evidence on which to base the claim, Justices Vanstone, Nicholson, and Bampton then argued that: "If she [Alison Fleming] was motivated to fashion her evidence to protect the appellant, then her evidence on other topics would be of little assistance." **If** she was motivated does not establish that she was so motivated. Assertion is not the same thing as fact. To repeat, there was no evidence offered to support such an extraordinary and damaging claim! And when Stuart Lindsay, a former Judge in the Federal Magistrates Court, was asked to give character witness for Alison Fleming, he was prevented from doing so on the grounds that it was irrelevant. Trial counsel for the appellant, Heywood-Smith, told Justice Gray, "If [Jane] is making totally unfounded allegations that have no basis, that may impact upon your Honour's assessment as to her reliability as a witness. This assertion was made by [Jane] and in my submission ..." At this point Justice Gray cut off counsel and ruled that "In the context in which it was made though, no, I don't think it's appropriate to obtain character evidence."[391]

It can be strongly argued that it would have been most appropriate to hear Stuart Lindsay on this matter since Justice Gray went on to make credibility findings in relation to Alison Fleming on no other basis than she disagreed with Sue Kay's memory on a relatively unimportant matter and because of the speculative possibility that she might fashion her evidence to protect her husband. The latter assertion is a particularly outrageous slur on the credibility of Alison Fleming. It was based upon a mere theory suggested/asserted by counsel for the defence, Andrew Harris, without any evidentiary base to support it. Nothing could logically be argued to follow on from it. The conclusion that on this basis Alison Fleming was a less credible witness than Jane is extraordinarily illogical.

In Chapter Six, third reason to mistrust the trial judge, reference was made to the failure of Justice Gray to take into account the admission by Jane that her memory was faulty and the fact that she told the Reverend David Richardson something very different from her final allegation about Meningie. To a Mr Witham, representing the Anglican Church, she said that

391 *Transcript of evidence given in Court* at page 2498 at lines 24-26.

> **I don't even actually remember him touching me. I don't actually remember in fact because I don't remember, I'm not reliable in that sense.**[392]

Justice Gray made no reference to what account should be taken of that very significant concession made by Jane herself in respect of her own credibility or, importantly to the disposition of this appeal, her reliability.[393]

To the Reverend David Richardson she said that the extent of the allegation Jane had made to him in the mid-2000s was that the appellant had "shown her his penis and expected her to admire it". The trial judge noted that Jane herself accepted that she may have said that to Mr Richardson. Tendentiously, trial judge Justice Gray excused this inconsistency by describing Mr Richardson's evidence that the allegation was "something of that sort" as being an "indefinite response" that did not necessarily reflect adversely upon Jane's account.

Equally, Justices Vanstone, Nicholson, and Bampton also took no account of Jane's admission that her memory was unreliable and did not rate the fact that the Reverend David Richardson agreed that his evidence represented **the extent** of Jane's allegation as made to him.

Justices Vanstone, Nicholson, and Bampton held that Justice Gray,

---

392 *Transcript of evidence given in Court* at page 1495 line 34 – page 1496 line 16, and particularly at page 1496 lines 4-7.

393 Justice Gray *judgement* at paragraph 377. Jane's evidence was clearly unreliable and this Court must bear in mind the distinction between honesty and unreliability *Waterways Authority v Fitzgibbon* (2005) 221 ALR 402 (HC).

> **was entitled to choose between the accounts and to take the view that her (Jane's) evidence could not prevent a finding that Jane's account was true.**[394]

But one can legitimately challenge this as there is arguably no evidence to justify rejecting the credibility of either Alison Fleming or Dr Fleming, but much to cast doubt on Jane's.

Justices Vanstone, Nicholson, and Bampton set out a few of the many inconsistencies, vagaries, uncertainties, and errors in Jane's evidence, including her inability to accurately recall events. Although imprecise and poorly assembled, these paragraphs contain a catalogue of Jane's inability to tell a consistent and sensible story. Notwithstanding this catalogue of evidence against Jane's reliability, Justices Vanstone, Nicholas, and Bampton went on to endorse Justice Gray's remarkable excusing of anything that would show that the defendant's case was not to be believed. This what the Full Court said:

> **The appellant contends that this inability told against Jane's credibility. However, the Judge was alive to this criticism and to its possible significance.**[395]
>
> **The Judge said at [407]:**
>
> **Jane was unable to say how arrangements were made for contact between her and**

394 *Fleming v Advertiser-News Weekend Publishing Company Pty Ltd & ANOR SASCFC* Judgment of The Full Court (The Honourable Justice Vanstone, The Honourable Justice Nicholson, and The Honourable Justice Bampton), 29 September 2016, at paragraph 143.

395 *bid.*, at paragraph 146.

> **the plaintiff after the incident at Meningie. Although in her statement to the police Jane said that the plaintiff would get in touch with her at the church choir practice, she said in crossexamination (*sic*) that with the benefit of hindsight she accepted that his tenure at St Jude's had ended and that it was at church functions that the contact would have been made.**
>
> **At [408] the Judge said he had to take into account:**
>
> **... the unlikelihood of there being an occasion involving a church function that the plaintiff had attended that would set the scene for the encounters in the Brighton area that Jane described.**
>
> **At [410] the Judge said:**
>
> **I have carefully considered both the fact that Jane is unable to say how the occasions of which she speaks about came about and her uncertainty about the cars that may have been involved but I regard her description of the occurrence of these occasions as compelling.**

Against this inability of Jane, the Judge placed his finding that there was an occasion after Meningie, as described by Jane, when the appellant told her he intended to marry Alison [411]. He also noted that the appellant had a motorcar (a Zephyr) and would, in the winter of 1971, drive to the Brighton area to pick up

Alison and her brother and take them to the football. [408]. His Honour weighed all these matters. **However tempting it was, he did not contemplate the possibility – contrary to Jane's evidence – that the Meningie incident might not have been the first of these incidents and that one or more of the meetings described by Jane could have preceded it.** What his Honour did find was that, such was his impression of Jane's evidence, her inability to describe how the other incidents began did not undermine his acceptance of the critical incidents said to have occurred at Meningie and St Mark's.[396]

> **We consider that the Judge was entitled to reach this position. There will always be inaccuracies, deficits and imponderables in the evidence of a witness looking back to events over such a long period. That the witness was young and plainly conflicted could only exacerbate such weaknesses. The Judge had ample opportunity to observe Jane in the witness box. She was there for seven days. Her evidence spans 375 pages of transcript, almost 70 per cent of it in crossexamination (*sic*). There was much documentary material bearing on her account, as well as the evidence of other witnesses which touched it. His Honour referred to most of the criticisms of her evidence. He explained why they did not undermine his faith in Jane. He did so at some length and with apparently great care.**

396 *Ibid.*, at paragraph 147.

> **He was not obliged to deal with every single argument mounted by the appellant. The Judge took the view that serious allegations such as those made by the respondents demanded clear and cogent evidence to support them. In Jane's evidence he found that clarity and cogency. The arguments put in this Court amounted to a recapitulation of the same arguments put to the trial Judge. As already explained, we do not agree that the Judge's approach to the question of proof was flawed. We have not found any error of a factual nature either. Our own appreciation of the transcript of Jane's evidence is that she was an intelligent and candid witness. There is nothing about her evidence which calls for its rejection on grounds of apparent dishonesty. It was a want of recollection and detail in relation to the Brighton beach incident where she could speak only of her feeling or assumption that sexual activity had preceded the walking along the beach, rather than any question of honesty, which led to the Judge not finding that incident proved.**[397]

Unwittingly, Justices Vanstone, Nicholson, and Bampton appeared to confirm the appellant's charge that Justice Gray was prejudiced in favour of Jane. They referred to Justice Gray as having "faith" in Jane, a most unusual term it is suggested in a judicial context.

---

397 *Ibid.*, at paragraph 148.

One would like to think that a somewhat more impartial stand would be at play, not a judge having "complete trust or confidence" in a witness despite so much evidence to the contrary.

The appeal judges accepted that Justice Gray was entitled to find that Jane's evidence provided the "clarity and cogency" needed to support the truth of the allegations. Jane is "honest" and honestly could not remember crucial (not incidental) details.

> **We have not found any error of a factual nature either. Our own appreciation of the transcript of Jane's evidence is that she was an intelligent and candid witness. There is nothing about her evidence which calls for its rejection on grounds of apparent dishonesty. It was a want of recollection and detail in relation to the Brighton beach incident where she could speak only of her feeling or assumption that sexual activity had preceded the walking along the beach, rather than any question of honesty, which led to the Judge not finding that incident proved.**[398]

This extraordinary statement is made in the face of many, many errors of fact demonstrated at trial and the expert evidence of Dr Arnold concerning the unreliability of Jane's evidence. That Justices Vanstone, Nicholson, and Bampton could hold that they found no errors in fact and that Jane's evidence was clear and cogent is extraordinary, so much so it is suggestive of

398 *Ibid.*, at paragraph 148

them not having read the evidence at all. Jane was wrong about almost all the facts associated with the alleged incidents at St Mark's College. It is not necessary to make statements about Jane's honesty. It was not alleged that she was knowingly a liar, just that by her own admission her memory could not be relied on. We should not confuse "seriously mistaken" with being an intentional liar, but at the very least her evidence was critically and crucially flawed.

Justices Vanstone, Nicholson, and Bampton also observed that Jane was in the witness box for seven days. They did not observe that the appellant was in the witness box for more than seven days and his errors were very few and minor. Jane's errors were many and major. Notwithstanding all of this, Justices Vanstone, Nicholson, and Bampton ultimately concluded:

> **In our view, it was open to the Judge to make the findings he did.**[399]

A final, but significant, observation regarding the appeal judgement was the assertion that any difficulties arising from the fact that some witnesses could not give evidence because of death or infirmity was a problem for the appellant to bear.

> **Furthermore, the analogy with the criminal courts is imperfect. There, persons have been brought before the courts many years after alleged offences to answer charges for sexual offences. Their liberty is at stake. On many occasions, the allegations have been**

399 Justices Vanstone, Nicholson, and Bampton *judgement* at paragraph 149.

> **made to police or prosecuting authorities earlier and not then proceeded with. A critical difference between those situations and the present is that the appellant has voluntarily initiated this litigation. Any forensic difficulties facing him due to the age of the respondents' allegations must have been apparent to him before he undertook that course.**[400]

It took some 37 years for Jane to make her complaints about the alleged activities of the appellant. Acting as investigator, prosecutor, judge and jury *The Advertiser* published these allegations which caused catastrophic harm to the appellant's reputation, health, employment, and financial security. *The Advertiser* continued its barrage of negative reporting. The only option in a one newspaper town was for the appellant to sue. Suing for damages is a civil matter not a criminal matter. But it is the right of every citizen to try to clear his or her name. It was a decision not lightly made, contrary to what is inferred by the phrase "voluntarily initiated this litigation". **The appellant did not "freely offer" to take legal action; he felt compelled to seek justice.**

In the application for leave to appeal to the High Court, the following observations were made about the significance of what Justices Vanstone, Nicholson, and Bampton held.

> **The Full Court erred in proceeding on the basis that the applicant as plaintiff was required to bear any prejudice associated**

---

400 *Ibid.*, at paragraph 183.

> **with the fact that events in excess of 40 years' antiquity were being assessed [FC183].**
>
> **It is a matter of public importance of general application that it is suggested by the Full Court that a person who is defamed by reference to an event of antiquity (40 years) should bear the prejudice associated with the loss of evidence consequent upon the passage of time by reason of his/her choosing to invoke the laws of defamation to defend his/her reputation [FC183]. This proposition by the Full Court is advanced without authority, effectively denies the remedy of defamation proceedings to a person defamed in circumstances such as these, and is plainly wrong.**

Finally, Justices Vanstone, Nicholson, and Bampton argued that in criminal cases an accused person's "liberty is at stake", the implication being, presumably, that a civil matter is much less serious. But that is not the case. Once allegations of this kind are published the person so accused, innocent as well as the guilty, may lose his or her reputation, perhaps even becoming unemployable for the rest of their lives. So it has been for me.

Chapter Eleven

High Court Refuses Application for Leave to Appeal

The rule of law is rightly regarded as being the foundation of any democratic society. But the rule of law is meaningless if there is no access to justice. It is pointless to be granted rights if you have no way of enforcing them.[401]

It is not unreasonable to suppose that most Australian citizens would consider that they were entitled to fair and reasonable access to the Australian court system. Even if things went pear-shaped in a lower court there were finer minds available who would listen and be susceptible to logical argument. In this instance, Dr Fleming, having unsuccessfully tried to restore his reputation in the Supreme Court of South Australia, before a single judge and at appeal before the Full Court, the possibility was raised by his legal advisers of an appeal to the High Court of Australia. Dr Fleming requested advice on not only whether he **may**, but

401 Andrew Caplen, President UK Law Society, 3 December 2014, "What use is the rule of law if there is no access to justice?" https://www.lawsociety.org.uk/news/speeches/access-to-justice/

whether he **should** seek leave to appeal to the highest court in the land? He was told that he **should**.

The High Court of Australia was established pursuant to the Australian Constitution.

> **Federal Judicature**
>
> **Chapter III of the Constitution (sections 71–80) provides for the establishment of the High Court of Australia. One of the High Court's principal functions is to decide disputes about the meaning of the Constitution. For example, it is the High Court which ultimately determines whether an Act passed by the Commonwealth Parliament is within the legislative powers of the Commonwealth. The power which the High Court has to interpret the Constitution means that it is a very important body. The High Court is also the final court of appeal within Australia in all other types of cases, even those dealing with purely State matters such as convictions under State criminal laws. Chapter III also gives the Commonwealth Parliament power to create other federal courts (for example, the Federal Court of Australia and the Family Court of Australia), and to vest federal judicial power in such courts and in courts of the States. 'Federal judicial power' is judicial power relating to one or more of the classes of dispute set out in sections 75 and 76.**[402]

---

402 The Australian Government Solicitor, *AUSTRALIA'S CONSTITUTION With Overview and Notes*, 2010, at page vii.

Section 73 of the Constitution states:

> **73. Appellate jurisdiction of High Court**
>
> **The High Court shall have jurisdiction, with such exceptions and subject to such regulations as the Parliament prescribes, to hear and determine appeals from all judgments, decrees, orders, and sentences:**
>
> **(i) of any Justice or Justices exercising the original jurisdiction of the High Court;**
>
> **(ii) of any other federal court, or court exercising federal jurisdiction; or of the Supreme Court of any State, or of any other court of any State from which at the establishment of the Commonwealth an appeal lies to the Queen in Council;**
>
> **(iii) of the Inter-State Commission, but as to questions of law only;**
>
> **and the judgment of the High Court in all such cases shall be final and conclusive.**
>
> **But no exception or regulation prescribed by the Parliament shall prevent the High Court from hearing and determining any appeal from the Supreme Court of a State in any matter in which at the establishment of the Commonwealth an appeal lies from such Supreme Court to the Queen in Council.**

After due consideration, Dr Fleming decided he would take the matter to the High Court. The "Application for Special Leave to Appeal" was prepared with the necessary diligence required for such an important matter. Dr Fleming's first Application for Special Leave to Appeal was refused but a further request was made that the High Court reopen the application following the decision in *Rush v Nationwide News Pty Ltd (No 7)* [2019] FCA 496.

Application to seek leave to appeal to the High Court

Notwithstanding one's right to apply for leave to appeal to the High Court, the High Court summarily dismissed that application in these terms:

> *Fleming v Advertiser News Weekend Publishing Company Pty Ltd & Anor [2017] HCASL 16 (9 February 2017)*
>
> *JOHN FLEMING*
>
> *v*
>
> *ADVERTISER NEWS WEEKEND PUBLISHING CO PTY LTD & ANOR*
>
> *[2017] HCASL 16 A44/2016*
>
> 1. *The application for special leave to appeal does not raise a question of general importance. None of the applicant's proposed appeal grounds enjoys sufficient prospects of success to warrant a grant of special leave. Special leave should be refused with costs.*

2. *Pursuant to r 41.08.1 of the High Court Rules 2004 (Cth), we direct the Registrar to draw up, sign and seal an order dismissing the application.*

S.M. Kiefel M.M. Gordon

9 February 2017

In seven lines, and without any supportive reasons, a citizen's right to appeal is dismissed. Not only has money been expended trying to exercise one's right to appeal, if one loses one pays the other side's costs as well. As has been argued in this book, there were many sound reasons why the High Court should have dealt with this. The application for leave to appeal was lodged in late December and dismissed in early February. One may be justified in speculating about just what kind of consideration the application received. How could Judges in the High Court simply deny that the issues over *Briginshaw* did not enjoy "sufficient prospects of success" and was not "a question of general importance"?

It has been suggested that because of under-funding, the High Court is, in practice, only open to a few appeal applications being agreed to. Applications for leave to appeal are dealt with summarily. Most are denied. It is a bit of a lottery to see whether your application has attracted the attention of whoever judges are appointed to look at it.

In this case, two grounds for rejection of the application were given, without justification:

1. The application did not raise a question of general importance, ie an unsettled matter of law; and

2. These judges did not consider that the appeal grounds enjoyed sufficient prospects of success.

The judges responsible for this decision were Chief Justice SM Kiefel and Justice MM Gordon.

Consideration will now be given as to whether this piece of summary justice is justified.

Questions of general importance

The Application for Special Leave to Appeal from the appeal judgment of the Full Court of the Supreme Court of South Australia set out several grounds of general importance for consideration which are summarised below.

The uncertainty of whether *Briginshaw v Briginshaw* is to be followed in a defamation case, where the defence pleads justification for having imputed the plaintiff was guilty of a serious criminal offence where the plaintiff has neither been charged nor convicted is a matter of public importance of general application. This is especially the case where:

- it was conclusively demonstrated the evidence of the principal complainant, Jane, was erroneous in material particulars; and
- in assessing Jane's evidence, the court brought to bear evidence given by a witness, Peter Kay, asserting (for the purposes of a contextual truth plea: [FC4] and [FC23-24]) consensual adult sexual conduct [FC119].

It is a matter of public importance of general application that at appeal the Supreme Court of South

Australia suggested that a person who is defamed by reference to an event of antiquity (in this instance 40 years) should bear the prejudice associated with the loss of evidence due to the passage of time on the grounds that the defendant "voluntarily" chose to invoke the laws of defamation to defend his reputation [FC183]. This proposition was advanced without authority and effectively significantly impinges upon, if not denies, the remedy of defamation proceedings to a person defamed in circumstances such as these.

It is in the interests of the administration of justice that both at trial and at appeal of a defamation case the court found there was sufficient evidence to support the defendant's claim that the applicant had committed serious sexual assaults some 40 years previously in respect of a teenage girl. The requisite standard of proof should not have been held to have been reached in circumstances where the story given by Jane, the said teenage girl, was not corroborated, had been described inconsistently by her on several prior occasions, and was shown to be erroneous in fundamental material particulars.

So, **there were** matters of general importance listed in the application for leave to appeal. They are and remain serious matters to which the High Court should have given its attention.

Briginshaw v Briginshaw and the 'balance of probabilities'

In *Briginshaw v Briginshaw* (1938) 60 CLR 336 Justice Dixon held:

> **But reasonable satisfaction is not a state of mind that is attained or established independently of nature and consequence of the fact or facts to be proved. The seriousness of an allegation made, the inherent unlikelihood of an occurrence of a given description, or the gravity of the consequences flowing from a particular finding are considerations which must affect the answer to the question whether the issue has been proved to the reasonable satisfaction of the tribunal. In such matters 'reasonable satisfaction' should not be produced by inexact proofs, indefinite testimony, or indirect inferences.**[403]

He further stated:

> **When, in a civil proceeding, a question arises whether a crime has been committed, the standard of persuasion is, according to the better opinion, the same as upon other civil issues ... But, consistently with this opinion, weight is given to the presumption of innocence and exactness of proof is expected.**[404]

The *Briginshaw* "principle", now codified in s 140 of the Commonwealth *Evidence Act 1995,* is largely viewed as the more serious the allegation, the more serious should be the consideration given by the decision maker and further, serious allegations with serious

---

403 *Briginshaw v Briginshaw* (1938) 60 CLR 336 at 362 per Dixon J.
404 *Ibid.,* at 363.

consequences require more compelling evidence to enable the decision maker to reach a state of reasonable satisfaction. As Justice Dixon held, how serious the allegation is, the likelihood of such an occurrence as described and the gravity of any consequences flowing from a finding are matters which must affect deciding whether the matter has been proved.

Any uncertainty in the way that *Briginshaw* is interpreted and applied is a very serious matter, and one that can only be clarified by the High Court or, if necessary, by the Parliament. After all, it is the High Court that is responsible for *Briginshaw* and how, in subsequent judgements, it is to be applied. That there is uncertainty as to precisely what the *Briginshaw* principles require is indicated by reference to several cases.

In *Rejfek v McElroy* (1965) 112 CLR 517 it was stated:

> **(T)he degree of satisfaction for which the civil standard of proof calls may vary according to the gravity of the fact to be proved.**

In *Neat Holdings v Karajan Holdings* (1992) 110 ALR 449 it was held:

> **(T)he strength of the evidence necessary to establish a fact or facts on the balance of probabilities may vary according to the nature of what it is sought to prove.**

The plaintiff presented to the trial court what it understood to be the proper application of *Briginshaw.*

> **The respondent media organisations carried the onus of proving justification of 'criminal sexual conduct'. That would necessarily require a high 'degree of**

> **satisfaction' or particularly strong evidence. That would follow from the fact that the media organizations made a deliberate decision to allege criminal sexual conduct and convict the applicant in the court of public opinion. And it is the more so when the alleged conduct is said to have occurred some 40 years ago. The case for a degree of satisfaction at least approaching the criminal standard seems as strong in those circumstances as the need for a high standard in respect of civil contempt. This case is different from a tortious action in deceit which is acknowledged to attract the *Briginshaw* onus. In this case, the allegations were being made against a man of the highest reputation, the then President of Campion College in Sydney.**

Hornal v Neuberger [1957] 1 QB 247 addressed the standard of proof in a civil action of alleged fraud. Lord Morris said:

> **The phrase 'balance of probabilities' is often employed as a convenient phrase to express the basis upon which civil issues are decided. ... In some criminal cases liberty may be involved; in some it may not. In some civil cases the issues may involve questions of reputation which can transcend in importance even questions of personal liberty. Good name in man or woman is 'the immediate jewel of their souls'.**[405]

405 Hornal v Neuberger [1957] 1 QB 266.

At both the trial and the appeal, standards such as the need for clear and cogent proofs were not applied. One expects from the judiciary clarity and certainty as to how such words would be interpreted, particularly when a man's entire life and livelihood are affected.

Briginshaw v Briginshaw and the 'onus of proof'

As the plaintiff understood the situation at the commencement of the proceedings against *The Advertiser*, the onus of proof would be on the defendant not on the plaintiff, and that the said standard of proof would necessarily have to meet a high 'degree of satisfaction' or for particularly strong evidence to be introduced in court.

In defamation matters, the defendant carries the onus of proving justification for having made the allegations being sued upon, in this case, justification for the claim that the defendant had committed 'criminal sexual conduct'. The standard of proof is to be in accordance with *Briginshaw* principles. The *Briginshaw* principles enable the Court to say to a defendant in the circumstances of a case such as this: you will be held to at least a burden approaching the criminal burden. For it to be otherwise would undermine the rule of law and constitutional protections upon which every member of society relies.

This position is also the case in other common law jurisdictions with Canada demanding even higher standards of proof.

The same position as to burden of proof pertains in the UK.

> (I)t is said that the more serious the allegation, the more cogent is the evidence required to prove it. In a juror's mind this may well come closer to the more familiar criminal standard of beyond reasonable doubt.[406]

Gibson DCJ in *Shandil v Sharma* [2010] NSWDC 273 at [252] refers to acclaimed English defamation lawyer, Peter Frederick Carter-Ruck (26 February 1914 – 19 December 2003), who said:

> If the imputation is one of a criminal offence the law requires unless the plaintiff has been convicted of the alleged offence that its justification should be proved as fully and as strictly as if the defamed person were on trial before a criminal court charged with that offence (Hornal v Neuberger Products Ltd [1957] 1 QB 247).[407]

As I have said, there is a good reason for the Court to say to the defendant, in the circumstances of a case involving the publication of allegations of a criminal offence, you will be held to at least a burden approaching the criminal burden. It is the police who are charged with the responsibility of investigating crime: *Police Act 1988* (SA), s.5. When the police investigate a case, they are bound by certain strict rules of conduct and procedure. Had police charged the plaintiff with an

406 David Price and Korieh Duodu, *Defamation Law, Procedure and Practice*, 3rd Edit., (2004), Sweet & Maxwell, para.8-03, at page 57. and cf Hornal v Neuberger Products [1957] 1QB, 247.

407 Carter-Ruck, *Libel and Slander*, Butterworths, 1985, 3rd ed, at page 94.

offence concerning Jane, the publications would almost certainly have been a contempt.[408] It is unlikely that the matters pertaining to Diane Lynch and Peter Kay could have been given in evidence in prosecuting the plaintiff in respect of an alleged offence involving Jane.

So, where the issue of the burden of proof is concerned, the decision does not boil down to "who does the Court believe?" as Justice Gray and Justices Vanstone, Nicholson, and Bampton wrongly claim. The real question is not one that requires the Court having to make a "choice" between the witnesses. The evidence of the complainant witnesses should be considered in conjunction with the content of the plaintiff's evidence and other evidence from witnesses for the plaintiff. Where there are contradictions, the question is not whose evidence is to be preferred, but whether the defendants have proved their case in accordance with *Briginshaw* principles.

No Presumption of Innocence – Justices Vanstone, Nicholson, and Bampton

Justices Vanstone, Nicholson, and Bampton did not accept that the *Briginshaw* principles provided for the presumption of innocence in civil matters when a criminal offence is being alleged. The appeal court ruled:

> **We would add that, although in *Briginshaw* Dixon J referred to a person against whom are alleged serious matters enjoying the**

408 *Hinch v AG* (1987) 164 CLR 15.

> **"presumption of innocence" and the consequent requirement of "exactness of proof", the later High Court judgments do not import that presumption into the civil arena. Furthermore, from the above it would appear that any references to *Briginshaw* as establishing an "onus" or a "standard" are incorrect. Additionally, in the several High Court cases referred to, there is no reference to *Briginshaw* establishing a "principle". Rather, reference is made to, for example, grave allegations being determined by reference to *Briginshaw* considerations: *G v H* at 400.**[409]

Justices Vanstone, Nicholson, and Bampton did not apply a correct understanding of the principles of *Briginshaw*.

The application of *Briginshaw* in civil matters such as defamation is a serious matter of general importance and should not have been so summarily dismissed by the High Court. Litigants have a right to reasonable certainty as to the meaning of the law and how it is to be applied by judges <u>**before**</u> they decide to litigate. If the High Court won't clarify the meaning, reach, and scope of the law, then the law makers in Federal and State Parliaments must do it for them.

It is suggested that there are also matters of general importance involved given the importation of popular anti-Catholic prejudice into the judgement

---

409 Justices Vanstone, Nicholson, and Bampton judgement, at paragraph 108.

of Justices Vanstone, Nicholson, and Bampton, and the extraordinary proposition by Justices Vanstone, Nicholson, and Bampton that it is the appellant Dr Fleming who must bear all the prejudice from a complaint delayed for some 40 years. This meant that his lack of access to exculpating witnesses who could give no evidence either through death or diminished capacity due to old age is something he, Dr Fleming, should have thought about before he initiated defamation proceedings.

The High Court refused to grant Dr Fleming's application for leave to appeal.

Rush, *Briginshaw*, and the second failure of the High Court to do its duty

On 8 December 2017, the actor Geoffrey Rush initiated defamation proceedings against the Daily Telegraph (Sydney, NSW). In his pleadings Rush claimed that material published in the Daily Telegraph carried serious defamatory allegations against him including allegations of sexual assault.

In *Rush v Nationwide News Pty Ltd (No 7)* [2019] FCA 496, Justice Wigney of the Federal Court held that Nationwide News and journalist Jonathan Moran failed to prove that the imputations published in two articles in late 2017 were true.

In his judgement, Justice Wigney explicitly referred to *Briginshaw v Briginshaw* and applied the principles contained therein:

Nationwide and Mr Moran bear the onus of proving that the balance of the imputations conveyed by the matters complained of were substantially true. The standard of proof is the balance of probabilities, even where the matter to be proved involves criminal conduct or fraud: Neat Holdings Pty Ltd v Karajan Holdings Pty Ltd (1992)110 ALR 449 at 449-450. In Neat, however, the majority (Mason CJ, Brennan, Deane and Gaudron JJ) went on to say as follows (at 450):

On the other hand, the strength of the evidence necessary to establish a fact or facts on the balance of probabilities may vary according to the nature of what it is sought to prove. Thus, authoritative statements have often been made to the effect that clear or cogent or strict proof is necessary "where so serious a matter as fraud is to be found". Statements to that effect should not, however, be understood as directed to the standard of proof. Rather, they should be understood as merely reflecting a conventional perception that members of our society do not ordinarily engage in fraudulent or criminal conduct and a judicial approach that a court should not lightly make a finding that, on the balance of probabilities, a party to civil litigation has been guilty of such conduct. (Footnotes omitted.)

Their Honours then referred to the following well-known observations of Dixon J in *Briginshaw v Briginshaw* [1938] HCA 34; (1938) 60 CLR 336 (at 362):

The seriousness of an allegation made, the inherent unlikelihood of an occurrence of a given description, or the gravity of the consequences flowing from a particular finding are considerations which must affect the answer to the question whether the issue has been proved ...

Those observations are now reflected in s 140 of the Evidence Act 1995 (Cth), which provides that in deciding whether it is satisfied that the case of a party has been proved on the balance of probabilities, the Court may take into account the nature of the cause of action or defence, the nature of the subject-matter of the proceeding and the gravity of the matters alleged.

There could be little doubt that the allegations that Nationwide and Mr Moran levelled against Mr Rush in their truth defence are grave allegations. That is a factor which must be borne in mind when considering whether Nationwide and Mr Moran have discharged the onus of proving, on the balance of probabilities, that the imputations were substantially true.[410]

410 *Rush v Nationwide News Pty Ltd* (No 7) [2019] FCA 496 (11 April 2019), 226-229.

Central to Justice Wigney's judgement was his finding that there was a lack of corroboration of the accusations made by the accusers.

This case of defamation, heard in the Federal Court of Australia, also contained allegations of serious criminal conduct. However, the rules used to assess the evidence given to prove those allegations, were different from the rules applied in *Fleming v The Advertiser* in the Supreme Court of South Australia.

Accordingly, Dr Fleming sought special leave to appeal in which compliance with the time limit in High Court Rules 2004, rule 41.02.1 would be dispensed. The application included the following:

> **2. The applicant says the uncertainty as to what the *Briginshaw* principle requires in a defamation justification defence that involves alleged criminal conduct is demonstrated by a comparison of the application of the principle in his case and in the recent case of *Rush v Nationwide News Pty Ltd* (No 7) [2019] FCA 496 (Wigney J).**
>
> **3. A consideration of the Rush reasons makes it apparent that his Honour considered that to establish the appropriate standard of proof it was necessary that in respect of the various allegations there be corroboration of same. Reference is made to the following paragraphs of the judgment in respect of the seven (7) allegations:**
>
> - **1st [462]**
> - **2nd and 3rd [506]**

- 4th [527]
- 5th [582], [592]
- 6th [622], [624]
- 7th [635], adopting [622] and [624].

4. The events the subject of the Rush case-occurred only one to two years prior to the proceedings. The events in the proceedings the subject of the application occurred some 40 years ago. The allegations by 'Jane' in those proceedings were totally uncorroborated. Indeed, the applicant's denials were corroborated by a number of witnesses and could have been corroborated by others since deceased. The applicant refers to page 11 and his submission on 'Prejudice consequent upon passage of time'.

5. In this matter, the word 'corroboration' does not appear in the reasons of the trial judge. Nor does the trial judge address the impact of a 'presumption of innocence' in the context of justification of criminal conduct.

6. In *Briginshaw* the High Court appears to recognise such a presumption: per Latham CJ at 344, Dixon J at 363, and McTiernan J at 372. Dixon J (at 363), when addressing a civil proceeding wherein a question of whether a crime has occurred, asserts that "weight is given to the presumption of innocence".

7. The Full Court in this matter at [108] addresses the reference by Dixon J to a

"presumption of innocence" in a dismissive way asserting that "later High Court judgments do not import that presumption into the civil arena". Whilst that might be the case, neither do they remove it.

8. The Full Court proceeds in [108): "Furthermore, from the above it would appear that any references to *Briginshaw* as establishing an 'onus' or a 'standard' are incorrect."

9. Justice Wigney in Rush ([227]) cites Dixon J in *Briginshaw* at 362 and not the passage at 363. Nevertheless, his Honour's apparent consideration that corroboration was required in Rush sits with the existence of a presumption of innocence. These are matters appropriate for consideration by the High Court.

10. Immediately below is a summary of critical differences in the way the law of defamation was applied in two different jurisdictions:

Rush	**Fleming**
Corroboration required of accuser	No corroboration provided by or required of accuser
	Corroboration for Fleming's evidence provided by third parties
Presumption of innocence applied	Presumption of innocence refused
Briginshaw fully applied	Briginshaw not applied as to 'onus' and to 'standard'

The High Court again rejects Dr Fleming without explanation

On 11 September 2019 the High Court of Australia handed down its decision, rejecting the Application. The reasons given by the High Court for this rejection are bald statements unaccompanied by any justification:

> First Reason: "The present application identifies no reason to conclude that the determination of the Court in February 2017 was attended by any error of fact or law that has occasioned a miscarriage of justice."
>
> Second Reason: "Nor does it appear that the exceptional course urged by the applicant is warranted by the prospects of success of the appeal foreshadowed by this application."

However, the applicant identified errors in law which made a definitive difference as to the finding of fact. It is difficult to understand the High Court's refusal to address the inconsistency in how the law was applied in the Supreme Court of South Australia compared to the way it was applied in the Federal Court of Australia. Does one assume that the High Court case of *Briginshaw v Briginshaw* applies in one jurisdiction but not in another, or worse in similar cases in the same jurisdiction?

The High Court rejected the first application for leave to appeal. The Rush judgement provided substantial reasons for the High Court to consider whether there had been a serious error in law in the Supreme Court of South Australia which they had overlooked when considering the previous application. In one case an impecunious Catholic priest is denied justice. In the other case an international celebrity is given the full benefit of the law.

For example, corroboration was not required when considering crucial evidence presented by the defence in *Fleming v The Advertiser.* It was deemed sufficient that the judge could choose to "believe" in, "have faith" in the witness alleging the offence while discounting the corroborating evidence which supported the plaintiff's account. However, such corroboration was rightly required in the case of Mr Rush. Further, in the defamation case of Mr Rush where there were allegations of criminal conduct it was for the defendant to prove the truth of the allegations, whereas in the case of Dr Fleming, it was for the plaintiff to prove his innocence.

There may be pressure under which a possibly underfunded High Court labours, with too few judges to handle the caseload. Nonetheless, it is suggested, that does not excuse a refusal to hear an appeal which includes a crucial matter, namely how differently the law of defamation is applied from one jurisdiction to another.

For citizens to have faith in our system of justice they need to know that the law is applied consistently and fairly to all. Where allegations of criminal acts are concerned, it should be those who make the allegations in the public way that newspapers and other media can or do, who should bear the onus of proving their allegations. In South Australia the plaintiff in a defamation matter faced a completely different way of assessing the evidence than that applied in a defamation case in the Federal Court.

Poniatowska v Channel Seven Sydney Pty Ltd

Shortly after the High Court refused Dr Fleming's second application for leave to appeal, the Full Court of the South Australian Supreme Court brought down their judgement in the defamation matter *Poniatowska v Channel Seven Sydney Pty Ltd* [2019] SASCFC 111 (27 September 2019).

Initially, Ms Poniatowska was charged in April 2008 with:

> **... 17 counts of obtaining a financial advantage by omission between August 2005 and May 2007, in contravention of section 135.2(1) of the Criminal Code (Cth).[411]**
>
> **The appellant foreshadowed a plea of not guilty to the charges and the matter was listed for trial in the Magistrates Court for July 2009. On the eve of trial the appellant accepted legal advice to plead guilty and she pleaded guilty on the morning of trial. Ultimately, she appealed to this Court against her conviction and her appeal was upheld. An appeal to the High Court by the Commonwealth Director of Public Prosecutions was dismissed on the morning of the day on which the Today Tonight story was broadcast.[412]**

---

411 *Poniatowska v Channel Seven Sydney Pty Ltd* [2019] SASCFC 111 (27 September 2019)

412 *Ibid.*

In the evening of the same day when the High Court brought down its decision, Channel Seven Sydney ran with their story about the matter. Justice Blue described what followed:

> **The story was prompted by a decision by the High Court earlier that day upholding a decision by this Court allowing an appeal against a conviction. Ms Poniatowska had been charged with 17 counts of obtaining a financial advantage between August 2005 and May 2007 in contravention of section 135.2(1) of the Criminal Code (Cth), to which she had pleaded guilty on the day of trial. Her appeal against conviction had been upheld because section 135.2(1) did not impose a duty to disclose and the prosecution did not contend that any other Commonwealth law required her to disclose her income to Centrelink.**[413]

Ms Poniatowska sued Channel Seven Sydney because of that broadcast in October 2011, a broadcast in which Channel Seven Sydney depicted **the appellant "as having defrauded and cheated Centrelink of $20,000 in single parent benefits while working for a building company and having avoided prosecution by finding a loophole in social security law that did not require her to disclose her income to Centrelink". The story was also published on the Channel Seven website.**"[414]

Ms Poniatowska lost her appeal before a single judge of the SA Supreme Court, Justice Greg Parker. On the

413 *Ibid.*, n. 15.

414 *Poniatotowska v Channel Seven Sydney Pty Ltd* [2019].

27th of November 2019 the Full Court of the SA Supreme Court overturned Justice Parker's judgement.

Both the trial and appeal judgements of *Fleming v The Advertiser* appear to be at odds with the judgement of the South Australian Supreme Court in the Poniatowska case, especially where the application of *Briginshaw* is concerned.[415]

First, the onus of proof. Justice Gray, and supported by Justices Vanstone, Nicholson, and Bampton, rejected the plaintiff's evidence, preferring the evidence of Jane (and Peter Kay). The rejection of the plaintiff's evidence provided a sufficient basis to find for the defendant according to Justice Gray and upheld on appeal. However, in *Poniatowska v Channel Seven Sydney Pty Ltd* Chief Justice Kourakis, and Justices Blue and Nicholson ruled that it is not a sufficient basis. Justice Blue wrote the judgement with the other two concurring. They held:

> **Secondly the Judge's approach involved a form of reversal of the onus of proof. The Judge addressed the question whether Ms Poniatowska's evidence should be rejected rather than the question whether Channel Seven had discharged the onus of proof. As juries are daily directed, the mere fact that evidence by a defendant in relation to an alleged offence is rejected does not entail that the offence has been proved by the prosecution to the requisite standard. For the reasons given above, Channel Seven had not discharged the onus of proof.**[416]

415 *Poniatowska v Channel Seven Sydney Pty Ltd* [2019], at nn 402, 474-477, 521-522, and cf 257, 277 and 301.

416 *Ibid.*, n. 522.

Conclusion

The Judge's conclusion that justification of the imputations had been established was vitiated by the matters referred to above.[417]

The question then arises whether this Court is in a position to make a finding whether Channel Seven proved that Ms Poniatowska was guilty of contraventions of section 135.2 and consequentially of fraud, having regard to the seriousness of the allegations in accordance with the *Briginshaw* principle.[418]

This Court did not see or hear Ms Poniatowska, or the other witnesses, give evidence. However, on appeal Ms Poniatowska does not challenge the adverse credit findings made by the trial Judge insofar as those findings were made or in general the findings of primary fact insofar as the Judge made such findings. I approach the assessment on the basis of assumptions of a general adverse credit finding being made against Ms Poniatowska, that the Judge's findings of primary fact are not disturbed, that Channel Seven proved the physical elements of section 135.2 contraventions and that a Centrelink officer did not explicitly give to Ms Poniatowska information about parenting payment that was objectively false.[419]

417 *Ibid.,* n. 523.

418 *Ibid.,* n. 524.

419 *Ibid.,* n. 525.

Earlier, Chief Justice Kourakis and Justices Blue and Nicholson had insisted on the need for Channel Seven Sydney to prove the truth of their allegations to the level prescribed by *Briginshaw*.

> **Thirdly, the onus remained on Channel Seven to prove that Ms Poniatowska was guilty of fraud, the discharge of which required taking into account *Briginshaw* considerations. For the reasons given below, such Centrelink documents as were tendered were of limited probative weight in the absence of explanations by a Centrelink witness of the system which created them, the meaning of the terms contained in them and the general practice which would inform an inference concerning the communications between Ms Poniatowska and Centrelink the subject of those records. The Judge did not take this into account.**[420]

And

> Discharge of onus of proof
>
> **In a prosecution for contravening section 135.2 of the Criminal Code relying upon circumstantial evidence, the prosecution would have been required to prove the prosecution case including negating any hypothesis consistent with Ms Poniatowska's innocence. The position on Channel Seven's justification defence was the same as if Ms Poniatowska had been**

420 *Ibid.*, n. 439.

> **prosecuted on the notional counts, except that the standard of proof was the civil standard taking into account *Briginshaw* considerations. The Judge was required to find proved, to the requisite standard, an affirmative prosecution case including that any hypothesis consistent with Ms Poniatowska's innocence was negated.**[421]

This application of *Briginshaw* is in stark contrast to the way the matter of proof was dealt with by the same Court in the case of *Fleming v The Advertiser,* particularly given that the circumstances were different. For example, the South Australian Police had advised Dr Fleming that they would not proceed against him so that prior to the defamation case there had been no criminal procedures.

Moreover, Dr Fleming had a much stronger case than that of Poniatowska since, as has been clearly identified earlier in this book, his evidence was corroborated by other witnesses and the contradictions in Jane's evidence were glaringly obvious. It should also be noted that the defendant failed to call two witnesses (Koop and Hyde) even though it had been promised they would be. The failure of a defendant to call witnesses was the cause of reprobation in Poniatowska.[422]

The Supreme Court of South Australia apparently now holds both that *Briginshaw* **does fully apply** in civil matters even when a judge rejects the credit of the appellant, **and that it does not fully apply** in civil matters.

---

421 *Ibid.,* n. 473.

422 *Ibid.,* nn. 440 - 441, 448, and 504.

The difference between the competence and inclinations of the relevant judges in the SA Supreme Court in deciding appeals on defamation matters involving a serious criminal offence is extraordinary. In *Fleming v The Advertiser Briginshaw* is held not to apply as establishing an 'onus' or a 'standard'. BUT … in *Poniatowska v Channel Seven Sydney Pty Ltd* the Full Court held that *Briginshaw* does apply in relation to 'onus' and 'standard'.

Moreover, how can the Australian High Court continue to refuse to do its duty by denying the undeniable, that there is a matter of both general application and importance in the way the law of defamation has been applied in the matter of *Fleming v The Advertiser*?

The allegations published by *The Advertiser* destroyed Dr Fleming's reputation and career. If those allegations had been tested properly, impartially, and logically then *The Advertiser* should have lost the case. In the SA Supreme Court, it seems that the uncorroborated evidence of one person, the accuser, trumps the denial of the priest even though that denial was corroborated by an eyewitness and other witnesses as well.

How is that not a miscarriage of justice?

Chapter Twelve

The Case Against the Judges in Brief – What is to be Done?

When injustice becomes law, resistance becomes duty.[423]

Injustice never rules forever.[424]

He who commits injustice is ever made more wretched than he who suffers it.[425]

It can be argued that there is much of which to be deeply critical regarding the performance of the four judges from the South Australian Supreme Court who presided over the defamation case of *Fleming v The Advertiser,* at trial and appeal. A discussion of how these judges carried out their duties as judges in this case now follows.

Prejudices

As has already been demonstrated there is considerable evidence of the four Supreme Court judges exhibiting prejudicial behaviour when considering this case:

1. An adult who alleges historical sexual abuse, in this instance claimed to have occurred more than

423 Thomas Jefferson [1743-1826].

424 Seneca [4 BC – AD 65].

425 Plato [428/427 or 424/423 – 348/347 BC].

40 years ago, is to be believed and protected. The evidence of the complainant is given more weight than any contrary evidence. Apparent lapses in memory which result in conflicting evidence being given by the complainant are excused. Evidence from the complainant, with no corroboration, is given more weight than conflicting evidence by the appellant despite the latter being corroborated.

2. Prejudice towards Roman Catholics was evident in the appeal judgement when considering the appeal and was used to support dismissing part of the grounds of appeal. The presence of such a prejudice was also evident in the trial at first instance. It could well be argued that such prejudice influenced the assessment by these judges of the other grounds of appeal.

Is the evidence of an adult complainant always to be preferred?

There is a growing disquiet among many in the legal profession that such a prejudice in favour of a complainant is not only wrong, but highly damaging to the accused no matter what the outcome of investigations. Barrister Barbara Hewson, (1 Gray's Inn Square, London) in her essay "False allegations of sexual abuse- The rise of the fine lie",[426] says "that victims of false accusations now deserve more consideration." She goes on to say:

---

426 *The Barrister Magazine*, 31st March, 2016, at http://www.barristermagazine.com/false-allegations-of-sexual-abuse-the-rise-of-the-fine-lie/

> **Even a nascent rebellion against the fashionable ideology of "believe the victim [of sexual abuse]" supported by former DPP Keir Starmer KC[427] is out of step with current CPS [Crown Prosecution Service] practice. A Manchester barrister who prosecutes allegations of sexual assault for the CPS was recently quoted[428] as saying: "Rape has become the bread and butter of the Crown Prosecution Service. Basically, if someone complains, we prosecute."**

Hewson ends her discussion of the unfairness of the prejudice shown by judicial and other authorities where allegations of sexual abuse, made by adults are concerned, in these terms.

> **In my opinion, far too little attention has been paid to the lure of the victim narrative, and the rewards of victimhood (for those who are competent). These rewards can include the sympathy and attention which those proclaiming to be victims can expect, and the seduction of the "truthful lie", both for its narrator and its audience.**
>
> **Those who confabulate about their past experience so as to come to terms with it may be expressing an emotional truth (such**

427 "Human rights, victims and the prosecution of crime in the 21st century", (2014) *Crim LR* 777, 782.

428 http://www.theglobeandmail.com/life/relationships/leah-mclaren-sadly-the-ghomeshi-trial-is-not-our-watershed-moment/article28730758/

> **as a perception of a violation of the self), but an actual lie. As the psychologist Professor Janice Haaken acknowledges:**
>
> **"The art of storytelling is not based merely on chronicling a sequence of facts but on the artful juxtaposition of dramatic elements. The power of the story to stir others... depends on its felt truth and plausibility rather than on its mere facticity."**
>
> **This may be the age of testimonial, as Elie Wiesel suggests, but testifiers do not inevitably speak the truth, as virtuous as they may perceive themselves to be.**[429]

In their discussion of this prejudice, Edward Hayes lawyers say this:

> **Historic and false allegation cases are a complex, unsettled area, where prosecutions are often based on the complainant's word against that of the defendant. Lack of corroborating evidence is unlikely to dissuade the police and CPS in our adversarial justice system. Victims should be protected and the guilty punished, but our system now encourages and even promotes miscarriages of justice.**[430]

In a comment relevant to the case of *Fleming v Advertiser,* these lawyers go on to remark:

---

429 Elie Wiesel, *Pillar of Salt: Gender, Memory and the Perils of Looking Back,* Rutgers University Press, 1998 at pages 185, 193.

430 Edward Hayes lawyers, "False and Historical Sexual Abuse", http://www.edwardhayes.co.uk/legal-services-for-you/false-allegation/false-and-historical-sexual-abuse

> **Complainants in historical abuse cases can appear to be sincere, truthful, and honest in giving their evidence. However, that does not necessarily make their evidence reliable. Memories are far from perfect. Even a witness that appears confident and convincing may not be accurate or reliable in the evidence they give. Where the evidence contains contradictions and inconsistencies, it is dangerous to place too much emphasis on the witness' demeanour. It is possible for an honest witness to convince their self of the correctness of their account though, in fact, it may be inaccurate. Such witnesses can be extremely persuasive in the manner they give their evidence. The police often concentrate on the development of witness statements rather than anything that may undermine "their case"**[431]

In South Australia, the police were not influenced by prejudicial thinking to simply believe whatever Jane told them. Dr Fleming was not charged with any offence concerning Jane. But the judges in *Fleming v The Advertiser* embraced the prejudiced view that the adult complainant of historic sex abuse allegations is always to be believed even though not only was there no corroboration of Jane's allegations, but the plaintiff's denial was corroborated. Further, Jane's story contained many contradictions and inconsistencies.

The same disquiet about the presumption that recovered memories of historic sex abuse are true

431 *Ibid.*

memories has also been expressed by the British Psychological Society. As was seen in the evidence that Dr Arnold gave, the whole notion of recovered memories is fraught. In 1993, the British Psychological Society convened a working party in response to the concern that some psychologists might be inadvertently implanting false memories of child sexual abuse in their clients. The working party's conclusions that both genuine recovered memories and false memories were likely to occur were endorsed in a subsequent article by Dan Wright, James Ost and Chris French, published in *The Psychologist* in June 2006, and a series of guidance documents have since been made available to members. The concerns reflected in these publications remain current, as accusations of historic child sexual abuse continue to increase in the wake of the revelations concerning Jimmy Savile and the setting up of the Independent Inquiry into Child Sexual Abuse by the UK government in 2015.[432]

In the June 2006 article cited above, Wright, Ost, and French made these observations:

> **We believe:**
>
> **that what appear to be newly remembered (i.e. recovered) memories of past trauma are sometimes accurate, sometimes inaccurate, and sometimes a mixture of accuracy and inaccuracy;**
>
> **that much of what is recalled cannot be confirmed or disconfirmed;**

---

432 Chris R. Brewin and Bernice Andrews, "False memories of childhood abuse: Are therapists to blame? *The Psychologist*, July 2017, at page 48.

> **that, because of these two beliefs, reports of past trauma based on such recovered memories are not reliable enough to be the sole basis for legal decisions.**[433]

Eleven years later, in 2017, Brewin and Andrews were able to report thus:

> **Recovered memories lie on a spectrum from being plainly false, being plausible but lacking in corroboration, to being independently corroborated. In seeking to explain those false memories that do arise within therapy, our account in no way excludes the possibility of therapists acting inappropriately, but places more weight on pre-therapy reality monitoring and on the interactions between a therapist and a client struggling to make sense of what are often distressing and confusing experiences.**[434]

In an outstanding report on "The Impact of Being Wrongly Accused of Abuse in Occupations of Trust: Victims' Voices" published by the *Centre For Criminality*, University of Oxford (2016) [*the University of Oxford Report*], the authors provide the context in which the assumption that alleged victims of sexual abuse are always to be believed became so widely adopted.

---

433 Daniel B. Wright, James Ost and Christopher C. French, "Recovered and false memories", *The Psychologist*, June 2006, at page 352.

434 Chris R. Brewin and Bernice Andrews, "False memories of childhood abuse: Are therapists to blame? *The Psychologist*, July 2017, at page 52.

In recent years, there has been some concern that allegations of sexual abuse, particularly non-recent abuse, have not received an appropriate response. Among politicians, criminal justice agencies and charities in the UK, there is a collective sense of remorse that reports of abuse were often not properly investigated and that those who reported it were often not believed. From this has emerged a new determination to correct past and prevent further injustices of this kind. For example, the Report of Her Majesty's Inspectorate of Constabulary (HMIC, 2013), *Mistakes Were Made,* recommended that each agency with a duty to safeguard children and vulnerable adults should implement regular and systematic checks to ensure they comply with relevant policies and that a system of mandatory reporting should be considered to ensure that those who become aware of evidence that a child has been or is being abused is under a legal obligation to notify their concerns to others.

It is argued that for some years the benefit of any doubt is now more likely to be given to the accuser (Webster, 1998; Burnett, 2013). Even in cases where the evidence only consists of testimony from the alleged victim and is strongly rebutted by the alleged perpetrator, the moral imperative not to 'let down another victim' or to leave

> **a possible sex offender free to cause further harm may be compelling (Webster, 1998; 2005). While this must, logically, reduce the chances of guilty persons avoiding prosecution ('false negatives'), it also risks increasing the likelihood of innocent people being presumed or found guilty ('false positives').**[435]

In their discussion of the evidence around this assumption, the authors of *the University of Oxford Report* demonstrated that this assumption is wrongly held, and has been the occasion of massive damage being done to innocent persons.[436] More than half of *the University of Oxford Report*[437] describes and discusses what the authors' research on the "Effects of False Allegations" on the "Legally Innocent" shows about the sufferings of those people who have been publicly accused and even arrested by the police.

The view that accusers should be believed was supported in many places of influence.

---

435 Carolyn Hoyle, Naomi-Ellen Speechley, and Ros Burnett, University of Oxford Centre for Criminology, *The Impact of Being Wrongly Accused of Abuse in Occupations of Trust: Victims' Voices*, 15 November 2016, at page 3. https://www.law.ox.ac.uk/sites/files/oxlaw/the_impact_of_being_wrongly_accused_of_abuse_hoyle_et_al_2016_15_may.pdf

436 Carolyn Hoyle, Naomi-Ellen Speechley, and Ros Burnett, University of Oxford Centre for Criminology, *The Impact of Being Wrongly Accused of Abuse in Occupations of Trust: Victims' Voices*, 15 November 2016, at pages 8-12.

437 Carolyn Hoyle, Naomi-Ellen Speechley, and Ros Burnett, University of Oxford Centre for Criminology, *The Impact of Being Wrongly Accused of Abuse in Occupations of Trust: Victims' Voices*, 15 November 2016, at pages 25-60.

> **February 2000 saw the publication of *Lost in Care*, the report of the judicial inquiry led by Sir Ronald Waterhouse into abuse in North Wales. On a BBC Newsnight programme that discussed the findings, Sir William Utting, the former Her Majesty's Chief Inspector Social Work, commented: 'It may be that innocent people are being convicted, but we ought to be more worried about the guilty who might get away'. This baleful remark implied that the abuse of children, no matter how long ago, was such a serious matter that it merited a reversal of the legal principle of the presumption of innocence in order to increase the prospects of securing convictions.**[438]

The damage done by the prejudice in favour of accusers is not confined to criminal cases. It has clear implications for civil matters as well, especially when someone is attempting to restore his or reputation in defamation proceedings.

This operational assumption, obvious throughout the present case, has the effect of reversing the onus of proof. The person accused must do the nigh on impossible, prove his innocence. And the consequences for a person wrongly accused, made worse by judicial embracing of the unfair assumption that the accuser is always to be believed, are totally devastating on the innocent person so publicly accused in the media.

---

438 Carolyn Hoyle, Naomi-Ellen Speechley, and Ros Burnett, University of Oxford Centre for Criminology, *The Impact of Being Wrongly Accused of Abuse in Occupations of Trust: Victims' Voices*, 15 November 2016, at page 9.

The evidence is that not all complaints by adults of historic sex abuse are true. Indeed, a presumption that they are true is unjust to the one complained of and blinds judges to the reality of what their obligations really are, namely, to get to the truth based upon fact. The judges Justice Gray and Justices Vanstone, Nicholson, and Bampton seemed not to be up to date where these matters are concerned and proceeded upon the basis of a false assumption or prejudice.

Weighing in the balance

The question of judges "weighing" probabilities, and "weighing" the evidence of one person against another is philosophically problematic. In his judgement, Justice Gray made many such references. These are some which are particularly problematic.

> **The emphatic nature of the plaintiff's denials of the use of the term "ménage à trois" to Monsignor Cappo and the evidence volunteered about the rumour, strongly tell against any confidence that I might have in accepting or giving weight to his emphatic and positive denials in other aspects of his evidence. [203]**
>
> **I have also expressed my concern in accepting or giving weight to the plaintiff's emphatic and positive denials. [425]**
>
> **I am satisfied on the balance of probabilities that it is an event that in fact took place. [392]**

I am satisfied that Jane's evidence of the incidents that took place at Meningie and St Mark's College establish on the balance of probabilities the commission by the plaintiff of the criminal offence of gross indecency contrary to s 58 of the Criminal Law Consolidation Act 1935 as it applied at the time. [425]

I balance that against the clarity of Dr Kay's recollection of the detail of the circumstances surrounding the incident and my impression that Dr Kay's evidence concerning this and the other incidents was not a fabrication. [242]

The least contentious use of "weighing" is the consideration of the "balance of probabilities" if by which we mean an objective assessment of the cogency of the evidence. Here the judge considers the reliability and probative value of evidence in terms of what is clearly and cogently shown to be probably true. However, whatever may be true in "theory", it is to the judicial practice we must turn.

First, consider what the terms are meant to mean. In his essay, "Proof on the balance of probabilities: what this means in practice", His Honour Judge Stephen Davies (UK) refers to several case judgements.

In a family case (Re B [2008] UKHL 35), Lord Hoffman answered that question using a mathematical analogy:

"If a legal rule requires a fact to be proved (a 'fact in issue'), a judge or jury must

decide whether or not it happened. There is no room for a finding that it might have happened. The law operates a binary system in which the only values are 0 and 1. The fact either happened or it did not. If the tribunal is left in doubt, the doubt is resolved by a rule that one party or the other carries the burden of proof. If the party who bears the burden of proof fails to discharge it, a value of 0 is returned and the fact is treated as not having happened. If he does discharge it, a value of 1 is returned and the fact is treated as having happened."

In another family case (In re H (Minors) [1996] AC 563 at 586), Lord Nicholls explained that it was a flexible test:

"The balance of probability standard means that a court is satisfied an event occurred if the court considers that, on the evidence, the occurrence of the event was more likely than not. When assessing the probabilities the court will have in mind as a factor, to whatever extent is appropriate in the particular case, that the more serious the allegation the less likely it is that the event occurred and, hence, the stronger should be the evidence before the court concludes that the allegation is established on the balance of probability. Fraud is usually less likely than negligence. Deliberate physical injury is usually less likely than accidental physical injury. A stepfather

is usually less likely to have repeatedly raped and had non-consensual oral sex with his under age stepdaughter than on some occasion to have lost his temper and slapped her. Built into the preponderance of probability standard is a generous degree of flexibility in respect of the seriousness of the allegation. Although the result is much the same, this does not mean that where a serious allegation is in issue the standard of proof required is higher. It means only that the inherent probability or improbability of an event is itself a matter to be taken into account when weighing the probabilities and deciding whether, on balance, the event occurred. The more improbable the event, the stronger must be the evidence that it did occur before, on the balance of probability, its occurrence will be established."

To quote again from Lord Hoffman, this time in a judicial review case (Secretary of State for the Home Department v Rehman [2001] UKHL 47):

"It would need more cogent evidence to satisfy [a judge] that the creature seen walking in Regent's Park was more likely than not to have been a lioness than to be satisfied to the same standard of probability that it was an Alsatian."

What is the difference between succeeding on the balance of probabilities and failing

on the balance of probabilities? In one case (Miller v Minister of Pensions [1947] 2 All ER 372) Denning J said:

"If the evidence is such that the tribunal can say 'we think it more probable than not' the burden is discharged, but if the probabilities are equal it is not."

Judge Davies goes on to remark that, if one is expressing "balance in percentage terms, if a judge concludes that it is 50% likely that the claimant's case is right, then the claimant will lose. By contrast, if the judge concludes that it is 51% likely that the claimant's case is right then the claimant will win. One may well ask how the judge is expected to measure the probabilities of a case to 1%!"[439]

The South Australian *Law Handbook* relevantly defines the "balance of probabilities" in these terms:

The standard of proof required in civil law cases, i.e. it is more probable than not that what the person says happened is true.[440]

The difficulty here is that there are no scales for weighing evidence or persons or probabilities because we are attempting to commensurate incommensurables. The device of "weighing" purports to attribute some kind of quasi-scientific basis to the process in which the judge

439 His Honour Judge Stephen Davies, *Proof on the balance of probabilities: what this means in practice*, 22nd October 2009. https://uk.practicallaw.thomsonreuters.com/2-500-6576?service=ld&__lrTS=20170430022322000&transitionType=Default&contextData=(sc.Default)&firstExhibit Page=true&bhcp=1

440 *Law Handbook*, Legal Services Commission of SA at http://www.lawhandbook.sa.gov.au/go01.php

is said to be engaging. Judge Davies asks the question: "One may well ask how the judge is expected to measure the probabilities of a case to 1%!" Another, possibly more important, question is to ask just what judges think they are doing when they are "weighing" and "balancing".

Justice Gray helpfully directed our attention to this passage from *Neat Holdings Pty Ltd v Karajan Holdings Pty Ltd*,

> **The ordinary** standard of proof required of a party who bears the onus in civil litigation in this country is proof on the balance of probabilities. That remains so even where the matter to be proved involves criminal conduct or fraud. On the other hand the strength of the evidence necessary to establish a fact or facts on the balance of probabilities may vary according to the nature of what it is sought to prove. Thus, authoritative statements have often been made to the effect that clear or cogent or strict proof is necessary "where so serious a matter as fraud is to be found". Statements to the effect should not, however, be understood as directed to the standard of proof. Rather they should be understood as merely reflecting a conventional perception that members of our society do not ordinarily engage in fraudulent or criminal conduct and a judicial approach that a court should not lightly make a finding that, on the balance of probabilities, a party to civil litigation has been guilty of **such conduct**.[441]

441 (1992) 110 ALR 449 at 450.

So, the judge is not just "balancing" but has also to consider evidence against standards of "clear and cogent proof" based on "a conventional perception that members of our society do not ordinarily engage in fraudulent or criminal conduct and a judicial approach that a court should not lightly make a finding that, on the balance of probabilities a party to civil litigation has been guilty of such conduct". How the judge is to carry out this process is not explained. Apparently, it is just up to the judge.

However, Justice Gray arguably moved well beyond the strictures he, himself, described. He spoke of "giving weight" to evidence, of being convinced on "the balance of probabilities" (without qualification), and resolving the contradictions in evidence given by Peter Kay by balancing "the confusion in Dr Kay's mind" against the "clarity of Dr Kay's recollection" concerning other details and Justice Gray's "impression that Dr Kay's evidence concerning this and the other incidents was not a fabrication".

This is pure fantasy. Such an approach leads to entirely subjective judgements. There are no scales capable of giving a measure here. Legal philosopher John Finnis, in his critique of consequentialism, put it this way:

> **... it is senseless to try to sum up the quantity of the size of this page, the quantity of the number six, and the quantity of the mass of this book.**[442]

442 John Finnis, *Natural Law and Natural Right,* Clarendon Press, Oxford, 1980, at page 115.

This is called trying to commensurate things which are incommensurable. In the context of moral philosophy, Alasdair MacIntyre described this kind of consequentialist thinking as:

> **a rhetoric which serves to conceal behind the masks of morality what are in fact the preferences of arbitrary will and desire.**[443]

MacIntyre's point is particularly appropriate when judges start talking about how much weight they will give to a piece of evidence. There are no scales with which to do this.

Justice Gray is apparently claiming to have a set of scales to weigh on one side Peter Kay's imprecisions, contradictions, and inconsistencies, against on the other side what Justice Gray considers to be the clarity of Peter Kay's recollections and, even more astonishingly, Justice Gray's personal impression or feeling that Kay was telling the truth. This is not justice so much as the rhetoric of arbitrariness, a rhetoric which serves to conceal behind the masks of justice what "are in fact the preferences of arbitrary will and desire".

It is established facts which should decide the issue, not a lottery as to whether a witness appeals personally to the judge or is a witness that the judge feels 'attracted to' or 'charmed by'. It is suggested that throughout his judgement one can perceive Justice Gray's personal preference to believe the allegations of the alleged victim. She and he must be believed unless proved otherwise.

Such prejudice helps explain the extraordinary lengths Justice Gray went to in his use of selective quotes to establish and support his preferred narrative.

443 Alasdair MacIntyre, *After Virtue*, (London: Duckworth, 1987), 71.

Add to this the philosophically dubious and untrustworthy nonsense of "weighing" and "balancing" quite different entities, then Justice Gray was able to make his subjective opinions appear more like an objective scientific evaluation. In fact, they are no more than an expression of his "preferences of arbitrary will and desire".

Errors in fact

Not only were there serious errors in logic in the judgements made in this case, there were also serious errors of fact and interpretation of evidence. Here are just seven examples of the many errors identified in the judgements.

Factual error 1

Justice Gray stated that Dr Fleming had "admitted that the evidence he gave of the rumour about having a child with a Member of Parliament was wrong". Justice Gray was wrong about that as the evidence demonstrated. When Counsel for Dr Fleming, Paul Heywood-Smith KC, began examining former MP and Minister Mark Brindal about the truth of whether there was such a rumour, Counsel for *The Advertiser* objected on the grounds of relevance because it was not being suggested by the defendant that that rumour was wrong.

> **MR HEYWOOD-SMITH: It's not for that purpose, it's for the purpose of explaining or supporting the witness's explanation as to his making a mistake about that, about making a mistake about what he told**

> **Monsignor Cappo and the fact that there had been such a rumour at that time which could have founded that mistake. If my friend is not going to take any issue about that, about the fact of there having been a rumour, then I won't press the evidence.**
>
> **MR HARRIS: The position is, as you would recall, I didn't put to the plaintiff that he invented the rumour, so it wouldn't be open to me, but I don't intend to do it anyway.**
>
> **HIS HONOUR: On that basis it's very difficult to justify the relevance.**[444]

That there was such a rumour, was not disputed by Harris or by Justice Gray. On that basis Justice Gray ruled that it would be "irrelevant" to further investigate the matter. Why, then, does Justice Gray say, in his judgement, that Dr Fleming had "admitted that the evidence he gave of the rumour about having a child with a Member of Parliament was wrong"?

Factual error 2

Justice Gray says that Dr Fleming wrongly denied using the term "ménage à trois" to Monsignor Cappo. It is Justice Gray who is wrong. Dr Fleming rightly denied using those words in the context in which it was put to him. When Monsignor Cappo made his notes of a meeting that took place more than 20 years previously, it transpired that Dr Fleming did utter that French term but

444 *Transcript of evidence given in Court* at page 2446 line 36 – page 2447 line 12

in an entirely different context. Dr Fleming's description of that other context, once it was revealed thanks to Monsignor Cappo's notes being produced by subpoena, was that there was no "rumour" but a misunderstanding of an innocent event that occurred and in an entirely different location on an entirely different date. This account was verified by two witnesses who gave evidence to that effect. In any case, a failure of memory should never be treated as the equivalent of a lie or general unreliability.

Factual error 3

One of the reasons why Justice Gray discredited expert witness Dr Michelle Arnold was that he thought she had got wrong a particular fact. But it was Justice Gray who got wrong this fact in evidence. Justice Gray asserts that the references provided by Dr Arnold provide "no support for Dr Arnold's hypothesis that Father Stephenson influenced Jane's memory in that or any other respect." However, when we go to the evidence itself it is clear that it is Justice Gray who has got wrong the sequence of events which in turn leads him to make the further mistake that the facts do not support Dr Arnold's conclusions.

All the references provided by Dr Arnold, taken together, provide ample support for Dr Arnold's conclusion that the Reverend John Stephenson influenced Jane's memory in that and in other respects. Having got that wrong Justice Gray then traduced the professionalism of Dr Arnold, thereby further undermining her evidence and allowing him to dismiss what she has to say.

This is crucial since it is the expert witness that gave scientific reasons why Jane's evidence should not be accepted in the way Justice Gray wants to accept it.

Factual error 4

Where the Anglican cleric the Reverend Alan Courtney is concerned, Justice Gray makes a series of errors. For example, he does not understand that Mr Courtney is an advocate for Peter Kay who stated he believed what Peter Kay told him but was not interested in discovering whether what he was being told was true.

Factual error 5

Justice Gray also wrongly asserts that Mr Courtney was free to choose what was his role in the pastoral issue he discovered. In fact, Mr Courtney had no right to deal with the Matter. Mr Courtney was a very newly ordained Deacon with little to no pastoral experience. Under Church law, he was obligated to take such a serious matter to the Rector of the Parish or, if not appropriate, to the Archbishop. That obligation was one of the promises that he swore at his ordination a month or two earlier. That Peter Kay didn't want him to take the matter to the Archbishop was irrelevant.

This was a case of mandatory reporting.

Factual error 6

Justice Gray manipulated the evidence to give credence to a very specific allegation by Peter Kay involving Dr Fleming sharing a room with him at University Anglican Society camps. The evidence from four independent witnesses was that such an arrangement never occurred it being Dr Fleming's policy that he would not share a room with a student or students. Against the evidence Justice Gray concluded that something must have happened and in a way that not even Peter Kay himself alleged.

Factual error 7

Justices Vanstone, Nicholson, and Bampton misrepresented a crucial part of Dr Fleming's appeal: "The appellant complains in ground 2.4 that, in accepting Jane's evidence of the Meningie incident, **the Judge "failed to consider" the contrary evidence of Mrs Alison Fleming** ...". But what Dr Fleming put in his written submissions to these judges was this:

> **Justice Gray "failed to consider the evidence of the third person involved in the Meningie incident before finding at [392] that Jane's allegation is true."**

Having misrepresented the ground of appeal, Justices Vanstone, Nicholson, and Bampton quarantined the actual ground of appeal from any kind of rational consideration.

Uncorroborated and based on hearsay

In nearly every important respect the witnesses called upon by *The Advertiser* were not in a position to corroborate the allegations made. Their evidence was nearly all based on hearsay, with an abundance of different versions of what they said they had been told by the complainants.

How any sensible judge could arrive at a conclusion that these allegations (by two of the three complainants) were substantially true to the level required by *Briginshaw* is beyond comprehension.

The hearsay rule has been described by the Legal Services Commission of South Australia:

> **Hearsay**
>
> A witness will be asked to tell the court only what she or he saw or heard, not what someone else told the witness had occurred. This is hearsay evidence.
>
> For example, a witness can say 'I saw Jill push Jack down the hill' but cannot say 'I wasn't there at the time, but Tom Piper told me that he saw Jill push Jack down the hill'.
>
> Whether a particular piece of evidence is hearsay or not is often a difficult question to answer, as this is a complex area of law and there are many exceptions to the general rule.[445]

This is the provision in the South Australia Evidence Act 1929

> Subject to this Act, this section does not apply to a statement made outside of a court admitted as evidence in any proceedings under an exception to the rule against hearsay at common law or under this Act.

Then we must know what the common law (judge-made law) regards as exceptions to the general rule against the admissibility of hearsay evidence.

445 http://www.lawhandbook.sa.gov.au/ch13s06s01s02.php

However, when a person tells another person or persons about something they say somebody else did with them many years previously, it is reasonable to suppose that that evidence, even if admitted, should be treated with rather more caution than was evident in this trial.

In so far as these matters are concerned, one can say with certainty that none of the allegations made about Dr Fleming were corroborated by any of the witnesses called by Peter Kay. On the other hand, Dr Fleming provided corroboration for what he said, a summary of which was given in Chapter Nine, in the section "Evaluation of Peter Kay's evidence".

The fact that Peter Kay told Sue Kay and Mr Courtney that Dr Fleming did certain sexual things with him in the past is not corroboration. Such evidence, which is an exception to the general rule against "hearsay", might be used to demonstrate whether there was consistency in what Kay is now saying and what he told others some time ago.

But that consistency was not there as the evidence revealed. In two matters, (mediation at St Peter's College and sharing a room with Peter Kay and Mr Courtney) his evidence was contradicted by Mr Courtney. And there were many other inconsistencies between what Peter Kay said to Mr Courtney and what he said to Sue Kay. Taking some 121 paragraphs, Justice Gray laboured mightily to explain away most of the multitude of inconsistencies between the evidence of Peter Kay, Sue Kay, and Mr Courtney discovered at trial.[446] But he had already found

446 Justice Gray *judgement*, at paragraphs 204-325.

against Fleming's credibility before he undertook the task of reviewing the evidence of Kay, Sue Kay, and Courtney.

Are these errors important?

These errors of logic and fact described above are very important to the outcome of the trial going, as they do, to the heart of the matter. It was Dr Fleming's case that the Meningie incident (in any of the three alleged different accounts) never occurred. Neither did any of the other incidents alleged by Jane, either at Brighton or St Mark's, occur. There was never proof based on probability of any kind, evidence needed to prove their substantial truth according to the *Briginshaw* standard.

The evidence presented concerning the issues where Peter Kay is concerned were all subject to serious doubt. In the end that evidence amounted to no more than Peter Kay's allegations, or what Peter Kay told other people who had no independent evidence of their own. The only exception to this was Mr Courtney's evidence that Dr Fleming made certain admissions to him, admissions contradicted by Dr Fleming's evidence and by the fact that Dr Fleming proceeded to ordination after these matters were investigated by Archbishop Faulkner.

There is more than one explanation for the events based upon the evidence provided to the Court. To none of these did Justice Gray give any serious consideration.

Further

There are other issues connected with the way this matter was handled by the Courts which ought to give the

Parliament and the community at large major cause for concern about the way these judges dealt with this case.

1. Justice Gray's intolerable delay in handing down his judgement (12 months) and the doubt that brings to the way he dealt with the matter at hand casts serious doubt on the reliability of his memory of the evidence given in the case.
2. The judges in the Supreme Court who heard the appeal were lazy and incompetent in failing to carry out their duties properly. Justices Vanstone, Nicholson, and Bampton made it quite clear that they sided with the presiding judge Justice Gray from beginning to end. They exhibited anti-Catholic prejudice (see n. 6 below) of an intolerable kind. They did not take seriously the grounds of appeal such that they would do the hard work in reviewing the evidence they needed to review in an independent manner. They misreported one of the most important grounds of appeal and so failed to deal with it. They hid behind cop out terms such as "it was open" to Justice Gray to conclude the way he did even when such conclusions were shown to be illogical and against the evidence at trial. The other favourite cop out term used by both Justice Gray and Justices Vanstone, Nicholson, and Bampton was that the judge was "not assisted" by the evidence. Do these judges not realise how pompous and how high-handed that sounds? It was clear that the judges in the Full Court hearing the appeal were never going to overturn Justice Gray. Was this because of judicial solidarity

together with certain assumptions common to them all?

3. The High Court, the highest Court in the land, is just not open for business where ordinary folk are concerned. The way in which the application for leave to appeal was dealt with seemed contemptuous of the very detailed material put to them. That Court gave no reasons for the decision beyond simply declaring that the appeal would be certain to fail. No reasons were provided by the judges in question as to why this would necessarily be the outcome. The Federal Government needs to look at the way things are handled in this Court as well. Is it the case that the High Court is, as many people have told the present writer, seriously underfunded such that it simply cannot deal with all the appeals that come its way? Justice is never served when Courts are understaffed, underfunded, and unable to discharge their responsibilities in the way they would wish. That the High Court is simply not equipped to deal with all the appeals that come to them because it is not sufficiently resourced to do what the Constitution requires of it is cold comfort to the litigator. If it is true that the High Court is forced to make choices as to which cases they will hear because of a lack of funding, then any fair-minded person would have sympathy with the judges concerned. The Federal Parliament has the duty to see that the Highest Court in the land is properly resourced to enable it to carry out fully its constitutional

responsibilities. The Parliament owes that to the Australian people. Notwithstanding any difficulties the High Court may face, and no matter how much sympathy one might have for the judges, those difficulties should not be visited upon persons who have a legitimate claim to appeal. **The dismissal out of hand of serious matters for appeal is intolerable in terms of the demands of justice.**

4. In fact, serious legal matters were raised for the High Court to deal with in relation to *Briginshaw*. It is undoubtedly the case that different judges in the SA Supreme Court apply *Briginshaw* in different ways. This is not the fault of Parliaments since *Briginshaw*, and other case judgements related to it, are a creation of the High Court itself. Those who wish to sue for defamation should have reasonable certainty as to what is the meaning of the law. If the High Court won't sort out the confusion that it has created, then the Federal Parliament should legislate to do it for them.
5. Justices Vanstone, Nicholson, and Bampton stated that any prejudice involved in witnesses unable to testify due to death or infirmity should be visited on the appellant. The reason behind why these witnesses were unavailable to testify is the extraordinarily long delay in the complainants making their complaints. This ruling by Justices Vanstone, Nicholson, and Bampton was not made on the basis of any stated authorities and may well now become a precedent for other cases. This is outrageous. Why did the High Court not

see that this was a matter of law crying out for clarification?

6. Justices Vanstone, Nicholson, and Bampton introduced into their reasoning public anti-Catholic prejudice in relation to the utility of Archbishop Faulkner's evidence (if it could have been given) and to the public record of what he did do which indicated that he found no fault in Dr Fleming that would stand in the way of his ordination. Again, it is not at all unreasonable to ask the High Court to deal with that. Will this use of prejudice find its way into other judgements now that the Full Court of the Supreme Court of South Australia has used prejudice in this way and the High Court has refused leave to appeal because the appellant would be certain to lose? This is another very serious matter with which the High Court was unwilling to deal.

Judges failing in their duties

The reason why, in the passage quoted, it is stated that the judges should first of all be asked their reasons, is to make it clear that the judges ought to judge the truth in accordance with the evidence.[447]

It is argued that the judges involved in *Fleming v The Advertiser* failed in their duties and failed spectacularly. The duties of judges were well set out in a paper delivered by the former Chief Justice of the High Court, The Hon Sir Gerard Brennan, AC KBE.

447 St Thomas Aquinas, *Summa Theologiae*, II-II, q. 67, a. 2, Reply Obj. 1.

Where arbitrariness is concerned, Sir Gerard said this:

> **Be cautious in the use of the umbrella phrases: "I prefer the evidence of X to the evidence of Y where their evidence conflicts". That smacks more of a formula than it does of reasoning, especially when the real choice may be as it often is between two defective recollections.**[448]

This is exactly what Justice Gray did in arbitrarily preferring the evidence of Sue Kay, one of his pantheon of "primary witnesses", to that of Alison Fleming, where there was only a relatively minor difference in memory of an unrecorded luncheon conversation which took place some 20 years previously. He used that arbitrary preference to conclude that this told against Alison Fleming being considered a reliable and truthful witness. In his judgement[449] Justice Gray failed to present an argument to justify his conclusion, instead using terms such as:

> **"The impression I got ..."**
>
> **"Doing the best I can with these varying versions and having regard to the impression each of the witnesses made upon me ..."**
>
> **"I accept Ms Kay's evidence ..."**
>
> **"I essentially accept ..."; "I do not accept ..."**

448 The Hon Sir Gerard Brennan, AC KBE, "The Role of the Judge", given at the *National Judicial Orientation Programme,* Novotel NorthBeach, Wollongong, NSW, Australia, 13th of October 1996.

449 Justice Gray judgement, at paragraphs 301-305.

"I do not consider …"

"I do not think…"; "I also do not think …"

All we have is the judge's feelings on the matter, seemingly based upon his undeclared assumptions. The judge is there to determine fact, not opinion, belief, consideration, or acceptance.

Justices Vanstone, Nicholson, and Bampton accepted Justice Gray's preference for Sue Kay's evidence, even though the evidence at stake condemned none of the parties (Sue Kay, Alison Fleming, or Dr Fleming) as a liar, unreliable, or deliberately misleading. They just didn't entirely agree where their recollections were concerned although it is obvious that they mostly agreed.

And finally, in addressing the issue of impartiality, Sir Gerard made these important observations:

> **I should say something about impartiality, the supreme judicial virtue, and the appearance of impartiality. They can be impaired in a variety of ways, some of which are too obvious to require comment. Those ways include too close a connection with, or expressions of support for, causes albeit the causes are laudable. Impartiality and its appearance can be impaired by such an intellectual predilection for one view of an issue falling for determination as precludes, or appears to preclude a fair consideration of contrary argument. And beware of expressions that emphasise forward-looking, right-thinking or politically correct attitudes, for such expressions might be**

> **thought to trim a judgment to the breeze of public or political approval.**[450]

It is contended that Justices Vanstone, Nicholson, and Bampton failed the test of impartiality by embracing anti-Catholic attitudes, particularly where the matter involves a Catholic priest facing allegations of sexual abuse, and the assumption that those who make historic claims of being sexually abused are telling the truth, thereby reversing the onus of proof in a defamation case. As discussed above and supported by the authoritative report of the Centre for Criminology at the University of Oxford (UK), the evidence is that not all complaints by adults of historic sex abuse are true. Indeed, a presumption that they are true is unjust to the one complained of and blinds judges to the reality of what their obligations really are.

It need hardly be said that Justice Gray's many errors are responsible for a serious miscarriage of justice. These failings include:

a) His delay in handing down judgement, a delay which is "intolerable" by any decent standards of judicial rectitude.
b) His apparent impaired capacity for rational thought where emotionally charged cases are concerned demonstrated by his embrace of logical fallacies.
c) His all-too-ready willingness 'to throw Mrs Fleming under the bus' by defaming her as an unreliable witness who does not tell the truth.

---

450 *Ibid.*

d) His willingness to excuse almost every demonstrated instance of self-contradiction and inconsistency in the witnesses for *The Advertiser* while affording no such consideration to minor inconsistencies by Dr Fleming and Mrs Fleming.
e) His general privileging of witnesses for *The Advertiser* as "principal witnesses".
f) His misunderstanding of evidence on key points which led him to take an unreasonable and toxic attitude to, for example, Dr Arnold, the expert witness in the case.

The Hon Justice M H McHugh

As long ago as the thirteenth century AD, St Thomas Aquinas referred to the important duty of a judge to provide reasons for their conclusions:

> **The reason why ... it is stated that the judges should first of all be asked their reasons, is to make it clear that the judges ought to judge the truth in accordance with the evidence.**[451]

His Honour Justice M H McHugh, a former judge of the High Court of Australia was of the same opinion as Aquinas. In a paper given at the Australian Bar Association Conference in 1998, Mr McHugh stated:

> **Reasons are therefore essential to the common law judicial method. Moreover,**

451 "Ad primum ergo dicendum quod ideo praemittitur in verbis illis de quaestione iudicibus facienda, ut intelligatur quod iudices debent veritatem iudicare secundum ea quae fuerunt sibi proposita." St Thomas Aquinas, *Summa Theologiae,* II-II, q. 67, a. 2, Reply Obj. 1.

> **those reasons must be so structured that they serve at least three purposes. First, they must permit the parties to see the extent to which their arguments have been understood and accepted. Lord MacMillan thought that the main object of a reasoned judgment "is not only to do but to seem to do justice." Second, they must be reasons that clearly explain the reasoning process and thereby further judicial accountability. Third, those reasons must declare and apply a principle or rule at a level of generality that transcends the facts of the case and enables other courts to decide other cases, identical in principle but not in detail, in the same way. It is necessary for a court to declare a rule or principle at this level of generality because, under the common law system of adjudication, courts not only resolve disputes but formulate rules and principles that can be used to decide comparable cases.**[452]

All the judges concerned in this matter failed the first test: "they must permit the parties to see the extent to which their arguments have been understood and accepted". If arguments are not understood they are unlikely to be accepted. As we have already seen, it is anything but clear that Justice Gray and Justices Vanstone, Nicholson, and Bampton understood the arguments put to them. The same may be said of the

452 The Hon Justice M H McHugh AC, "The Judicial Method", *The Australian Bar Association Conference, London, England*, 5 July 1998.

High Court judges who, without explanation, refused to hear an appeal in the case of *Fleming v The Advertiser*.

That the same judges failed the second of the McHugh purposes is also clear. When a judge makes egregious logical errors, misinterprets evidence, and gets some evidence wrong, he or she is hardly likely to be described as one who has provided reasons "that clearly explain the reasoning process and thereby further judicial accountability".

Justices Vanstone, Nicholson, and Bampton formulated a principle that a person who chooses to defend his reputation in Court must bear the prejudice that arises because of the death and incapacity of crucial witnesses, because that choice was freely made. That principle was applied to this case even though it is a formulation that lacks legal precedence and contravenes common sense.

Moreover, Justice Gray and Justices Vanstone, Nicholson, and Bampton adopted a long-since overturned legal principle, that a wife is not competent to give true and objective evidence in a civil case involving her husband. How this would be in accord with McHugh's third purpose for legal reasoning has defeated the present writer.

That Justices Vanstone, Nicholson, and Bampton seem not to have examined the evidence available to them dispassionately is a disgrace.

What is to be done?

The answer to that question is far from clear. All legal avenues seem to have been closed to Dr Fleming.

Could the High Court reconsider its position? After all the bench contains men and women of the highest integrity and are said to have been chosen from among the best legal brains in the country, and there would not appear to be any rule barring them from revisiting a purely procedural question.

Could the Federal Parliament (or State Parliaments) act? Yes, they could. They could legislate to clarify *Briginshaw,* to clarify what should be the correct principles of proof that apply in civil matters such as defamation where the person suing is doing so because of allegations of a serious criminal offence. The Federal Government could better fund and staff the High Court. All Parliaments could legislate to make it clear to judges that the intrusion of religious or any other form of unjust prejudice into their judgement will not be tolerated with the punishment being that such judges would be removed from their position and the matter being required to be heard again. It could make clear that many of the difficulties where witnesses are concerned in historical cases should not be visited upon the appellant in defamation cases.

There are two other possible ways forward. The High Court could be urged to hear the matter by either the Attorney-General or the Chief Justice of the Supreme Court. Both have been asked. Both have refused.

The Attorney-General

Where the then Attorney-General, the Honorable Vickie Chapman, is concerned, she gave a short answer to the question put to her on my behalf. She indicated that she was not minded to intervene to support an application for special leave to the High Court. Why not? She didn't say.

The Chief Justice of the Supreme Court of South Australia

On 6 February 2021 I wrote to the Chief Justice of the Supreme Court, the Honourable C Kourakis. Chief Justice Kourakis was one of the three judges which heard the appeal in the Poniatowska matter, and which had correctly and fully applied *Briginshaw*. I thought that once he was aware that the law had been incorrectly applied in my matter, he might draw it to the attention of the High Court perhaps asking the High Court to look again at my applications for leave to appeal

> **... Recalling that the judgement in *Poniatowska* by Blue J is supported by Kourakis CJ and Nicholson J and that the dismissal of Fleming's appeal by the same SA Supreme Court involved Nicholson J, a further question arises. How can Nicholson J have concurred with *Vanstone* in the terms of the rejection of the appeal against the *Gra*y judgement while later endorsing the judgement written by Blue J? Does this mean that Nicholson has two minds depending upon the case he is hearing, and which might be thought of as prejudice against the Catholic party in *Fleming v The Advertiser*? Or is it the practice in the SA Supreme Court for one of the three judges to do the work with the other two signing off**

on the judgement after only a very cursory look at what the judgement actually says and how it is argued? ...

This is only the beginning of my complaints about the way I was treated by judges in the SA Supreme Court. The major errors in logic, the arbitrary favouring of the defendant's witnesses (none of whom corroborated allegations) as "principal witnesses" or "main witnesses" while ignoring the evidence given by the plethora of witnesses who corroborated Fleming's evidence, the rejection without sound reason of the evidence of an independent expert witness on memory, together with the major errors pointed out above cries out for action.

I am appealing to you as Chief Justice to do something about this because my life has been unjustly ruined by the manifest failures of our judicial system over which you preside. I have no reason to, and nor do I, include you in that observation. My family has been badly affected. So too has the reputation of the Court been badly affected as some legal scholars are now noticing, and because, in any case, truth and justice are meant to count for something. Would that I had had, as judges in my matter, Blue J, et al who dealt with the *Poniatowska* matter.

I write in trust that you will want to see fairness and justice triumph in my matter

> **and in the hope that you will be able to do something about the fact that the law has not been equally applied in my case and to my great disadvantage.**

He did not reply. Instead, on the 11 February 2021, I received a response from someone to whom I did not write, his Associate, Patrick Schaefer.

> **The Chief Justice cannot intervene in, interfere with, or reverse decisions made by the independent judicial officers of this Court. The proper avenue for challenging a judgement of this Court is by way of appeal to the High Court of Australia.**

With respect I think that the Chief Justice's Associate is quite wrong in what he says in the first sentence. And assuming the Chief Justice read my letter (and I have no idea whether he did), I further assume he agreed with his Mr Schaefer.

I consulted the *Supreme Court Act 1935* which defined the role of Chief Justice in these terms:

> **9A—The Chief Justice**
>
> **(1) The Chief Justice is the principal judicial officer of the court.**
>
> **(2) The Chief Justice is responsible for the administration of the court.**

I also consulted the Rules which seem to be interested mainly in fees.

Further, the *Constitution Act 1934* defines Chief Justice thus:

76—Definitions

(1) In this Part, unless the contrary intention appears—

the Chief Justice means the Chief Justice of the Supreme Court and includes any other judge of the Supreme Court who is acting in the office of Chief Justice;

In his Foreword to the book *First Among Equals,* the Hon JJ Doyle AC, former Chief Justice of the SA Supreme Court, acknowledges that the role of Chief Justice is not tightly defined apart from referencing one or two of his duties which in subsequent times have been shed. Crucially, The Honourable JJ Doyle makes this observation about the strategy used by the author of the book, Dr John Emerson. "Dr Emerson's study of the lives of the five Chief Justices who have held office since Federation is an attempt to remedy the lack of information about this office." The Hon JJ Doyle then cites Dr Emerson himself on the way he has gone about structuring his book.

Because the importance of personal interpretation of the role, the book is divided accordingly into chapters on each successive Chief Justice. This biographical structure acts as a foundation for a more socio-historical exploration of the way each Chief Justice dealt with not only changing community expectations of justice but broader changes in society as well.[453]

453 John Emerson, *First Among Equals,* Adelaide, the University of Adelaide Barr Smith Press, 2006, vi -vii.

In his subsequent Introduction to the book, The Hon JJ Doyle again refers to what he calls

> **the importance of personal interpretation of the role ...**[454]

The title of the book, *First Among Equals,* is a translation of the of Latin tag, *primus inter pares*. The term itself proves little about how the "First" exercises his powers/authority. For example

> **Just as the monarch is first among equals in the ruling family, the ruling family itself is first among equals among the tribes of a given country.**[455]

And since the Chief Justice "is responsible for the administration of the court", and the Court is meant to be about justice, I don't see why he **cannot** intervene to assist in having the application for leave to appeal to the High Court granted and the appeal heard. He just chooses not to. In this matter, Chief Justice C Kourakis should be aware that a mistake in the application of *Briginshaw* has occurred. He only has to compare the judgement in which he concurred concerning Poniatowska with the judgments in *Fleming v The Advertiser.*

That being the case then, given his legal right to interpret his role in new ways in changing social circumstances, it is entirely open to the Chief Justice to intervene in this and other matters where an injustice has occurred. As the name of his office implies, his role is about the administration of **justice**.

---

454 *Ibid.*, 9.

455 https://www.britannica.com/topic/primus-inter-pares

Chapter Thirteen

Allegations of Bias or Improper Motive

In this book, the judges concerned (Justice Gray and Justices Vanstone, Nicholson, and Bampton) have been accused of embracing prejudice based on evidence contained within their own written judgements. Those prejudices are three in number:

1. The adult complainant of sexual abuse alleged to have occurred when the complainant was underage some 40 years previously, is presumed to be telling the truth in all relevant respects. Any conflict in accounts between witnesses must be resolved in favour of the complainant.
2. The wife of the one accused cannot give independent and unbiased evidence. This belief, shared by all the judges concerned as revealed in their judgements, is now an outdated belief belonging to the nineteenth and early twentieth centuries. Nevertheless, it is a belief/prejudice seemingly still held by Justice Gray and Justices Vanstone, Nicholson, and Bampton.
3. A Catholic priest *qua* Catholic priest is not to be believed.
4. Catholic Archbishop Faulkner is presumed by Justices Vanstone, Nicholas, and Bampton to have

> been incompetent in dealing with allegations of sex abuse even though no evidence was led to support that view and based solely on the unproved theory that Catholic leaders are in general unreliable in such matters. Such anti-Catholic prejudice in a case involving the alleged defamation of a Catholic priest, is particularly scandalous.

As I have indicated in this book, all three prejudices clearly influenced the outcome of the trials.

Reiteration of the main thesis of this book

In the year 2008 *The Advertiser/Sunday Mail* published stories which seriously defamed Dr John Fleming. Dr Fleming sought to exercise his legal right to, at least in some measure, restore his public reputation. He was thwarted in that endeavour when Justice Malcolm Gray of the South Australian Supreme Court found in favour of *The Advertiser/Sunday Mail.*

It is the thesis of this book that Justice Gray's written judgement was incompetent in several respects. First and foremost, it seems to the present writer that Justice Gray decided that he was going to believe the person whose pseudonym is Jane who was the person at the centre of the defamation matter, and that decision was formed by his prejudice in favour of adult women who accuse a Catholic priest of sexual misconduct said to have occurred many decades earlier. He reached his decision on emotional grounds and governed by the popular prejudice that such persons making these allegations are bound to be telling the truth.

Having decided that he would "believe in" Jane, "have faith in" Jane, it seems that Justice Gray then set about making the evidence fit his conclusion. He achieved this end by:

1. Asserting on illogical grounds that Dr Fleming was not a credible witness.
2. Asserting on illogical grounds that Mrs Fleming was not a witness of credit.
3. Asserting on illogical grounds that the expert witness on memory, Dr Michelle Arnold, was not a witness to be relied on.
4. Ignoring the strength of the evidence of many witnesses called by Dr Fleming who corroborated what he had to say.
5. Explicitly favouring witnesses for *The Advertiser/Sunday Mail* even though those witnesses could not corroborate any of the accusations made against Fleming.
6. Explicitly rationalising away the multitude of serious inconsistencies and errors of fact by the witnesses for *The Advertiser/Sunday Mail* to sustain his preferred narrative.
7. Explicitly using minor disagreements between witnesses' memory of certain undocumented conversations or events as reasons to call into question the credibility of witnesses for Dr Fleming, and Dr Fleming himself.
8. Getting wrong his account of the evidence on several crucial points.

9. Employing many logical fallacies to make his prejudged conclusions work.
10. Appearing to embrace the anti-Catholic prejudices which flowed from the tongue of the barrister representing *The Advertiser/Sunday Mail.*

The three judges of the South Australian Supreme Court who heard the appeal produced a judgement that was

1. Lazy and incompetent.
2. Misrepresented the law by arguing that later High Court judgments no longer import the "presumption of innocence" and the consequent requirement of "exactness of proof" into the civil arena and, furthermore, that any references to *Briginshaw* as establishing an "onus" or a "standard" are incorrect.
3. Misrepresented matters of fact.
4. Misrepresented one of the most important grounds of appeal and therefore being able to demolish their 'straw man'.
5. Imported popular anti-Catholic prejudice into their judgement.
6. Showed the same level of intellectual incompetence where ordinary standards of logic are concerned; and
7. Failed in their duty to fully and objectively examine the evidence and take seriously the grounds of appeal.

Justice Gray gave the appearance of understanding that *Briginshaw* should be applied.

> I do not take the Court in Neat Holdings as detracting from the remarks concerning the

> requirement for clear or cogent or strict proof in appropriate cases, of which I regard this as one, dependent, as it is, upon the acceptance or otherwise of the direct evidence of particular witnesses. In Rejfek v McElroy,7° the Court confirmed that proof in a civil case of a serious criminal allegation such as fraud, "should be clear and cogent such as to induce on a balance of probabilities an actual persuasion of the mind as to the existence of the fraud". The Court went on to observe: ... the 'clarity' of the proof required, where so serious a matter as fraud is to be found, is an acknowledgement that the degree of satisfaction for which the civil standard of proof calls may vary according to the gravity of the fact to be proved: see Briginshaw v Briginshaw per Dixon J, Helton v Allen per Starke J, Smith Bros v Madden per Dixon J. (Footnotes omitted) I accept that those remarks apply to the proof required in this case in respect of the sexual misconduct alleged both criminal and otherwise. In addition, the defendants say that the contextual imputations which I have found conveyed by the publications are substantially true. Again, they must make out their case in that regard on the civil onus.[456]

In practice he did not do so. But the Full Court under Justices Vanstone, Nicholas, and Bampton stated that,

456 Justice Malcolm Gray, *Fleming v Advertiser-News Weekend Publishing CO P/L & ANOR (No 2) [2016] SASC 26, 2016,* at paragraphs 184-186

in any case, *Briginshaw* no longer imposed the onus of proof on the respondent (ie no presumption of innocence for the appellant) or even the standard of proof which is to be applied beyond mere balance of probabilities.[457] They effectively abandoned *Briginshaw* as relevant in this matter.

Moreover, the Justice Gray judgement and that of Justices Vanstone, Nicholson and Bampton are clearly at variance with the way the law of defamation was contemporaneously applied in another jurisdiction (the Federal Court of Australia in NSW), concerning Geoffrey Rush, and even in the same Court, the South Australian Supreme Court, in the matter of Poniatowska.

From where is justice to be found in a legal system in which all kinds of prejudices are applied, and where the highest court in the land refuses to grant leave to appeal?

Dr Fleming defamation case: is it unique?

It seems that the case of *Fleming v The Advertiser* is the ONLY civil case where the *Briginshaw* principle has been held not to apply. In all the cases before this one, and in all of those afterwards, judges have applied the *Briginshaw* principle or rule as they were in duty bound so to do.

How is it then that the High Court of Australia could say "The application for special leave to appeal does not raise a question of general importance. None of the

457 Justices Vanstone, Nicholson, and Bampton judgement, at paragraph 108

applicant's proposed appeal grounds enjoys sufficient prospects of success to warrant a grant of special leave."?

Pace the judges of the High Court, how could it not be a "question of general importance" for the well-established common law *Briginshaw* principle not to have been applied in the case of Fleming (unlike any other defamation case) with disastrous consequences for Dr Fleming? How can it not be a matter of general importance for judges in the Supreme Court of South Australia to explicitly deny that ***Briginshaw*** **should not apply in one case while saying that it does apply in all other cases?**

Chapter Fourteen

Afterword

Dr Fleming submits to a lie detector test (polygraph)

Some 18 months before the trial, on the 15th of July 2014, Dr Fleming submitted to a polygraph examination (lie detector test). While Justice Gray chose to disbelieve him on no fair or objective grounds, the polygraph vindicated him as a truth-teller. The specific issue was Jane and whether Fleming had been truthful in his denials of her allegations.

The test was carried out by Steven Van Aperen, a former policeman and Australia's best qualified forensic polygraph examiner. The statements Dr Fleming made in a written and signed declaration, and upon which he was tested, were these:

1. At no time have I performed fellatio on [Jane], conversely at no time has [Jane] performed fellatio on me.
2. In fact, I have never engaged in fellatio with anyone.
3. At no time has [Jane] masturbated me.

Van Aperen then conducted the polygraph in which he put to me the following questions among many others:

Question R5: Have you lied to any of the information contained within your signed declaration form? Response NO

Question R7: Regarding the information contained within your signed declaration form have you lied to any part of it? Response NO

In his written report, Van Aperen concluded that:

> Mr Fleming's polygrams showed no strong or consistent unresolved responses to the aforementioned relevant questions.
>
> After careful evaluation of the physiological responses made by Mr Fleming, **it is the opinion of this examiner that Mr Fleming was truthful when he gave the above indicated answers to relevant questions R5 and R7**.
>
> On the basis of the scientific research cited above **the confidence in the truthful outcome by Mr Fleming is approximately 96%.**

Of course, Australian Courts do not accept lie detector tests as hard evidence, and for good reason.[458] But most reasonable people in the "Court of Public Opinion" do accept that *some account* of these tests should be taken seriously.

458 Contemporary research on polygraph tests suggests they significantly improve the chance to detect deception (NRC, 2013; Honts & Thurber, 2019), but several shortcomings make the application of this technology inefficient and unreliable (Iacono & Ben-Shakhar, 2019; NRC, 2003; Synnott et al., 2015).

Chapter Fifteen

The Behaviour of journalists for *The Advertiser* and *The Sunday Mail*

This book would be incomplete if I did not make some critical comments on the performance of *The Advertiser/Sunday Mail*, and two of its reporters, Nigel Hunt and Sean Fewster, especially given the misleading and inaccurate account of events which Fewster has now used for a further public attack. These two persons have, in my opinion, not behaved in an ethically responsible manner in this matter. In the case of Hunt from the beginning. In the case of Fewster from the beginning of the defamation trial in 2016 to the present day.[459] Indeed, the fact that Fewster continues to prosecute his case against me on his radio programme is a major reason why I have felt it necessary to publish this book – to defend myself.

Some history

Nigel Hunt sent me emails in the days after World Youth Day 2008. In those emails, he said that he was coming to

459 https://www.fiveaa.com.au/podcast/just-lawful

Sydney the next day and wanted to talk to me about my "activities" when I was an Anglican priest in Adelaide. I took his email to be a friendly email, but I had to tell him that I could not see him that week because my schedule was already full.

Subsequently, I received a tip-off from phone calls from Archbishop John Hepworth and lawyer Arlene Macdonald telling me in broad terms what Hunt was up to and that he wanted to talk to me because he was, within a few days, going to run a story accusing me of sexual misconduct.

I cancelled my appointments and stayed at home the following day. Hunt arrived at Campion College with a photographer. He was told I was not in. He then drove to my home and parked his car a couple of doors away from our house where he remained for several hours.

At one point, Hunt and his photographer came to the door of my home and asked to speak to me. Through my wife, I declined because Hunt would not provide me with the full substance of the matters he wished to talk about. In any case, my solicitor strongly advised me not to speak to Hunt. My wife asked Hunt what he really wanted, and whether he would be considering anything that I might have to say before he published his story. He replied that the story was already written, and he just wanted me to respond to it, sight unseen.

At that point, while I knew there were allegations, I wasn't sure from where those allegations were coming. I certainly had no inkling of accusations of a threesome or any suggestion of fellatio, and the stories when first published did not suggest those things. I wasn't advised of the threesome allegation until I was interviewed by the police.

In short, Hunt wanted an immediate response from me to a story that I had not read, the details of which I did not know, and to do so without advanced notice of exactly what he wanted to discuss with me. In the end, he provided a scrappy piece of paper on which he had written a short dot-point list of things he wanted to discuss in the hope that I might change my mind. That shortlist was, by no means, full disclosure. Crucial elements (such as names of complainants and all relevant details) were withheld from me.

Nigel Hunt and unsubstantiated accusations

It should be clear, even to journalists at *The Advertiser*, that public accusations of the kind they were making against me, would have a devastating effect on the person being accused. This is the case whether the accusations are true or not true. *The Advertiser* provided no corroboration for the accusations being made, nor did they investigate the motives of the people concerned. Seemingly adopting the slogan "always believe the accuser", Nigel Hunt did his worst. Where the principal accuser is concerned, there was available to Nigel Hunt an abundance of persons who could, and later did, corroborate my account, and were in a good position to be able to explain the mental instability of the accuser and what her motivations would almost certainly be.

I can find no evidence that Nigel Hunt did anything more than just believe this person with the pseudonym "Jane". Similarly, Peter Kay. Even worse for him was the fact that several people were there at the relevant times, and who could and did corroborate my evidence. Again, there is no evidence that Hunt bothered to explore the character and motivations of this man.

Media, Entertainment & Arts Alliance (MEAA) Journalist Code of Ethics

In its Preamble, this document tells us that journalists not only "scrutinise power, but also exercise it, and should be responsible and accountable". But accountable to whom? The Code doesn't say, so one assumes they are mainly accountable to themselves and their employers. In its first paragraph of "standards", the Code says this:

> Report and interpret honestly, striving for accuracy, fairness and disclosure of all essential facts. **Do not suppress relevant available facts, or give distorting emphasis. Do your utmost to give a fair opportunity for reply.** [their emphasis]

The Advertiser/Sunday Mail did not live up to this standard. Hunt had written a hit piece in which he simply believed the complainants and, without entering into a proper conversation with anyone in a position to know if these uncorroborated claims were objectively true. All that the target of the allegations would be allowed to do was to respond to a case made against him. Nigel Hunt acted as police, judge, and jury and did that very badly. No police officer would make a public claim without first speaking to the "person of interest" and following up on that evidence.

In paragraph 3 of these standards:

> Aim to attribute information to its source. Where a source seeks anonymity, do not agree without first considering the source's motives and any alternative attributable source.

Hunt appeared to fail this test. Two of the three were adults at the time when they said abuse took place. They were allowed to shelter behind false names. Hunt sought no corroboration (because he could find none?) or, if he did, it was unacknowledged that he tried and failed to find corroborating evidence.

News Corp Australia Editorial Professional Conduct Policy

Further evidence of the lack of ethics followed by Hunt as he investigated and reported this story may be seen in News Corp's own code of conduct. For example:

> 1.5 Try always to tell all sides of the story when reporting on disputes and with such stories, reasonable steps should be taken to contact adversely named parties.
>
> 1.6 Journalists should rely only on credible sources.

To whom did Hunt refer to test the credibility of his sources? There is no evidence that he did that. And he certainly was not interested in telling all sides of the story allowing me only to comment on his sensationalized account which occupied several pages of *The Sunday Mail*. Hunt made it clear to my wife that the story was written, and he was not going to change it no matter what I might say.

Why would I talk to journalists who come at me with unsubstantiated accusations? Now that would be silly. So, I followed the legal advice provided to me.

Sean Fewster

Throughout the defamation trial, another journalist for *The Advertiser*, Sean Fewster, wrote daily reports which promoted the accusations and save for one piece, did not give equal and fair coverage of the evidence provided by my witnesses. After the loss of the appeal, and the refusal of the High Court to hear my appeal, the same Sean Fewster engaged in a vile and malicious personal attack on me. How dare I sue his Lord and Master, News Corp. I was "evil", "vile", and so on

The article by Sean Fewster ("Evil in a Robe")[460] is an example of the personal and vindictive trial by media perpetrated by *The Advertiser/Sunday Mail*.

Fewster defends the behaviour of his colleague, Nigel Hunt, in these terms:

1. You hear accusations against a prominent person.
2. You choose to believe what they say.
3. You decide to publish these unproved allegations and write the stories accordingly.
4. Only then do you find it necessary to consult the one accused and any others he names who might throw some light on the subject while insisting on holding to the accuracy of the story no matter what the subject of the story tells them.

To quote Fewster:

460 *The Sunday Mail*, 12 February 2017, at page 28

> Informing the subject of a story about that story, prior to print, and offering them right of reply **is among the most basic of a journalist's responsibilities**.

Now compare that with the relevant sections of *The Advertiser*'s *Code of Conduct*, a "policy [which] applies to News Corp Australia and its editorial employees."[461]

> 1.0 Accuracy and Reporting
>
> 1.1 **Publications should take reasonable steps to ensure reports are accurate and not misleading.**
>
> 1.2 Publications are free to editorialise, campaign and take stances on issues provided they take reasonable steps to fulfil the requirements of 1.3 and 1.4.
>
> 1.3 Comment, conjecture and opinion are acceptable in reports to provide perspective on an issue, or explain the significance of an issue, or to allow readers to recognise what the publication's standpoint is on the matter being reported.
>
> 1.4 However, this does not allow us to knowingly publish inaccurate or misleading information and publications should correct significant inaccuracies or misleading material once they have been recognised as detailed in Section 2.0 – Mistakes.

---

461 https://www.adelaidenow.com.au/help/code-of-conduct

> 1.5 **Try always to tell all sides of the story when reporting on disputes and with such stories, reasonable steps should be taken to contact adversely named parties.**
>
> 1.6 **Journalists should rely only on credible sources.**
>
> 1.7 Direct quotations should not be altered except to delete offensive language, protect against defamation, or to make minor changes for clarity.

I say that Nigel Hunt did not act in accordance with each of the above provisions of the Code marked in bold.

Hunt had heard stories he believed. There seems to be no evidence that he tested the accuracy of the stories, relying only on the accusations of three anonymous people. Having written his stories ready for publication he came to Sydney to seek a response from Dr Fleming. When asked by Dr Fleming's wife whether he would change those articles in the light of what Dr Fleming might say, Hunt replied that he would not, but he just wanted to give Dr Fleming a right of reply. As I said before, no one in their right mind would agree to be interviewed under these fixed conditions.

This was gotcha journalism. If he had done his homework properly, taking into consideration what Dr Fleming would have said together with speaking to any witnesses he might have suggested, Hunt's story may well have been very different. But he did not. And no amount of rationalisation by Fewster can change the fact that Hunt had behaved unethically even by the limited standards of *The Advertiser*'s *Code of Conduct.*

In his article "Evil in a Robe"[462], Fewster exemplifies the personal and vindictive trial by media perpetrated by *The Advertiser/Sunday Mail* by acting in variance with the same *Code of Conduct*, by which he, himself, is bound. He makes assertions which are not factually based.

1. Fewster's claim that Dr Fleming refused to speak is untrue. He chose not to speak to Nigel Hunt under the conditions laid down by Hunt. He refused to be part of a *Sunday Mail* hatchet job.
2. Dr Fleming released his own statement. *The Advertiser/Sunday Mail* simply used that statement to double down on their story by publishing the accusers' response to this statement.
3. Dr Fleming exercised his legal right to sue. Fewster's version of this right is that "Fleming not only refused to speak, he doubled down – as cowards and bullies do – by filing a million-dollar lawsuit against the paper". This is the response of a player, not an objective reporter operating only in the public interest. It is Fewster who is the "coward and bully". He uses the power of *The Advertiser*'s monopoly of the market in Adelaide where print journalism is concerned, to justify the brutal way in which Hunt and his newspaper decided to behave.
4. Fewster asserted that "he [Fleming] wanted to ruin them in court". That, too, is patently untrue. The three accusers were all hidden from public sight by their use of pseudonyms. Dr Fleming did not sue any of the accusers. He only sought to sue the newspaper. The truth is

462 *The Sunday Mail*, 12 February 2017, at page 28

that it is *The Advertiser/Sunday Mail* who chose to "ruin Fleming in court" and out of what I can only judge to be sheer malice, Fewster wishes to continue its witch hunt.

5. Fewster said no one believed Fleming. That is untrue. Many people who gave direct evidence in Court, corroborating evidence at that, were simply dismissed by judges without cause because they, the judges, seemed to proceed on the same basis as the journalists; believe accusers where sexual allegations are made no matter what and certainly where a Catholic priest is concerned.

But perhaps the most egregiously untrue statement made by Fewster, and *The Sunday Mail* was this: "Those abused … were Fleming's own parishioners – **some mere children** …".

Fewster must have known that was untrue. There was only one case of alleged child abuse, the very matter upon which Fleming sued. To say that there were "children" exhibits bad faith by Fewster and the newspaper for which he works.

The Advertiser and conflict of interest

The Advertiser ran reportage of the trial in which it was a key player. That seems to be a clear case of a conflict of interest. Hunt and Fewster were invested in the matter as was the newspaper itself. They were not disinterested reporters, and The Advertiser was not a disinterested publisher. They had axes to grind.

Why did they not employ someone unconnected with the case to write objective reports and without being subject to conditions on how the reports would be written? That's a good question. After all, *The Advertiser/ Sunday Mail* is the only daily newspaper in South Australia. The electronic media to their credit did not get involved and dispassionately reported the outcome.

And now, some 15 years after the first publication, Sean Fewster has conducted eleven hours of radio time discrediting me all over again with these false allegations.

Chapter Sixteen

Churches Respond to Allegations Against Father Fleming 2008-2022

With the agreement of Archbishop Philip Wilson, the then Catholic Archbishop of Adelaide, I was appointed the founding President of Campion College, Australia's first liberal arts tertiary institution. This necessitated my wife and I leaving Adelaide, South Australia in May 2004, to live in Sydney. The task was an enormous one. The first phase, 2004 to 2006, was hard work. First, it required the bringing up to current building standards of the old Marist Seminary in Old Toongabbie and fitting it out for purpose as a residential tertiary College for men and women. It also involved developing academic curricula fit for a university degree in the liberal arts, applying for registration and accreditation as a state recognised tertiary institute able to grant degrees. That was all achieved in time for the first intake of students in 2006.

Trouble brews

The first hint of trouble from Adelaide came in the middle of 2004. I received a request from the then Archbishop of Adelaide, Philip Wilson, to see him in his Adelaide Office.

At that meeting, Archbishop Wilson informed me of a complaint made against me by social worker Diane Lynch. He told me that it was a complaint of sexual misconduct, that the complaint was non-specific, and that she had been invited several times to make her complaint formal through the Church's officer who dealt with these things. Diane Lynch did not respond to those invitations. The Archbishop then asked to hear from me what I knew of this woman and her complaint.

Diane Lynch before 2004

I told the Archbishop that Lynch had made this accusation once before to his predecessor. At that time, Lynch said she was not interested in complaining to the police, was not interested in going through a formal complaints process in the Church, but only wanted a meeting with me in the presence of others. That meeting took place in the Archbishop's House, West Terrace, Adelaide in, I think, about 1995. Lynch made some vague and non-specific accusations of an event she said had occurred at some unspecified time when I was an Anglican Minister. I forcefully denied her accusation. I also pointed out how much of a nuisance Lynch had been to me at that time, how she stalked me, and would turn up to public places where I was due to speak uninvited. I kept her at arm's distance. When Alison and I became engaged she stopped me in King William Street (Adelaide) near the Beehive Corner, to tell me how displeased she was and that "we have not yet worked out our relationship". I replied at that time: "Diane, we have no relationship." Later, when Alison and I had gone to live in London she wrote me letters, telling me of her engagement and still later sending me photos of her wedding day. Not long after, she wrote to tell me that her marriage had irretrievably broken down and they were now separated.

After we had returned to Adelaide where I had been appointed as Rector of the Plympton Parish, Lynch began to harass me with phone calls, and demanded that I see her and help her with an assignment she had on psychology for her degree. I refused. After midnight Mass Christmas 1979, Lynch turned up on her motor bike at the Church where I had celebrated the Midnight Mass. She was in a rage complaining that her local parish had used a modern liturgy rather than the traditional 1662 Prayer Book. She expressed these views to me and before a large gathering of parishioners who were still at the Church after Mass. I told Lynch she would need to discuss that with her parish Minister, and that I had no role to play in what happened at her parish church.

In the late 1980s I was approached by Lynch in a restaurant where Alison and I were dining with another couple. She was a photographer and asked if she could take our photos. We agreed. I then rose from the table and spoke to her quietly at some distance from the table. I inquired after her well-being. She told me she was at university doing a social work degree. I congratulated her on that positive development and wished her well.

Then came her complaint, the meeting in 2004, and her intensified campaign against me.

After that meeting at the Archbishop's House, I did not set eyes on her again until her appearance in Court in the defamation proceedings in 2015.

Towards the end of this conversation, Archbishop Wilson thanked me for my candour and said that as far as he was concerned the matter was concluded.

The next time I was to hear about Diane Lynch was through an article written about me by journalist Nigel Hunt and published in the Sunday Mail at the end of August 2008. Her accusations were, in the end, set aside by Justice Gray as they had been earlier by the Anglican Church.

Peter Kay and Jane

Jane, and Peter Kay have already been dealt with in this book.

The story is published in 2008

At the end of August 2008, the *Sunday Mail* ran a story making certain allegations against me. Archbishop Wilson knew the story was coming as the published story itself made clear, **but he made no attempt to warn me**. I was in hospital on the day of publication when the Archbishop rang me on my mobile phone. He did not enquire after my health. He simply referred to the published stories, said "now this is very serious", and ordered me to return to Adelaide. He then hung up. **Moreover, Wilson at no time told The Advertiser what he knew of Lynch and Kay. I was hung out to dry.**

From that time, Wilson made no attempt to discuss any of these things with me. Instead, he made sure that my career at Campion College was over, indeed that my priestly pastoral ministry was over. Archbishop Wilson at no time made pastoral contact with me, relying on reports to him by the Vicar General who had occasional interactions with me.

Catholic Church inquiry led by Michael Abbott KC

In August 2008 Wilson had "commissioned an inquiry to be conducted by Michael Abbott KC into various allegations which had been made in the print media concerning Fr John Fleming and the knowledge of the Archdiocese of Adelaide about those allegations."[463] That inquiry lasted well over a year, thereby occasioning me maximum damage. Bishop Manning of Parramatta intervened with Archbishop Wilson to get him to move the inquiry along, especially as the inquiry was not into Dr Fleming but into the way in which the Archdiocese of Adelaide handled such matters. After the report had been concluded, he made a public statement.

Prior to Archbishop Wilson making his public statement, my canon lawyer, the Reverend Doctor John Doherty, PP, DCL had written to the Archbishop in these terms:

> **1. Fr Fleming has not been provided by you with a copy of the Abbott Report. In the circumstances, it is reasonable that Fr Fleming be provided by you with a copy. I request that you do so immediately, in particular, before any public statement by you.**

463 Public Statement by Archbishop Philip Wilson Catholic Archbishop of Adelaide concerning "*Mr Michael Abbott KC - Report on Findings*", 23rd October 2009.

> **2. As to your proposed public statement, I request that beforehand, you consult Fr Fleming's civil lawyer (Michael Sykes, Sykes Bidstrup, 77 Angas Street, Adelaide SA 5000, msykes@sykesbidstrup.com.au, 08 8223 4186). You will appreciate, based on the Abbott Report, the allegations against Fr Fleming appear tenuous indeed. No doubt you share my concern that any public statement by you does not, directly or indirectly, give currency or weight to those allegations.**
>
> **The Archdiocese has a duty of care to Fr Fleming which includes prompt resolution of this matter.**[464]

Neither I nor my canon lawyer have ever been shown the Abbott Report, nor was my civil lawyer consulted. In fact, the duty of care owed me by the Archdiocese of Adelaide did not extend to a "prompt resolution" of the matter.

In his public statement (23rd October 2009) made after this inquiry had been completed, he said this:

> **In the circumstances, I am now satisfied on the basis of Mr Abbott's comprehensive findings, that the steps taken by the Archdiocese were appropriate having regard, amongst other things, to the wishes of the persons who came forward at the time. In many ways the response which the**

464 Dr John Doherty, *Letter to Archbishop Wilson*, 23 October 2009.

> **Archdiocese did make was based almost wholly on the wishes of the complainants at the time.**[465]

It is curious that Archbishop Wilson would say that the response of the Archdiocese was "based almost entirely on the wishes of the complainants at the time" with no reference to anything that Dr Fleming might want to happen. Believe the accuser, no matter what?

Archbishop Wilson's intentions made clear?

At a meeting with the then Vicar-General, Monsignor David Cappo, Alison and I were informed by him that Archbishop Wilson was working towards getting me back into pastoral work. That was the reason why I was expected to undertake a psychological assessment.[466] I undertook that assessment and a report by Dr A Diment was sent to the Archdiocese of Adelaide.

Dr Diment said:

> **Father John Fleming has formally assessed (on reliable, valid instruments – BAI, BDI-II, CAQ) with average (minimal) levels of clinical anxiety and depression. He would (in the past) fit diagnostic criteria (DSM-IV-TR, 296.36) for a major depressive condition (chronic, moderate) but this is currently in**

465 Public Statement by Archbishop Philip Wilson, *ibid.*

466 From notes of meeting held at 8 Greygum Terrace, Northmead, NSW 2152, between 1000 hrs to 1230 hours, 14th of November 2009.

remission and appropriately controlled. (I note Dr. Yenson's opinion that a return to Adelaide may exacerbate this).

He has formally assessed (the main focus of this report) with a well-adjusted, well-integrated personality structure (I consider this broader term is more appropriate than a "type") and there was no evidence of personality traits which are problematic in his role as a Priest.

There was no evidence of a personality disorder or psychosis and the higher scoring traits or those furthest from average and trait descriptors (see table)- Conformity, Warmth, Impulsivity ("seeking relationships with others"), "reality-oriented", Superego strength, Extraversion and "very well-integrated" (low on Psychoticism) taken as a whole form a pattern that could readily be considered as desirable "priestly qualities."

I am not aware of any psychological tests in general use that measure personality/ behavioural traits relating to "spirituality" in the context of Priestly vocation (I believe some have been designed but I am not sure of their validity) but given his ordination was obtained after a lengthy process I believe the Catholic Church was the best judge of his "successful" application and using its own criteria for this quality. His communication and administrative skills are

> **well-documented, and he had been given an extension of his College Presidency-there is nothing in my assessment that would compromise these aspects of his vocation.**
>
> **Father Fleming is currently well-motivated, is very eager to resume his former roles and he has very good family support which is important for his good prognosis.**
>
> **I hope this is useful and would be happy to provide any further information you may require.**[467]

Although Adelaide had agreed to my excardination, the Diocese of Parramatta under its new bishop, Anthony Fisher OP, reneged on his predecessor's undertaking to incardinate me in that Diocese. So, Alison and I returned to Adelaide. In the event I was not, in fact, given any pastoral appointment in the Archdiocese of Adelaide. I was a "supply" priest only, often saying Mass in Italian for the relevant congregations.

Some five years after the publication of the allegations and the refusal of the police to take the matter further, and about four years after the Archbishop's inquiry led to a similar conclusion, I was called to see the Archbishop at his West Terrace residence on the 20th August 2013. **The purpose of the meeting was not for pastoral purposes or meaningful open discussion but to hand over an official letter from him requesting my immediate retirement from the priesthood. He would not discuss its contents with me.**

---

467 Anthony D Diment BSc. MA(Qual), Letter of Report to Archbishop Wilson, 17th December 2009.

In that letter, he reiterated his concerns that the matters alleged against me were "very serious", that those matters have not been "resolved" because the Catholic Church has no jurisdiction to deal with matters said to have taken place while I was an Anglican, and that the Anglican Church had deferred any further consideration of the matter until after the defamation case had been heard and decided. He knew that SAPOL were no longer investigating the matter.

Because of these "factors", he said he "was also very concerned about the impact this is having on the complainants themselves" even though he had said in his public statement that "the response which the Archdiocese did make was based almost wholly on the wishes of the complainants at the time".

Archbishop Wilson said that he recognised that the time had also been stressful for me, acknowledged that I had "vehemently denied the allegations from the outset" and that I was bringing defamation proceedings against the newspaper concerned.

Even though he believed I "posed no risk to children" and that I had the right to the presumption of innocence, he concluded that the "allegations are such that they can no longer be allowed to remain unresolved". He then went on to say that "because the allegations are very serious **and have never been definitively resolved**" that I should "immediately stand down from all ministry *ad cautelam* and *pro bono Ecclesiae*".[468]

---

468 *Ad abundantiorem cautelam,* or *ad cautelam* means "out of an abundance of caution" against the possibility of negative outcomes, while *pro bono Ecclesiae* means "for the good of the Church".

He concluded his letter:

> **Given the importance of this matter I ask that you submit your letter of retirement from all ministry within 14 days of the date of this letter.**

I put the matter in the hands of my canon lawyer who wrote to Archbishop Wilson. This what Dr Doherty wrote:

> **On behalf of Fr Fleming, I am asking Your Grace to rescind that request for the following reasons:**
>
> - **You have posited as your reason for issuing this request "whilst I consider how best to deal with these complex questions" (i.e., the definitive resolution of the allegations). However, canon law provides for the issuing of such a request only within a formal penal process. Your Grace has not initiated such a process and, absent this process, cannot issue this sort of request. Canon 1722 is relevant here. This canon gives the right to a bishop to remove an accused priest from ministry during a penal process. However, with respect, I must assert that the requirements of that canon have not been met. Canon 18 states that laws that restrict the free exercise of rights are subject to a strict interpretation. Further, canon 87 says that procedural and penal laws cannot be dispensed. Fr Fleming**

could be placed on leave only after the penal process has started and no such process is in train here. Your request, then, lacks its proper legal basis.

- The norm of the Code in this matter is substantially that found in the revised 2010 version of *Sacramentorum Sanctitatis Tutela* [The Safeguarding of the Sanctity of the Sacraments]. Article 19 of SST refers to canon 1722 and other related canons. This means that the conditions in those canons must be fulfilled. In light of SST, then, Your Grace's request lacks its proper legal basis.
- As to Your Grace's reference to the Congregation for the Doctrine of the Faith's support for this request, the first point that I must make is that the CDF does not have competence in this case. This is because the accusations concern events alleged to have happened before Fr Fleming became a Catholic. It is my understanding that it is the Congregation for the Clergy that has competence.
- And, even if the CDF did have competence, the advice Your Grace has relied upon would be at odds with the Church's universal law and the CDF's praxis in these matters in similar cases. I have seen letters of the CDF in such cases advising bishops how to act.

The CDF has asked bishops to deal with allegations using an administrative penal process. Within such a process, a bishop can place the accused priest on "administrative leave," but it can only be during that process and not otherwise.

- However, without studying the CDF advice I am unable to advise Fr Fleming and to address Your Grace in more precise terms on this point. Accordingly, I would be most grateful if Your Grace would send me your correspondence with the CDF so that I can study the CDF advice, the context in which that advice was given, and the reasons for it, so as to advise Fr Fleming how he can best exercise his right of defence.
- Moving to substantive considerations, the allegations have already been the subject of serious and thorough investigations by the police and in Your Grace's own process conducted by Mr Abbott. Both investigations failed to discern evidence of wrongdoing. You were happy to allow Fr Fleming to return to ministry in 2009 after receiving the Abbott Report, and having fulfilled your duty to investigate such an allegation. I would be surprised if the police and Mr Abbott failed to follow any line of investigation. And, as far as I know, nothing new has emerged since then.

Given this, it is unjust to propose a completely open-ended period of reflection about some possible process or action when the matter has already been fully examined.

- I will now comment on what appears to be the standard of proof implied in Your Grace's letter. The phrase "definitively resolved" is positing a totally impossible standard of proof. No allegations, especially historic ones, can ever be definitively resolved. The canonical standard of proof in such cases is moral certitude and this is broadly comparable to the criminal law standard of beyond reasonable doubt. To posit the higher standard of "definitively resolved" will mean that the allegations will never be resolved and, presumably, Fr Fleming will be permanently excluded from ministry. This would be, in effect, a permanent penalty and even a quasi-laicisation, something totally at odds with the Church's law and its praxis in such cases.
- Finally, I will appeal on behalf of Fr Fleming to Your Grace as bishop and pastor, as one who, in Church theology and law, is a father to his priest-collaborators and the person entrusted with the responsibility of protecting his priests' rights (Canon 384). I will

do so using the words of Fr John Beal (Rev. John P. Beal, "Administrative Leave: Canon 1722 Revisited," in *Studia canonica*, 27 [1993], pp. 293-320, concluding remarks): *"Expanding the extrajudicial coercive power of Church authorities by broad provisions for imposing 'administrative leave' in particular law also reverses the direction of the postconciliar development of penal law and opens the door to the perception, if not the reality, of arbitrariness. One cannot fault Church authorities for seeking to respond to the demands of victims and of the Church community for justice, but the course of justice is not served by running roughshod over the rights of clerics. Even accused clerics retain their right to a good reputation (c. 220), to decent support (c. 281, §' 1-2), to exercise orders in carrying out the duties of their offices (c. 274, § 2), and not to be punished except according to the norm of law (c. 221, § 3). While one cannot absolutize the rights of clerics, those rights must be at least part of the calculus by which decisions about 'administrative leave' are reached. Otherwise, in an ironic reversal of the dictum of the Council of Trent, bishops will find themselves perceived more as percussores* **[English: thugs]** *than as pastores* **(Sess. XIII, de ref, cap. 1)."**

> **It is for these reasons that I now formally ask Your Grace to withdraw your request.**[469]

Archbishop Wilson's response was a three-sentence letter:

> **I have received your letter of September 2, 2013, regarding Father John Fleming.**
>
> **I have referred your letter to the Congregation for the Doctrine of the Faith for advice.**
>
> **I will not comment further on this matter until I have received advice from the said Congregation.**[470]

I never heard anything more on the subject from the Archdiocese of Adelaide, or from Rome, even up to the time of publication of this book.

Impact of Archbishop Wilson's request that I retire

The consequence of these manoeuvrings by Archbishop Wilson made it impossible for me to settle with News Corp because the law of the Church was not being followed, and even though SA Police had said that it would not proceed against me, the Anglican Church had adjourned consideration of the matter. None of these things were of my doing. Moreover, the Archbishop

469 Letter from Dr Doherty to Archbishop Wilson, 2nd of September 2013.

470 Letter from Archbishop Wilson to Dr Doherty, 4th of September 2013

wanted these matters to be "definitively resolved", an impossible standard.

The only way to clear my name was to continue with the defamation process since Archbishop Wilson, while accepting my right to the presumption of innocence, wished me to retire thereby bypassing my right to that presumption. By his actions, Archbishop Wilson had "locked me in" to defamation proceedings there now being no other way left open for me to prove my innocence. A further aggravating factor was the determination of the Anglican Church to continue a process against me in the context of that Church having already paid money to two of the accusers and the apparent bias against me by two of the South Australian Anglican bishops including Archbishop Driver. I was cornered.

The Anglican Church in the Diocese of Adelaide

The Anglican Church decided to proceed against me with its own inquiry even though they had already paid compensation to two of the complainants, and even though I had long ago relinquished Anglican Orders and was not under their authority. I had effectively resigned Anglican orders when I was received into Full Communion with the Catholic Church. Their professional standards board had not followed its own procedures which required the Board to advise me of the allegations at the time when they were made to them. And to cap it all off they waited until 12 months after the police inquiry to make their first official notification to me of complaints they said they had received from at least two of the accusers years before.

It is interesting to note the performance of the Anglican Church in this matter. It seems that there were some who wished to destroy me.

The John Stephenson intervention

First, there is the matter of the sermon preached by the Reverend John Stephenson in his parish Church on the morning of the publication of the story, the 31st of August 2008. At the time Mr Stephenson preached this homily he was honorary Chaplain to Archbishop Driver and had been since 1985. He had prepared that sermon before publication and had advance copies of this homily distributed throughout the Anglican parishes of this state and to other Anglican agencies in South Australia and elsewhere in the country via the Diocesan Intranet. The distribution of the homily needed to be made by him by, at the latest, close of business Friday, 29th August, two days before the Sunday Mail publication.

Mr Stephenson had, then, the agreement of the Archdiocese, for the publication of this document.

This suggests a high degree of co-ordination between Stephenson, the Anglican Diocese of Adelaide, and the Sunday Mail journalist Hunt which is amplified in the outrageous and defamatory remarks Stephenson made in his homily.

Mr Stephenson was the counsellor to "Jane". He had no university degrees as far as I can ascertain. He had completed some course work at COPE (Hutt Street) in transactional analysis which in turn is associated with the recovered memories technique.

Mr Stephenson referred to himself as an authority on these matters having "served with the Professional Standards Committee" of the Adelaide Anglican Diocese. Referring directly to the Sunday Mail article he said:

> **Some of you know John well and may have been his or Alison's friend. Many people will be deeply shocked by the article; many will feel angry and betrayed.**
>
> **One survivor tells me how difficult she finds it to make moral decisions. Her abuser, a priest whom the church endorsed as a spokesman on ethical issues, not only stole her innocence; he stole her capacity to judge between right and wrong.**
>
> **The latest instance of human failure is likely to provoke scepticism because of John's high profile as an ethicist and a spokesperson for the hierarchy, with a particular hard line on authority and stem-cell research and contraception.**

Throughout this homily Mr Stephenson assumes my guilt, publicly interferes in the "Jane" matter while a police investigation is underway, all the time acting as agent of the Anglican Church and close adviser to his Archbishop.

The Driver/Weatherill intervention

When I returned to Adelaide, I was invited to dinner by Mr Ross Davies and his wife. Davies was the former Anglican Bishop of The Murray. That evening Mr Davies [by then a Catholic layman] told me of what he knew of the matter. He then put those details into a written statement [subsequently resolved into a statutory declaration]. My emphases have been added to that statement.

> I Ross Owen Davies of 302A Cross Road Clarence Park South Australia, formerly Bishop of The Murray in the Anglican Church of Australia do solemnly state that the following is my recollection of a conversation between myself and the Right Reverend Gary Weatherill[471], Bishop of Willochra in the Anglican Church of Australia and the Most Reverend Jeffrey Driver,[472] Archbishop of Adelaide in the Anglican Church of Australia on the 5th June 2007 held at the Adelaide Club Dining Room.
>
> This conversation occurred at a point of time before any allegations against Fr John Fleming were known publicly or to me personally.
>
> **Over lunch Bishop Weatherill brought up the topic of John Fleming and stated that they were going to get John Fleming at last.**
>
> I asked what he was referring to with such a comment.
>
> Archbishop Driver seemed uneasy with the topic and commented that it was very serious indeed.
>
> **Weatherill informed me of 2 complaints against Fleming, one by a woman & one by a man.**

471 Weatherill is now the Bishop of Ballarat

472 Driver has now retired

I said I was surprised and shocked.

Driver affirmed this was so & that justice would be done against him.

Weatherill then expressed a second time but more vehemently & aggressively that John Fleming was getting what he deserved at last.

I said I was a friend and felt compromised and found what I was hearing difficult to believe. I said I thought it best if we moved on to another subject.

We sat in embarrassed silence and moved on!

I am prepared to issue this statement in the form of a Statutory Declaration if required by legal counsel for Fr Fleming.

R O Davies

17th June 2011

Mr Weatherill and Dr Driver seemed to have no compunction in publicly discussing, with a third party, matters guarded at that time by strict confidentiality. Dr Fleming wrote to Dr Driver on the 7th of August 2011.

Dear Archbishop

Enclosed with this letter please find a statement by Mr Ross Davies, former Bishop of The Murray.

I am anxious to discuss this statement with you as soon as possible and in any case within the next seven days.

I am prepared to meet with you at your office. I wish to be accompanied by Stuart Lindsay,

> my friend and counsellor throughout the inquiry your Church continues to pursue against me.
>
> Please confirm your willingness to meet with me by calling me on XXXXX

Later, Mr Davies was to commit what he had earlier written into a formal statutory declaration. See next page.

Archbishop Driver replied to my letter on the 11th August 2011. In that letter, Dr Driver said he was not willing to engage with me and said that it would not

> ...be proper to express any comment regarding the unsigned "statement" of Bishop Davies, a copy of which you sent to me under cover of your letter. The occasion to which Bishop Davies makes reference would appear to have been a private meeting between the three Provincial Bishops (something that happened regularly before meetings of the Provincial Council). That said, I have no independent memory of the matters to which Bishop Davies refers and, in any event, I fail to understand your purpose in providing me with a copy of this document. **The matters raised with me in your letter, or conversations I may or may not have had in the past, are incapable of affecting the outcome of the Professional Standards processes of the Diocese of Adelaide.**

This was a brush off. **I was not seeking to discuss with Dr Driver allegations about <u>my</u> alleged behaviour. I wanted to discuss with him the allegations made**

STATUTORY DECLARATION

State of South Australia - *Oaths Act 1936*

I Ross Owen Davies, formerly Bishop of The Murray in the Anglican Church of Australia

of 302A Cross Road Clarence Park South Australia

do solemnly and sincerely declare that

1. The following is my recollection of a conversation between myself and the Rt Reverend Gary Weatherill, Bishop of Willochra in the Anglican Church of Australia and the Most Reverend Jeffrey Driver, Archbishop of Adelaide in the Anglican Church of Australia on the 5th June 2007 held at the Adelaide Club Dining Room.

2. The occasion for the meeting was the Provincial Council of the Church, which met twice a year. The 3 Bishops attended and in some years (though not in this particular year) an Assistant Bishop from Adelaide also attended. The lunch occurred during a break in the Council's business on that day. I do not recall that alcohol was consumed by any of us at the lunch.

3. This conversation occurred at a point of time before any allegations against Fr John Fleming were known publicly. I was not aware that John was the subject of any allegations of this nature. This is the first I had heard of them.

4. Over lunch Bishop Weatherill brought up the topic of John Fleming and stated that they were going to get John Fleming at last. I had never discussed the Fleming allegations with Weatherill previously. I can't recall what we were discussing just prior to this topic being introduced. I recall that the PSA procedure and protocol were relatively new to our Church at this time. He made it clear to me in Driver's presence he thought Fleming was going to get his just deserts. I asked what he was referring to with such a comment. He explained that Fleming was the subject of a church inquiry about sexual misconduct, and that there were 2 complainants, one a man and one a woman. The man was a married man, he said. The woman was someone Fleming had known through college; I gathered he meant St Marks: she was someone he had counselled. It involved improper sexual advances in each case. He didn't tell me their names. I was subsequently told by John Harley that the man was Peter Kaye. I specifically recall these details being given by Weatherill, because I told my wife of them when I got home that night.

5. Driver confirmed what Weatherill had said. I cannot recall the precise words that Driver used to do this but the effect of the words was plain to me. I have thought very carefully about this. He said more than words indicating that there was a process and that it would take its course. He said the allegations were serious. He told me that the allegations had substance. He said words that indicated that justice would be done in the sense that Fleming would be held to account for what he had done. He specifically told me that the details Weatherill had mentioned were accurate-that these were the allegations against Fleming.

6. At no stage did Driver attempt to rein Weatherill in, when he was giving me this information. Weatherill spoke with an air of vitriol; I would say he was gleeful when he recounted these matters to me. Driver could not but have seen that. I was also struck by the fact that Driver seemed very comfortable with Weatherill providing information to

Statutory declaration from Mr Ross Davies.

about <u>his</u> behaviour at a luncheon in the Adelaide Club, hardly to be described as a "private meeting". Indeed, it was no more than a social luncheon these bishops enjoyed before the real meeting which was a meeting of the Provincial Council.

Stretching credulity, Driver did not deny that he had engaged in that conversation, only that he couldn't recall it, and so ducked for cover. Not innocent until proved guilty but, as Mr Davies reported in his statutory Declaration, he and Bishop Weatherill had determined that I was guilty as alleged and that "Fleming was going to get his just deserts".

No doubt the presumption that I was guilty was behind the Anglican Church's decision to pay compensation monies to at least two of the three complainants before any process to determine truth had been engaged. **On the face of it, that would seem to construct a financial incentive for the complainants to continue with their allegations come what may, a fact of which Justice Gray took no account.**

Resolution of the Anglican Church's involvement

In the event, the Anglican Church resolved not to proceed further in this matter.

> In this case, the Board has not proceeded beyond the directions hearing stage in these proceedings. As outlined above, if a finding of misconduct were to be made under section 61 of the Ordinance, the Board is satisfied that there is now no meaningful course of action that the Board could take under section 61 in relation to the matter.
>
> It is on this basis that the Board considers that this matter should now be laid aside and so determines that no further action in relation to the complaint should be taken.
>
> Despite the significance of the Supreme Court action, as indicated earlier, the Board

> considers that these proceedings should now be brought to an end. It is acknowledged that it has not formally considered evidence or received submissions as to the nature and effect of the conduct of the respondent. It recognises that aspects of the complaints in these proceedings involve serious allegations and potential grave consequences in relation to the respondent. The Board notes that the respondent has consistently denied the allegations that have been made against him in this matter, but the Board also notes that the original complainants find support in the decision in the Supreme Court action.
>
> This decision is made by unanimous resolution of the Board, after taking into account the requirement that any question of law **or procedure has been determined by the presiding member of the Board**.[473]

Episcopal pastoral care in the Catholic Church

The pastoral care of priests is a major responsibility of Catholic diocesan bishops. Canon law describes the duty of pastoral care in these terms:

> **Canon 384 With special solicitude, a diocesan bishop is to attend to presbyters and listen to them as assistants and counsellors.**

473 Decision of the Professional Standards Board, *In the matter of Dr John Fleming*, 24 September 2020.

> **He is to protect their rights and take care that they correctly fulfill the obligations proper to their state and that the means and institutions which they need to foster spiritual and intellectual life are available to them.**

Personal pastoral care was provided to me by some bishops, but not by some of those who were obliged to protect my rights.

1. I always received excellent pastoral care from the Most Reverend Leonard Faulkner [1926-2018] who ordained me as a priest.
2. From August 2008, I had no personal conversations with Archbishop Wilson [1950-2021] about the accusations made against me. Being prevented by the Archbishop from going back to work after the police had finalized their inquiries in my favour, occurred without the allegations being properly tested by any process in the Archdiocese.
3. After Wilson resigned as Archbishop on the 3rd of June 2018, Bishop Greg O'Kelly was appointed Apostolic Administrator *sede vacante* of the Archdiocese of Adelaide. I received one phone call from Bishop O'Kelly which lasted about a minute. Otherwise, he communicated a few times by email. He formally banned me from public ministry.
4. On the 19th of March 2020, Pope Francis announced that he had translated Bishop Patrick O'Regan to the Archdiocese of Adelaide as its

ninth Archbishop. I have met with Archbishop O'Regan on one occasion after he granted my request for a meeting.

5. Outstanding pastoral support came to me from the then Bishop of Parramatta, the Most Reverend Kevin Manning [1933-2019], in whose Diocese I worked when I was at Campion College, and Archbishop John Hepworth who was not a bishop of the Roman Catholic Church. Bishop Manning had reached an agreement with the Archdiocese of Adelaide that I would be incardinated into the Diocese of Parramatta. Before that matter could be settled Bishop Anthony Fisher OP was appointed as the new Bishop of Parramatta. Bishop Fisher did not follow through on certain undertakings which had been made by his predecessor where I was concerned and, despite our friendship over many years, I have had no contact with him for many years now.
6. From my admittedly limited experience I would say that **many Catholic diocesan bishops in this country "don't do" pastoral work personally, keeping most priests at arms' length**. They do not personally support their priests when they are in trouble and are still even now more concerned with themselves and what they see as the reputation of the Church.
7. The same is not true of many senior priests who have been particularly solicitous of my well-being, especially Father Philip Marshall VG, Father Peter Joseph, Father Greg Pritchard, Father Michael McCaffrey FSSP, Mons. Robert Egar,

Mons Robert Aitken and too many others for me to mention here. I also received some support from Mons David Cappo.

8. I received great support from many of the Catholic laity.

And in the end ...

The evidence reveals that the heads of the two Churches (Philip Wilson and Jeffrey Driver) abjectly failed properly to discharge their duties. They appear to have acted on the presumption of guilt. The Anglican Archbishop paid significant money to complainants even though they had not communicated with me in any shape or form before doing so. The consequence of all this meant that I had to put my faith in the State for justice, a faith, as it turned out, that was completely misplaced.

I am still a Catholic priest, but without faculties to perform any form of public ministry. I celebrate the Holy Mass in my home. Beyond that, I try to live my life as a priest, saying my prayers, reading widely, and, just recently, having my book on euthanasia published.[474]

And, of course, I have the great joy of being married to Alison, my best friend and wife. So, I live the life of a priest without faculties except to be able to say Mass privately, husband, father, and grandfather.

---

474 John Fleming, *To Kill or Not to Kill: Euthanasia in a Society with a Cultural Death Wish*, Austin Macauley Publishers, 2021.

Appendix A

Timeline

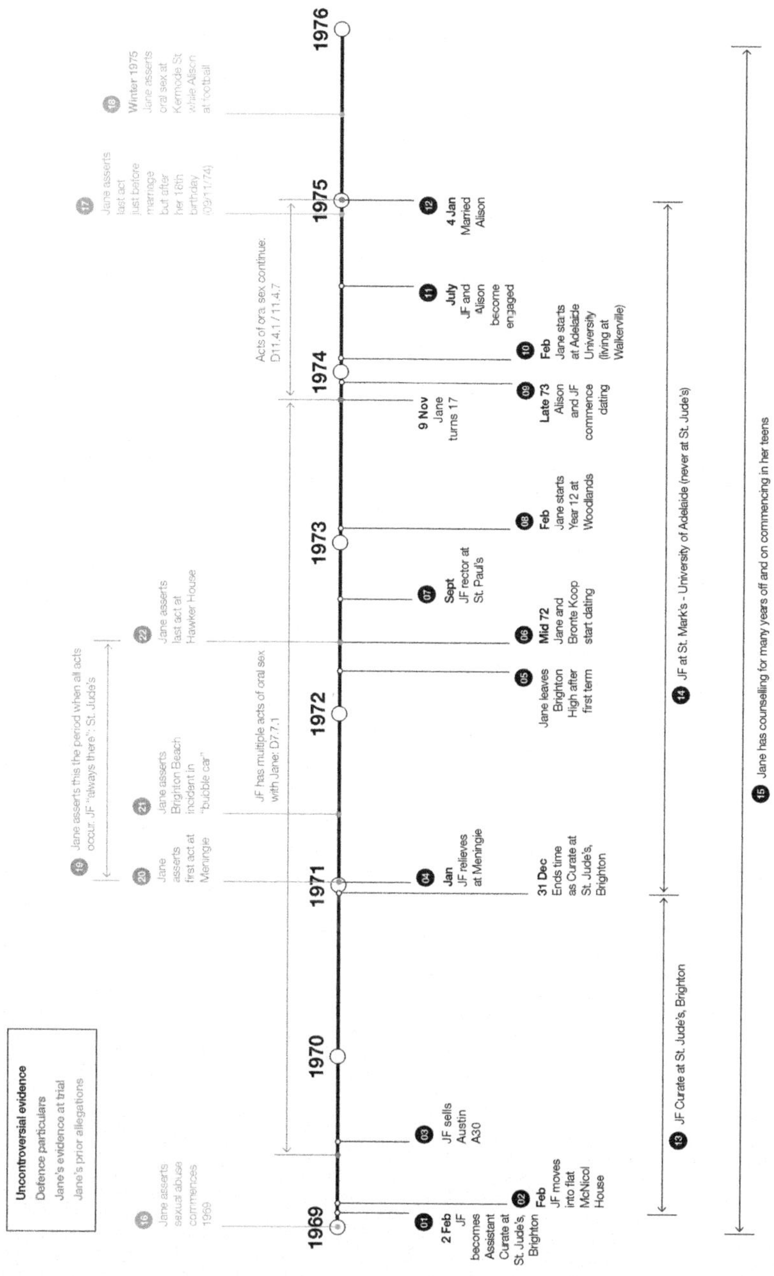

The grounds for appeal against the two judgements of Justice Gray and Justices Vanstone, Nicholson, and Brampton, together with the second application for leave to appeal to the High Court of Australia, are clearly set out in the second applicant application to the High Court for special leave to appeal. These grounds for appeal, never considered by the High Court, also contain a fresh ground of appeal in light of the judgement of the Federal Court which ruled in favour of actor Geoffrey Rush when he sued for defamation.

Application to the High Court of Australia Special for Leave to Appeal

IN THE HIGH COURT OF AUSTRALIA
ADELAIDE REGISTRY No. of 2019

BETWEEN: **JOHN IRVING FLEMING**
Applicant

and

ADVERTISER-NEWS WEEKEND PUBLISHING COMPANY PTY LTD & ADVERTISER NEWSPAPERS PTY LTD
Respondents

APPLICATION FOR SPECIAL LEAVE TO APPEAL

The applicant applies for special leave to appeal from the whole of the judgment of the Full Court of the Supreme Court of South Australia given on 29 September 2016.

The applicant seeks an order that compliance with the time limit in High Court Rules 2004, rule 41.02.1 be dispensed with.

On 27 October 2016 in action number A44 of 2016 the applicant made an application for special leave to appeal from this judgment, which application was refused with costs by this Honorable Court on 9 February 2017.

Part I: Proposed grounds of appeal

1. The Full Court misapplied the principles of appellate review in not allowing the appeal from the trial judge on the basis that Jane's evidence as to the Meningie incident and the St. Mark's College incident is glaringly improbable and inconsistent with the uncontroverted facts clearly established at trial [FC149].
2. The Full Court erred in proceeding on the basis that the applicant as plaintiff was required to bear any prejudice associated with the fact that events in excess of 40 years antiquity were being assessed [FC183].
3. The Full Court misapplied the principles of appellate review in finding that the trial judge was correct to find the imputations of serious criminality against the applicant were justified, as being substantially

true, by placing significance upon findings made in relation to the conduct of the applicant involving a witness (Kay) [FC143], [FC151] and another witness (Courtney) [FC129] in support of a contextual truth imputation when such defence was no longer available to the respondent following the decision of the trial judge during final submissions to reverse his decision made on the first day of trial and to permit the applicant to adopt the respondent's imputation of general criminality [FC23].

4. The Full Court erred in finding that the applicant's good reputation, had it been assessed by the trial judge, could have made no difference to the findings [FC178].

Orders sought if special leave is granted

1. The appeal is allowed;
2. The question of damages be remitted to the Full Court of the Supreme Court for damages to be assessed;
3. Costs.

Part II: A concise statement of the leave or special leave questions said to arise.

1. The uncertainty concerning the application of *Briginshaw v Briginshaw* in the context of a plea of justification in a defamation case, to an imputation of guilt of a serious criminal offence in circumstances where the plaintiff was neither charged nor

convicted is a matter of public importance of general application especially where:

1.1 It was conclusively demonstrated the evidence of the principal complainant (Jane) was erroneous in material particulars; and

1.2 In assessing Jane's evidence the court brought to bear evidence given by Peter Kay asserting (for the purposes of contextual truth plea: [FC4] and [FC23-24]) consensual adult sexual conduct [FC199].

2. It is a matter of public importance of general application that the Full Court suggest that a person who is defamed by reference to an event of antiquity (40 years) should bear the prejudice associated with the loss of evidence consequent upon the passage of time by reason of his/her choosing to invoke the laws of defamation to defend his/her reputation [FC183]. This proposition by the Full Court is advanced without authority, effectively denies the remedy of defamation proceedings to a person defamed in circumstances such as these, and is plainly wrong.

3. For the reasons set out in Part III, it is in the interest of the administration of justice that the applicant have the opportunity to restore his reputation where it has been that found serious sexual assaults occurred 40 years ago in respect of a teenage girl. In circumstances where Jane's story was uncorroborated, was stated inconsistently on prior occasions, and was shown to be erroneous in fundamental material particulars, the requisite standard of persuasion should not have been reached.

Part III: The applicant's argument in support of the grant of special leave

1. The High Court has power to reopen an application for special leave. The Court is referred to the following authorities:
   1.1 *Re Sinanovic's Application* [2001] HCA 40 (2001) 180 ALR 448, 450-451 at [7];
   1.2 *Postigilone v The Queen* (1997) 189 CLR 295 at 305;
   1.3 *Fischer v Cth.* [1997] 2 Leg Rep SL 1.
2. The applicant says the uncertainty as to what the *Briginshaw* principle requires in a defamation justification defence that involves alleged criminal conduct is demonstrated by a comparison of the application of the principle in his case and in the recent case of *Rush v Nationwide News Pty Ltd (No 7)* [2019] FCA 496 (Wigney J).
3. A consideration of the *Rush* reasons makes it apparent that his Honour considered that to establish the appropriate standard of proof it was necessary that in respect of the various allegations there be corroboration of same. Reference is made to the following paragraphs of the judgment in respect of the seven (7) allegations:
   - 1st [462]
   - 2nd and 3rd [506]
   - 4th [527]
   - 5th [582], [592]
   - 6th [622], [624]
   - 7th [635], adopting [622] and [624].
4. The events the subject of the *Rush* case occurred only one to two years prior to the proceedings. The events

in the proceedings the subject of the application occurred some 40 years ago. The allegations by 'Jane' in those proceedings were totally uncorroborated. Indeed, the applicant's denials were corroborated by a number of witnesses and could have been corroborated by others since deceased. The applicant refers to page 11 and his submission on 'Prejudice consequent upon passage of time'.

5. In this matter, the word 'corroboration' does not appear in the reasons of the trial judge. Nor does the trial judge address the impact of a 'presumption of innocence' in the context of justification of criminal conduct.
6. In *Briginshaw* the High Court appears to recognise such a presumption: per Latham CJ at 344, Dixon J at 363, and McTiernan J at 372. Dixon J (at 363), when addressing a civil proceeding wherein a question of whether a crime has occurred, asserts that "weight is given to the presumption of innocence".
7. The Full Court in this matter at [108] addresses the reference by Dixon J to a "presumption of innocence" in a dismissive way asserting that "later High Court judgments do not import that presumption into the civil arena". Whilst that might be the case, neither do they remove it.
8. The Full Court proceeds in [108]: "Furthermore, from the above it would appear that any references to *Briginshaw* as establishing an 'onus' or a 'standard' are incorrect."
9. Justice Wigney in *Rush* ([227]) cites Dixon J in *Briginshaw* at 362 and not the passage at 363. Nevertheless, his Honour's apparent consideration

that corroboration was required in *Rush* sits with the existence of a presumption of innocence. These are matters appropriate for consideration by the High Court.

10. Immediately below is a summary of critical differences in the way the law of defamation was applied in two different jurisdictions:

Rush	**Fleming**
Corroboration required of accuser	No corroboration provided by or required of accuser
	Corroboration for Fleming's evidence provided by third parties
Presumption of innocence applied	Presumption of innocence refused
Briginshaw fully applied	Briginshaw not applied as to 'onus' and to 'standard'

11. The proceedings the subject of the application arose out of the respondent media organisations becoming aware of a police investigation into the applicant's relations with a number of young persons many years in the past. The respondents chose not to await the outcome of the police investigations but rather published allegations in *The Sunday Mail,* a South Australian newspaper. (The first publication appears in the attached Supporting Materials document).
12. The respondent sought to justify an imputation of "criminal sexual behavior" by particulars given in respect of one person, given the pseudonym 'Jane'. Lesser imputations, not involving any criminal conduct, were raised as contextual truth imputations, and should not have been even considered following the decision made during submissions (refused in

Opening) that the applicant should have leave to amend to adopt the respondent's contextual truth imputation of "criminal sexual behavior".

13. The applicant says there is uncertainty as to what the *Briginshaw* principle requires. In *Rejfek v McElroy* (1965) 112 CLR 517 at [10] the Court spoke of :

    (T)he degree of satisfaction for which the civil standard of proof calls may vary according to the gravity of the fact to be proved.

    In *Neat Holdings v Karajan Holdings* (1992) 110 ALR 449 the Court expresses it thus:

    (T)he strength of the evidence necessary to establish a fact or facts on the balance of probabilities may vary according to the nature of what it is sought to prove.

    Emphasis is placed on the need for 'clear' or 'cogent' evidence to bring about the reasonable degree of satisfaction required in the particular case. The following passage from Dixon J's judgment in *Briginshaw* continues to be cited:

    In such matters 'reasonable satisfaction' should not be produced by inexact proofs, indefinite testimony or indirect inferences.

    The uncertainty derives from judicial officers having different views as to what is 'clear' or 'cogent', whilst insisting that the standard of proof remains the civil standard.

14. In the case at bar the respondent media organisations carried the onus of proving justification of 'criminal sexual conduct'. That would necessarily require a

high 'degree of satisfaction' or particularly strong evidence. That would follow from the fact that the media organizations made a deliberate decision to allege criminal sexual conduct and convict the applicant in the court of public opinion. That is the more so when the alleged conduct is said to have occurred some 40 years ago. The case for a degree of satisfaction at least approaching the criminal standard seems as strong in those circumstances as the need for a high standard in respect of civil contempt.[475] This case is different from a tortious action in deceit which is acknowledged to attract the *Briginshaw* onus. The case at bar had the allegations being made against a man of the highest reputation, the then President of Campion College in Sydney. The speech of Lord Morris in *Hornal v Neuberger* [1957] 1 QB 247 assists. That case addressed the standard of proof in a civil action where fraud (fraudulent misrepresentation) was alleged. At 266 Lord Morris said:

> *The phrase 'balance of probabilities' is often employed as a convenient phrase to express the basis upon which civil issues are decided. ... In some criminal cases liberty may be involved; in some it may not. In some civil cases the issues may involve questions of reputation which can transcend in importance even questions of personal liberty. Good name in man or woman is 'the immediate jewel of their souls'.*

475 In respect of the discrete issue of civil contempt the High Court has taken the view that civil contempt, as with criminal contempt, has to be proved beyond reasonable doubt: *Witham v Holloway* [1995] 183 CLR 525.

15. The Full Court should not have been satisfied as to the requisite standard of persuasion for the reasons hereafter appearing.

<u>The Meningie Incident</u>

16. Contrary to the trial judge's acceptance of Jane's evidence regarding Meningie and the rejection of Alison's evidence where it was found [J392] – [J395]:
    16.1 Jane's evidence was "inherently credible and compelling";
    16.2 "I am satisfied on the balance of probabilities that it is an event that in fact took place"; and
    16.3 "I am satisfied Jane's allegation is true";

    there was nothing "inherently credible" about Jane's story. Her account is inherently implausible or glaringly improbable.

17. There are seven reasons why that is so.
18. **First**, the trial judge made his Meningie incident finding based on a consideration of Jane's evidence in isolation from the evidence of Alison and the evidence of the applicant, the two other people said to be present. On Jane's evidence, she and Alison slept in the applicant's bedroom and the alleged incident took place just before settling for the night. Alison denied that she and Jane slept in the same bedroom as the applicant and she denied kissing the applicant. The applicant denied Jane and Alison slept in his bedroom and denied kissing Alison and denied that Jane touched his penis.
19. **Second**, the other person said to be in the room at the time of the Meningie incident (Alison) denies the event in fact occurred. The trial judge's rejection

of Alison's evidence is unreasoned and, indeed, a non-sequitur [J143]. The trial judge's dismissal of her evidence sets at naught the value of her evidence on the basis she is married to the applicant. The Full Court does not advert to the impact that *Briginshaw* principles might have on the issue. [FC150-154]

20. **Third**, in considering the requisite strength of the evidence to find that, in fact, the sexual assault at Meningie took place, the trial judge gave no proper regard to the fact that Alison's parents and brother who are dead but could have given evidence that the girls did not sleep in the applicant's bedroom; and the evidence given by Alison's surviving younger brother that while he could not recall the sleeping arrangements at Meningie their "mum was really conservative and dad was very protective" .

21. **Fourth**, Jane had given accounts to, inter alia, the police and church authorities, which accounts were grossly inconsistent with her evidence at trial as to the incident.

    21.1 To Father Stephenson – to the effect that concerning Meningie "she was juvenile when [Fr Fleming] got her to perform oral sex on the beach. This occurred at the country location in the South East. After the incident they rejoined the McNicol family further down the beach" ;

    21.2 To Mr. Witham (Anglican Church enquiry) concerning Meningie: "I don't even actually remember him touching me. I don't actually remember in fact because I don't remember, I'm not reliable in that sense."

    21.3 To Fr. David Richardson (respondents' witness) concerning Meningie that the applicant had "shown her his penis and expected her to admire it" which was "the extent of her cause for anger at John Fleming".

22. In considering the quality or strength of Jane's evidence, the trial judge and the Full Court failed to attach any significance to these prior statements concerning Meningie. None of this evidence was addressed by the Full Court [J138-140].
23. **Fifth**, the memory expert raised doubts about the reliability of Jane's account of the alleged Meningie incident, but the trial judge gave no proper regard to it before he found [J392] that Jane's account was "inherently credible and compelling" [J155-160].
24. **Sixth**, the trial judge and the Full Court erred in assessing the reliability of Jane's evidence consequent upon her evidence as to how alleged assignations were made with the applicant in the 18 months after the Meningie incident [J407] and [FC144].
    a) A timeline of Jane's evidence, overlaid against objective evidence, evidence of independent witnesses, the respondents' pleadings and Jane's prior statements shows the impossibility of the allegations she makes. (The 'Timeline' appears as part of the Supporting Materials). Such impossibility cannot be explained away by "getting the dates wrong". Jane's timeline cannot stand with other evidence in the trial. Jane says multiple incidents occurred between the Meningie incident and the last incident (St. Mark's) arising from meetings with the applicant at St. Jude's Church functions during 1971-1972. The clear evidence, however, is the applicant did

not attend St Jude functions after he moved to St. Mark's (T599/9-12). Jane's evidence that he was "always there" cannot be accepted. It was not put to the applicant that he was "always there". It was not put to him that he was ever there.

b) Jane told police she would see the applicant at choir practice each week. However, by this time the appellant had ceased his curacy at St Jude's. When confronted with this in cross-examination, Jane claimed she saw the applicant at church functions. When pressed further, Jane claimed the applicant "was always there. He didn't finish his curacy and then go. He still came back. He came back many times."
c) Every other witness from St Jude's who was questioned on the topic controverted this. In particular, Russell Simmonds, the applicant's successor as curate at St Jude's, gave evidence that he had no recollection of the applicant's return to the parish whatsoever, and that to do so was not an accepted or acceptable practice.
d) This evidence told against Jane's reliability. The trial judge did not address it adequately and merely noted "it is clear that the plaintiff maintained contact with the Brighton area and the McNicol family in particular." However, there was no evidence of the applicant 'maintaining contact with the Brighton area'. Again: it was not put to Fr Fleming that he was ever there after he had completed his curacy.

At [FC144] the Full Court mistreats this evidence in much the same way as the trial judge at

[J408]. It is not to the point that he was "rarely in Brighton and its environs". Jane did not assert 'chance' meetings. She did not suggest meetings were arranged by phone or letter. Her evidence was meetings occurred at 'church functions' and that the applicant was 'always there'. There were no such 'church functions' at which the applicant was present. The Full Court simply ignores a fundamental flaw in Jane's allegations going to the reliability of her story. [FC148]

25. It is an incontrovertible fact, proved through Church records that in January 1971 the applicant was a locum priest for about a week at Meningie. Jane steadfastly maintained the Meningie incident was the first sexual contact. She however alleged sexual encounters in the applicant's "rice bubble" car which the evidence revealed was disposed of in 1969. The year 1969 was a year when the applicant was the curate at St. Jude's and Jane knew him. She has reconstructed, inaccurately, a story in her mind.

26. **Seven**, in opening the respondents' case at trial, the respondents' counsel said:

> Bronte Koop was a friend of [Jane] in her late teens. They went out together. He will tell the court that in the 1970s she confided in him about the fact of the sexual relationship she had had with the plaintiff. We will also call a person by the name Candice Hyde, who will also tell the court that the witness Jane confided in her about her relationship with the plaintiff. I can't give you the precise date but it was the late 1970s they shared a house together.

During the course of the trial, the respondents' counsel told the trial judge:

> He [Bronte Koop] is a witness from whom I propose to lead evidence of complaint being made or evidence of the fact that [Jane] in conversations with Bronte Koop while they were going out, so in the period sometime around the middle of 1972 to sometime in 1973, which was the duration of when they were boyfriend and girlfriend, that she told Bronte Koop about the fact of having had a sexual relationship with the plaintiff.

Neither Koop nor Hyde were called to give evidence and the respondents offered no explanation for their failure to call them. Despite the submissions at trial that an adverse inference ought to be drawn, the trial judge made no reference to Koop or Hyde. Neither did the Full Court refer to this matter.

<u>St Mark's College incident</u>

27. The trial judge also found there was one other criminal sexual incident involving the applicant and Jane – the St Mark's College incident [FC424]. As with the Meningie incident, Jane's evidence was uncorroborated, and inconsistent with prior statements and with other evidence.
28. Contrary to the trial judge's finding, Jane's account of the "last occasion" of having oral sex with the applicant is glaringly improbable for the following reasons:
29. **First**, the applicant denied it. His evidence was he had never engaged in oral sex.

30. **Second**, Jane's evidence at trial was that in mid-1972 on a Saturday afternoon in the football season, she caught the train from Brighton to the Adelaide Railway Station, walked to the applicant's flat at St Mark's College and performed oral sex on the applicant, who wore red tracksuits pants with a white strip. She said this was the last occasion of sexual contact with the applicant. Jane said she went on Saturday afternoon because she knew Alison was at the football. The uncontradicted evidence was:
    30.1 the applicant was an avid follower and went to the football on Saturdays; and
    30.2 when Alison watched the football it was with the applicant or he was present.
31. **Third**, Jane's evidence at trial was inconsistent with her having told police that an incident involving red tracksuit pants was a separate event from the last occasion of sexual contact. (Neither the trial judge nor Full Court addressed this inconsistency).
32. **Fourth**, following the respondent's publications, Jane told Mr Abbott KC, who conducted an inquiry on behalf of the Catholic Church, that the last sexual contact occurred when she was 18 and just before the applicant married. (This inconsistency was not addressed by the trial judge or the Full Court). It was not an isolated assertion. She told police (July 2008) that the 'last time' was "relatively shortly before he married Alison, so I would have been 17 years old".
33. **Fifth**, according to what she told Abbott KC, Jane's last sexual contact must have occurred between November 1974 and January 1975 – well outside the football season.

34. **Sixth**, Jane's description of the layout of the applicant's St Mark's College flat was vague and bore no resemblance to the uncontradicted evidence of its actual layout.
35. **Seventh**, Jane's evidence to Mr Cannons, an Anglican Church investigator, was that she did not remember what occurred and to the police that she could see "the red tracksuit bottom, and I, I've blocked the rest – ".
36. **Finally**, Jane told the trial judge this last occasion of sexual contact occurred when she was aged 15, not long before she commenced a relationship with Bronte Koop. The applicant repeats para. 26 hereof and the respondent's failure to call Mr Koop.

<u>The Kay Allegations</u>

37. This finding is of lesser significance as it does not go to 'criminal sexual conduct' but relates to the contextual imputations only. The finding also relates to ground 3 (Part I). When applying the *Briginshaw* standard to serious criminality it is not appropriate to rely upon evidence relating to non-criminal conduct which could only have been admissible consequent upon a ruling, subsequently reversed, that the applicant not have leave to adopt the respondent's contextual truth imputation of general criminality.
38. The applicant asks rhetorically: how do Mr Kay's allegations assist in proving Jane's allegations? The two matters are not connected in time or space. It is simple prejudice.
39. The Peter Kay allegations were made in the early 1990s and investigated at the time by the then

Catholic Archbishop (Faulkner) who then proceeded to ordain the applicant.

40. The applicant's case was that Peter Kay had embellished the story now given to the one advanced by him in 1994 and that he should not be believed.
41. The Full Court failed to have proper regard to the prejudice the applicant suffered due to the passage of time (Archbishop Faulkner's diminished mental capacity precluded him from giving evidence) [FC183]. It dismissed the fact that the Archbishop allowed the applicant's ordination to proceed in the face of an alleged allegation concerning Peter Kay because, inter alia, "the response of church officials to complaints of sexual misconduct by church functionaries is, now notoriously, problematic". [FC120]
42. The Full Court erred in the assessment of the applicant's response to Mr Kay's allegations by mistakenly approaching the applicant's interview with Abbott KC on the basis that Abbott was investigating Kay's complaint. He was not. Rather his remit was to investigate the Church's response to the complaints of Jane and Jenny [FC130-1]. The applicant's advisor at the interview took the position that the applicant should not raise matters which he and the applicant understood were not part of Abbott's enquiry.

The applicant's good reputation

43. The Full Court erred in finding that the applicant's good reputation, had it been assessed could have made no difference to the findings [FC178] and, in particular, that this was so because allegations

had been made by three separate persons thereby 'swamping' evidence of good reputation: [FC177]. This is simple prejudice.

Prejudice consequent upon passage of time

44. The trial judge and the Full Court gave the benefit of lack of memory over many years to the respondent media organizations rather than to the applicant. Examples are [FC141], [FC143], [FC148], and [FC179-184]. The Full Court did so because the applicant had voluntarily initiated the litigation.
45. The observations of the High Court in *Prince Alfred College Inc. v ADC* [2016] HCA 37 at [100] to [105] are apposite.
46. The potential for gross injustice exists in this matter if the applicant is denied an appeal to this Court. The plaintiff is a person of hitherto good reputation, Catholic priest, author, academic of international reputation, former President of Campion College in Sydney. The plaintiff's life, and that of his wife, has been shattered by the Supreme Court as he has been deprived of academic postings, his previous level of remuneration such that he is now a bankrupt, and his ability to function as a Catholic priest.

Part IV

The applicant is an impecunious Catholic priest seeking to restore his reputation.

Part V

Briginshaw v Briginshaw (1938) 60 CLR 336 at 347, 350, 353, 362, 363

Rush v Nationwide News Pty Ltd (No 7) [2019] FCA 496 at [227], [462], [506], [527], [582], [592], [622], [624], [635]

Rejfek v McElroy (1965) 112 CLR 517 at [10]

Neat Holdings v Karajan Holdings (1992) 110 ALR 449 at 450

Witham v Holloway [1995] 183 CLR 525 at 534, 535

Fox v Percy (2003) 214 CLR 118 at [25]

Chakravarti v Advertiser Newspapers Ltd (1998) 193 CLR 519 at [134]

Lewis v Daily Telegraph [1964] AC 234 at 285

Prince Alfred College Incorporated v ADC [2016] HCA 37 at [100] – [105]

Defamation Act, 2005 (SA), s.24

Index of Proper Names

Abbott KC, Michael	32, 160, 168, 195, 215, 216, 220, 222, 344, 459-460, 467, 500, 502
Aitken, Mons Robert	482
Andrews, Bernice	396, 397
Aquinas, Saint Thomas	420, 424
Arnold, Michelle	16, 53, 118, 144, 172, 187, 189-192, 198, 229-357 *passim*, 396, 411, 424, 435
Aspilcueta, Martin	72
Augustine, Saint	70, 71
Bampton, J	See Vanstone J
Black, Tanya	247
Blue, J	384, 385, 387, 428, 429
Brennan, Sir Gerard	278, 376, 420, 421
Brewin, Chris	396, 397
Briginshaw	8, 9, 14-16, 44-48, 51, 52, 123, 158, 163, 173, 174, 176, 183, 202, 231, 297, 298. 301, 365-501 *passim*

Brindal, The Hon Mark	96, 101, 102, 164, 223, 409
Browne v Dunn	122
Burley, J	64, 65, 67
Burnett, Ros	398, 399, 400
Campion College	6, 19, 25, 27, 39, 370, 444, 455, 458, 481, 493, 503
Cannons, Greg	161, 220, 232-236, 263, 342, 501
Caporaso, Peter	194, 195, 200
Cappo, Monsignor David	90-101, 103, 104, 109, 110, 124, 164, 223, 307, 308, 401, 410, 411, 461, 482
Carrig, Helen	199
Centre For Criminality	397, 399, 400, 423
Chapman, Vickie	427
Chicknaiken, Walter	235, 236
Claring-Bould, Rev Joan	102, 164, 223, 310, 334, 340
Collits, Paul	3, 6, 20, 21, 23
Courtney, Rev Alan	306, 309, 310, 313, 334-340, 412, 415, 416, 487
Dart, J	43
Davies, Ross	472-477
Davies, Stephen	402, 405, 406

Dershowitz, Alan	40, 41
Diment, A	461-463
Doherty, Dr John	215, 459, 460, 465, 470
Dohnt, Lorraine	102
Doyle, JJ	431, 432
Driver, Archbishop Jeffrey	200, 471-477, 482
Duncan, The Hon Peter	135
Egar, Monsignor Robert	481
Emerson, Dr John	431
Faulkner, Archbishop Leonard	90, 91, 94-96, 126-127, 129-130, 307, 311-313, 315-318, 334, 335, 416, 420, 433; 480, 502
Fewster, Sean	443, 447-448, 450-453
Finnis, John	407
Fisher OP, Archbishop Anthony	463, 481
Fleming, Peter,	164, 220-223
Flint AM, David	3, 5, 9, 23
Fox v Percy	276, 303, 305, 330, 504
French, Chris	396, 397
Gaudron, J	186, 278, 376
Gladstone, William Ewart	79, 80
Gordon, J	365, 366
Gray, Justice Malcolm	20, 33, 48, 49, 50, 52, 53, 79, 81-83, 85, 88-90, 97- 113, 115-117-121, 123-135, 138, 141-146,

	148-152, 154, 156, 159-162, 165, 169-178, 180-199 *passim*, 201, 202, 205-207, 211, 212, 214, 216, 217, 220, 222, 227-231, 246, 248-251, 266, 272-274, 278-282, 285, 286-90, 294-297, 303, 305-311, 318, 319, 321-324, 327, 330-332, 337, 340, 345, 347, 349-353, 356, 357, 373, 385, 401, 406, 407-413, 415-417, 421-423, 425, 426, 428, 433, 434, 436-438, 441, 458, 478, 485
Gummow, J	186, 276, 303
Helton v Allen	299, 437
Henning, Kirsty	102, 164, 210, 211, 217, 223, 310, 334, 340
Hepworth, John	444, 481
Hewson, Barbara	392, 393
Heydon, J	114, 119, 303
High Court of Australia	20, 51, 113, 304, 361-362, 381, 424, 430, 438, 485, 487
Hilton, Daryl	161
Hoyle, Carolyn	399, 400
Hudson, Alan	160, 161

Hunt, Nigel	19, 26-28, 34, 35, 140, 193, 443-452 *passim*, 458, 472
Hyde, Candice	188, 189, 388, 498, 499
Innocent XI, Pope	73
Jackson v John Fairfax	57
Jones v Dunkel	122, 157
Joseph, Peter,	481
Kiefel, CJ	365, 366
Kingsley, Charles	69, 70, 73, 79
Kirby, J	186, 276, 303
Koop, Bronte	188, 189, 246-248, 250, 388, 483, 498, 499, 501
Kourakis, Chris	112, 385, 387, 428, 432
Layman SJ, Paul	73
Lindsay, Stuart	102, 142, 143, 350, 351, 475
Lunn, J	65-67
Macdonald, Arlene	97, 102, 123, 164, 218, 223, 310, 334, 340, 444
MacIntye, Alasdair	408
Maloney SDB, Francis J	317
Manning, Kevin	459, 481
Marshall, Philip	481
McCaffrey FSSP, Michael	481
McGowan, Glenn	304

McHugh AC, J	205, 277, 278, 424, 425, 426
McKenzie, Malcolm	102
McNicol, Douglas	157, 164, 203, 223
McNicol, Jean	164, 223
McNicol, Malcolm	164, 223
McNicol, Tom	153, 164, 223
Milligan, Louise	35
Moens, Gabriël A	3, 6, 11-18
Munro, Debra	150, 164, 223
Neat Holdings	47, 297, 298, 369, 376, 406, 436, 492, 504
Newman, Saint J H	69, 70, 73, 79
Nicholson, J	See Vanstone J
O'Kelly, Greg	480
O'Regan, Patrick	480
Ormerod, Neil	314-317
Ost, James	396, 397
Paul, Saint	70
Peek, J	44, 65-67, 121, 298
Pell, George	7, 9, 13, 23, 25, 28, 31, 35
Pennafort, St Raymond of	70
Pepper, Rachel	47
Perreall, Judith	289

Poniatowska[476]	8, 383-389, 428, 429, 432, 438
Porter, Christian	13
Pritchard, Greg,	481
Rejfek v McElroy	46, 299, 369, 437, 492, 504
Richardson, David	150, 151, 171, 176, 180-182, 197, 247,309, 313, 351, 352, 495
Romilly, Sir John[477]	273, 274
Royal Commission[478]	7, 9, 24, 25, 270, 314, 315, 316, 317
Rush, Geoffrey[479]	8, 364, 375, 377-382, 438, 485, 489, 490, 491, 504
Schaefer, Patrick	430
Schumann, Claus	233
Simmonds, Russell	164, 209, 210, 223, 497
Smith, Stuart	326
Sobels, Amy	290-294
Speechley, Naomi-Ellen	399, 400
Stanley, J	305
Stephens, Keith	200

476 Poniatowska v Channel Seven Sydney Pty Ltd [2019]

477 Crouch v Hooper (1852) 16 Beav. 182 at 184-5: 51 ER 747 at 748

478 Royal Commission into Institutional Responses into Child Sexual Abuse

479 Rush v Nationwide News Pty Ltd (No 7) [2019]

Stephenson, John	122, 171, 176-182, 190-192, 197, 244, 246, 249, 250, 257, 259, 260, 280, 281-286, 300, 301, 323-330, 332, 411, 471-473, 495
Stevens, Fiona	86
Sykes, Michael	112, 113, 290, 460
The Advertiser	7, 11, 25-28, 34, 38, 39, 41-43, 49, 50, 53, 56, 63, 81-84, 89, 90, 101, 110, 112, 113, 119, 130, 132, 135, 146, 155, 156, 178, 179, 190, 214, 216, 239, 269, 275, 279, 285, 289, 293, 294, 305, 348, 359, 371, 378, 382, 385, 388, 389, 391, 395, 409, 413, 420, 424, 426, 428, 432, 434-436, 438, 443, 445, 446, 448, 4449, 450, 452, 453, 458
The Sunday Mail	7, 19, 20, 26, 29, 33, 37, 56, 245, 447, 448, 451, 452, 457, 458, 472, 473, 491
Van Aperen, Steven	441, 442
Vanstone, J, *et al*[480]	48, 85, 115, 116, 120,

480 The Full Court of the Supreme Court of South Australia was comprised of Justices Vanstone, Nicholson, and Bampton

	121, 142, 170, 194, 266, 274, 278, 305-321 *passim*, 330-360 *passim*, 373-375, 385, 401-438, *passim*
Wass, J	266-270, 272, 274, 275, 277
Watson v Foxman[481]	271, 273
Weatherill, Gary	473, 474, 475, 478
Weinberg, Mark	7, 9
Wigney, J	375, 378, 380, 489, 490
Wilson, Philip	24, 32, 38, 39, 215, 315-318, 455, 456, 458, 459, 460-461, 463, 464, 465, 470, 471, 480, 482
Wright, Dan	396, 397
Zimmermann, Augusto	3, 19, 21

481 Watson v Foxman (1995) 49 NSWLR 315

Made in the USA
Monee, IL
08 November 2026

68060663R00285